FOOD
OF
JAPAN

SHIRLEY BOOTH

Grub Street • London

To Hitomi and Seiji Kimura of Daitō In Temple
who first encouraged me to cook and teach.

Published by Grub Street
The Basement
10 Chivalry Road
London SW11 1HT

Copyright this edition © Grub Street 2000
Text copyright © Shirley Booth 2000

The moral right of the author has been asserted

British Library Cataloguing in Publication Data

Booth, Shirley
Food of Japan
1. Cookery, Japanese
I.Title
641.5'952

ISBN 1902304160

Photography: Simon Smith
Line illustrations: Jun Baba
Design: GDAdesign
Design: Adam Denchfield Design

Printed and bound in Great Britain by Biddles Ltd, Guildford and King's Lynn

CONTENTS

ACKNOWLEDGEMENTS

My gratitude to the numerous people who have helped and supported me, both during the writing of this book and in the years of learning that preceded it, knows no bounds. Whether in Japan or Britain I hope they know how much I have appreciated their kindness and support.

There are a number of people I want to thank for their help specifically during the making of this book. Some contributions were enormous, others smaller, but all were humbly and gratefully received.

My first thanks go to Hitomi and Seiji Kimura of Daito In Temple, for eating my first attempts at *Shōjin Ryōri* and for their help in setting up classes at their beautiful temple in Kashiwa; the nuns of Sanko In Temple for teaching me about *Shōjin Ryōri*, and so much more. In Britain, my thanks to my publisher and editor, Anne Dolamore, for her critical eye, her sense of fun, her encouraging attitude, and for taking on a first time writer; Colin and Manami Sloley and Ian Shipley for their introduction to Anne; the Baba family for their enduring friendship, and specifically to Adrienne Baba for her beautiful pottery used in many of the photographs, her husband Togo Igawa for the back cover calligraphy, and to their son Jun Baba for his detailed and informative drawings; Eico Kanno for help with preparing the food for the photography, for answering my questions and checking my Japanese; Mr Takabatake for help with terminology; Alison Scott and Christine Booth for help on the shoot; Mari Inui and Marie Stroud for helping to translate recipes; David Windle for making the gluten; Bob Lloyd for permission to use his recipes, his help with printing the manuscript and for his support over several years; Yasko Yokoyama, and Tsutomu Sahara of Publishers Year 2001 Limited, for the book *Edō Ryōri* and permission to use recipes from it; Atsushi Momose for his early instruction in Japanese food and culture; Nobuko Takano and the Ikeda family, for over twenty years of friendship, countless gifts of food and kitchen items, and for putting up with me hanging around in their kitchens and asking questions. I must also thank my bosses at NHK Enterprises in London, Tsunehiko Ikegami and Kiyomi Sukegawa, for allowing me a flexible timetable to finish my writing.

More generally I also want to thank Yasushi Taguchi, Robbie Swinnerton, Andy Lunt, Christopher and Setsuko Dawson, Bill Benfield, Mark Hammond, Hideo Isso, Masafumi Harube, Christopher Fryman, Michiko Mimura, Hiromi and Chieko Yamagami, Yutaka Yamazaki, Mieko Kuroiwa, Setsuko Sakakibara, Liane Grundberg, Gareth Jones, Mustard Catering, Stuart Andrews, Sue Aron, Sue Sareen, Di Holmes, Kazuko Hohki, Tertia Goodwin at the Authentic Ethnic Cookery School in London, and to all the students who have attended my classes, both in Japan and Britain, for their enthusiasm.

My thanks and apologies go also to people I have forgotten to name here.

Finally, a big thank you to my father and all my family, for their constant love, support and encouragement.

INTRODUCTION

The first food I ate in Japan was the food that most Japanese have to begin their day: miso soup. The elderly *obaasan* (grandmother) who was looking after me woke me up and kindly offered me breakfast. It was to be the first of many culinary discoveries but, at seven in the morning with jet lag, a soup that looked like a stagnant pond wasn't my idea of breakfast. The taste however was a revelation, and soon I couldn't get enough of it. My longing for cheese-on-toast was soon eclipsed by my fascination for the strange and surprisingly delicious foods I was discovering. Soon I was hooked on miso, and in the following months I discovered something else: miso soup was just the thing for a hangover – hangovers being something else I quickly became familiar with, after long evenings knocking back the saké, the local rice wine.

Another early encounter was with the smell of grilled fish. Walking home from the public bath in the early evening, my washing bowl and towel in my hand, warm and tired, the smell of fish being grilled over charcoal braziers would waft before me. Even now, over twenty years later, I need only catch a brief noseful of the aroma of grilled mackerel and I am instantly transported to how I felt on one of those early summer evenings in Tokyo, on my first big adventure thousands of miles from home.

Such smells often emanated from the *yatai*, or street vendors – Japan's original fast food sellers. *Yatai* have been around for hundreds of years, as evidenced by old woodblock prints showing *yakitori* carts and noodle trucks, and are still everywhere, day and night. Stumbling off the last train at way past midnight you'll often find at the station exit the *takoyaki* man – selling little pancake balls filled with bits of squid and octopus, and served with shredded nori seaweed called *aonori*. When I lived in Togoshi in downtown Tokyo I never feared walking home after catching the last train – the ten minute walk was enlivened by the sight of inebriated and hungry, but never aggressive, salarymen on their way home, slurping down huge bowls of steaming hot noodles being dispensed by the *rāmen* seller from his mobile kitchen.

One of the best ways of meeting ordinary Japanese people, once you have a smattering of Japanese, and one of the best ways to learn about the food is in the *izakaya* – the small local bars. They are relaxed and informal places, full of laughter and ribaldry. My local in Togoshi couldn't have been more local – it was exactly opposite my house on a narrow street. In fact it was so close that one night my flat mate complained that he could hear my laughter bursting forth from the bar whilst he was trying to sleep. The type of food served there was simply cooked traditional fare, to accompany drinking, and most of the recipes in this book are the type of thing you'd be served in any *izakaya* in Japan. *Izakaya* are not like pubs or American bars, where people dress up just to drink. Think of a country style tapas bar in Spain and you'd be nearer the mark. Loud laughter. Activity. Orders being shouted. Sounds of frying, steaming and stir frying. You don't find traditional *izakaya* blasting out pop music either – although there may be a TV in the corner, with some traditional *enka* folk singer warbling away.

Another early memory was the absolute wonder I felt at wandering around Japanese department stores for the first time. The food section is always in the basement, and what a feast for the senses. Huge wooden tubs of miso (fermented soybean paste) in twenty different colours and tastes. Pickled vegetables of every shape and colour. Mounds of dark stringy seaweeds piled high, and glistening in the artificial light. The best thing is that samples of everything are available to taste. I found it a great way of trying out new and unfamiliar foods – and very effective at keeping hunger pangs at bay whilst shopping. At first I felt guilty about eating so many free samples, but soon realised that the white capped assistants eagerly thrusting strange looking morsels at me, with cries of *Irrashai irrashai* (welcome) wanted me to taste them. This was Asia after all!

A less thrusting or commercialised aspect of Japan lies 500 miles to the west of Japan's biggest city, Tokyo. Here sits the old capital of Kyoto and the spiritual heart of Japan. Before the capital moved to Tokyo this was where the Imperial family lived and was the seat of government. It is still regarded as the religious capital. Buddhist temples are to be found everywhere in Japan, but Kyoto has the highest concentration of temples, and it is here that the largest and most famous temples are to be found. A trip to Kyoto is a part of every school child's curriculum, and something everyone tries to do at least once in their lifetime.

It's a tradition for temples to provide food for visitors, and eating the temple specialities is all part of the experience. Okutan and Junsei are two of many restaurants in the grounds of Nanzenji temple which are famous for their tofu dishes, cooked in a myriad of different ways. When I was filming there some years ago for my first documentary on Japanese food I, together with my film crew, was thrilled to be treated to a full banquet, or procession, of Nanzenji's famous tofu dishes. The sound man was a traditionally-minded Japanese fellow who tucked in with gusto – an opportunity for a special feast that comes along only rarely. Unfortunately the poor cameraman, who was not Japanese, wasn't keen on Japanese food at all, least of all tofu, and with every dish that was brought to our table he looked more and more crestfallen... "not more tofu" "*tofu bakkari*" he exclaimed "nothing but tofu." But watching the excitement of the soundman, who was eagerly tucking in like a kid in a candy store, made up for his own disappointment. Another restaurant in Kyoto specialises in dishes made only with wheat gluten (called *fu* in Japanese), but, as is usual in magical Japan, the cooking styles are so varied, and the presentation so ingenious, that you wouldn't recognise each dish as being made from the same ingredient.

In the stifling heat of a Japanese summer, low tables are set outside in the temple grounds, spread with red cloths and shielded from the sun by paper parasols. The only sounds are the occasional plop of carp in a nearby stream, the distant reverberation of a temple bell, and the incessant chatter of the cicadas in the trees. In such surroundings a large glass bowl with cubes of silken tofu floating in iced water is a refreshing and welcome sight. This tofu is eaten just as it is, with a selection of condiments such as grated fresh ginger root, ground sesame seeds and *katsuobushi* (flakes of dried bonito fish which seem to dance on top of the pure white cubes). A dribble of light soy sauce completes the experience. In winter tofu is served in a bowl of steaming hot broth, and served with the same condiments. Slices of tofu grilled with a coating of miso paste and served on little kebab sticks are called *dengaku* and are another temple favourite.

"Strong wine, fat meat, peppery things, very sweet things, these have not real taste; real taste is plain and simple. Supernatural, extraordinary feats do not characterize a real man; a real man is quite ordinary in behaviour."

From the *saikontan*, written by Kojisei around the seventeenth century, a prose poem which encompasses the philosophies of Zen, Taoism and Confucianism.

This simplicity is one of the surprising and pleasing things about Japanese cooking. The techniques are not difficult, and easily acquired. It is similar to the way that good Italian cooking relies on fresh ingredients simply prepared. The freshness of the ingredients is paramount. After that there are three basic principles to adhere to: colour, taste and cooking method. Japanese traditional cooking is based on 'the five colours', 'the five cooking methods', and 'the six tastes'. A good cook will try to get a balance of each of these in one meal.

The five methods are boiling, grilling, deep frying, steaming and raw (including pickled or vinegared). Although a simple meal may not include all of these, it wouldn't duplicate any cooking style. A more elaborate meal certainly would include each style. There is more detail about this in the next section.

The colours are black (or purple), white, red (or orange), yellow and green. For example, a good blend of colours would be a meal that included green (spinach), black (*hijiki* seaweed), red (carrot), white (tofu) and yellow (pumpkin or corn).

The five tastes are sweet, salty, spicy, sour and bitter. Contrary to what one may think, bitterness is not a taste to be despised. In occasional and small amounts it can balance the diet, and a few foods are eaten specifically for their bitterness, such as *myōga* a type of shoot or bud, some types of *tōhgan* (wax or winter gourd), and of course the famous green tea of Japan. (Similarly in the West, for example, it is the very bitterness of Campari and Angostura that is desired.) In addition to these five tastes the Japanese reckon they have a taste all their own – it's *awai*, which roughly translated means delicate, transitory or faint, and is an important part of Japanese cooking. Chilled fresh tofu could be described as *awai*. Understanding this 'understatement' is one of the keys to appreciating Japanese cuisine, and in the process Japanese culture. Similarly, *umami* is a much used word when discussing food amongst Japanese people, and translates as deliciousness, or tastiness. In fact some Japanese argue that *umami* as well is a separate taste, akin to sweet and sour. (For a fascinating debate on this question see Richard Hosking's book, A *Dictionary of Japanese Food*.)

Another taste which is a key to understanding Japanese culture is *shibui*. It's not something to aim for in food, as it means astringent (for example, the inside of a banana skin is *shibui* and occasionally a persimmon can be *shibui* – when it sticks to the roof of your mouth). But *shibui* , when used to describe design or style, expresses a Zen Buddhist notion, of asceticism – such as the simple arrangement of stones in a garden. Through such an ascetic or 'astringent' approach is considered the way to enlightenment.

So, from originally being affronted by the strange and wonderful foods I encountered I began to learn about them. This process took me to a Zen Buddhist nunnery, and although I hadn't planned to visit Japan to attain enlightenment, I soon found that traditional Japanese food owed much to Zen Buddhism.

From Shinjuku station in the heart of the capital a train carries you west for 20 minutes or so to the suburb of Musashi Koganei. Here, nestled behind a plain and unremarkable looking apartment block stands Sanko In Temple, an oasis of tranquility minutes from the hustle and bustle of the city centre. It was here that I came to learn from the abbess of the temple, Koei Hoshino, a remarkable woman who taught me not only techniques, but about the true spiritual value of food, and how preparing it and eating it can indeed become a route to enlightenment.

The strictly vegetarian diet of the monks and nuns of Japan is called *Shōjin Ryōri*, which means "food to progress the spirit", and this was to be the basis of my odyssey into Japanese food, and Japanese culture. At Sankō In I discovered that, not only is Japanese food good for the body, it's also good for the soul. Learning to cook and serve Japanese dishes then was my personal route to understanding something of the soul of Japan.

Buddhism took hold in Japan as a result of contact with China in the 7th and 8th centuries. This greatly influenced cooking style, as it was forbidden, by Buddhist doctrine, to kill any living thing. It was at this time that tofu and other soybean products became the main source of protein, not only for monks but for the lay people too, who became practising Buddhists.

The nobility, and people who lived in coastal areas where fish was plentiful, took a less rigid view of the Buddhist precept, and interpreted it as applying only to four legged creatures. Thus they could eat fish and fowl with, as they saw it, impunity. In mountain areas this bending of the rules was taken even further: in order to allow themselves the luxury of wild boar meat it was referred to as 'mountain whale' *yamakujira*, (whale in their book being allowed). Nevertheless the basic prohibition on eating meat, and a preference for vegetable and soy products, was to remain unchanged for over a thousand years, until the Meiji restoration in the nineteenth century, and the growth of Westernisation.

The first Western foreigners to visit Japan were the Portuguese in the sixteenth century, who came first as traders and later as missionaries, and stayed in the area around Nagasaki on the southern island of Kyushu. At first they lived there reasonably harmoniously, but then Spanish missionaries and Dutch traders arrived. Eventually Japan began to feel threatened by so many Western visitors and their efforts to convert the Japanese to Christianity, so further contact with Westerners was forbidden, and the missionaries, as well as Christianity itself, banned. (Fascinatingly a small group of Japanese Christians remained in the Nagasaki area, and for centuries followed their faith in secret. To this day they are called the Hidden Christians, and practise a unique type of silent worship.) After most of the foreigners were expelled there remained only a small group of Dutch traders, confined to a small island called

Dejima near Nagasaki. And that is how it remained until the nineteenth century. For 200 years Japan was closed to outsiders, and the Japanese themselves were forbidden to leave. Then in 1853 Commodore Perry sailed in to Japan from America with his infamous Black Ships, and anchored at Uraga in Edō (now Tokyo) Bay and the following year a treaty was signed. There then followed several years of rebellion and unrest, until at last, in 1868, the Emperor of the time, Meiji, opened Japan's doors to trade, and so ended 200 years of Japan's isolation from the rest of the world. This was known as the Meiji Restoration. At first the strange looking foreigners, with their long noses, whiskery faces and gigantic bodies were distrusted, and were known as 'hairy barbarians'. Most Japanese had never seen such big people before. (They were gradually to realise that this was a result of their weird eating habits – eating meat of all things.) Soon all things Western became fashionable. Men were seen sporting top hats and shoes with their kimonos, and those who could afford it wore complete Western attire – including short hair and moustaches with their suits. Another of the fashions quickly adopted was meat eating. In fact the Emperor actually decreed that people *had* to start eating meat – thus overturning over a thousand years of Buddhist tradition. Luckily for the health of the Japanese, although meat eating was no longer forbidden, it still wasn't readily available, so it was eaten sensibly, in small quantities, and never became the main dish in a meal, as in the West. Sukiyaki is probably the most meat-centred dish in Japanese cuisine, and one of the most well known, but is a good example of a dish that didn't exist in Japan until the Meiji Restoration 131 years ago.

Healthiness of Japanese food

"Neither have they yet any flocks of sheep and goats, any droves of geese, turkey or pigs. Even cattle are comparatively scarce, and neither flesh nor their milk is in general use. The pasture meadow and the farmyard are alike lacking."

Basil Hall Chamberlain, *Things Japanese*

In addition to the religious beliefs which dictated such a healthy and low fat diet, the geography of the country reinforced a dependence on healthy food. Japan is mainly mountainous, surrounded by small coastal plains. Only 15% of the land is cultivable, so this land has to be used wisely, and is too precious to give over to cattle grazing.

The cultivation of rice and soy beans though was a good use of the space available: a high protein return for minimal land use.

"The wheat is sown in rows with wide spaces between them, which are utilized for beans and other crops, and no sooner is it removed than daikon (Raphanus sativus) *cucumbers, or some other vegetable, takes its place, as the land under careful tillage and copious manuring bears two, and even three, crops in the year."*

Isabella Bird, *Unbeaten Tracks in Japan*

Surrounded by coastline the fruits of the sea became another important element of the diet. Fish of course, both raw and cooked were eaten (but not by the devout) and in addition an array of different sea vegetables were incorporated into traditional Japanese cooking.

As a rice growing nation the traditional Japanese meal has always been based around rice. Unlike bread and potatoes in the West, in Japan rice is seen as the main dish. All other dishes are side dishes, known as *o-kazu*. There is a growing understanding in the West that healthy eating means more carbohydrates, less saturated fat, – i.e. smaller portions of meat – and much more fatty fish, such as mackerel and sardines, which are rich in Omega 3 fatty acids; and a good proportion of vegetables. The Japanese have been eating this way for centuries. The evidence of the benefits of such a diet is readily visible. The Japanese people are slim. Obesity is uncommon, although sadly it is increasing in the younger generation who are adopting Western eating habits of hamburgers, pizzas and ice cream. Twenty years ago it was rare to see anyone who was overweight. Traditionally there has been a low incidence of heart disease, breast cancer and diabetes in Japan – all diseases which have been linked to the high saturated fat diet which is common to Western industrialized nations.

Soy bean products, in many different guises, appear in every meal, usually as soy sauce, miso or tofu, and good use is made of sea vegetables, which are chock full of essential minerals, such as calcium, iron, zinc and glutamic acid. Side players such as sesame (a rich source of calcium), *umeboshi* (a type of pickled plum which is reckoned to be good for acid stomachs), *katsuo* (dried bonito fish) and ginger all give flavour and goodness, taking us into a realm of flavours unlike any you've ever known!

Japanese cuisine then is rich in foods which are good for you, have been shown to prevent disease, and are above all tasty. The style of eating too is conducive to good health. Lots of little dishes: small portions eaten slowly over the course of an evening. It's very similar to Spanish tapas or Greek meze, and just as convivial, especially when saké is consumed!

Historically speaking Japanese cooking can be divided into two main styles. The style of cooking that was popularised at the Imperial court in Kyoto and around the Kansai region is characterised by its lighter and saltier flavours. Light soy sauce, called *usukuchi* is popular here, and helps give food a lighter appearance. Sweet white miso is also a feature of Kansai, and temple, cooking. Imperial cooking and temple cooking influenced each other, having originated in the same geographical region.

With the rise in power of the samurai class in the sixteenth and seventeenth centuries, a simpler and more robust style of cooking emerged – a style more characteristic of the Kanto region around Tokyo. This book is a blend of both – the basic *izakaya* style cooking is more reminiscent of Tokyo cooking, whilst the lighter temple dishes are Kansai style. This is not an important issue however – most probably you won't be able to tell the difference – struggling as you may be to simply keep track of miso, *umeboshi* and *konnyaku*.

"The rice bowl contained a calculated quantity of one-fifth to each guest, and etiquette demanded that all the rice must be eaten. Other courses included a small quantity of cooked fish, egg plant and various pickles, and the meal came to an end with delicious clear, sweet jelly, cut into squares and served on bamboo leaves."

Grace James, *Japan Recollections and Impressions*

One of the popular images of Japanese food is of tiny portions beautifully presented. This image is especially characteristic of *kaiseki* food, which is the food that accompanies the tea ceremony. Tea ceremony and *kaiseki* cuisine is not within the scope of this book but its influence is felt in all Japanese cooking. Tea ceremony evolved around the fifteenth century, and was a poetic response to nature, a way of celebrating and appreciating the natural environment. Specially built tiny houses were constructed for the purpose, set amid traditional Japanese gardens. Inside, the rooms were decorated with flowers of the season, and poems were read celebrating the season. Naturally the food served was not only seasonal in itself but represented the seasons too. Dumplings were made to look like chestnuts in autumn. Rice cakes resembled bamboo shoots in spring. Wheat gluten was shaped into red maple leaves for autumn, and cherry blossoms in spring. Although tea ceremony cooking is an enchanting and unforgettable experience, my aim is to introduce you to Japanese ingredients, flavours and textures, by the same route that I took: that is, eating family cooking at my friends' homes, experiencing simple country food at modest *minshuku* (country B&Bs), and eating at humble *izakaya* and *nomiya* (drinking places). All these recipes are inspired by memories of places such as Kanae in Shinjuku, Shinhinomoto in Yurakucho, and at my previously-mentioned local bar in Togoshi (which unfortunately is no longer there). In addition I've included recipes I learned at Sankō In Temple, to give you a flavour of simple Zen Buddhist cookery, which in many ways is the heart of Japanese cuisine.

For anyone who wants to eat healthily, simply and stylishly, Japanese cuisine is the perfect choice. It's not a weight loss diet, to be followed for a week or two, but a way of life. Incorporating Japanese foods and habits into your eating can be a way of staying slim and healthy, living long, and enjoying yourself into the bargain.

The best news though is that Japanese cooking is simple. The techniques are easily acquired. Once you are familiar with the ingredients and what to do with them, the rest is easy! I hope this book will show you how easy it can be, and that one day soon, nori, miso and mirin will sit in our cupboards alongside the sun dried tomatoes and olive oil which we now take for granted.

Shirley Booth

ESSENTIAL JAPANESE INGREDIENTS

SOYBEAN PRODUCTS

TOFU (bean curd) is no longer a stranger to Westerners, but Japanese ways of using it may be. It is the coagulated curd of soy milk, which itself is made by crushing whole soy beans. Tofu is exceptionally high in protein, and an excellent food for vegetarians. It can be eaten just as it is, or used in a variety of cooked dishes. See section on soy products for a more detailed description and ways of using it.

Silken tofu (kinugoshi) is soft and falls apart easily. This silky smooth texture is what gives it its name. I think it is the best tofu for eating plain, either chilled or slightly warmed, and for dressings and dips.

Cotton tofu (momendōfu) is the firmer tofu most easily available in the West. It gets its name from the cotton indentations which result from the cotton lining the tubs in which it is set. Cotton tofu is best for cooking with, but in most cases it shouldn't be overcooked, as it becomes spongy after long cooking.

Deep fried tofu pouches (abura-age or usu-age) These are the little pouches that most often appear stuffed with rice in sushi bars or lunch boxes. In fact they are thick blocks of tofu that have been pressed and deep fried. They can be purchased ready made and frozen in the West, fresh in Japan. The pouch shape of course is crying out to be stuffed, and indeed this is a classic way of using them. However, they are also often cut into strips and added to soups, and are good sautéed with *hijiki* and root vegetables, as they add a little oiliness (and protein) to a dish.

Deep fried tofu cakes (atsuage) These are thick blocks of tofu which have been deep fried. They are excellent for long cooking (as in *o-den*) as they don't fall apart, and don't absorb moisture as readily as fresh tofu.

Freeze dried tofu (koya-dōfu) is exactly that. When tofu freezes, the structure and texture of it completely changes (which is why you never put it in your freezer). These hard, dry, blocks are commercially freeze dried, and very versatile. They keep for months, and, once re-hydrated, although the texture is completely different from fresh tofu, it has the same goodness. The sponge like texture absorbs flavours readily, so it's good for dishes which require long simmering in broth. The dry cake can even be finely grated and used as an unusual coating for deep fried foods.

O-kara is the fibrous residue from making tofu. These days it's regarded as animal food, but traditionally it was eaten at home. It's high in fibre and quite delicious when simmered slowly, as it absorbs the flavours of what it is cooked with. It's included here as a country style food.

MISO is a rich savoury paste made from fermented soybeans. Cooked soybeans are mixed with salt and grain (barley or rice) which has been fermented with *aspergillus koji*. The enzymes from the *koji* break down the beans and grains, resulting in a strongly aromatic, versatile and healthy food. It is the main ingredient in miso soup, and is used in a variety of dishes. It's a must for Japanese cookery – it keeps for years and is widely used. There are several different types, which are described further in Soy Products and some of the basics, but in most cases which miso you use is not critical. Just keep trying different ones until you find the one you like the best. Briefly they are:

Mugi miso made with barley – all purpose.

Genmai miso made with brown rice, chunky and rich.

Shinshu good all purpose medium miso – my recommendation for beginners. Sometimes called yellow miso.

Hatcho miso very salty, good for winter cooking. The only miso that is made only with soybeans, without grain.

Sweet white miso (Saikyō miso) is made using a higher proportion of rice *koji* to soybeans, a lower proportion of salt, and is fermented for a shorter time. This results in a smooth and very sweet miso. Used as a pickling agent, in New Year soup called *ozōni*, and in dressings. Popular in Kyoto temple cookery. Doesn't keep.

Akadashi red miso – rich and dark.

Awasemiso a mixture of different misos, so a good all purpose choice, especially for soup.

NATTO is another type of fermented soybean, but completely different from miso. It's a sticky gooey mass, traditionally eaten with rice at breakfast. It's one of the few vegetable products that contain Vitamin B12, so an important food for vegetarians – if you can get used to the texture. Unlike miso, *natto* doesn't keep for longer than a week in the fridge – if it starts to acquire a strong ammonia smell it should be thrown away. It freezes well though, and this is how you are most likely to buy it. It's sold in small polystyrene containers – each is one portion. *Hikiwari natto* is *natto* where the beans are slightly chopped up, rather than whole beans – and I prefer it.

SOY SAUCE (shōyu) the ubiquitous oriental flavouring, is made from soybeans, wheat and salt. There are basically two types – light and dark. The darker one (*koi kuchi*) is popular in the Tokyo area, and the lighter one (*usu kuchi*) in Western Japan in the Kansai area. In addition the light one is often used when colour and appearance is important and you don't want to darken food too much. Contrary to what you may imagine, the light one is actually saltier than the dark, so you can use less when cooking. The dark is all purpose, good for simmering and marinades, is the one most used in this book, and most widely available abroad. Japanese soy sauce, which is naturally brewed, should always be used. Never substitute with the artificially brewed and coloured Chinese soy sauces which are sold widely.

Tamari is a soy sauce favoured by macrobiotic cooks – it's made without wheat, so is good for people with wheat allergies.

SOY MILK SKIN (yuba) Fresh *yuba* is a speciality of Kyoto and temple cookery, although the dried version is used a lot in Chinese cooking. Soy milk is left on a low heat to form a skin, and this skin is *yuba*. Although a simple food, it is time consuming to make so it's regarded as something of a delicacy. Dried *yuba* is available in this country in Chinese and Japanese stores. It can be reconstituted in water and added to soups or simmered in Japanese stock. Dried *yuba* can be simply deep fried, in which case it expands and puffs up in the same way that prawn crackers or Indian popadoms do.

RICE AND RICE PRODUCTS

Kome is the Japanese word for uncooked rice. Japanese rice is short grained and sticks together, making it easy to eat with chopsticks. Some types of Japanese rice available abroad are Koshihikari and Nishiki, and some brands are Kokuho Rose and California Rose. Most will have been grown in the U.S.

Sweet rice (*mochi kome*) is glutinous rice, specifically used for pounded rice cakes called *mochi*, and for the red bean rice called *sekihan*.

'Spring rain' noodles (*Harusame*) are very fine transparent noodles which are variously made from mung bean starch, rice starch or potato starch. They are a common feature of one-pot dishes, good in vinegared salads, and easily available.

Mochi refers to rice cakes made from sweet rice, which is steamed and then pounded into a sticky glutinous cake.

Rice flour dumplings (*dango*) are made with glutinous rice flour, called *shiratamako*. Confusingly, some types of rice flour cakes are also called *mochi*.

The two basic types of rice flour are:

Joshinko is ground from ordinary short grain rice, which is non-glutinous. Used for sweet making.

Shiratamako is raw glutinous rice flour, usually sold in small lumps or granules. Used for sweets or dumplings which are then cooked either by steaming or boiling.

VEGETABLES

Many Japanese vegetables are the same or similar to those in Europe. Some of the more unusual ingredients are available in Chinese stores, and some only in Japanese stores. In many cases I have suggested more readily available alternatives which can be used. You can also try growing them yourself. Joy Larkom's book *Oriental Vegetables* is an invaluable guide for anyone tempted to do so, with probably more information than you'd ever need.

Aubergines (*nasu*) These are the smaller ones which are now more readily available here. Popular in summer they are served grilled, pan fried, steamed and deep fried (as in tempura).

Bamboo shoot (*takenoko*) The fresh young shoots of bamboo herald spring. Although rather ugly looking in their fresh state, as they are covered in a rough brown husk, the Japanese go all poetic and romantic about them. (In spring sweet cakes made from rice flour are shaped, and decorated, to resemble young shoots.) If you can get hold of the fresh shoots they need long boiling, to remove bitterness, and the husks removed afterwards. Even the canned and water packed variety needs to be well washed before use, to remove any white residue. Bamboo shoot can be used in many ways – simmered, sautéed, deep fried and stir fried to name a few.

Burdock (*gobō*) *Arctium lappa*. A plant of the cooler northern hemisphere which grows wild in Britain but is cultivated for its long tasty root in Japan. Do not peel, but simply scrape the fine skin off. Place the cut root in cold water immediately after cutting to get rid of any strong taste and stop discoloration. It is related to Scorzonera, which is black, and salsify which is white, so if burdock itself is difficult to find it may be worth experimenting with these as substitutes. Jerusalem artichoke, although a different shape and softer texture, has a similar earthy taste. Burdock is rich in vitamin B and various minerals. It's most usually made into *kimpira*, a sesame flavoured, sautéed and simmered side dish. Very young tender roots are also pickled, and are heavenly.

Carrot (*ninjin*) *Daucus carota* are much the same as the carrots we use in the West, although there is an attractive Japanese variety, *takonogawa*, which is a dark almost red colour, and much used in Kyoto cooking. Carrots are important in simmered dishes (*nimono*), but are also sautéed, pickled and salted.

Chestnuts (*kuri*) *Castanea crenata* are very popular in Japan, especially in autumn when they are seen as a symbol of the changing seasons. Cooked chestnuts are made into a paste and into sweet confections. At New Year sweet chestnut purée (*kuri kinton*) is eaten.

Chinese cabbage (*hakusai*) *Brassica rapa* var. *pekinensis* has been eaten in the East since the fifth century, and is now widely available in the UK. It needs very little cooking, and is therefore added to one-pot dishes, such as sukiyaki, right at the last moment. It is also a popular ingredient in pickles. In Korea, Chinese cabbage is the main ingredient in the highly pungent *kimchee* pickle, which also contains loads of garlic and chilli, and which is eaten in every meal. It's mentioned here, in a book on Japanese food, as Korean food is now a part of Japanese culture (like curry in Britain). Also, I have included one or two 'fusion' dishes which have recently appeared in Japan and which utilise *kimchee*. Anyway – it's so delicious that I want everyone to know about it. I have therefore sneaked in a recipe on how to make your own *kimchee* in the pickle section.

Chinese chives (*nira*) *Allium tuberosum*. A member of the onion family, *nira* resembles chives, but thicker stemmed and with a stronger garlicky flavour. It is used as garnish and flavouring but also as a vegetable in itself. I first ate *nira* stir fried with chicken liver in a noodle bar in Koenji – that was twenty years ago and I still remember it. In Japan, garlicky type foods were usually introduced from China – you'll therefore be most likely to find *nira* in Chinese markets.

Chinese pear (*nashi*) *Pyrus pyrifolia*. This is a most delicious fruit, although its looks are uninspiring – with the shape of an apple and the skin of a pear. The flesh is crisp, white and juicy – like a cross betwen an apple and pear in fact. The Japanese are fond of it in summer, served sliced and chilled, with a sprinkling of salt to bring out its sweetness.

Chinese yam (*nagaimo* or *yamaimo*) *Dioscorea japonica*. The Japanese names translate as long potato or mountain potato, as one variety is indeed long, and the other looks a bit like ginseng – a fist-shaped tuber with five fat 'fingers'. They are not easily available in Britain (although I have seen imported ones in Japanese stores – at a price), but for readers in Japan I have included them. The tubers actually grow on vines, and in some parts of the United States, where it's referred to as *jinenjo*, it grows wild. Grated raw *nagaimo* is called *tororo* and is served on top of bowls of noodles, or mixed with raw tuna. The texture takes some getting used to, as it's viscous and sticky, but the taste is not in the least offensive. It can also be cooked, which removes its viscosity, resulting in just a slight and attractive stickiness. Like *daikon*, raw *nagaimo* contains diastase, an enzyme that digests starch. It also has a reputation for efficacy in helping to heal stomach ulcers, and even asthma, which is attributed to the fact that it contains alantoin

– one of the few plants that does.

Chrysanthemum leaves (shungiku or **kikuna)** *Chrysanthemum coronarium*. This is a particular edible variety, so I don't recommend you start tucking in to your prize blooms. Fresh leaves are available in some Japanese markets, but again, if you are adventurous you could try growing your own. The younger leaves have a mild, but distinctive flavour, which intensifies the older the plants become. The taste may take a bit of getting used to, but it's such a typical Japanese vegetable that it's definitely worth trying. It's also rich in vitamins and minerals. Like spinach, chrysanthemum leaves don't need much cooking – overcooking makes them bitter. They are a common ingredient in sukiyaki and other one-pot (*nabe*) dishes, and can also be served *ohitashi* style, simply boiled with a drizzle of soy sauce and *katsuo* (bonito flakes) on top. Chrysanthemum petals are also edible. The whole flower is often used as a garnish, and the petals are sold dried and can be used in salads and pickles.

Cucumbers (kyūri) *Cucumis sativus* are smaller in Japan, have fewer seeds in proportion, and therefore are less watery than the large ones common in the West. Mainly they are used for pressed salad and pickles, but occasionally they are simmered. Fresh cucumber is often eaten as it is with a dip of miso.

Daikon **radish** *Raphanus sativus* is sometimes known as mooli radish. *Daikon* means great root, and it is – sometimes growing up to two or three feet in length. Other varieties, instead of being long and thin, are short and fat. The flavour varies from mild to quite spicy, depending on the variety and the season. In Japan itself winter *daikon* are the best – large and juicy. The variety grown is influenced by the soil and the climate. In general, short and thick ones, which are more associated with China, are coarse and more suited to cooking, whereas the longer and thinner ones, more common in Japan, are good for grating and pickling. In the West you probably won't have a choice – you'll be using whatever is available, and that's just fine! Nutritionally, *daikon* contains some Vitamin C. Grated raw *daikon* is a traditional accompaniment to greasy food (such as deep fried tempura, and oily fish) as it is believed that it helps 'cut the oil'. This is due to the presence of enzymes, such as diastase, which are said to help break down carbohydrates and fats. In fact there are many uses of *daikon* in Japanese traditional and folk medicine – perhaps another reason, apart from its size, that it has been named great root. *Daikon* is also commonly simmered as a vegetable, in dishes like o-den (a one-pot type of stew). Because its flesh is dense it needs long cooking, but this is when its flavour is best and its natural sweetness released.

Kiriboshi daikon is dried strips of *daikon*. Reconstituted it can be used in pickles or salads, or sautéed and stewed. The texture of course is different from fresh *daikon*, but the flavour is good and more intense than the fresh type.

Ginger (shōga) *Zingiber officinale* is used in Japanese cooking in many ways. The fresh young pink shoot is eaten as it is, with a miso dip, to accompany drinking. Thin, pink, slivers of the root, pickled in sweet vinegar, are eaten in sushi bars to refresh the palate in between courses, where, in sushi-shop parlance, it's known as *gari*. A similar pickled ginger, but shredded, is eaten with o-konomiyaki (a thick savoury pancake) and also with *kare raisu* (a particularly bland Japanese version of – well – curry and rice). Freshly grated ginger root (and its juice) is used in tempura dipping sauce, in dressings, dips and to flavour sautéed foods. Try to find the freshest and juiciest root you can. Ginger root is also used medicinally in folk medicine, added to hot drinks or mixed with *kuzu* starch to aid digestion. A delicious warming winter drink can be made by mixing *amazake* (sweet fermented rice paste) ginger and hot water.

Ginkgo nuts *(ginnan)* *Ginkgo biloba.* This is the fruit of the female ginkgo or maidenhair tree, an extract of which has recently gained popularity as a health food supplement. It is said to improve the flow of blood to the brain, and therefore aid the memory (hence its other name, the memory tree). The fruit, or nut, however, is eaten as a food in China and Japan. Part of its attraction is the beautiful green colour of the nuts when shelled, but also, because its preparation is labour intensive it is regarded as a luxury food. In autumn it is an ingredient in a special tempura, and it's commonly used in the steamed savoury egg custard called *chawan mushi.* Canned nuts are available but I don't recommended them as they are too mushy. Fresh nuts are available in Chinese markets. When the nuts ripen on the tree they are covered in a sticky outer coating which absolutely stinks – something like a paraffin smell. Anyway you can always tell if you are anywhere near a female ginkgo in autumn because you'll smell it yards away. These sticky nuts fall off the tree, and you can then either squelch them underfoot by mistake, or do as I did and go collecting them. I have many happy memories of gathering them from the grounds of Daitō In Temple, where I first started teaching Japanese cookery. I'd go out armed with a plastic bowl and rubber gloves, and come back with my treasure. The next stage was to rub off the sticky and smelly fleshy coating, to reveal the hard shell underneath. A vigorous wash in cold water would follow, and then I'd leave them in the sun to dry off. This is the stage at which you'd buy them in the market. You can also try germinating them from the nut. I brought several back from Japan for my dad to germinate, and now have several small trees of my own. They do eventually grow huge – they are commonly found in the grounds of temples, and here in London there are two guarding the gates of South Park in Fulham, near my flat.

Gourd strips *(kanpyō)* are made from the gourd *yūgao.* The flesh is dried into long thin strips which are used variously for tying up sushi parcels, cabbage rolls and for a filling in sushi rolls themselves. It requires softening and long cooking, but is a brilliant way of tying bundles of food, especially if they are to be simmered, as it is edible.

Green peppers *(piiman)* are a relatively recent introduction to Japanese cuisine but are now widely used, especially in *yakitori* and tempura. Japanese peppers are smaller and thin skinned – try to use them if you can find them. Another important difference is that in Japanese cooking peppers are only ever grilled (or barbecued) and quickly pan fried or deep fried. They are never simmered in liquid or steamed (as they are in Mediterranean cooking). The loss of colour, shape and texture is considered unappealing – and I agree!

Hokkaido Pumpkin (*kabocha*) *Curcubita moschata* and *Curcubita maxima.* The small dark green *kabocha* is now fairly easily obtainable outside of Japan, for which I am thankful. It has thicker creamier flesh than most pumpkins, is much less watery and really sweet and tasty. Turks Cap and Butternut squash are fairly similar and can be used instead – but they may be even more difficult to get hold of. *Kabocha* is delicious baked, boiled, steamed, deep fried and even puréed and used in sweets. Uncooked *kabocha* can be cubed and successfully deep frozen.

Japanese leek, long onion, Welsh onion or bunching onions (negi) *Allium fistulosum*. The Japanese long onion called *naganegi* is smaller than a leek but bigger than a spring onion. If you are using this book in the West you may find such onions difficult to get hold of. In some recipes the best alternative would be the largest spring onions you can find (usually available at Chinese stores) and in others young tender leeks would be more suitable (in sukiyaki or one-pot dishes for example). One other point to note is that it is the white bulbous part that is used in Japanese cooking (if you were using leeks the green tops would be too tough in any case). Without wanting to confuse the life out of my readers, and putting them off Japanese cooking for ever, I will also add that in the Kansai region of Japan a different type of onion is used, and it is the green part that is eaten. So I suggest you use your judgement depending on whether you substitute leeks or spring onions. Of course you could try growing your own. In Japan fields of *negi* are an impressive sight – long neat rows which are gradually 'earthed up' to a height of about a foot. As a result the green tops are visible, and the stem section below the soil is blanched, creating the long white edible part.

Lotus root (renkon) is the rhizome of the water plant *Nelumbo nucifera*, which is a type of water lily. The rhizome grows in muddy ponds under water, and is distinguished by the holes that are visible when the root is sliced across. This distinctive shape lends itself perfectly to artful arrangements, and the holes can also be stuffed (for example with red bean paste) to great effect. In the colder seasons lotus root is available fresh in Chinese markets. Frozen sliced root can be obtained from Japanese stores, and is an acceptable alternative to fresh. Dried lotus root is available from health food shops and macrobiotic suppliers, but it's not suitable for all recipes. It can also be found canned, which I think isn't worth having. Half the point of *renkon* is its crunchiness, and as you know crunchiness is the last word that springs to mind when talking of canned vegetables. Water packed lotus root can also be found in Japanese shops, although it tends to be a bit pricey. However, once opened it will keep in the fridge for about two weeks, but needs to be boiled in clean water every two days. Whole fresh links will keep relatively well, but cut portions should be used within a couple of days. To stop fresh cut roots from turning brown steep them in water with a little vinegar or lemon juice added. In any case don't buy roots that have turned dark – they should be a creamy colour. Lotus root has a long history in the East of having been used medicinally, and is said to be especially effective for respiratory problems. Lotus root tea is often taken to alleviate a cough or symptoms of a cold.

Mustard spinach (komatsuna) *Brassica rapa* var *komatsuna*. This is considered an indigenous Japanese vegetable, neither mustard nor spinach actually. The green bunches are often sold with the flowers attached which are mildly spicy, thus the mustard in its name. Again they are popular for pickling.

Mugwort (yomogi) *Artemesia princeps* is a wild grass or herb, and is traditionally used to flavour buckwheat noodles (*yomogi soba*) and *mochi* – pounded rice cake, which is then called *yomogi mochi*. Festivals in Japan are nearly always associated with the eating of some special food, and March 3rd, which is Girls Day or the Doll Festival

(*Hinamatsuri*) is celebrated with the eating of *yomogi mochi*. Perhaps the Japanese instinctively knew that mugwort contains nutrients especially beneficial to girls – iron and calcium. Mugwort grows wild in Japan in much the same way as it does here, and as you're not likely to find it in the shops you'll have to pick it yourself. Dried mugwort is sold for use in cake making, in some Japanese stores. (Dried mugwort is also the herb used by acupuncturists for the process known as moxibustion, whereby small mounds of the dried herb are burned on top of the skin to heat a particular area.)

MUSHROOMS

Shiitake mushroom *Lentinus lidodes* are grown on the *shii* tree, a type of oak. Studies have revealed the presence of a substance called lenitan in *shiitake* mushrooms, which has been shown to boost the immune system. Some researchers believe that *shiitake* may help to prevent and even fight cancer, and there is quite a body of research on the subject. In any case they are delicious, and becoming more widely available. Dried *shiitake* keep for years, and have a very intense flavour. The soaking water from dried *shiitake* is used as a vegetarian basis for stock, containing as it does sodium guanylate, a flavour enhancer.

Enokitake (enokidake, or enoki) mushroom *Flammulina velutipes* grows on the *enoki* tree – the Chinese hackberry, which is where it gets its name. These days though they are produced commercially, and have recently made an appearance in Britain. These are the thin stringy white mushrooms sold in little bunches, sometimes with the mycelium still attached. This should be cut off and the mushrooms rinsed before use. The flavour is not strong, and *enokitake* are a favourite for soups, and one-pot dishes like sukiyaki. Be careful to chew them well – I find them a bit stringy and they can get stuck in your teeth or throat.

Shimeji mushroom *Lyophyllum aggregatum* are small mushrooms with white flesh and a brown top. Like *enokitake* they are sold in Japan with the mycelium attached, and have a mild flavour.

Matsutake mushroom *Armillaria edodes* are the truffles of Japan. They appear in the stores for only a few feverish weeks in autumn. They are one of the best indicators of the season – one of the few foods left that cannot (as yet) be cultivated, and thus produced to order. They must be gathered in the wild, from the pine forests where they grow. It's the forests that give them their distinctive, and appealing, pine forest aroma.

Maitake *Grifola frondosa* is a large aromatic mushroom with frond like sections. Available dried it has recently been recognised as possibly having anti-viral and immune-enhancing properties. If you can get the fresh one it makes delicious tempura (the batter clings to the folds of the fronds).

Nameko *Pholiota nameko* are small slippery mushrooms, usually sold preserved in jars. They are rarely sold fresh even in Japan as they do not keep well. The only time I've seen the fresh mushroom on sale was at roadside stalls, temporarily set up during the mushroom gathering season. In country areas like Nagano (which is where I experienced mushroom madness!) locals scour the woods for wild mushrooms and then set up their wares by the side of the road. Sometimes makeshift eating tents are erected, serving mushrooms in everything – mushroom noodles, mushroom rice, mushroom hot pot, grilled mushrooms, etc. *Nameko* are often used in clear soups where their woody flavour and delicate amber colour can be fully appreciated. They may be a bit too slippery for some Western tastes, but as is so often in Japanese food, it is the texture that intrigues as much as the taste, and often that texture is slippery.

Myōga *Zingiber mioga.* Although related to the ginger plant it is the young shoots and leaves of this variety which are eaten, and not the tuberous root. It can be found growing wild in the mountains in Japan, and is a harbinger of spring. The fresh variety is available for only a short time. Pickled shoots are sold in jars, but the fresh shoots, finely sliced, are incomparable for taste and crunchiness.

Pak Choi (chingensai or **shakushina)** *Brassica rapa* var. *chinensis.* If a Chinese market has nothing else it will have pak choi – a leafy green vegetable. The whole thing can be eaten, upper leaves, stems and flowers. There are several varieties, but suffice to say that although the green leaf is more flavoursome than the stem the crisp texture of the white stem section is very appealing. Use it as you would Chinese cabbage, with very little cooking. The green parts can be used as an alternative in recipes that call for spinach.

Perilla or Beefsteak plant (shiso) *Perilla frutescens.* There are two types of this highly aromatic plant, which is a part of the mint family, but looks more like it is related to the nettle family. The green leafed shiso (*ao jiso*) is eaten fresh, most usually as an accompaniment to sashimi (some say that it protects against any possible parasites in the fish). It is also used as an ingredient in sophisticated tempura – coated in batter and deep fried. The dark purple variety (*aka shiso*) is used primarily for pickling, and it is this that gives the infamous pickled *umeboshi* plum both its red colour, and flavour. The taste of both varieties is highly distinctive – I've always thought it resembles cumin. In Japan it is readily available – an everyday item like parsley to us, but here you may have to grow your own. It's not difficult to grow – most Japanese emigrés, posted abroad by their company, keep a pot of *shiso* on the front porch, whether in London or Los Angeles.

Shishitō *Capsicum annuum* var *angulosum.* Although this looks like a lethally hot chilli it is actually a rather mild and sweet, small, green pepper. They are eaten whole, and are popularly grilled on skewers as part of *yakitori* or deep fried as tempura.

Sweet potatoes (satsumaimo) *Ipomoea batatas.* This potato gets its Japanese name from the Southern Kyushu area of Japan which was previously dominated by the Satsuma clan, and which was the first area to import it from Okinawa island. Sweet potatoes are now widely available in the West, even though the varieties may slightly differ – some being paler and less sweet than the Japanese varieties, but any of them will suffice. If you can get the one with deep yellow flesh so much the better.

Takuan is *daikon* radish that has been pickled, through the process of lactic acid fermentation, with rice bran and salt, rice lees or just salt. In any case, all over Japan it appears as the ubiquitous (and aromatic) yellow pickle served alongside rice at traditional breakfasts, and almost every other meal as well. It's named after the monk Takuan Osho, who is supposed to have invented it in the seventeenth century. That's one story of its etymology, another being simply that it comes from the Japanese word for preserve – *takuwae*, but that's not half as interesting is it?

Taro potato (*satoimo*) *Colocasia esculenta.* Sometimes called eddoe or yam. In the West Indies the green tops are called callalloo and are a popular vegetable (like spinach) in their own right. In Japan the roots are eaten as a cooked vegetable, and are an important ingredient in *o-den*. The hairy brown skin can cause your hands to itch, so it's advisable to wear rubber gloves when you peel them. Peel thickly and place into lightly vinegared water to stop from discolouring. The raw tuber must not be eaten as it contains a poison, which is only destroyed by cooking. The cooked texture is rather like a slightly gooey and creamy potato. Look for the smallest ones you can find in Oriental, Indian and Caribbean stores. If you are cooking them on their own, not as part of a simmered dish, you can boil them whole in their skins. The skin then slips off easily after cooking.

Trefoil (*mitsuba*) *Cryptotaenia japonica* is sometimes called Japanese wild parsley. In appearance it resembles flat leafed parsley, (*mitsuba* means three leaves) but it has a much better taste – delicate and distinctive. I first tasted it as a garnish on *o-zoni* – a soup containing pieces of *mochi* (rice cake) which is traditionally eaten at New Year. Apart from adding piquancy to soups, the leaves and tender young stems are added to steamed savoury custard, one-pot dishes and lightly steamed vegetables. It can be easily grown if you can't find it in the shops.

Turnip (*kabu*) *Brassica rapa* var. *rapifera*. Some popular varieties are Tokyo Cross, which is small, round and white and *Hinina kabu* which is a longer red skinned variety. All are sweeter, crisper and more tender than the traditional British turnip. I have seen them in this country, sometimes imported from Italy. The tops are eaten as a green, and the roots steamed or simmered, although the widest use is probably for pickles. Whole raw turnip is commonly cut into a chrysanthemum shape, then salted and vinegared and served as an exceptionally pretty pickle.

Udo *Aralia cordata.* I have no idea if there is a common name in English for this – probably not as I have never seen it here. The young stalks of this plant are blanched, either by earthing up (in the same way that *negi* are grown) or by growing them in the dark. It's usually sliced thinly and added to dressed salads, floated on top of soups or simmered. Soak in cold water for a few minutes before using to get rid of any bitterness.

Wax gourd or Winter melon (*tōhgan*) *Benincasa hispida* is available in Chinese markets. It's usually eaten cut into chunks and boiled or steamed.

Yam Cake (*Konnyaku*) is a gelatinous cake made from the starchy root of the *Amorphallus konjac* plant – so although it looks nothing like a vegetable (and doesn't smell like one either – it smells fishy) it is included here. It contains glucomannan, a highly absorbent dietary fibre, which is supposed to reduce appetite, and stabilise blood sugar levels. In fact a sweetened *konnyaku* is now being promoted in the West as a slimming aid. Personally I prefer the traditional ways of eating it, and this book contains several suggestions of how to prepare it. It's also supposed to be good for prostate problems, although I haven't personally been able to test that theory! *Konnyaku* is available in Japanese stores in the chill cabinet in water packs, and keeps unopened for several weeks.

Shirataki is *konnyaku* which has been further processed into long noodle-like strands.

It's used in simmered dishes such as sukiyaki and *shabu shabu*, but is also delicious sautéed with *hijiki*. It's sold in water-packed plastic pouches, which keep well unopened. I have also used dried *shirataki*, which re-hydrates well and is very convenient.

Ito konnyaku is similar to *shirataki*, but thicker.

OTHER INGREDIENTS

Amazake is a sweet thick liquid made from rice, fermented with *kōji* (*Aspergillus oryzae*). Traditionally it is mixed with hot water, and drunk on midnight visits to shrines and temples to celebrate New Year, when its warming qualities are most welcome. It's particularly delicious with some grated fresh ginger. A brown rice version and a variety made from millet are available in the UK, marketed by Clearspring, and are used by macrobiotic cooks (and me) as a natural sweetener.

Bean paste (*an*) is a sweet paste made from *azuki* beans, and much used in the manufacture of sweet cakes. It's an essential ingredient in the ubiquitous *yōkan* – a cloyingly sweet confection made with bean paste and agar agar (*kanten*) into a thick jelly, which is eaten with green tea. *An* can be made at home fairly easily or purchased in tins.

Chirimen, sometimes called **shirasuboshi,** are tiny dried sardines or anchovies. They are used as an ingredient in the sprinkle for eating with rice, called *furikake*, which also contains sesame seeds and bits of *nori* seaweed amongst other things. Larger *shirasuboshi* can be used in vinegared salads – a classic one being *wakame* and cucumber salad.

Kamaboko is a processed fish cake. Fish (different kinds are used) is pounded into a paste and mixed with starch. *Kamaboko* is often coloured a ghastly pink, (which can be off-putting) and slices of it are used in one-pot dishes, such as *nabeyaki udon* and *o-den*. At New Year celebrations it's one of the ingredients in the special New Year food called *o-sechi ryōri*, which is beautifully assembled in layered lacquered boxes. Other types of fish cake used for *o-den* are *hanpen*, which is fluffy white and comes in square cakes, and *chikuwa*, a fish paste sausage.

Karashi (Japanese mustard) is similar to hot English mustard. It's sold in powder form and also ready made in tubes. English mustard powder (although slightly milder) when mixed with water is a decent substitute. *Karashi* is an essential to accompany *o-den*, and is delicious added to simmering liquids.

Kōji *Aspergillus kōji* is the fermenting agent used to make miso, saké and rice vinegar. It is available in health food stores here, but making foods from scratch in this way is beyond the scope of this book.

Kuzu starch *Pueriara lobata*. A superior (and accordingly expensive) thickening agent as it thickens into a deep clear glaze. Traditionally *kuzu* was used to make a digestive remedy, as it's reckoned to be excellent for acid stomachs. For cooking purposes potato starch, called *katakuriko* in Japanese, is often substituted. Apart from medicinal reasons, *kuzu* is preferable because it remains solid – *katakuriko* gives off liquid after standing. Although the price of *kuzu* prohibits its use on a daily basis it's good to have some for special dishes where its particular qualities are appreciated, such as Sesame 'Tofu' (*goma dōfu*) or Persimmons in Saké Sauce.

Potato starch (katakuriko) Although these days *katakuriko* usually refers to potato starch, *katakuri* is actually the dog tooth violet (*Erythronium japonicum*) – which is where this starch was obtained many years ago before the availability and price became too prohibitive to process commercially. You need to use less *katakuriko* than you would cornstarch or *kuzu*, as it is stronger than either. *Katakuriko* is fine for thickening sauces which are to be eaten immediately, not so good for thick 'puddings' which are set in a mould (see **kuzu** above).

Roasted soybean powder (kinako) is used as a coating for cakes and *mochi* (rice cakes). It's sometimes mixed with sugar and has an appealing nutty flavour.

FLAVOURS, CONDIMENTS AND SEASONINGS

Dashi is the stock which is the basis of all Japanese cooking. It's used for soups, flavouring, dipping sauces, dressings and simmering. This is the rock on which everything depends. The simplest *dashi* is made with only *kombu* (kelp sea vegetable), but more usually it's also flavoured with dried bonito shavings (*katsuobushi* – see below) or dried sardines (*niboshi*). The soaking water from dried *shiitake* makes an excellent basis for a stock which is also suitable for vegetarians. Home made *dashi* has the best flavour, and is simple to make. However, these days many housewives in Japan use an instant *dashi* powder (*dashi no moto*) which is also widely available abroad, very quick to use and an acceptable substitute. (See the section on Soy and Miso for more on *dashi*.)

Katsuobushi is dried and salted fillet of bonito fish. An extensive drying and fermentation process results in fillets which are as hard as wood, and which keep for years. The fillets are shaved into thin flakes and used as a flavouring – the basis of *dashi* (see above). Very fine flakes, called *hana katsuo,* and shredded flakes called *ito-kezuri katsuo* are also used as a condiment – sprinkled on top of cooked vegetable or tofu.

Mirin is usually described as 'sweet cooking saké'. It's actually made from distilled spirit and *Aspergillus oryzae* mixed with rice – the same culture used in making miso and soy sauce. It is a sweet syrupy liquid, with an alcohol content of about 13%, which is often burned off by the cook. It is used to add sweetness and for marinading and glazing, as in *teriyaki*. It's readily available in both Japanese stores and in the bigger supermarket chains.

Pickled plum (umeboshi) *Prunus mume* is not actually a plum at all but a type of apricot. The unripe fruit is picked when green, dried in the sun and then pickled in salt – a method of preserving them which is at least 1000 years old in Japan. The salted plums are pickled with red perilla (*shiso* leaves), which turns them a dark pink colour, and they become mouth-puckeringly tart. The Japanese though reckon that this tartness is just the thing to wake up the day, so they eat one every morning for breakfast with their rice and miso soup. The effect is to jolt you awake – rather like the culinary equivalent of a cold shower! However, as *umeboshi* have long been used in folk medicine to aid digestion and alkalise an acid stomach, then this practise is probably very sensible. Placed on top of a bed of white rice, one single plum resembles the Japanese flag – red circle on white base – so this food retains a spiritual as well as nutritional place in the nation's heart.

Ume paste (bainiku) is the mashed up flesh of the plums. This form is exceptionally convenient, as you don't have to fiddle about with skin and stones. I use it a lot to add flavour, especially to salad dressings. Clearspring market it in the UK, and it's available in jars at most health food stores. It lasts a long long time.

Ume su is a by-product of making *umeboshi* – a salty vinegar – and I use it in salad dressings – sparingly – as it's very salty.

Ume extract is a medicinal product obtained without adding salt. In Japan it's a popular folk medicine, used to neutralize acid in the stomach and to aid the liver and kidneys in ridding the body of impurities. A concentrated tablet form is sold under the name *meitan*.

Prickly ash pepper (sanshō) *Zanthoxylum piperitum*. This spice is made from the ground pods (not seeds) of the prickly ash tree. In spring the leaves (called *kinome*) are also used and in autumn the berries are pickled. This is not really a pepper as it isn't hot, just sort of – well, tangy. Its fragrance masks greasiness, so it's used with fried and grilled foods.

Rice vinegar (komesu) is much milder than the vinegars we are used to in the West, being low in acid. Rice vinegar is essential for making sushi rice and vinegared salads, but is generally not used for pickling as in the West.

Rice wine (saké) is the national tipple of Japan, brewed from rice mixed with *Aspergillus oryzae*. In cooking, saké is used to lessen strong smells, especially from fish, and to help tenderise foods. If you object to alcohol you can burn it off first by igniting it, and the flavour will remain, many cooks do so anyway.

Sesame (goma) *Sesamum indicum* is as popular in Japan as it is in the Middle East or China. High in calcium, sesame is a useful food for non-dairy eating peoples. Light or white sesame seeds are usually toasted before use to release their flavour. Most often the seeds are then ground and used as a dressing. **Goma dōfu** is a type of savoury sesame custard which is a speciality of Zen temple food – and delicious (see Sweets and Beverages).

Black sesame seeds are used as a garnish because of their striking appearance and in *furikake*, a dried condiment which is sprinkled on rice.

Goma shio is a mixture of salt and sesame and used as a condiment on rice.

Seven spice pepper (shichimi tōgarashi) is hot and spicy, being a mixture of red chilli pepper (*togarashi*), *sanshō*, dried citron peel, white poppy seeds, white sesame seeds, hemp seed, and bits of nori sea vegetable. Sometimes perilla is added (making eight-spice) but the name stays the same. It's used for spicing up bowls of hot *udon* (wheat) noodles, added to soups and a variety of other things, according to taste.

Sudachi *Citrus sudachi* is a citrus similar to *yuzu* (see below) but used whilst still green, and the juice as well as the rind is used.

Wasabi *Wasabia japonica* is the ground root of what is known as Japanese horseradish, although it's not a part of the horseradish family at all, and is unique to Japan. This is the innocent-looking dollop of green paste that can blow your head off in sushi bars. The fresh item is a knobbly root that grows on the edges of streams and ponds. In high class eating places in Japan, you'll be presented with a piece of root to grate yourself on a fine toothed grater, to accompany your meal. More likely it will be ready grated, and in economy restaurants it will be a commercially produced paste. In the West, tubes of paste are available (look for *nama wasabi* – 'fresh' *wasabi*) or a powder which can be mixed up, much like English mustard. (English mustard by the way is not a substitute.) *Wasabi* is essential for sushi and sashimi (raw fish) and is used in this book once or twice to add piquancy to dressings.

Yuzu *Citrus junos* is a Japanese citrus, with no English equivalent. As far as I know it is indigenous to Japan. Lucky Japanese. It has a unique and compelling aroma, which is concentrated in the rind, and which I adore. The flesh is never used, and the juice only occasionally. It is used as much for its aroma as flavour, and is usually encountered as a sliver of peel floating on top of a clear soup. As the lid of the lacquer bowl is lifted the sweet scent of *yuzu* envelops one's nostrils. As I have never seen fresh *yuzu* in the UK, I made sure I brought a good supply of dried peel back from Japan the last time I was there. A powdered *yuzu* 'sprinkle' is available and it too is a decent substitute.

OILS

Safflower (benihana), sunflower (himawari) and rapeseed oils are all popular for deep frying and sautéeing in Japan. Rapeseed oil **(natane abura)** is becoming more widely available in Britain, and I recommended it for its health benefits. It has a better ratio of the 'good' Omega 3 fatty acids to the 'bad' Omega 6 (of which corn oil, sunflower and safflower have more). Olive oil is not recommended for Japanese cooking as the flavour is too distinctive and obliterates delicate tastes.

Sesame Oil (goma abura) when toasted is a highly aromatic oil with a strong nutty flavour. It's used in small quantities for sautéeing root vegetables, such as burdock (*gobo*) and *hijiki* sea vegetable, and sometimes a little is added to the oil used for frying tempura. It has a low smoking point so burns easily. Untoasted cold pressed sesame oil has a mild taste.

SEA VEGETABLES

Sea vegetables contain 10 to 20 times the mineral content of land vegetables, and are good sources of calcium, potassium, magnesium, iron and zinc. **Kombu** and **arame** are particularly rich in iodine, which is not found in many foods. Incidentally, the best way of cutting dried sea vegetables is with scissors, before you soak them in water.

Agar agar (kanten) *Gelidium amansii* is a traditional gelling agent made from the gelidium type of sea vegetable. It is particularly useful in summer as it sets quickly at room temperature, and doesn't melt as readily as gelatin made from animal products. When set it has a sharper line than gelatine, so it takes the shape of moulds well. Agar agar-based jellies are popular in Japan's stifling summer heat – even looking at the crystal clear gel makes you feel cool. Traditionally the production of agar agar (*kanten*) takes place in winter, by cooking the raw sea vegetable down to a gel, which is then left to set in bar-shaped moulds. The bars are left outside on a cold winter's night to freeze. In the daytime the sunlight melts them, and at night they freeze again. This freeze drying process goes on for a week or two, and the result is a very light bar of gel, with its moisture eliminated. *Kanten* can be purchased in this bar form (in which case it can also be used as a fun and nutritious salad ingredient), or in flakes or granules.

Arame *Eisenia bicyclis*. Although at first glance *arame* looks like *hijiki* it is in fact different, being more slippery with a less chewy texture. It's one of those foods that you can slip into any dish to add a little extra flavour. It can be added to rice dishes and salads to make them extra nutritious, or briefly sautéed with other vegetables, stir fry style. *Arame* is usually sold partly processed that is, it is pre-cooked, and cut into thin shreds, ready for brief soaking before use. *Arame*, like *kombu*, is highest of all the sea vegetables in iodine.

Dulse *Palmaria palmata* is an Atlantic sea vegetable, which is not used in Japan, but adapts well to Japanese cookery. It contains all the 56 minerals and trace elements necessary for health, being particularly rich in iron. It also contains vitamins A and B. Apart from all that it is very tasty. Because it's quite soft it can be eaten dried, right out of the packet, as a snack. Re-hydrated it goes well with green vegetables, and chopped finely combines well with grains. I use it in this way to make millet croquettes. It's available in health food shops.

Hijiki *Hizikia fusiforme*. The texture of *hijiki* is quite different from other sea vegetables – it's not slimy at all, but thick and chewy – like soft twigs. *Hijiki* is especially rich in calcium, and combines well with root vegetables such as carrot or lotus root. It's also good sautéed with deep fried tofu, *shirataki* noodles, or soybeans.

Kombu *Laminaria* is rich in iodine, and high in glutamic acid which softens fibres and increases digestibility of foods. The most important use of *kombu* is in making **dashi**, the stock which is the basis of all Japanese cooking (see *dashi*). Putting a piece of *kombu* in with the water when cooking beans helps to make them more digestible, and cuts down cooking time. Dried *kombu* keeps indefinitely, but should be protected from damp. Although the Japanese pronunciation is nearer to *konbu*, it is generally called *kombu* by non-Japanese.

Tororo kombu is a very finely shredded kelp (*kombu*) which is sprinkled on top of soups, whereupon it becomes instantly soft and edible. It's an original fast food, and an excellent way of serving a healthy dish with no effort. It has a strong taste reminiscent of the seaside.

Nori *laver* or *porphyra genus/porphyra tenera*. This is the dark green 'skin' wrapped around sushi. The harvested sea vegetable is cooked to a soupy gluey paste, stretched across large frames, and dried to create thin crisp sheets, that look like carbon paper. These are made in a standard size – 20.5 x 17.5 cm/ 8 x 6 ⅞ inches, and are essential for making sushi rolls (*norimaki*). Cut into strips *nori* is used as a garnish and sprinkled on top of soups, noodles and these days even spaghetti.

When I first stayed in a *minshuku*, a traditional B&B, I was intrigued to discover a little cellophane packet on top of my rice bowl at the breakfast table. It contained about five miniature sheets of *nori*, just the right size for wrapping around a mouthful of hot rice, which, of course, is exactly what they were for. Delicious. The individual packaging ensures the *nori* stays fresh and crisp.

Aonori *Monostrama latissima* or *enteromorpha* is another type of *nori* which is sold as small dried green flakes. In this form it is sprinkled on soups, and is an essential component of *okonomiyaki*, the pancake/pizza popular in Osaka.

Wakame *Undaria pinnatifida* is a mild and delicate sea vegetable, much used in miso soup. It's also commonly made into a vinegared salad mixed with thinly sliced and salted cucumber. Available dried it's very easy to reconstitute. Large pieces should be left for 5 minutes in cold water, and the hard spine cut off before using. Packets of dried, ready cut *wakame* are exceptionally convenient as they can be sprinkled directly into hot soup. The dried product swells impressively when it's re-hydrated, so you always need less than you think.

Mekabu is the sporophylls, or base section of *wakame*, which is exceptionally high in minerals. It has a stronger and saltier flavour than *wakame*, and has been popularised in the West by macrobiotic cooks.

WHEAT PRODUCTS AND NOODLES

Hiyamugi noodles are finer than *udon* but thicker than *sōmen*, and, like both, made from wheat flour. Usually eaten cold in summer like *sōmen*.

Soba are buckwheat noodles, made with nothing more than flour and salt. As buckwheat contains no gluten it's usually mixed with wheat flour, and the proportion of buckwheat to wheat is reflected in the price. 100% buckwheat is for those who must have as much of the distinctive buckwheat taste as possible and don't mind paying for it. However, another reason for eating buckwheat is that it is high in rutin, which helps thin the blood, so *soba* is a good food for helping to avoid heart disease. As Japanese men probably eat *soba* noodles about 3 or 4 times a week it could be one of the contributory factors to Japan's traditionally low incidence of heart disease. *Soba* noodles are eaten both hot and cold.

Sōmen noodles are very fine wheat flour noodles, eaten cold in summer.

Udon noodles are made with wheat flour, and usually eaten in hot broth. They are quite thick and chewy, and are essential in *nabeyaki udon* – a one-pot dish cooked and served in an individual miniature casserole.

Wheat Gluten (fu) Most popularly this is available dried. It is sold in either rectangular biscuit-like pieces, or in circular pieces with a hole in the middle, in which case it is called *kuruma fu* (meaning wheel shaped). It is added to soups and stews. It is often shaped into small pieces resembling flowers or vegetables to reflect the season, such as *hyotan* or gourds, and red maple leaves, to symbolise autumn, and in spring it's made into pink cherry blossom shapes.

Nama bu is fresh gluten. It's not available outside Japan, and even in Japan it's a speciality of Kyoto cooking. It is pure protein, used in traditional vegetarian cooking instead of meat, usually simmered in some way. You can make wheat gluten easily at home.

DRIED FOODS

Luckily for us in the West many Japanese ingredients are available dried. This is not just for export, the Japanese themselves use a great deal of dried food. Blessed with sunny dry weather in winter, and hot sunny days in spring and autumn, the drying of food became an essential and efficient method for preserving food for the winter months. Mushrooms, sea vegetables, freeze dried tofu, fish, and gluten are all available dried.

BEVERAGES

Tea (o-cha) is the national beverage of Japan, the green tea which is drunk without milk or sugar. Japanese tea comes in several grades.

Bancha is coarse grade tea for drinking in quantity, to slake your thirst. This is the tea which is drunk with family and friends, and in ordinary restaurants. It's always served free, and must be served hot. In Northern areas of Japan frequent tea drinking is accompanied by pickle eating.

Genmaicha is ordinary grade *bancha* which is mixed with roasted grains of brown rice (they look like popcorn in the packet). This is a nice mild combination and I find it a good way of introducing foreigners to the taste of green tea.

Hōjicha is roasted *bancha* tea which can be drunk either hot or cold. It has a smokey flavour and is less bitter than green tea. It's a good tea to quench thirst, and usually quite acceptable to Westerners who may be apprehensive about green tea.

Kukicha is similar to *hōjicha*, but contains no leaves – only twigs and stems. It is therefore low in caffeine, and so appeals to macrobiotic eaters and people who wish to regulate their caffeine intake. Unlike other Japanese teas *kukicha* is actually simmered, not merely steeped. It's also quite delicious.

Senchais is high grade green tea picked from young bushes. This is tea for guests – the tea which is served to special visitors, and in formal situations such as business meetings. Often served with sweet bean cakes such as *yōkan*.

Gyokuro is the finest tea of all, the tenderest leaves being picked under optimum conditions. To be offered this tea is an honour and it must therefore be drunk with expressions of appropriate gratitude.

Matcha is the powdered green tea of the tea ceremony.

Mugicha is made from roasted barley, and is a popular and refreshing drink in summer, when it's drunk chilled.

ALCOHOL

Saké The national drink, brewed from rice. Used in many ceremonial occasions but also to simply get drunk.

Shōchū A white spirit distilled from grain, or starch, variously potato, barley, millet or buckwheat. Considered less refined than saké – a workman's drink. It's drunk cold in summer, with various mixers, such as lime, lemon etc., a recent fashion being *shōchu* mixed with oolong tea. In winter it is often drunk with hot water, with an *umeboshi* plum in the bottom of the glass.

Umeshu is a delicious plum-flavoured liqueur, made by flavouring alcohol with the *umeboshi* plum. It's a popular and refreshing summer drink. It's sold in liquor stores in large bottles, sometimes with several plums settled in the bottom, and also in cans pre-mixed with soft drink, such as soda or lemonade.

FISH GLOSSARY

Some of the most commonly used fish for sushi, with their English approximations, follow. The latin names are for the varieties found in Japan. I am indebted to Richard Hosking's book *A Dictionary of Japanese Food*, which provided me with many of these translations and latin names.

akagai	ark shell *(Anadara broughtonii)*
anago	conger eel *(Anago anago)*
aoyagi	round clam *(Mactra chinensis)*
ayu	sweetfish *(Plecoglossus altivelis)*
awabi	abalone *(Nordotis* spp.*)*
buri	yellowtail *(Seriola quinqueradiata)*
hamachi	younger yellowtail
hamaguri	Venus clam *(Meretrix lusoria)*
hirame/karei	flounder *(Paralichthys olivaceus)*
hotategai	scallops *(Patinopecten yessoensis)*
ika	squid *(Dibranchiate cephalopod)*
ikura	salmon roe
kaki	oyster *(Crassostrea gigas)*
kani	crab
maguro	tuna *(Thunnus thynnus)*
saba	mackerel
sake	salmon
sayori	halfbeak/garfish *(Hyporhamphus sajori)*
suzuki	sea bass *(Lateolabrax japonicus)*
tako	octopus *(Octopus vulgaris)*
torigai	cockle *(Fulvia mutica)*
unagi	freshwater eel *(Anguilla japonica)*
uni	sea urchin

Some other cooking fish are :

aji	horse mackerel *(Trachurus japonicus)*
amadai	red tilefish *(Branchiostegus japonicus)*
bora	striped mullet, grey mullet *(Mugilcephalus cephalus)*
kamasu	saury pike *(Sphyraea japonica)*
hamo	pike conger *(Muraenesox cinereus)* *has lots of tiny bones. Don't recommend.
iwashi	sardine
kajiki	swordfish
kisu	sillago/ Japanese whiting *(Sillago japonica)*
masu	sea trout *(Oncorhynchus masou masou)*
matodai	John Dory/flatfish *(Zeus faber)*
mejina	blackfish *(Girella punctata)*
sayori	half beak/garfish *(Hyporhamphus sajori)*
sanma	Pacific saury *(Cololabis saira)*
shirauo	whitebait
suzuki	sea bass
wakasoji	smelt

SOME USEFUL JAPANESE UTENSILS

Although it's far from difficult to cook Japanese with a Western style *batterie de cuisine*, there are a few items which will make your cooking either slightly easier, or simply more fun. If you are like me you'll be pleased of the excuse to purchase even more interesting kitchen utensils. Every time I go to Japan I come back with more bamboo spoons, bamboo scrapers, graters, cutters and assorted low-tech gadgets. I lovingly treasure my cedar sushi bowl (*sushi oke*) and rice pot, both bound with bands of copper, my blue-glazed grinding bowl (*suribachi*), ginkgo-leaf-shaped cutters and a mountain of other bits and pieces. The best place in Tokyo to find all these things is an area called Kappabashi, which is right by the Tokyo fish market at Tsukiji. A trip to Kappabashi is a cook's dream: streets of shops piled high with kitchen utensils of all shapes and sizes, lots of bamboo, lots of cedar, wire skimmers bound with copper, stainless steel and of course lacquer ware and ceramics. It's my idea of heaven.

Bamboo rolling mat (*makisu*) A small slatted mat of bamboo strips (like a smaller version of the bamboo window blinds called *sudare*). This is an essential for making *norimaki* – rolled sushi with a *nori* wrapping. It's also useful for squeezing moisture out of cooked vegetables, such as spinach.

Charcoal brazier (*shichirin*) A small table top stove, made of unglazed clay which is filled with charcoal. A metal grid is placed over the top and used for cooking at the table. The clay is usually decorated with Chinese characters, making them decorative, and, these days, rather old fashioned items. High class restaurants still use them and they are readily purchased at neighbourhood pottery stores in Japan. At home people are more likely to use portable table top gas burners.

Chawan mushi cups *Chawan* is a bowl or cup, and *mushi* means 'to steam'. *Chawan mushi* is a steamed savoury egg custard. If you come across handleless cups with lids in a Japanese store this is what they are for. Any medium size tea cup, or mug, will do the job.

Chopsticks (*hashi*) are a most efficient tool, as they can be shovel, whisk, tongs, knife and fork, all in one. A pair of long chopsticks is useful for cooking, and inexpensive. The precision afforded is also helpful for arranging food delicately (Japanese chopsticks are more pointed than Chinese ones). Metal tipped chopsticks are used for retrieving fried foods (as in tempura) and thicker wooden ones are used for mixing tempura batter. Lacquered chopsticks are elegant, for use in a formal meal, and in most families each person has their own favourite pair. A popular present for couples is a decorated pair of 'his and hers' chopsticks, presented in an attractive box (with 'his' being longer than 'hers'). **Waribashi** are the disposable chopsticks used in restaurants. Although hygienic they cause some concern to environmentalists, (including me) who decry the cavalier way in which the wood is used only once then discarded. When I was working at NHK in Japan in the 1980s there was a move to introduce re-usable chopsticks in the staff restaurants. One day, instead of the disposable wooden *waribashi*, we were offered re-usable plastic ones in a common pot placed on the table. Activism worked even in Japan.

Cutter (*nukigata*) Small metal cutters in flower shapes are used to cut food into seasonally appropriate shapes. Cherry blossoms for spring, bamboo leaves for summer, maple or ginkgo leaves for autumn, and plum blossoms for winter, are some of the most common. Boxes of four (one for each season) can be purchased.

Deep frying pot (*agemono nabe*) This is not an essential item as any heavy bottomed pot will do, but dedicated tempura cooking pots are nice as they have a wire drainer which fits on the side. Although woks are sometimes suggested for deep frying I don't recommend them. They are thin, and conduct heat quickly, which is what you need for stir frying, but when used for deep frying the oil can become too hot. What you need is a steady, even temperature, which is why a heavy pot is better.

Donabe *Nabe* is actually the Japanese word for cooking pot, so refers to saucepans of all kinds, including cast iron and aluminium ones. However, when talking of *nabemono* – one-pot dishes cooked at the table – ***donabe*** particularly refers to large earthenware cooking pots which can be put directly on to a flame, usually a portable gas ring which is placed in the centre of the table. Smaller *nabe*, with lids, are used to prepare dishes such as *nabeyaki – udon*, which is cooked individually. Earthenware *nabe* must be completely dry on the outside before they are put on a flame, otherwise they will crack. Wash and dry thoroughly, therefore, after use.

Japanese grater (*oroshigane*) Fairly essential for Japanese cooking as the teeth are finer than on a Western style grater. Grates root vegetables such as *daikon* and turnip into a pulp. One style, made from plastic, has a dish underneath to hold the gratings, and is good for larger quantities. Another style is made from aluminium with very sharp teeth, and is best for smaller things such as ginger. Ceramic graters are also available but slightly less efficient as they aren't as sharp as the other types.

Knives (*hōchō*) The most important tool in a Japanese chef's kitchen, along with his cutting board, is his knife. Indeed, a Japanese chef is referred to as "one who is skilled with the knife." Japanese knives are varied, but the most useful all purpose knife you can buy is a *nakiri bōchō*– a vegetable knife. This is big, almost like a cleaver, but lighter, and will do most things you need, from peeling to chopping. Just make sure it's sharp. The other difference is that Japanese knives are sharpened on one side only – this is most efficient for making paper thin slices. Small paring knives are not much used, as even peeling is done with a large knife (see cutting notes below). Extremely long, thin and sharp knives (*sashimi bōchō*) are used for slicing raw fish, but any very sharp knife will do. If you try to cut raw fish with a blunt knife you get a horrible ragged edge – not attractive at all. Cleavers (*deba bōchō*) which are heavier than vegetable knives, and have a pointed end, are used for fish, chicken and meat. Japanese knives are famous for their craftsmanship, developed through a long tradition of sword making. The most expensive knives are made from hard steel, and are practically unaffordable for the home cook. The knives commonly used in homes in Japan are either carbon steel, made from a thin layer of hard steel sandwiched in between a softer steel, or stainless steel. I recommend a carbon steel knife as it is so much easier to keep sharp. The hard steel 'sandwich' inside is what gives the sharp edge. Stainless steel knives look nice, but lose their edge too quickly. The edge of a carbon steel knife can be easily honed with a whetstone, and should be sharpened after each use. Just be sure to dry it well to prevent rusting.

Drop lids (otoshibuta) are made from cedar and are made to fit inside the saucepan, sitting on top of the foods being cooked, when simmering and boiling. This stops the foods from moving around and breaking up, and also acts to contain the heat and concentrate it into the food. You can improvise with a circle of aluminium foil (or find an enterprising carpenter to make you some).

Wooden pickle lids (oshibuta) look similar to drop lids, but are thicker and have a small hole in the middle, for liquid to seep through. They are placed on top of vegetables that are to be pickled, and a heavy weight (traditionally a stone) is placed on top.

Metal mould (nagashibakō) These square sided moulds with a removable lining are perfect for making straight sided gelled items. Use them for making sesame custard (goma dōfu) and for both sweet and savoury kanten 'jellies'.

Omelette pan (makiyakinabe) A small rectangular pan for making the rolled omelette which is a feature of sushi making. Their advantage is the shape – producing straight sided omelettes of the correct size.

Pestle and mortar (suribachi) (grinding bowl) and **surikogi** (grinding stick). The great thing about Japanese pestle and mortars is that the inside surface of the bowl has tiny grooves 'combed' into it. This assists the grinding process most efficiently, making light work of sesame seeds, walnuts and the like. Because the surface is slightly porous I never use mine for garlic or Indian style spices, as I don't want to contaminate it – I keep it purely for Japanese cooking. It can also be used to mix tofu or mash potatoes and other ingredients.

Rice paddle (shamoji) A flat spoon for serving rice, made from bamboo. Wood is a good material for this as it absorbs moisture from the rice. The paddle is an essential for 'cutting through' and cooling sushi rice. Elegant versions, for serving at table, are lacquered.

Rice shaper (o-nigiri no oshigata) Small plastic moulds for shaping cooked rice into the traditional triangular shape required for o-nigiri (or musubi) rice balls. (For children's lunch boxes other fancy shapes such as animals and flowers are sold.) I use mine often, and it gives a really neat professional looking finish to your Japanese cooking. Keep a bowl of water handy when using it, and rinse between each use – this stops the rice sticking to it.

Sesame roaster Not really an essential, it's a ceramic bowl-shaped vessel which is almost completely enclosed. It has a hole in the top, and a hollow handle. The enclosed top stops the seeds from popping right out of the bowl, and the hollow handle enables you to pour the seeds out once they are roasted.

Skewers (kushi) are much used in Japanese cookery. Metal skewers are used for grilling fish, and they must be sharp. Bamboo skewers are used for grilling vegetables, tofu and yakitori (chicken morsels). The other point to make regarding skewers, is that when using bamboo ones you have to be careful not to burn them. A Japanese style charcoal grill is built up between brick supports. The skewers themselves rest on the supports, so only the skewered food is exposed to the heat (unlike a

Western style barbecue). Bear this in mind when you are barbecuing, otherwise you'll have charred bits of stick falling in to the fire, along with the food. You may have to build an improvised one. For more information on skewering see the section on fish and chicken.

Skimmer (ami shakushi) – both fine mesh and coarser mesh are available. They are used for skimming oil during deep frying, and for removing scum (*aku*) from simmering foods, especially meat. This was an important aspect of traditional cooking, as the scum was seen as harbouring bad spirts (bad *ki*) in the food. Traditionally made skimmers are works of art, hand-made by craftsmen and women, who carefully shape the wire and bind it with copper. Similar items can easily be found in Chinese stores, but if you find yourself in Kappabashi buy the original Japanese article.

Small and wider-spaced mesh scoops are for retrieving soft foods like tofu from a cooking pot.

Steamer (mushiki) is flat bottomed and square, not circular, and readily holds ceramic cups for making *chawan mushi*. **Seirō** is a traditional large wooden or bamboo steamer, still used for steaming glutinous rice and rice cakes.

Wooden sushi mould (oshiwaku) Used to make the pressed sushi, called *battera zushi,* popular in Western Japan. A useful item to help you make professional looking sushi, but any small rectangular container could be used instead.

WHAT IS A JAPANESE MEAL?

A Japanese meal has been described as a succession of hors d'oeuvres. It's quite a good description, although I prefer to liken it to eating in a tapas bar in Spain. Lots of small quantities of many things. The one rule that is steadfast in Japanese cuisine of all types is that you don't serve a lot of one thing – and each dish is served on a separate plate or bowl. The plate itself is specially chosen to best enhance the food being served. This may be because the Japanese have been used to making do with little – so what they have has always been appreciated, worshipped and enhanced. They have been forced, by necessity, to cultivate a sense of gratitude for the gifts of nature. Whatever the reason, the fact is that whatever you are served in Japan is almost always served beautifully. Food never crowds the plate. In fact the plate itself is part of the meal. Any old plate won't do. For a lover of ceramics like me this is a dream. Perhaps this is why I fell in love with Japanese cookery – now I have an excuse to buy even more plates and dishes. If you are a beginner though don't be put off – a simple white plate or dish will suffice. The important thing is that each dish has its own receptacle and plenty of space around it. I could never understand why American portions are so huge, and the plates overflowing. To me, a lover of Japanese minimalism, American platefuls seemed so gross. Then one day I was cooking with an American woman, and I specifically chose larger plates on which to display my food – so that the portions would sit daintily in the middle. My American friend couldn't understand that at all – to her an overflowing plate was a symbol of abundance! Which to me perfectly illustrates two completely different attitudes to past deprivation. Both countries are reacting to a memory of a time when they had little, but whereas the Americans celebrate their current prosperity by loading up the plate, the Japanese show their appreciation of what they have by celebrating and contemplating each morsel. Japanese extravagance or abundance is not shown by overflowing the plate but by the number of dishes served.

SO WHAT IS A BASIC MEAL?

A basic meal is known as *ichijū sansai* 'soup and three'. This means: soup, three dishes plus rice and pickles. The three dishes will each be prepared in a different cooking style – chosen from the following: grilled (*yakimono*), steamed (*mushimono*), simmered (*nimono*), deep fried (*agemono*), sautéed (*itamemono*), vinegared (*sunomono*) or dressed salad (*aemono*). All of the recipes in this book have a small symbol beside them, denoting which cooking style they are prepared with. A balanced meal will therefore have a selection of icons, and not too many of the same one. You can serve the dishes all together, as you would at home, or in succession as you would be served in an *izakaya* (like tapas in Spain).

A formal meal would begin with up to three 'starters': an appetizer (a small dish of seasonally prepared titbits or a vinegared salad), a clear soup (to show off the delicacy of the basic *dashi* stock) and raw fish (sashimi). Following this, the 'three middle dishes' could number up to five or more , incorporating one of each cooking style. The finish would then be another soup, usually miso (not clear), rice and pickles.

The important points to note are to avoid duplicating ingredients, and to pay attention to colour and presentation. The aim is to try and get a balance of colour, cooking style and ingredients. Common sense will show you the way.

COOKING METHODS

 Aemono Dressed things, as in *horenso no goma **ae*** (spinach with sesame dressing), *nasu no soramame **ae*** (aubergine with broad bean dressing).

 Agemono Deep fried things.

 Itamemono Sautéed/pan fried, such as *no miso itame* (sautéed with miso).

 Mushimono Steamed things. *Mushi* is steam. *Mushiyaki* is steam grilled, meaning to steam in a foil parcel which itself is grilled, cooked over or under a flame.

 Nimono Simmered (or poached) things.

 Sunomono Vinegared things (*su* is vinegar, and becomes *zu* at the end of a word as in *karashi zu*, mustard vinegar).

 Yakimono Grilled, cooked over charcoal or a flame, as in *yakitori* (grilled chicken kebabs).

COOKING TECHNIQUES

Arai Means to wash. Used for river (freshwater) fish. Wash with cool water and then plunge into iced water and leave it for a minute to chill.

Sarasu Soaking in a lightly vinegared water to prevent discolouration and remove bitterness. Used with burdock, lotus root, taro potato and sometimes sweet potato. Use 1 teaspoon rice vinegar to ½ litre of water.

Shimofuri To freshen meat and fish by pouring boiling water and then plunging into iced water to chill. Reduces odour and freshens the flesh.

Tataki Actually means to pound, and refers to the ground ingredients (such as garlic or ginger) which are wrapped around fish or meat to flavour it. The fish is first quickly seared on the outside (the inside should still be uncooked), wrapped in the garlic or ginger then left to chill. It's a common technique for serving bonito (to make *katsuo tataki*), *aji* (horse mackerel) and tender fresh beef.

Yugaku Parboiling. For green leafy vegetables this means plunging into boiling water briefly and then straight into cold to arrest the cooking process and retain colour (also called *irodashi* – colour giving technique). Sliced root vegetables can also be put straight into boiling water but are usually left to cool naturally. Chunkier root vegetables are placed in cold water and brought to the boil, to allow them to cook evenly all the way through and prevent the surface from falling part.

Quick cooking such as grilling (yakimono) and sautéeing (itamemono) are suitable for:

Shellfish (scallops, prawns, squid etc.) and firm white fish – cook quickly over a high heat, as long cooking makes them rubbery. You need only a light seasoning to enhance the flavour – not to penetrate the food.

Meat and chicken are usually basted (or sautéed) with a strongly flavoured sweet liquid and cooked quickly – until just cooked through, (as in *yakitori,* chicken, liver and salmon *teriyaki,* sukiyaki etc.).

Charcoal grilling: Japanese charcoal burners are either little pots with a wire over the top (so you can have the bamboo skewers jutting over the edge) or small troughs, built up either side so you can rest the bamboo protuberances on bricks, whilst the food in between cooks on the coals. Soak the skewers in water for half an hour before using.

If you cook like this over coals then cook the side which will be uppermost when served first.

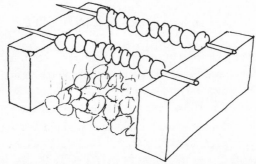

Longer cooking, simmering (nimono) is suitable for:

Oily fish which generally benefits from a longer simmering in a heavily seasoned liquid which will eliminate odour and oiliness, and where the seasoning will impart flavour – for example, mackerel simmered in miso, sardines in saké and plum.

Root vegetables such as *daikon,* potatoes, burdock and items that will absorb flavour such as freeze dried tofu, *konnyaku* (yam cake) and fish cake.

Chicken and light fish when simmered are cooked for a shorter time.

Gluten products and tofu products are usually only briefly simmered until flavour is absorbed.

Uses for fish common in the UK

Cod and **haddock** can be used for one-pot dishes, and short simmering. Fillets can be used for grilling, such as *teriyaki* style.

Dab – grill the whole thing. Deep fry or simmer fillets.

Herring, **mackerel** and **sardines** – use whole for salt grilling, use fillets for longer simmering in strong flavoured stock. Marinade for *sashimi*. Smoked mackerel can be used for rolled sushi.

Monkfish – use for steaming or deep frying.

Plaice, **Flounder** – deep fry or steam-grill fillets.

Red mullet – salt grill whole fish. Use steaks in soups and one-pot dishes.

Sea bass – use in soups, one-pot dishes, for grilling and for sashimi.

Sea bream – grill the whole thing *shioyaki* style. Use steaks for one-pot dishes and soups.

Sole – grill whole or deep fry fillets.

Squid – makes lovely *sashimi* when fresh. Can be marinated in vinegar, grilled, simmered and deep fried.

Swordfish – steaks can be grilled *teriyaki* style.

Tuna – makes delectable *sashimi*, especially the fatty tuna (*toro*). Can also be simmered, grilled and seared.

Salmon – smoked salmon is excellent for faint hearted *sashimi*-eaters. Fresh salmon can be also eaten as *sashimi*. Steaks can be poached in one-pot dishes, steamed or grilled, and make lovely salmon *teriyaki*.

Trout – whole trout can be salt grilled, fillets poached or steamed quickly in light flavoured stock. If very fresh they can be used for *sashimi* (after giving them the *arai* washing treatment).

CUTTING STYLES AND STROKES

Cutting strokes

Once you've selected your fresh ingredients, made a meal plan and know what you are going to cook; you have to actually prepare the ingredients, and the first stage of course is cutting. The way you cut determines how pleasurable your cooking will be, how well the foods cook and how attractive the finished result will be. There are three basic cutting strokes, all simple to master, and each with a different purpose.

Hira giri: *giri* means to cut, and *hira* is to pull, thus this is a pulling or drawing cut, where the knife is pulled towards you. It's used for *sashimi* and delicate cooked foods and is a gentle cut designed to preserve the shape of the food. The best way to see it in action is to go to a sushi bar and watch the chef slicing fish for sashimi. **Oshi giri:** *Osu* means to push, so this is a pushing cut, where the knife is steadied by the left hand above it and forced down firmly. It's used for things with resistance like *mochi* rice cakes, raw pumpkin, cutting sheets of nori seaweed and for mincing. **Tsuki giri:** *tsuki* means to thrust, so this is a thrusting cut. The knife is pushed forward, and this is the most common cut, used for cutting raw vegetables and thinly slicing. This is the cut I most have to instruct when I'm teaching Japanese cooking. The mistake most students make is to push down or pull the knife towards them. Wrong! Once you have mastered this you can make those wafer thin slices so admired in Japanese cooking, and you can make them quickly. Steady the food to be cut in your left hand, with the knuckles tucked under resting on top of the food (this is so you don't slice your fingers off). As you slice, the knuckles move to the left along the length of the vegetable.

Cutting styles

Katsura muki are thin continuous sheets. To be honest this is difficult. A top chef can peel a whole *daikon* radish into one long continuous sheet in this way, but I confess that I can't. It takes nerve and an enormous amount of skill. Basically the radish is 'fed' through the blade, and the procedure is executed in mid air. This cutting style is used to make shredded *daikon* radish, which accompanies *sashimi*. The resulting long thin sheet is further sliced into thin strands, but you can get a similar result using a Japanese shredder.

KATSURA MUKI

Circles, half moons are used for root vegetables such as *daikon*, carrots and lotus root. Half moons are then **quartered** and used for smaller and uneven vegetables such as bamboo shoots or carrots. These cuts are used for simmering, sautéeing, deep frying, for some salads and for pickling, depending on thickness.

RAN GIRI

Rolling wedges called **ran giri**. *Ran* means chaos, so this is a random cut, used for long thin root vegetables such as leeks, burdock, and carrots, and for pumpkin.

It is used for simmered dishes, which need longer cooking. The vegetable is rotated 90 degrees between diagonal cuts.

SASAGAKI

Shavings (sasagaki) are made by rotating a long thin vegetable – like sharpening a pencil. It's commonly used for cutting burdock.

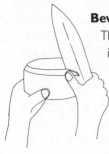

Bevel cut cylinders are used for *daikon*, turnips, carrot and pumpkin. The top and bottom edge are bevelled to stop the food falling apart in cooking.

Clapper cut (*hyōshigi giri*). *Hyōshigi* are wooden 'clappers' which were used in the past by night watchmen, or firemen, who roamed the streets, knocking together bits of wood and crying out,

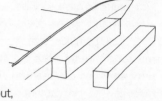

warning householders to be careful of fire, and remind them to tend their charcoal braziers, or paraffin stoves. The thick rectangles (about ½ to 1 cm) resulting from this cut are reminiscent of these wooden clappers, and this is why this cut is so named. Root vegetables such as burdock and carrot can be cut this way, for simmering, and courgettes and pumpkin can be cut like this for tempura. Thinner rectangles or slabs are made for vinegared dishes.

Juliennes are made from thin slabs, which are stacked and cut through again. One of their uses is for vinegared dishes and salted garnishes.

SAINOME GIRI

Cubing (*sainome giri*) and **mincing (*mijin giri*)** are created by stacking slices, as above, and used for vegetables, meat and sometimes fish (cubes of tuna for example for simmering).

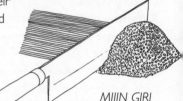

MIJIN GIRI

TABLEWARE AND PRESENTATION

"As each popular tree and flower comes into season and the people flock to country resort or city park, the streets of Tokyo are quick to reflect the feeling of the moment. The Ginza (Silver Way) the famous modernized shopping street of central Tokyo bursts into seasonable decorations four times a year at least. Shopkeepers and householders combine to defray expenses and the thoroughfare is decorated as a whole, not piecemeal, with rows of lanterns, each hanging from its stand of white wood with penthouse roof. The pine, bamboo and plum blossom which celebrate New Year give place to cherry and weeping willow which hardly seem dusty before wistaria and iris appear."

Grace James, *Japan Recollections and Impressions*

Although millions of Japanese now live in urban areas, many of them still have a romantic attachment to the countryside, to where they came from (even if it was a generation or two back) and thus to nature. This attitude can be seen in the high streets of cities which are decorated four times a year (at least) with plastic representations of the changing seasons such as cherry blossoms (in spring) and maple leaves (in autumn). In spring the arrival of cherry blossoms is most importantly celebrated by everyone visiting the local parks to sit under the pink canopy of the blossom trees – a ritual called *hanami* or flower viewing. There they drink plenty of saké and beer, accompanied by picnic lunches, and once the effects of the saké begin to kick in, they dance and sing and generally enjoy themselves. Such is their devotion to this activity that office juniors are sent out from the office in the early morning to 'bag' a pitch under a tree. Later in the day the rest of the office staff will appear, and work will be forgotten for the rest of the day.

So important is the blossoming of the flowers that it is reported on the news – along with the weather charts. The whole nation follows the progress of the 'cherry blossom line' as it travels northwards – the blossoms opening first in the south, and then maybe two or three weeks later in the northern areas. In autumn a similar (but more subdued) frenzy accompanies the viewing of maple leaves as they change colour. Excursions are made to mountain areas where the leaves are at their most colourful and abundant. All this preamble is to illustrate what could be called an institutionalisation of an appreciation of nature in Japan. And it translates itself to the way that food is presented. The Japanese word for food presentation is *moritsuke*, and it means 'to heap'. Food is always heaped in an attractive pile on the plate, and the resulting arrangement is meant to symbolise natural features of the landscape. Mountains (larger pieces of food) are always at the back, with rivers, valleys and streams, rocks and stones at the forefront. This is why Japanese food is almost never presented in a symmetrical, circular or geometric pattern (in the way that *nouvelle cuisine* often is in the West). Think of a Japanese garden. There are no clipped hedges or dead straight pathways, as there are in formal French or English gardens. All is meandering, off centre, uneven and natural. This is what you should aim for in your presentation. Luckily it can be simple, and because much Japanese food is served at room temperature it can also be prepared in advance.

Presentation ideas: Serve a single grilled fish on a piece of slate, or even bed of small pebbles, or just scatter a few around the edge, placing the fish with the head facing left.

Tempura is commonly served on a bamboo basket, but you can try placing a few morsels on a fallen autumn leaf, or decorate with a ginkgo leaf or two.

Lay a few pine needles across deep fried food in autumn or winter.

In summer present food in glass dishes or on glass plates for a cooling effect. Float two or three green maple leaves on top of cold tofu in iced water.

Use natural items for presentation such as a slab of wood or marble. Large scallop or abalone shells can be used as a small side plate, to hold pickles or small portions of salad. Smaller shells can be used to hold dollops of *wasabi* paste or mustard, or a small mound of grated ginger or *daikon*. A wonderful lively fish restaurant in Nakano in Tokyo called Okajyoki seats its customers around a long square counter and places in front of each diner a large slab of slate on which freshly grilled fish is served. You can do the same. Just be sure anything you use is clean, and any leaves you use aren't poisonous!

Tableware

As a visit to any Japanese pottery store will teach you, there is no such thing as a matching dinner service in Japan. There is however an enormous variety of dishes, bowls, cups, pots and plates. There are shallow bowls and deep bowls, small and large, tiny saucer like plates and large square or oblong plates. Dishes are sold in sets of five, and an average home will have a least ten different sets if not many more. Each shape and size of dish has a different purpose as described below.

How to eat – table manners

"How the hell do you eat soup with chopsticks?" is a common cry amongst new-comers to Japanese food. The answer of course lies in the fact that the soup is served in a lacquer bowl, which has a little stand on the bottom, and in the fact that the bowl is never brim full. The bowl is designed so that you can lift it to your mouth, holding the top rim with your thumb and with the base of the bowl resting on your fingers. Lift it to your mouth and use your chopsticks to pick out the solids from the soup. Sip the liquid from the rim of the bowl. This is why soup bowls are not made of china – otherwise they'd be too hot to hold. Rice is eaten in a similar way, lifting the bowl to your mouth and 'shovelling' the rice in with the chopsticks. Large flat plates which hold grilled and deep fried dishes are not lifted to the mouth, but pieces are broken off and conveyed to the mouth with chopsticks (this is also why food is prepared in bite size pieces). This is easy with softer food like grilled fish, or simmered *daikon* radish. Sometimes you can place pieces of cooked food on top of your rice bowl and carry them in the bowl to your mouth in that way. It is bad manners to leave the rice bowl on the table and take food from it.

   The small dish used for soy sauce which accompanies *sashimi* can also be lifted to the mouth if necessary. When dipping sushi in to soy sauce dip the fish side only. If you dip the rice side then it'll all fall apart and you'll have a horrible mess.

Chopstick etiquette

There are a few things it's useful to know when dining with Japanese people, especially concerning chopsticks. It's frowned upon to wave your chopsticks around gesticulating, and definitely not done to suck them or have them touch your mouth. Chopsticks are also used for picking up foods from a communal plate, and in polite circles one turns the sticks around and uses the non-eating end to select pieces (sometimes serving chopsticks are set instead). Stabbing food with chopsticks is also considered bad manners, although many a poor *gaijin* (foreigner) in Japan has been known to resort to such a gesture in frustration at not being able to pick something up. The most heinous crimes of all though are to pass food from chopstick to chopstick, and to leave chopsticks sticking in a bowl of rice. Both of these are associated with death rituals, so naturally they aren't welcome at the dinner table. As well as being superstitious the Japanese are a tidy people and like to leave things looking neat – chopsticks are placed on rests in front of the diner (facing left) and replaced there after eating. At formal tea ceremony meals the rice bowl is washed out with tea, and actually wiped clean with a cloth or tissue at the table, by the guest.

"At the close of the meal the guest swills out his own vessels with hot water, and drinks the water afterwards. Taking a piece of hanshi (white paper) he wipes everything until it is perfectly dry and clean. The used paper he folds small and wrapping it in a clean sheet, hides it in his sleeve. My own sleeve being unsuitable for the purpose I deposited my papers in my handbag, and I noticed that my brother quietly stowed his in his pocket."

Grace James, *Japan Recollections and Impressions*

The best example of this though is the way the Japanese wrap up 'take away' lunch boxes after eating the contents. Even on trains (which is one of the commonest places to eat lunch boxes or *bentō*), people go to the trouble of wrapping all the little bits up again, and carefully replacing the elaborate tie, before throwing it away. It's just another way of showing respect for their food.

Some of the things we in the West find abhorrent however are perfectly acceptable in Japan, and slurping is one of them. Soup is slurped, and noodles are sucked in noisily from the bowl. I have to admit it's hard to get used to – I had to train myself to make a noise when eating noodles – if you don't they think you're not enjoying them. Picking ones teeth with a toothpick at table is also acceptable, so long as it's done coyly – with the left hand shielding the mouth, while the right digs away. Some of these habits were criticised by Grace James in her book, *Japan Recollections and Impressions*.

"Guzzling, gobbling, soup-sucking noises are strictly de rigueur, *as is the loud hiss of delight over a good cup of tea, the windy sigh after drinking (still heard in English nurseries), the hand laid on the stomach, as well as more startling indications of happy repletion. All this banquet etiquette is established national custom, and cannot fairly be stigmatized as a blot, but what of the really dreadful tooth-pickings and suckings, hawkings, throat clearing, gargling and spittings? The inexperienced have no conception what this can be like, and although foreign residents in this country accustom themselves with surprising rapidity, these unfortunate personal habits are shocking to strangers."*

I hope that little passage hasn't put you off, and you are still keen to read on and learn how easy Japanese cooking can be. I have not divided the book into sections such as starters and main meals, because, as previously explained, Japanese meals are made up of several dishes, and can be assembled however you like. In reality you'd probably be choosing at least one dish from each section.

All recipes serve four unless otherwise stated. Sometimes the portions will seem small by Western standards, but most of the recipes do not constitute an entire meal. Several dishes would be served at once, enabling you to enlarge or reduce a meal according to your appetite, or generosity.

I have included sugar in most recipes, just as the Japanese do. However, feel free to omit it if you don't like using refined sugar. Alternatively you can substitute with grain syrup, such as barley malt syrup or rice syrup, which will add a mild and healthy sweetness.

A note on the pronunciation of Japanese words

Japanese pronunciation is easy. Briefly, there are 101 sounds or syllables, most comprising a consonant and vowel, thus: *a, i, u, e, o, ka, ki, ku, ke, ko* (the o is hard, as in 'cot' not the typical English 'eau' sound, as in mow or sow); *ma, mi* (mee), *mu, me, mo, na, ni, nu, ne, no*, and so on. *Ha, hi, hu* (halfway between *hu* and *fu*, but usually transcribed as *fu*), *he, ho*. Exceptions are *tsu* (not tu) *chi* (not ti), *shi* (not si), and a lone consonant '*n*' as in *shu-n-gi-ku* and *da-i-ko-n*. This means that in all Japanese words consonants and vowels alternate, exactly as they are written (in roman script), for example *u-su-a-ge, a-tsu-a- ge, na-ma-bu*. The syllables are also equally stressed. Some letters change their pronunciation when preceded by another word. For example, *nama fū* becomes *nama bu; battera sushi* becomes *battera zushi*, and *chirashi sushi* becomes *chirashi zushi*. Long or doubled vowels are indicated by a macron, as in *shōjin ryōri, tōfu, shōga, sōmen, shōyu* etc.

Occasionally a consonant is doubled, and therefore held a beat longer, as in *battera ba-t-te-ra*. Some sounds are combined to create a glide betwen the consonant and vowel, for example, *kya* (as well as *ka*) *shya* and *shyu* in addition to *sa* and *tsu*.

SOY – THE PROTEAN PROTEIN

As the olive tree is to the Mediterranean, so the soybean is to Japan. It is one of the true staples of Japanese cooking – the entire cuisine is unimaginable without it. Soybeans have been cultivated in China for thousands of years – some records show soybeans as having been grown as early as 2800 BC. In any event they soon found their way to Japan, along with various methods of preparing them, which originated in China, and were refined by the Japanese. In fact the actual whole bean appears in Japanese cooking only occasionally – most usually the bean will have been transformed into something else. This is because, although nutritious, the texture of the bean is rather indigestible, so low technology processing of the bean makes it easier to eat.

However, soybeans in their raw state are an important part of the festival known as Setsubun. At this festival, which takes place every year in early February, (at the time of the old New Year observance) soybeans are thrown around the house, to drive bad spirits away, and invite good spirits in, for the coming year. The throwing is accompanied by cries of *oniwa soto* (bad demons out!) *fukuwa uchi* (good spirits in!). As well as scattering the beans in the house, they are thrown by Shinto priests at local shrines. Huge crowds gather to await the throwing, and erupt into complete madness as they scramble and fall over each other to pick up the fallen beans, as doing so is supposed to bring good fortune in the year to come.

With its high protein content soya is also an ideal food for non-meat eaters – soybean products were developed by monks as an alternative protein source. The Buddhist scriptures state that he who eats meat will be reborn as cattle in the next life – small wonder that the devout were keen to explore other protein sources. Methods of processing soybeans are numerous, and result in an array of delicious and nutritious foods which don't resemble each other at all, and which can be divided into fermented and non-fermented products. Tofu is made from soy milk, and, far from being fermented, it must be eaten fresh, so it is traditionally prepared daily. Miso is just the opposite – a rich dark paste made from soybeans which have fermented for as long as three summers. *Natto* is another product of fermentation, using the agent *bacillus natto*, and is a sticky and pungent mass of bean. These products are dealt with in further detail under separate sections.

There are sound environmental reasons today why we should eat more soy. Although a great deal of agricultural activity is devoted to the growth of soybeans, especially in the United States, most of the crop is not fed directly to humans. Oil is extracted from the beans, for assorted manufacturing purposes, and the de-fatted soybeans are used as animal fodder. Using land to grow soybeans for human consumption, rather than for cattle food, would seem to be a more efficient use of resources. If land is used directly for growing soy protein for human consumption the yield is 20 times more usable protein than if land is used for grazing or growing cattle fodder. The protein return from animals is 20% of the protein fed to them. Compared to other grains or beans, soybeans give a higher protein yield per land area unit.

William Shurtleff is an American who has devoted his life to promoting the production and use of soy products in the West. He firmly believes that the answer to world hunger, and some health problems besetting the West, such as obesity, lies in this humble little bean. He could well be right. His books The Book of Miso and The Book of Tofu are the most well researched books I have ever come across on one food. His passion is so great that he has set up the Soyfoods Center in the U.S., to promote knowledge of soybeans. In any event the two books mentioned contain a myriad of recipes on how to use miso and tofu in both Japanese and Western style ways.

Apart from the much touted protein content, soybeans contain cellulose which, like other fibres, is good for 'keeping you regular', and may prevent certain cancers. Soybeans are high in alpha-linolenic acid, one of the fatty acids needed for health and a possible defence against heart disease. In a French study reported in The European in June 1994, Professor Serge Renaud wrote "It is very interesting that the two populations with the lowest coronary heart disease mortality in the world have a similar high intake of alpha-linolenic acid." He was referring to Crete, which has a high intake due to its high consumption of walnuts, and Japan, with its high consumption of soybeans. The Japanese eat soybeans in some form every day. Miso, tofu and soy sauce are eaten daily. Recent studies have also shown the importance of soybean products specifically to women. The abundance of natural plant oestrogens in soy products are especially helpful in offsetting menopausal symptoms, such as hot flushes and mood swings – symptoms more or less unknown amongst Japanese women. Note that these plant oestrogens are not found in soy sauce or soybeans oil, but in full bean products like tofu, miso, natto, tempeh and soybeans.

Some other lesser known soybean products have even higher concentrations of protein. Per 100 grams, tofu contains about 6 grammes of protein. Freeze dried tofu and yuba, which is the protein rich skin of soy milk (like evaporated milk) are especially concentrated – 50% protein. Roasted soybean powder, called kinako, is 35% protein, and delicious too.

Soy Sauce (shōyu)

The best soy sauce is traditionally made from soybeans, wheat and salt. Like miso, which is described at length next, this mixture is fermented with an aspergillus mould, and mixed with a brine solution which is then left for one or two years. The mash is finally pressed and the resulting dark liquid is shōyu – soy sauce. Traditionally made sauce soy like this will be found in a natural foods store. Elsewhere, what you are most likely to find is a soy sauce made by a similar but speeded up process. The mixture will be fermented at higher temperatures over 6 months. This is the soy sauce you are most likely to find in Japanese stores, and which most Japanese use daily.

Soy sauce is high in glutamic acid, which is the natural form of monosodium glutamate. so it's a flavour enhancer (which is why food tastes so good with a drizzle of soy sauce over it).

A lighter soy sauce (called usukuchi) is popular in the western Kansai region of Japan (around Kyoto). This may be because Kansai people are even more particular about the appearance of their food than other Japanese – they like it to look as attractive as possible. Light soy sauce discolours food less, so it's sometimes more suitable for certain dishes. However, the lighter one is actually saltier than the dark, so use less of it when cooking. Use light soy sauce when colour and appearance is important and you don't want to darken the food too much. However, if you only ever use the dark one you won't go far wrong. When you will go wrong is if you use the artificial concoctions on sale as soy sauce under Chinese names. They do not resemble real shōyu, and usually contain hydrochloric acid and caramel colouring. I never use them. Look for 'naturally brewed' on the label.

Tamari is a type of soy sauce favoured by macrobiotic cooks and available in health food stores. It is made with soybeans only, without wheat, so it's good for people with wheat allergies. Although it looks dark and rich, the flavour is slightly less strong than soy sauce, but it imparts its flavour well over long cooking. It's good for foods like freeze dried tofu, o-den and marinades, which are cooked over a long period and absorb flavours.

MISO – GIFT OF THE GODS

Miso is a paste made from soybeans and grain, usually rice, but sometimes barley or wheat, and occasionally it's made with a mixture of several grains. In all miso cooked soybeans are mixed with salt and kōji. Kōji itself is made by fermenting grain (or beans) with aspergillus oryzae, to produce a fluffy mold covered grain. The final mixture is left to ferment in wooden vats for two or three years, and it's this long process which gives an unremarkable looking food quite magical properties.

The enzymes from the kōji break down the beans and grains, resulting in a strongly aromatic, and supremely healthy food. The Japanese believe miso to be a gift of the gods, sent for the health and happiness of humanity, and indeed it is one of nature's wonder foods.

Like yogurt, miso contains living enzymes which are excellent for the digestion, but miso also seems to have a unique ability to rid the body of toxins. After the bombing of Hiroshima in the last war, doctors in Japan found that victims who ate lots of miso were better protected from radiation sickness. Although they couldn't have been aware that it might protect them from such unimaginable horrors, the Japanese have been eating miso as an essential part of their daily diet for centuries.

Because it's high in B vitamins and protein, miso is a valuable food for non-dairy eating vegetarians. It was introduced to Japan from China by Buddhist monks, who were forbidden to eat meat. Along with tofu, to which miso is related because of its soybean content, miso is a welcome source of protein. The deep rich misos, such as genmai or akadashi can imitate the heartiness of a meat stew. And although no self-respecting monk would eat pork, I have discovered that a Sunday roast can be jazzed up by adding sweet white miso to the apple sauce.

To the Japanese the aroma of miso evokes memories of the innocence and security of childhood: brands of miso soup are sold in Japan under slogans such as 'The Taste of Mama'. It's akin to the British nostalgic fondness for Marmite (and the Aussie's for Vegemite) maybe because, like both products, miso is also a product of fermentation.

But these days it's not only the Japanese who feel passionate about miso. Miso is now being made outside of Japan. There are several makers in America, and South River Miso Company, where I went to film the process, is one of them. Thousands of miles from Japan, in the heart of the New England countryside, Christian Elwell and his wife Gail live a simple hardworking existence, making miso. Their wooden two storey house is both home and workplace, and it's fragrant with the heady smell of fermenting soya beans.

In the small pine clad 'spore' room, Christian, as carefully as a Buddhist monk raking the pebbles in a Zen stone garden, pushes his hands through trays of kōji, the rice 'starter'. For it to work well the kōji must be disturbed daily, but in a set pattern and rhythm, a pattern decreed by thousands of years of experience.

When it is ready the fermented rice starter is added to cooked soybeans and, like wine, the mixture is trodden to a mash. Family and friends join in, singing together as they work. It is then left to mature in wooden tubs, the biggest of which could easily hold ten men. After fermenting over two or even three summers, the miso is ready to be eaten.

Nutritionally miso is around 15% protein. It also contains carbohydrate, fat, minerals and vitamins, most significantly vitamin B12. The lactic acid bacteria it contains aids digestion and settles the stomach. In fact miso soup is just the thing for hangovers, as any life-long saké-drinker will tell you. When you just can't face anything – miso soup will go down. Believe me.

Another of miso's virtues is that it keeps for years, so it's easy to have some handy for those moments when you want to make something out of nothing, and it's easier to use than many so-called convenience foods. It doesn't even need to be cooked.

When you have nothing but a couple of aubergines, you can still make an exotic starter by spreading slices of the aubergine with miso and popping them under the grill to make *dengaku,* an authentic Zen Buddhist dish, as served in the temples of Japan. You can do the same thing with slices of tofu (see *Tōfu Dengaku*). You can also add flavourings to the miso itself, such as lemon juice, sesame seeds, ground pepper or – one of my favourites – mustard.

For lazy cooks, busy housewives, gourmets or even monks, miso does indeed seem to be a gift of the gods.

TYPES OF MISO

Hatcho miso gets its name from the street in Okazaki, near Nagoya (eighth street or *hatcho*) in which it originated, and where it is still made. *Hatcho* miso is different from others in that it is made only with soybeans, without grain. The starter is also unique to the area, *aspergillus hatcho,* instead of the usual *aspergillus oryzae.* The resulting miso is almost solid – thick, firm and dark, and was said to be Emperor Hirohito's favourite. Indeed *hatcho* miso is almost as revered as the Emperor himself, and with almost as lofty a pedigree. It combines well with fish and all grains, such as barley or rice, and is good in hearty winter stews and soups.

Medium miso (Shinshu) Again this miso is named after the area in which it is made, in this case, Shinshu , the central area of Japan, north west of Tokyo, not a street corner. *Shinshu* miso is light yellow, and made with rice. It is an excellent all purpose miso – this is the one to buy if you are a newcomer to Japanese food, as it's savoury enough for soups yet mild enough for dressings and dips. This is the type of miso you'll find in Japanese supermarkets, rather than in health food shops. Sometimes called yellow miso.

Brown rice miso (genmai miso) is a rich salty miso made from brown rice (*genmai*). In this country it's more likely to be found in health food stores than Japanese stores.

Red miso (usually Sendai miso) *Sendai* is one of the famous miso producing towns, specialising in a dark red miso, made with rice, barley and soybeans. Like *genmai* it is chunky and rich, better for soups and stews than dressings.

Sweet white miso (Saikyō miso) is made using a higher proportion of rice *koji* to soybeans, and a lower proportion of salt, resulting in a smooth sweet miso which is delicious in salad dressings and summer style dishes. It is much sweeter and lighter than any of the other misos, partly because its fermentation period is much shorter – weeks rather than months or years. Because it is barely fermented it doesn't keep as well, and must be refrigerated once opened. Sweet miso is much used in Kyoto temple cooking and complements fruit, especially apple and orange. It is also used as a pickling agent, in a New Year soup called o-zōni, and as a dengaku topping.

Barley miso (mugi miso), as the name suggests, is made with barley and soybeans. It is darker, saltier and chunkier than other misos, as it is aged for longer. Barley miso is considered a bit of a country food. Its heavy chunky appearance doesn't seem to suit modern sophisticated palates, and it is in much less general use than the other misos. In the West it is popular with macrobiotic cooks. In Japan barley has long been considered a poor man's grain – what you ate if you couldn't afford rice – so perhaps that association has rubbed off, which is rather a pity, as it's tasty and healthy.

Soybean miso is the miso equivalent of tamari – made only with soybeans and no grain of any kind. It is most popular in central areas of Japan, and does not constitute a significant proportion of Japan's misos (see Hatcho miso above). It is considered more of a regional farmhouse product, to be enjoyed when visiting country areas.

Awasemiso is a combination of different miso types, in appearance slightly darker than Shinshu miso, and a good all purpose miso, especially good for miso soup.

Most of the miso on sale in Japanese stores is pasteurized, a process which arrests fermentation, and ensures that the miso keeps well. Unpasteurized miso does not export well, because it continues to ferment, eventually blowing the lid off its packaging! However, this unpasteurized variety is extremely good for the digestion, so if you can get it I recommend it. Source Foods (who are based in Wales) make fresh miso (their barley miso is especially delicious) and it can be found in small yoghurt size cartons in the refrigerated section of health food shops. Another company in Sussex, called 'Full of Beans' also makes fresh miso (and other soybean products).

MISO BASED RECIPES

To begin our recipes at the beginning means starting with the food with which most Japanese begin their day – miso soup. Miso soup is the food most associated with miso, and by far the most usual way that Japanese get their daily dose of miso. If they don't have it at breakfast they'll have it at lunchtime (possibly as part of a teishoku – set lunch) or with the evening meal. However, before we learn how to make miso soup we have to know how to make **dashi**.

Dashi – basic stock

Dashi is the fond de cuisine of Japanese cookery – the basis on which everything else depends. Dashi is a seaweed and fish based stock, used for simmering, poaching, flavouring and marinading, dipping sauces and stews. And it's an essential for soups. As it is the basis of nearly all Japanese recipes, it is important to get it right. In Japan, the quality of the dashi is regarded as the real test of a chef. For this reason, in a formal meal a clear soup, called suimono, is served first. This soup is an indicator of the quality of what is to follow, as it is essentially just dashi (the stock) with a little soy sauce, and a few solid items floating in it. Drinking this clear soup will tell you how good (or bad) the rest of the meal will be.

Like many things in Japan a whole mystique surrounds the making of *dashi*, and it's not supposed to be easy, but actually you can make a very acceptable one without a great deal of effort. The ingredients are simple – dried kelp (*kombu*) and dried bonito flakes (*katsuobushi*). The skill lies in selecting the best grades of kelp and bonito, and the timing – how long you leave the ingredients in the water. Unlike Western style stocks *dashi* isn't left to simmer for hours. The flakes of dried bonito are shaved from a block of bonito fillet which, after a long process of fermentation (with *Aspergillus glaucus*) and drying, results in a fillet which is as hard as wood. Although ready-made flakes are available in small cellophane packets, the best flavour comes from bonito which is shaved off the fillet immediately before use. There is a beautiful tool, called a *katsuobako*, or *katsuo kezuri-ki*, which is like a carpenter's plane, with a box underneath to catch the shavings, especially for this purpose. I was lucky enough to be given one, in beautiful Zelkova wood, as a goodbye gift from my friends, Hitomi and Seiji Kimura of Daitō In Temple. Shaving the fillet on this box correctly takes skill and practice – which I haven't quite mastered yet – but I persevere.

In the shops the packaged flakes are sold as *kezuri katsuo*, which are generally rough thick flakes used especially for making *dashi* or *hana katsuo* (flower bonito) which may also include the finer flakes used as a garnish on top of tofu, or cooked vegetables.

There are two types of *dashi*: Primary *dashi* has a delicate flavour, is used for clear soups, and is the one regarded as the chef's signature. Secondary *dashi*, where the *kombu* kelp is simmered, has a stronger flavour and is used for miso soups and simmering foods – in fact for most things apart from delicate clear soups (*suimono*).

OTHER *DASHIS*

A stronger saltier stock called **niboshi dashi** is made with tiny dried sardines (called *niboshi*). This is a tasty base for rich and thick miso soups and noodle broth. Like *katsuo*, *niboshi* contain a flavour enhancer called sodium isonate, which is why they make food taste good, especially if used together.

Shiitake dashi The soaking water from dried *shiitake* mushrooms is too good to throw away and is also used for stock. It's particularly useful for vegetarians who may not want to use fish based products, such as the bonito or sardines, in their cooking.

PRIMARY DASHI

I piece of dried *kombu* (kelp) about 10 cm/ 3-4 inches long	A handful of *katsuo* (dried bonito flakes) about 25 g/ I oz
I litre / I¾ pints cold water	

Gently wipe the *kombu* with a damp cloth, removing any white salt deposits. Do not wash it, as you will remove the flavour. Place the *kombu*, together with the water, in a large cooking pot. Heat for about 10 minutes until it reaches boiling point. The fleshiest part of the *kombu* should be slightly soft. If it isn't, add a little more cold water to keep it from boiling, and keep on the heat. Remove the *kombu* and bring the pot to a boil. Add four tablespoons of cold water and the *katsuo* flakes. Bring back to the boil and remove from the heat.

When the flakes have settled at the bottom of the pan remove them by straining the *dashi* through muslin to obtain a clear and delicate stock for use in clear soups.

SECONDARY *DASHI*

You can make this using the *kombu* and *katsuo* that have been retrieved from the primary *dashi*, above, or you can use fresh *kombu* and *katsuo*. The difference here is that more water is used (1½ litres/2¾ pints) and the *kombu* is kept on a low simmer for 15-20 minutes, until the liquid is reduced. As above the *katsuo* flakes are added just as you finish boiling the *kombu* and taken off the heat. This gives a stronger stock, and is the one most used in this book. The *katsuo* and *kombu* are now thrown away. If you want to be very economical you can keep the *kombu* and use it for *o-den* (Hot-Pot – see section on fish and meat) where it will be simmered until edible, or it can even be simmered with a little soy sauce and sugar to make a condiment.

Dashi can be successfully frozen for future use, if you desire, although there will be some loss of aroma and flavour.

Commercially produced dashi

When you are in a hurry and don't have time to make *dashi* from scratch you can use one of the excellent instant *dashi* powders that are now on the market (ask for *dashi no moto*). The flavour is extremely good, in fact most Japanese housewives use it, and it gives your cooking an authentic Japanese taste. Beware that it does contain monosodium glutamate.

CLEAR SOUP
SUIMONO – "SOMETHING TO DRINK"

This is the ultimate test of your primary *dashi* – a clear soup. When this soup is served in high class restaurants in Japan it would typically be presented to the guest in an exquisitely decorated lacquer bowl. As the lid is lifted a gentle cloud of steam rises and the delicate flavour envelops the nostrils. Nestling in the bottom of the black lacquer bowl would be a beautiful arrangement of some kind – a bamboo or maple leaf fashioned from gluten, a piece of carrot in the shape of a cherry blossom, or perhaps silken white tofu cut to resemble a chrysanthemum in bloom. Such artifice is more easily attainable than you may think, as you will soon learn.

CLEAR SOUP WITH TOFU AND SPINACH
TŌFU NO SUIMONO

I block silk bean curd (tofu)	850 ml / I ¼ pint primary *dashi*
50 g / 2 oz fresh young spinach leaves, washed	I tablespoon soy sauce
pinch salt	

If you have a large flower shape cutter use it to cut four flowers from the tofu. Place each piece carefully, without breaking, into the bottom of a lacquer soup bowl (preferably black for contrast). Par boil the spinach briefly for I minute in a pan of salted boiling water. Remove and plunge in to cold water immediately. Squeeze the excess water from the spinach and divide into four. Drape a piece of spinach alongside or over the tofu in each bowl. In a saucepan bring the *dashi* to boil, and add the soy sauce. Taste, and add a pinch of salt if necessary. Take off the heat and pour into each bowl, making sure the items are covered. Don't fill the bowl, but leave a 2 cm / I inch gap at the top. Place a lid on and serve at once. This is a nice light soup for summer.

VARIATION 1: SHIITAKE AND EGG-DROP SOUP
TOKITAMA JIRU

For an autumn style soup, using mushrooms instead of the tofu and spinach, place a *shiitake* mushroom in the bottom of each bowl:

4 large dried *shiitake* mushrooms (or fresh – in which case don't soak them)	*dashi* and seasonings as before
	I egg, beaten

Soak the mushrooms in warm water for at least 30 minutes until soft. Remove stems. Cut a cross in the centre of each mushroom. Place the mushrooms in with the *dashi* and bring to the boil (this ensures that the mushrooms are heated through). Add the seasonings as before. Take off the heat and pour in the beaten egg slowly in a stream. Remove immediately and divide between four bowls, with one mushroom per person. (You can add the mushroom soaking water to the *dashi*, but strain it first to remove any dirt particles.)

VARIATION 2: CHICKEN AND DAIKON RADISH
TORINIKU TO DAIKON NO SUIMONO

Instead of tofu and spinach a winter style soup can be made with tender pieces of chicken breast and thin slices of *daikon* radish. The chicken must be marinated and cooked separately first, and the *daikon* boiled until tender.

I medium chicken breast fillet, without skin	8 cm/ 3 inch piece *daikon*, peeled and cut into wafer thin slices
I tablespoon saké	*dashi* and seasonings as before
I tablespoon *mirin*	I sheet nori cut into strips
pinch salt	2 cm/ I inch to garnish

Cut the chicken into 12 small strips (3 per person). Marinate the chicken in the saké, *mirin* and salt for 30 minutes. Meanwhile bring the *daikon* to a boil in clear water, and cook until tender, but not falling apart. Remove the *daikon* with a slotted spoon and put aside. You can now use this water to cook the chicken in. Pop the chicken and the marinade into the water and simmer over medium heat for about 10 minutes until the chicken is cooked. Skim off any scum as it appears. Arrange 3 pieces of chicken and a few slices of *daikon* in each bowl and pour over the heated seasoned *dashi* as before. Garnish each bowl with the *nori*.

SHIRUMONO – MISO AND OTHER THICK SOUPS

CLASSIC MISO SOUP WITH TOFU AND WAKAME
TŌFU TO WAKAME NO MISO SHIRU

Miso soup is not in the 'clear soup' class. It's considered a 'thick' soup, and therefore in the general soup category – *shirumono*. It's not necessary to use primary *dashi* for this soup – if you've boiled your *dashi* for too long and inadvertently made a secondary *dashi* – don't worry. It'll be perfect for miso soup, and indeed for anything other than the clear soups. It's rare to find a Japanese who doesn't love miso soup, and as it is so popular there are as many different recipes as there are families. This is a classic combination with tofu and *wakame* sea vegetable, but you can vary the solid ingredients, using whatever is seasonally available. In winter you can add root vegetables or onions, in summer water cress, spinach or bean sprouts (cook them first). Once you have added the miso don't let the soup boil, as it will destroy the beneficial enzymes in the miso.

2 tablespoons dried *wakame* (or 2 lengths of fresh, well washed, and the hard spine cut away)	5 tablespoons miso (*awasemiso* or *Shinshu* – medium)
I block silken (soft) tofu cut into small cubes	I litre / 1¾ pints *dashi* stock
	2 chopped spring onions to garnish

Soak the dried *wakame* in cold water for about 5 minutes until soft, squeeze water away and chop in to 3 cm/1 inch lengths. (You can buy small packets of ready cut *wakame*, which you don't even need to soak – just sprinkle it in to the hot soup.)

Divide the *wakame* and tofu evenly between the four lacquer soup bowls. Put the miso into a small bowl or cup. Bring the *dashi* to boil in a saucepan, and use a couple of tablespoons of it to mix the miso to a thin paste. Blend thoroughly, then pour into the *dashi*. Remove from the heat and ladle soup carefully on top of the ingredients in each bowl. Garnish with chopped spring onion.

WINTER MISO SOUP WITH ONION AND DAIKON
DAIKON TO TAMANEGI NO AKAMISO JITATE

½ *daikon*, peeled, thinly sliced and cut into half moons	1 litre/ 1¾ pints *dashi* stock (secondary or *niboshi* sardine stock)
1 onion, thinly sliced and cut into half moons	5 tablespoons *Hatcho* miso
	2 tablespoons dried *nori* sea vegetable

Simmer the *daikon* and onions in the *dashi* stock until just tender. Cut the *nori* into thin short strips about 3 cm/1 inch long. In a small bowl mix the miso to a cream with a few tablespoons of the hot stock. Add the miso to the soup. Serve in lacquer bowls, and garnish with the *nori*.

BUTTER BEAN SOUP WITH YELLOW MISO
SHIROINGEN NO MISO SHIRU

150 g/5 oz dried butter beans (or one 400 g/14 oz can – in which case you omit the cooking beans stage in the recipe)	1 litre/1¾ pints *dashi*
	500 ml/18 fl oz water (if cooking dried beans. Omit if using canned)
7 cm/3 inch piece of dried *kombu*	2 sticks celery, de-stringed and chopped finely
3 onions, chopped finely	3 tablespoons medium (yellow) miso
2 tablespoons vegetable oil	1 teaspoon salt
1 teaspoon toasted sesame oil	*Ao nori* to garnish

If using dried beans soak them overnight. Drain, then place them in a large saucepan with plenty of fresh cold water. (Do not add salt – it makes the beans tough.) Bring to a rapid boil for ten minutes then drain. In a large saucepan heat the oils, add the onion and sauté, covered, until soft. Add half the *dashi* and the same amount of water, the drained beans, and the chopped celery. Now pop in the piece of *kombu* – it will help to break down the beans and make them more digestible – it can be removed later. Simmer slowly until almost cooked (about an hour). Add the rest of the *dashi* and simmer for a further 20-30 minutes until the beans are soft and mushy. Remove the piece of *kombu*, which will be quite soft. Now you can either leave the soup as it is or mash it with a potato masher, so it's partly smooth but still got bits of solid in. (You can put the soup in a blender if you want a really smooth soup, and if you do you can leave the *kombu* in as well – it'll disperse and add goodness and flavour.) Finally mix the miso to a paste with some of the hot liquid (or hot water if the liquid is too thick), and add to the soup. Bring to the boil and take off the heat immediately. Garnish with *ao nori* sprinkled on top.

MISO SOUP WITH BEAN SPROUTS AND DEEP FRIED TOFU
ABURA-AGE TO MOYASHI NO MISO SHIRU

This is a nice light soup for summer, using a light miso such as *Shinshu*, or mellow barley miso.

I deep fried tofu pouch (*usu-age* or *abura-age*)	4 tablespoons light miso
100 g / 4 oz bean sprouts	Japanese chilli pepper (*shichimi togarashi*) to serve
I litre / 2 pints *dashi*	

In a colander pour boiling water over the tofu to get rid of excess oil. Drain on paper. Cut into thin strips widthways. In a separate saucepan bring ½ litre / I pint water to a boil. Dunk the bean sprouts in for 30 seconds, then remove and drain. Place a few pieces of tofu and a generous amount of bean sprouts in the bottom of each lacquer soup bowl. In a large pot bring the *dashi* to a boil. In a separate bowl mix the miso to a paste with a few spoons of the hot *dashi*. Add the miso, and turn off the heat just as it starts to boil again. Pour the soup over the contents of each bowl. Sprinkle with pepper and serve.

OTHER MISO RECIPES

 ## SIMMERED DAIKON RADISH WITH MISO SAUCE
FUROFUKI DAIKON

This recipe uses the sweet white miso called *saikyō* miso, which is used frequently in temple cookery, and in the Kansai region of Japan, to the west of Tokyo. This is an extremely simple but interesting way of serving the large white radish called *daikon*. *Daikon* are at their best during winter, and also this is simmered, so it's considered cold weather food.

I large *daikon* radish	2 tablespoons saké
10 cm/ 4 inch piece *kombu* (kelp)	I tablespoon *mirin*
SAUCE:	2 tablespoons water
8 tablespoons sweet white miso	slivers of *yuzu* rind or lemon zest to
I tablespoon darker medium miso	garnish

Peel the *daikon* and cut into 8 thick rounds, about 3 cm/1 inch thick. With a small knife bevel the edges of each round. This stops the *daikon* from falling apart in the cooking. Cut a cross all the way through the depth of the round, but keeping the edges intact. This helps the *daikon* to cook all the way through and also makes it easier to eat with chopsticks. Place the *daikon* in a large covered pot with plenty of water (or *dashi* stock) and bring to a boil. If you have a drop lid use it here, to stop the food from rolling around in the pot. Simmer until tender – about 20-30 minutes. In a small saucepan mix the misos together with the saké, *mirin* and water, keeping over a low flame, until blended and hot. Place two rounds of *daikon* per person on a plate and spread the miso on top of each. Garnish with a sliver of *yuzu* rind (if you have it) or lemon zest. Eat immediately while hot.

GRILLED VEGETABLES WITH FLAVOURED MISO
DENGAKU

This is a simple and quick way to dress up vegetables. A slightly more elaborate version of the topping, using egg, is used with tofu (see *Tōfu Dengaku*). This eggless version is more traditional in the temples where eggs are not eaten. Slices of aubergine, *konnyaku*, and tofu as well as large mushrooms are all suitable for this treatment. You can either grill or lightly pan fry the vegetables.

2 small aubergines, sliced in half lengthways (or one large aubergine cut into thick rings)	**TOPPING:**
	I tablespoon caster sugar (optional)
	4 tablespoons *dashi*
½ block *konnyaku* (yam cake) cut into four	2 tablespoons mellow barley miso
	4 tablespoons *mirin*
a little vegetable oil to brush on before grilling	I teaspoon Japanese mustard (*karashi*)
	I tablespoon lemon juice (or *yuzu* seasoning)

Lightly brush the aubergines with oil and place under a medium grill and grill each side for a few minutes until soft. Bring the *konnyaku* slices to a boil in a saucepan, then drain and cool. Place under grill to slightly brown, then remove. In a small saucepan, dissolve the sugar in the *dashi*. Use this liquid to mix the miso to a paste, then add the other ingredients, and bring to almost boiling. Take off the heat. Spread the miso topping evenly on the aubergine and *konnyaku*. Place under medium hot grill until just bubbling. Serve immediately.

 ## AUBERGINE AND PEPPER IN MISO
NASU NO MISO ITAME

A tasty and simple way of using green peppers and aubergines in summer, when they are plentiful. The richness of the miso complements the delicate taste of aubergine, and the green pepper provides a little crunchiness and sweetness, although this dish is often made with just aubergine. Japanese aubergines and peppers are much smaller than most of the ones you find in British shops, and the peppers have a much thinner skin. You can sometimes find similar small ones here, but if you can't, just use the larger ones and cut into 5 cm/2 inch pieces. As this can be eaten at room temperature I often serve a large bowl of it at parties alongside pasta and rice salads.

3 small aubergines	1 tablespoon sugar
3 small Japanese style green peppers	125 ml/ 4 fl oz water
4 cm/ 1½ inch piece fresh ginger	1 teaspoon *kuzu* or other starch
2 tablespoons miso (a medium one)	3 tablespoons vegetable oil
1 tablespoon soy sauce	1 tablespoon saké

Wash and trim the aubergines and cut into chunks (using the *han giri*, rolling wedge technique). If large, sprinkle with salt and leave for 30 minutes, then rinse and pat dry.

Wash the peppers and remove the seeds. Cut the flesh into irregular shaped bite-size pieces. Pat dry. Peel then grate the ginger on a fine grater.

Mix the miso, soy sauce, sugar and water, gradually adding the water to the miso whilst stirring. Dissolve a teaspoon of *kuzu* powder (or *katakuriko* – potato starch) separately in water, ready to thicken the sauce at the end.

Heat the oil in a large frying pan and sauté the aubergine, pepper and grated ginger for around 5 minutes until the vegetables are soft (keep moving the vegetables around and make sure the ginger doesn't stick to the base of the pan). Add a splash of saké and cook for a further 30 seconds. Add the miso mixture and bring to a simmer. Thicken with the starch, stirring thoroughly and take off the heat.

TOFU – MEAT OF THE FIELDS

"I took my lunch – a wretched meal of a tasteless white curd made from beans, with some condensed milk added to it..."   Isabella Bird, *Unbeaten Tracks in Japan*

Poor Isabella. Unfortunately she made the mistake of doing what some Westerners continue to do – putting sweeteners with tofu to change the taste. I have never understood why people try to make cheesecake and mousses and the like from tofu. If, instead of using tofu as a dairy substitute (or whatever it was she was trying to do), she had simply eaten tofu the way the Japanese eat it she would have been pleasantly surprised – and maybe even enjoyed her lunch. Here are some ideas for doing it the Japanese way, and avoiding the 'Isabella effect'.

Tofu, or bean curd originated in China where it's called "the meat of the fields" because it's so rich in protein. For this reason it became especially important in Japan, where meat eating has been acceptable for only 150 years, since the Meiji restoration. One legend has it that tofu was invented by a government official in China, who, unlike his fellows was not open to bribery or corruption. So honest was he that he never had enough money to buy meat – so, needing a cheaper, alternative protein source he developed tofu. True or not, it explains why, to this day, overly honest (or just poorly paid) officials in Japan are called 'tofu officials'.

Tofu is the milk of soybeans to which a coagulant is added, resulting in a custard-like curd which is virtually tasteless but full of protein. The protein rich milk is made by first wet milling raw soybeans to produce a slurry called '*go*'. (In the past this was added to miso soup, but this is now considered rather old fashioned.) This slurry is then boiled and pressed, and filtered through cloth to produce a protein rich 'milk'.

In the old University neighbourhood of Tokyo, I observed Saitama-ya tofu makers making tofu the old fashioned way – completely by hand, using natural *nigari* or bittern for the coagulant (commercially produced tofu is made these days with calcium sulphate). The tofu maker and his wife began the day at three in the morning, and the next four hours were gruelling. It was a cold February morning when I filmed them, and it was not a comfortable way to start the day. Small wonder that such traditional methods of food production are dying out. Young Japanese these days have loftier ambitions than to get up in the early hours of the morning to slosh around in cold water on the stone floor of an unheated kitchen. It was freezing, but fascinating to watch the process at such close quarters: boiling and mashing of soybeans; extracting the milk with an old fashioned hand press; and finally adding a coagulant and leaving it to set in worn wooden moulds lined with cotton. By seven o'clock the tofu was ready for the first customers, who, like the French with their bread, expect fresh tofu daily for the morning's miso soup. Even though Tokyo is in some ways a sophisticated and modern place, with modern buildings and hi-tech gadgetry galore, small neighbourhood food industries like the tofu maker can still be found. The tofu shop is recognisable by the deep troughs of cold water at the front, with white blocks of tofu floating around in them. Tofu spoils easily so it's kept under water until it's sold. You can keep it in the refrigerator at home for up to 5 days so long as you keep it in water and change the water daily. It can also be revived in boiling water if it's less than fresh, but if it shows any sign of being sour it should be thrown away.

Cotton tofu (*momendōfu*) is the firmer tofu most easily available in the West. It gets its name from the indentations from the cotton lining the tubs in which it is set. Cotton tofu is best for cooking with, but even this tofu shouldn't be overcooked, as it becomes spongy after long cooking. After the coagulant is added cotton tofu is placed into moulds, with holes around the bottom edge. Weights are placed on top, and, as the curds and whey separate, the whey drains off and only the curds remain. Cotton tofu is also referred to as regular or firm tofu.

Silken tofu (*kinugoshi*) is made from a richer milk than regular cotton tofu, and is not pressed. After the coagulant is added to the milk it's poured into a smooth sided mould, without holes, to set. The proportion of coagulant, and temperature of the soy milk is crucial if this tofu is to set without separating, so proportionally more coagulant is used than in cotton tofu. The resulting tofu is soft and falls apart easily, with a silky smooth texture from which it gets its name (no, the moulds are not lined with silk). I much prefer this tofu for eating plain, either chilled, as *hiya yakko*, or slightly warmed, as *yudōfu*. It's also good for making dressings and dips. Apparently tofu aficionados regard cotton (*momen*) tofu as more authentic, but that doesn't worry me!

TO PREPARE TOFU

For cooking, frying or making in to dressings, some of the water in tofu must be removed. There are two ways of doing this, either by first boiling and then pressing the tofu under weights, or simply just pressing. To do this place the tofu in a saucepan of boiling water and boil for a couple of minutes. Remove and wrap it in a clean tea towel. Place on a slightly tilted board, (the draining board is a good idea, next to the sink) put a small plate on top with a 1 kilo/ 2 pound weight (or can) on top, and leave to drain for about half an hour, or until some of the water has drained away. Or you can omit the pre-boiling and leave it to drain under weights for a bit longer.

HOW TO CUT TOFU

Although the chopping board and knife reign supreme in Japanese cooking, this is one instance where African style cutting is often employed – without a board. Holding the tofu in the palm of your left hand, cut carefully through crosswise into little blocks. Your hand will hold it together, and you can then carefully slide the tofu into soup or bowls. This is especially handy for the soft tofu.

Deep fried tofu pouches (*usu-age*). Also referred to as *abura-age*, these are the little pouches that most often appear stuffed with rice in sushi bars or lunch boxes. In fact they are thick blocks of tofu that have been pressed and deep fried. They can be purchased ready made and frozen in the West, fresh in Japan. Cut into strips they are good sautéed with sea vegetable and root vegetables, as they impart a little oiliness (and protein) to a dish, and are often added to soups.

Deep fried tofu cakes (*atsuage*). These are thick blocks of tofu which have been deep fried. They are excellent for long cooking (as in *o-den*) as they don't fall apart, and don't absorb moisture so readily. Fried tofu keeps fresher much longer than fresh tofu. It also absorbs flavours better and holds its shape so it's perfect for stewed and simmered dishes.

Grilled tofu (*yakidōfu*). This is firm tofu that has been lightly grilled or toasted. Again, it holds its shape well so it's used in dishes like *sukiyaki* and *mizutaki* – one-pot dishes, where a firmer texture is required.

Freeze dried tofu (*koyadōfu*) is exactly that. When tofu freezes, the structure and texture of it completely changes (which is why you never put fresh tofu in your freezer). These hard little blocks are commercially freeze dried, and very versatile. They keep for months, and, once re-hydrated, although the texture is completely different from fresh tofu, it has the same goodness (more actually, because the protein is concentrated). The sponge like texture absorbs flavours readily, so it's also good for dishes which require long simmering in broth. In addition the dry cake can be finely grated and used as an unusual and protein rich crispy coating for deep fried foods.

To re-constitute dried tofu do the following: Cover the tofu with hot water in a bowl or saucepan. It will float to the top because it's so light, so put a small plate (that fits inside the pan or bowl) on top, to keep the tofu under water. Soak it for 5 minutes until it's absorbed water, and then squeeze it out – a milky liquid should come out. Soak again, and squeeze again, doing this two or three times until the liquid squeezed out is less milky. It is now ready to add to simmering liquids in a variety of dishes.

TOFU RECIPES

CHILLED SILKEN TOFU WITH CONDIMENTS
HIYYA YAKKO

This is a dish to show off the quality of the tofu used: one for the aficionados, as the flavour is pure and not masked by other ingredients or flavourings. You can have as little or as much condiment as you like.

DIPPING SAUCE:	CONDIMENTS:
4 tablespoons soy sauce	2 tablespoons white sesame seeds
1 tablespoon sugar (optional)	2 spring onions
4 tablespoons saké	5 cm/ 2 inch piece fresh ginger
250 ml/ 9 fl oz *dashi*	
2 blocks fresh silken tofu (*kinugoshi*)	

Combine the dipping sauce ingredients in a small saucepan and heat to dissolve sugar and eliminate alcohol. Put aside to chill. Just before serving divide evenly between four small bowls. Cut each block of tofu into six, and place 3 pieces for each person in the bottom of a deep bowl (or place family style in one large glass bowl). Roast the sesame seeds gently in a heavy bottom frying pan (or sesame roaster if you have one). Chop the spring onions finely. Peel and grate the ginger to a pulp. Place each condiment into small individual bowls for everyone to share. Each person dips their tofu into their own bowl of dipping sauce, adding condiments to taste.

Simple variation

A quick and easy way of serving this – it could make an instant starter – is to sprinkle a tablespoonful of bonito flakes (*katsuo*) on top of each serving of tofu, drizzle a little soy sauce over, and hey presto! Grated ginger goes well with this also.

EXOTIC VARIATION: CRYSTAL TOFU
SUISHO DŌFU

Because Japanese summers are so hot and humid various methods have been devised of serving food which looks cool. In this variation the tofu pieces are glazed in a transparent gel-like coating, creating an iced and therefore cooling effect. To heighten this feeling it's served in a glass bowl, with chunks of ice to keep the tofu chilled.

2 blocks regular (firm/cotton) tofu	**DIPPING SAUCE AND CONDIMENTS:**
6 tablespoons (approx) potato starch (*katakuriko*) to dust the tofu	as for page 59

Place the tofu in a saucepan of boiling water and boil for a couple of minutes. Remove and wrap it in a clean tea towel. Place on a slightly tilted board, put a small plate on top with a heavy weight (such as a couple of cans) on top of the plate. Leave to drain for about half an hour, or until some of the water has drained away. Cut each block of tofu into 6 pieces and dust each piece in potato starch, making sure each surface is well covered. Bring a large saucepan of lightly salted water to the boil. Drop the tofu pieces in and cook for one minute, until the starchy coating has become translucent. Remove carefully and chill in cold water. Serve family style in an attractive glass bowl, with ice cubes scattered over, 3 pieces per person.

SIMMERED TOFU
YUDŌFU

Tofu is so much a part of Japanese life that it's the subject of proverbs and words of wisdom. One of them is "Religious faith should be like tofu – good in any circumstance." To illustrate this the Japanese also eat tofu in winter, with the same condiments as *hiyya yakko*, but heated. For this you can use either firm or soft tofu, depending on taste (and dexterity with chopsticks). This dish is usually brought to the table in the pot in which it is heated, usually an earthenware *nabe* or a cast iron cooking pot. If you don't have either, a shallow saucepan will do, but the pot should be kept warm on a food warmer at the table. Diners then help themselves directly from the pot, taking one piece at a time and dipping it in a small dish of soy sauce and various condiments. The condiments are also laid out separately so people can help themselves. I actually prefer the texture of soft (silken) tofu for this dish, but it is a bit tricky lifting it without breaking the tofu. If you can get hold of one of the beautiful small slotted spoons made for this task I recommend them. I have several – stainless steel with bamboo handles, and others hand made from twisted wire, bound with copper.

2 blocks tofu	DIPPING SAUCE – COMBINE THE
CONDIMENTS:	**FOLLOWING:**
2 spring onions, chopped finely	4 tablespoons soy sauce
I tablespoon sesame seeds, lightly	I tablespoon sugar
toasted	4 tablespoons saké
4 cm/1½ inch piece fresh ginger, peeled	250 ml/ 9 fl oz *dashi*
and grated	

Cut the tofu into large cubes – a standard size block can be cut into 6 or 8 pieces. Put enough water in the pot to just cover the tofu. Bring slowly to a simmer. Serve immediately the tofu is heated through – do not allow it to boil or it will become tough. That's it. Serve with condiments and dipping sauce as in *hiyya yakko* (page 59-60).

TOFU WITH PEANUT AND PUMPKIN SAUCE
TŌFU NO PIINATSU DENGAKU

This recipe was given to me by Bob Lloyd who is a master macrobiotic cook, based in west London but currently getting something of an international reputation. Bob is never afraid to experiment with putting traditional Japanese foods with Western ones – in this case good ol' US style peanut butter. Bob usually bakes his tofu and sauce together in the oven, but here I've pan fried the tofu, and poured the sauce over, keeping to the traditional Japanese style an of oven-less kitchen.

I pack firm tofu	I tablespoon *Shinshu* medium miso
2 onions, diced	I tablespoon peanut butter
450 g/ I lb peeled and diced pumpkin	pinch sea salt
(must be a variety with dense yellow	juice of half a lemon
flesh, such as Hokkaido pumpkin	parsley to garnish
kabocha, Turk's Turban or Butternut	I tablespoon vegetable oil
squash) – about 2 cm/ ¾ inch cubes	

Drain the tofu as before, to get rid of excess moisture. Put the chopped onion and pumpkin in a saucepan with water to half cover. Bring to a boil and simmer until the pumpkin is soft – between 10 and 20 minutes. Drain, but keep the cooking liquid. In a large bowl (or the same saucepan) blend the miso, peanut butter and a little of the hot cooking liquid to a paste. Add the pumpkin and onion and mash well until you have a smooth sauce. You may need to add more of the cooking liquid – it needs to be slightly runny. (You can use a food processor if you like, although I never do.)

In a heavy bottom frying pan or skillet heat up the oil to medium. Cut the tofu into 4 or 8 pieces. Pan fry each side for about 3 minutes until heated through and slightly golden. Whilst this is cooking heat up the sauce if necessary, but do not boil it. Stir in the lemon juice. Put one or two pieces of tofu on each person's plate and pour over the sauce. Garnish with parsley. This can be served as a protein rich (and rich tasting) main dish in a vegetarian meal. It could be served with something light and green – such as simmered broad beans and *wakame*, or a green vegetable based cooked salad, and of course rice. This must be eaten hot.

TOFU WITH MISO TOPPING
TŌFU DENGAKU

Dengaku was originally the name of a public performance or entertainment in medieval Japan, usually as part of a festival. At these performances were *dengaku-hoshi*, dancers who pranced around on stilts. The bamboo skewers that are used here somehow resemble the stilts and thus they were named. You will also need either a double boiler (*bain marie*) or a basin in a saucepan of boiling water, to stop the egg scrambling. Or you can leave out the egg altogether, in which case you'll have a *dengaku* similar to the one on page 55. The idea here is to make three different coloured miso toppings, by adding different flavourings to a basic mix.

If you have a Japanese style charcoal grill you can use it to brown the tofu, or you can just pop the pieces under a medium grill, and insert the bamboo skewers afterwards.

2 blocks firm tofu

double pronged *dengaku* skewers

MISO TOPPINGS:

Basic white topping –

  100 g/ 3½ oz white miso

  1 tablespoon sugar

  1 tablespoon *mirin*

  1 egg yolk*

  4 tablespoons *dashi*

  Flavouring

  1 teaspoon fresh ginger juice

Green miso topping –

  100 g/ 3½ oz white miso,

  1 tablespoon sugar

  1 tablespoon *mirin*

  1 egg yolk*

  4 tablespoons *dashi*

  1 tablespoon cooked puréed spinach

  (frozen would be OK)

Red miso topping –

  75 g/ 3 oz red miso

  2 tablespoons white miso

  2 teaspoons sugar

  1 tablespoon *mirin*

  1 egg yolk

  3 tablespoons *dashi*

  2 teaspoons white sesame seeds,

    toasted and ground

  Black sesame seeds to garnish

* use the egg whites to make Snowy Kanten Jelly, page 245

Basic method

In the basin (or top boiler) put the miso, sugar and *mirin*. Do not put over water or heat yet. Blend all together with the egg yolks. Place over heat simmering water, and add the *dashi* slowly. Keep stirring until it's smooth and creamy.

For the white miso: add the freshly grated ginger juice now.

For the green miso: Add the spinach purée to the prepared miso sauce and beat well. It doesn't matter if the purée is not completely smooth – bits of spinach in it is fine.

Red miso: Blend the miso as before, but in this case flavour with toasted and ground white sesame seeds.

To prepare the tofu for the toppings

Wrap and press the tofu for at least an hour (see 'How to prepare tofu', page 58). Cut each block into 6 pieces. Insert bamboo skewers and grill on both sides for about 5 minutes (2½ minutes each side). The tofu needs to be heated through and lightly speckled, but still soft. Remove from heat and spread one side with the topping. Spread it fairly thickly – about ¼ cm / ⅟₁₆ inch. Grill again for another minute, with the miso side near the heat. If you are grilling Japanese style this means your tofu will be topping side down. If the topping is too runny this will not be a success, in which case pop them under the grill instead.

Although traditionally eaten directly off the bamboo skewer, this dish can be prepared without skewers at all – you can even quickly pan fry the tofu, and simply spread the miso dressing on top before serving, without heating up again. You can also vary the size of the pieces – giving small canapé style portions if you prefer.

As well as tofu you can use this to dress vegetables, such as thick rounds of grilled aubergine, or large field mushrooms – the rich tasting miso combines well with their delicate tastes.

DEEP FRIED 'TREASURE BALLS' IN THICK SAUCE
GANMODOKI NO ANKAKE

Fresh tofu is only offered for sale on the day it is made, so this is a way of using up unsold tofu from the previous day, by combining it with vegetables and flavouring and deep frying it. At Saitama-ya tofu shop in Tokyo I watched the tofu makers' wife as she mashed left over tofu with an assortment of chopped vegetables and shaped it into large round patties, which she then deep fried. In neighbourhood tofu shops these golden cakes are sold from a cool cabinet at the open front of the small shop, along with the other deep fried tofu products mentioned here. The ingredients vary from shop to shop, but nearly always contain some kind of vegetable and sea vegetable, and often a ginkgo nut (but I haven't included them here, as they are not easy to get hold of, and a fiddle to prepare). The mushroom and carrot here are cooked and flavoured before adding to the tofu – it's a bit of extra work but worth it, I think, in terms of adding taste. If you don't want to do this you can just add the items uncooked and unflavoured, in which case omit the carrot, as it may not cook well enough with just the deep frying.

2 blocks tofu	10 g/ ¼ oz dried arame sea vegetable,
½ medium carrot	soaked in cold water to re-hydrate
4 dried *shiitake* mushrooms, soaked in	(or *hijiki*)
warm water to soften	**SAUCE** (optional):
FLAVOURING FOR CARROT AND	2 tablespoons potato starch
MUSHROOM:	(*katakuriko*) or *kuzu*
I teaspoon sugar	240 ml/ 8½ fl oz *dashi* (made up with
2 tablespoons soy sauce	the *shiitake* soaking water)
I teaspoon toasted sesame oil	2 tablespoons soy sauce
I tablespoon white sesame seeds	I tablespoon *mirin*
	I teaspoon fresh ginger juice

Place the tofu in a saucepan of boiling water and boil for a couple of minutes. Remove and wrap it in a clean tea towel. Place on a slightly tilted board, put a small plate on top with a heavy weight (or can) on top, and leave for about half an hour, or until some of the water has drained away.

Peel and then finely mince the carrot by chopping into small matchsticks, stacking and then cutting across. Finely mince the *shiitake* and discard the stems. (Keep the soaking water for the *dashi* stock.) Dissolve the sugar in the soy sauce. In a small pan heat the sesame oil and add the carrot and *shiitake*. Keep it moving to stop it sticking. After 30 seconds add the sweetened soy sauce, and simmer, uncovered, over a low heat, until the liquid is absorbed and the contents slightly sticky. Remove from heat and leave to cool.

Drain the *arame* or *hijiki* (throw away the soaking water) and chop into small strands (about ½ cm/ ⅛ inch). Lightly toast the sesame seeds in a dry frying pan or skillet (or sesame roaster if you have one).

Now put the drained tofu into a large *suribachi* (or bowl). Using the *surikogi*, wooden pestle (or a wooden spoon) mash up the tofu, and then add the flavoured carrot and mushroom, the chopped *arame* and sesame seeds. Now, using your fingers so as not to mash up the ingredients, combine them well. Keep mixing and kneading until the mixture holds together. Take about 2-3 tablespoons of the mixture and form into round flat cakes. The cakes should be about 5-7 cm/ 2-3 inches in diameter – quite large.

Heat some oil for deep frying to medium (170C/ 340F), and drop one or two cakes in at a time. Fry for 4-5 minutes until golden. Drain on kitchen paper.

To make the sauce mix the starch with a little cold water to make a thin paste. Put the *dashi*, soy sauce and *mirin* in a small saucepan. Add the starch liquid and bring to a boil and simmer, stirring vigorously for a few minutes until the mixture thickens. Add the ginger juice. Place one tofu cake per person in a dish and pour over one to two tablespoons of the hot sauce. These can be eaten as a vegetarian main dish, a side dish in a bigger feast, or as a snack.

Variation: simmer the deep fried cakes in a broth of *dashi* and soy sauce. Add two tablespoons soy sauce to 350 ml/12 fl oz *dashi*. A blob of Japanese mustard mixed in with this broth adds extra piquancy.

 ## DEEP FRIED TOFU IN BROTH
AGEDASHI DŌFU

"When stuck for what to prepare, just make tofu" is another saying. The Japanese must have been saying this since at least 1782, as this was the year a recipe book was published in Osaka, entitled *One Hundred Rare Tofu Recipes*. It proved so popular that the author wrote another hundred! It just goes to show how important tofu was as a protein source for the Japanese people. This is one of my favourite dishes, and something I always order when I am in an *izakaya* in Japan. After cooking the starchy coating becomes stretchy and gelatinous – lovely. Be sure it's served piping hot.

1 block firm tofu	3 tablespoons *mirin*
3 tablespoons *kuzu* or potato starch (*katakuriko*)	**CONDIMENT:**
oil for deep frying	5 tablespoons grated *daikon* radish with chilli (see *momiji-oroshi*, page 188) or plain grated *daikon* and 1 tablespoon freshly grated ginger
BROTH:	
225 ml/ 8 fl oz *dashi*	
3 tablespoons soy sauce	

Wrap the tofu in a clean tea towel, and place on a slightly tilted board on the draining board. Put a small plate on top with a heavy weight (or can) on top. Leave for about half an hour until some of the water has drained away, and tofu is dryish. Cut into 8 large cubes. If using *kuzu* starch you will need to break up the lumps to make a fine powder. To do this put the *kuzu* into a strong paper bag and roll a rolling pin over until you have a fairly fine powder. If using potato starch simply sprinkle on to a plate, and dust each piece of tofu in the starch, making sure every surface is covered. Heat the oil to medium (170C/ 340F) and drop the tofu pieces in. Fry until a light golden colour. Meanwhile combine the ingredients for the broth in a saucepan, bring to a boil and take off the heat.

Put two pieces of tofu per person into a medium size deep bowl. Pour the hot broth over, until it's about a third of the way up the tofu (it shouldn't be swimming). Shape the grated *daikon* into four little cone shapes and place on top of the tofu in each bowl. If using ginger also make that into little cone shapes, and place another smaller cone of ginger on top of the *daikon*.

Note: You can also sprinkle bonito flakes (*hana katsuo*) on top if you like.

TOFU POUCHES
ABURA-AGE OR USU-AGE

Making these little tofu pouches is traditionally another of the tofu maker's wife's tasks. They are made with tofu which is cut into thin sheets, and which are then pressed between bamboo mats and deep fried twice. The first frying is in a low temperature oil, when the tofu expands and lightens. They are then fried more briefly at a higher temperature, which removes moisture from the tofu and fixes the shape. The result is crispy on the outside and soft on the inside. I watched Mrs Saitama test the temperature of the oil by dipping her bare fingers into it – at the same time her husband was up to his elbows in icy water! What a hard working pair they were. Anyway, the result of the careful double frying is crisp pouches which can be split open (like pitta bread) and stuffed. (See page12).

STUFFED TOFU POUCHES
FUKUBUKURO

These are similar to *inarizushi* – the little pouches of rice served in sushi shops, but instead of being stuffed with rice they are stuffed with vegetables and tofu. In fact it's tofu stuffed with tofu. The pouches are tied at the top with *kanpyō* – dried gourd strips – and the effect is of small money pouches. Which is where they get their name – *bukuro* means bag or pouch, and *fuku* means happiness or good fortune – I suppose you could call them lucky bags. They can be served on their own, or included in the simmered Hot Pot (*o-den*), page 206. The gourd strips serve two purposes – as a tie for the bags, and as food – as they absorb the flavours of the simmering broth they become especially juicy and delicious.

---

4 tofu pouches (*usu-age* or *abura-age*)	4 cm/ 2 inch length *daikon* radish
8 x15 cm/ 6 inch long strips of dried gourd (*kanpyō*)	½ carrot
	SIMMERING INGREDIENTS:
salt	450 ml/16 fl oz *dashi*
FILLING:	6 tablespoons *mirin*
1 block firm tofu	6 tablespoons soy sauce
8 dried *shiitake* mushrooms, soaked in water to soften	

Place the deep fried tofu pouches in a colander and pour boiling water over, to eliminate oiliness. Place on kitchen paper to drain. Cut each piece in half and carefully pull apart to create little pouches.

To soften the gourd strips wash them, place them on a cutting board and rub vigorously in salt. Wash them again and place in clean water in a saucepan and bring to a boil. Boil until soft. Drain, and set aside.

Press the tofu under a plate as before. When well pressed dice into ½ cm/ ¼ inch pieces. Drain the softened *shiitake* mushrooms, then cut off the stalks and dice roughly.

Peel the *daikon* radish and carrot and dice (about 1cm/ ⅜ inch cubes). Boil them separately until just beginning to get soft. Cool and mince roughly.

Combine the tofu, mushrooms and vegetables and put about a dessertspoonful of the mixture into each pouch. The pouch should be bulging (in other words look enticing – like a bag of treasure), but with enough room at the top to gather it together and tie it, without the mixture splurging out. Tie each bag with a gourd strip.

Add the simmering ingredients to a large cooking pot, and bring to a boil. The pot should have a wide enough base for the pouches to sit upright without being piled on top of each other, but not so wide that they fall over. Place the pouches in the liquid carefully – they should fit snugly against each other in the pot. This is an opportunity to use one of your drop lids if you have one. Place it on top of the pouches, inside the pan, so the contents don't move around, but steam can escape. Simmer gently for 30 minutes, after which the flavours will be well combined, and the contents soft. Serve hot with a little of the simmering liquid spooned over. However, they are also nice served at room temperature, so they can be prepared ahead of time. They could be served as part of a buffet style spread, or as a starter. Again this is another excellent dish to serve to non-meat eaters. You can spice it up by adding ginger or mustard to the simmering liquid.

TOFU POUCHES WITH BEAN SPROUTS IN VINEGAR DRESSING
USU-AGE TO MOYASHI NO SUNOMONO

This makes a quick and easy side salad. The pouches here are not stuffed but cut into thin strips.

1 pack bean sprouts	2 tablespoons *mirin*
1 deep fried tofu pouch (*usu-age*)	1 tablespoon vinegar
15 g/ ½ oz *arame*	1 teaspoon light soy sauce
DRESSING:	2 tablespoons *dashi* or water
3 tablespoons sesame seeds	

Wash the bean sprouts then plunge them into a saucepan of boiling water for 30 seconds so they lose some of their crispness. Drain and immediately plunge into cold water to arrest any further cooking. Drain well and gently squeeze out excess water. In a colander pour boiling water over the deep fried tofu to get rid of excess oil, drain on kitchen paper and then squeeze it well. Cut crosswise into thin slivers (about 1 cm/ ⅜ inch wide). Soften the *arame* sea vegetable in cold water for about five minutes then drain.

Now make the dressing. Lightly toast the sesame seeds in a heavy frying pan, keeping them moving to prevent them burning. When they start popping and jumping remove from the heat. Grind them to a rough paste in a *suribachi* (grinding bowl). Scrape them out of the bowl and put them in a small saucepan together with the liquid ingredients.

Heat gently for a minute or two until slightly thickened. Combine the *arame*, bean sprouts and tofu, and gently mix in the sauce, using chopsticks or fingers.

Note: To make this even speedier you can use tahini (sesame paste) instead of the toasted sesame seeds. The texture is smoother, but the taste still good. Serve at room temperature as a side dish.

THAI MARINATED TOFU STEAK
TAI FŪ TŌFU SUTEIKI

The trick here is to allow plenty of time for the tofu to marinate and absorb the flavours. Although garlic isn't a traditional Japanese flavouring (it's not used in temple cooking for example), it is now used in modern Japanese cooking which is absorbing influences from other parts of south east Asia as well as from the West. This is influenced by Thai flavouring.

I block firm (cotton) tofu	3 cloves garlic, minced or crushed and
I tablespoon chopped fresh coriander	chopped
to garnish	I teaspoon grated ginger
MARINADE:	pinch dried coriander leaf (cilantro)
120 ml/ 5 fl oz water	½ red chilli – seeds removed and finely
4 tablespoons soy sauce	chopped
2 tablespoons *mirin*	2 tablespoons fresh coriander to
2 teaspoons lime juice	garnish

Drain and press the tofu, as before. Combine the marinade ingredients. When the tofu is well pressed cut into 4 thick slices and place in a flat bottomed dish. Pour the marinade over, making sure each piece is well covered and leave for at least an hour. (You can even marinade overnight so long as it's in the fridge.) When ready to cook transfer the tofu to a heavy bottomed frying pan and pour the marinade over. Simmer gently, uncovered, for about 15 minutes until some of the juice is gone. Serve hot with the fresh coriander sprinkled over.

TOFU STEAK WITH KIMCHEE DRESSING
KANKOKU FŪ TŌFU SUTEIKI

I first tasted this in a funky little jazz bar in Ebisu in Tokyo, which serves lots of interesting bar snacks marrying traditional Japanese ingredients with un-traditional flavours. Kimchee is the ubiquitous pickled cabbage of Korea – searingly hot and spicy from the chilli and garlic in which it is pickled. This is my approximation, from memory, of the resulting combination.

I block firm tofu	½ teaspoon toasted sesame oil
I tablespoon vegetable oil	120 g/ 4 oz kimchee (page 179)

Boil the tofu for 2 minutes in clean water. Remove, wrap in a clean cloth and drain under weights for 30 minutes to remove excess water.

In a heavy bottom frying pan or skillet, heat the two oils to medium heat. Cut the tofu into four slices (or chunks if you prefer). Pan fry the pieces, until lightly brown (not crisp) on each side. Turn them carefully using a spatula so they don't break up. Remove the tofu and quickly heat up the kimchee in the same pan, turning quickly so it doesn't burn. Spoon the kimchee equally over each piece of tofu and serve immediately.

MIXED VEGETABLES WITH TOFU DRESSING
SHIRA AE

This is a classic Japanese recipe using tofu to make a creamy dressing for vegetables. You can vary the vegetables according to what is available, but be sure to separately cook them, as shown here. The flavouring liquid for the vegetables gives flavour and penetrates the tofu dressing. Sesame seeds and *shiitake* mushrooms help to add even more depth and richness.

---

1 block firm tofu

6-8 dried *shiitake* mushrooms, soaked in warm water, the stalks trimmed, and sliced thinly

SIMMER THE MUSHROOMS IN:

250 ml/9 fl oz *dashi* (made up with *shiitake* soaking water)

3 tablespoons soy sauce

2 tablespoons *mirin*

1 teaspoon sugar

1 carrot, cut on the diagonal and into thin juliennes, about 2 cm/ ¾ inch long

20 green beans, topped and tailed, and cut on the diagonal into thin strips

SIMMER THE CARROT AND BEANS IN:

250 ml/ 9 fl oz *dashi*

2 teaspoons sugar

2 tablespoons soy sauce

TO FLAVOUR THE TOFU DRESSING:

1 tablespoon caster sugar

1½ tablespoons soy sauce

½ tablespoon *mirin*

2 tablespoons sesame seeds, lightly toasted and ground in *suribachi*

3 cm/1 inch piece of fresh ginger, peeled and chopped into small matchsticks, to garnish

---

Plunge the tofu into boiling water in a saucepan and boil for a minute or two, remove, wrap in a cloth and drain (as described on page 58, 'To prepare tofu') for 30 minutes. Combine the flavouring ingredients for the mushrooms in a small saucepan, then simmer gently for 10 minutes or until most of the liquid has disappeared, and the mushrooms are coated with the sticky soy sauce. Allow to cool. Combine the simmering ingredients for the carrots and beans, and simmer together, until the carrots are just softening, and the beans cooked. Remove with a slotted spoon and allow to cool. (There may be some liquid left here, in which case reserve it in case you need it later.) Now you need to flavour the tofu for the dressing. To do this dissolve the caster sugar in the soy sauce and add the *mirin*. Grind the sesame seeds to a paste in a grinding bowl (*suribachi*). Break up the tofu into the sesame and mash with the wooden pestle. Add the soy sauce and *mirin* mixture. Just before serving toss the previously simmered and cooled vegetables in the mashed tofu dressing and coat well. If the mixture is a bit too dry you can add a bit of any left over simmering liquid. You can serve individually, by placing a small mound in the bottom of a small deep dish for each person, or you can serve it family style, piled into a larger dish and set in the centre of the table. Garnish with two or three matchsticks of fresh ginger. This is protein rich which would therefore be suitable as a main dish in a vegetarian meal, or can be eaten as a side dish.

TOFU WALNUT PÂTÉ
KURUMI TO TŌFU NO PÂTÉ

This is another of Bob Lloyd's recipes – he's very inventive with tofu. It's not something you'd be served in Japan, but uses Japanese ingredients in a delightfully interesting way. It's quite rich, so a little goes a long way. Served on top of mini rice crackers it makes a tasty and healthy vegetarian canapé, or it can be used as a stuffing – for mushrooms, peppers, tomatoes or even squid.

1 block firm (cotton) tofu	2-3 tablespoons *natto* miso chutney
40 g/ 1½ oz shelled walnuts	(available from most health food
4 small spring onions, finely chopped	shops, amongst the macrobiotic
	ingredients)

Place the tofu in a saucepan of boiling water and boil for a couple of minutes. Remove and wrap it in a clean tea towel. Place on a slightly tilted board, put a small plate on top with a heavy weight (or can) and leave to drain for about half an hour, or until some of the water has drained away. Gently roast the walnuts in a clean dry frying pan until lightly toasted. Remove and grind well in a grinding bowl (*suribachi*). Add the drained tofu, broken up into pieces, and grind together to a rough paste. Add the *natto* miso chutney and mix well (do not grind – the chutney has slivers of kelp [*kombu*] in it, which are nice as they are). Fold in the finely chopped spring onions, and it's ready to use however you fancy.

TOFU AND CARROT BALLS
MARIDŌFU

I devised this recipe as a way of using the left over pulp from making carrot juice. It seemed too good to simply throw away, and, unlike freshly grated carrot which has a high water content, it is quite dry which makes it perfect for mixing with tofu and deep frying. The resulting balls are a lovely orangey colour – quite jolly. I tried them out on my Japanese friend Naho who heartily approved of both the taste and texture, but collapsed in to fits of embarrassed giggles when I suggested we call them golden balls! After further thought I came up with the idea of naming them after the gaily coloured balls of multi-coloured cotton, called *mari,* that are a traditional toy for Japanese children. This then is a recipe for those of you who have a juicer (the centrifugal type).

I block regular tofu (drained as in the previous recipe above)	I teaspoon ginger juice (squeezed from freshly grated ginger)
8 tablespoons carrot pulp left over from making juice	I tablespoon white sesame seeds
	oil for deep frying

Drain the tofu under weights for half an hour. Place in a *suribachi* or bowl and mash. Add the carrot pulp and mix together well (you can use your fingers). Add the ginger juice and sesame seeds and combine well. Using your hands form about one tablespoonful of the mixture at a time into small balls, making sure the mixture sticks together well. Deep fry in medium hot oil (about 170C/ 340F) for 2-3 minutes until golden. Serve on bright childishly-decorated plates (or plain dark plates to show off the colour) with a drizzle of soy sauce.

DEEP-FRIED TOFU AND SHIITAKE 'PINE CONES'
MATSUKASA

In this dish, which I first ate at Sankō In Temple, deep fried tofu is shaped into little cone shapes, to resemble fallen pine cones (*matsukasa*) and is a dish to celebrate autumn. The seasonal effect is completed by scattering real pine needles over the finished dish (not to be eaten of course). The *shiitake* mushroom is separately flavoured in sweetened soy sauce.

I block regular or cotton tofu	oil for deep frying
3 large dried *shiitake* mushrooms	**DIPPING SAUCE:**
½ teaspoon caster sugar	I teaspoon fresh ginger juice
I tablespoon soy sauce	I tablespoon soy sauce
I teaspoon vegetable oil	

Boil the tofu in clean water for 2 minutes remove, wrap in a clean cloth and drain with a weight on for 30 minutes, to remove excess water. Soak the mushrooms in warm water until soft, chop off the stalks and finely mince the flesh. Dissolve the sugar in the soy sauce. In a small pan heat the oil, add the *shiitake* and briefly sauté. Add the sweetened soy sauce mixture to the mushrooms and keep the mixture moving on a medium heat until the liquid is absorbed and the mushrooms sticky. Remove from the heat. Break up the tofu into a *suribachi* and grind to a paste, using a mashing and grinding motion. Add the flavoured mushroom and mix well. Take about I tablespoonful of mixture and press it into a cone shape (make a ball first and then sharpen one end). This should make about a dozen. Heat the oil for deep frying to medium, about 170C/ 340F and drop the cones in to fry. They should be golden, and not too dry on the outside. They don't need much cooking, so better to underdo them than overdo them (unless you like a very crispy coating). Drain and serve 3 per person with a dip of soy sauce and ginger juice. They make an interesting starter, or a protein side dish in a Japanese meal. Serve hot.

Note: You can make edible pine needles from lengths of noodles. Take two pieces of *soba* buckwheat noodle about 6 cm/ 2 ½ inches long and bind them together with a small strip of *nori* at the base (the piece of *nori* should be small, about 1 cm/ ⅜ inch). Dampen the *nori* to secure it. Deep fry for 30 seconds. The noodles spread out creating a pine needle shape, which can be used to garnish autumnal dishes. Carrot 'maple leaves' can also be scattered on the plate.

SIMMERED DRIED TOFU WITH SHIITAKE AND CARROT
KOYADŌFU TO SHIITAKE NO NIMONO

Legend has it that this method of preserving tofu was discovered by accident, by a forgetful monk, who left his tofu outside on a cold night on Mount Koya, near Kyoto. Mount Koya has a beautiful temple on top of it, is a well known retreat for monks, and it is very cold in winter, so it could well be true. The texture of tofu changes completely when it is frozen (because it's mainly water), and after repeated freezing and thawing it becomes like a dry sponge. This makes it an excellent choice for dishes which are simmered for a long time as the tofu soaks up flavours, and becomes quite delicious. Not only that, the drying process concentrates the protein in tofu, to about 50%, so it's good for you as well.

4 pieces dried tōfu (*Koyadōfu*)	1 ½ teaspoons toasted sesame oil
5 dried *shiitake* mushrooms	2 tablespoons soy sauce
25 g/ 1 oz dried hijiki sea vegetable	2 teaspoons *mirin*
1 carrot	

Soak the tofu in hot water (weighted down with a plate to stop it floating, as described in the introduction to freeze dried tofu). Squeeze out and soak a couple more times. Meanwhile, place the *shiitake* in warm water and leave to soak for at least half an hour (adding a tablespoon of sugar will speed up the softening process). Separately soak the *hijiki* in cold water, and leave until soft and the volume increased. Peel the carrot (or simply scrape or scrub if organic). Slice into diagonal circles. Drain the *shiitake*, but keep the soaking water – it will be used to add flavour. Cut off the stalks (they are too tough) and slice the caps thickly.

When the *hijiki* is softened pour off the soaking water (you can use some of it to cook in if you like, but it's rather strong and salty – I prefer to throw it away). If the *hijiki* is in large stringy pieces chop it up a little. Heat the sesame oil in a large frying or sauté pan and add the *shiitake*, and sauté briefly. Add the chopped *hijiki*, and sauté for a couple more minutes. Add the *shiitake* soaking water (make it up to 300 ml/ 10 fl oz with water or *dashi* if necessary), and simmer for 5 minutes. Cut the tofu into thick strips and add to the *hijiki* mixture in the pan, mixing well. Add the flavouring ingredients – the soy sauce and *mirin* and simmer for 20 minutes. Finally add the carrots and simmer for another 10 minutes until the carrots are cooked, and not much liquid remains. (Add more water or *dashi* during cooking if it dries up, and keep testing for doneness, and flavour.) The richness of the stock and flavour of the *hijiki* and mushroom will be absorbed by the tofu.

FREEZE DRIED TOFU TEMPURA
KOYADŌFU NO TEMPURA

Traditionally *koyadōfu* was made by leaving blocks of tofu outside on a freezing night, and then allowing the daytime sunshine to thaw them out. Japanese winters lend themselves perfectly to this process – very cold at night and dry and sunny in the daytime – which is why several foods are preserved in this way. (Agar agar the seaweed jelly, and *konnyaku* are both produced in a similar way.) Luckily there are places in Japan, high in the mountains, where these traditional and natural methods are still used. Try to use such naturally made products if you can – you'll find them in natural health food shops. Packaged dried tofu will keep for a few months, but starts to discolour and turn a little rancid with age. The dried tofu has to be both re-constituted and cooked (simmered) before making this dish, so you could soak and simmer more pieces than you need for the previous recipe, and keep some over for deep frying a day or two later. Cooked dried tofu keeps well, about 4 days in the fridge.

4 pieces dried tofu	pinch salt
TO SIMMER:	1 small egg
1 tablespoon soy sauce	125 ml/ 4 fl oz ice cold water
600 ml/1 pint water	1 tablespoon very finely chopped perilla
1 tablespoon caster sugar	(*shiso*), coriander or parsley
1 teaspoon salt	oil for deep frying
TEMPURA BATTER:	
75 g/ 3 oz plain flour	

First prepare the tofu as described in the previous recipe. Cut each piece into three, widthways. Place tofu in a saucepan with the soy sauce, salt, water and sugar. Make sure the sugar is dissolved. Bring to a boil, and then simmer uncovered, on a low heat for 15 minutes. The tofu needs to keep its shape, so don't overcook it. Most of the liquid will have been absorbed. Cool the tofu pieces and then press out excess liquid. Put aside and prepare the tempura batter. The batter for this dish is not as lacy and light as regular tempura batter – it is more of a substantial coating (this is because you don't want the tofu inside to touch the oil and burn). Mix the flour, salt and egg with the water until just combined but no lumps remain. Fold in the finely chopped parsley or perilla. Heat the oil to medium (170C/ 340F). Dip the tofu pieces in the batter and slide carefully in to the oil. Fry for about 3 minutes until lightly golden. Keep using a finely slotted or mesh spoon to remove bits of batter and perilla (or parsley) that escape into the oil and burn. Serve 3 pieces to each person whilst hot.

O-KARA – SOYBEAN MASH

This is the fibrous residue left over when soy milk is squeezed from the pulp. It's mashed up beans, so it's actually quite nutritious – about 20% protein and full of fibre. Try to ignore the fact that it looks like damp sawdust! Traditionally it was a food in its own right, but these days it's considered peasant or country food, not sophisticated enough for urbanites. Consequently most of the *O-kara* produced in Japan (which is a lot) is now either fed to animals or wasted. However, cooked judiciously it makes a cheap and tasty meal, so I've included a typical *O-kara* recipe here. It's also great for adding to croquettes and bulking out soups – or even hamburgers.

O-KARA SIMMERED WITH CHICKEN AND VEGETABLES
UNOHANA

The fluffiness of *o-kara* is reckoned to remind the Japanese of a small white flower called *unohana*. This dish then has an extravagantly poetic name which was employed to disguise a very basic and cheap meal. *O-kara* is virtually tasteless, but because it's light and spongy it absorbs flavours well. The sweet soy sauce simmering broth imparts a hearty deliciousness to this dish, which can be made without the chicken if you prefer. *O-kara* is about 20% vegetable protein, so it's good for you even without the chicken.

2 large dried *shiitake* mushrooms	I teaspoon salt
I large skinless chicken breast fillet	I tablespoon sesame oil
I large carrot	250 ml/ 8oz *dashi* (made up with *shiitake*
25 g/ I oz green beans	soaking water
I tablespoon caster sugar	250 g/ 9 oz *o-kara* soybean mash
I tablespoon soy sauce	2 spring onions
I tablespoon *mirin*	

Soak the mushrooms in warm water for 2 hours until soft. Discard stems and chop flesh into thin strips. Shred the chicken into thin strips. Peel and cut the carrot into small juliennes (matchsticks), and cut the beans on the diagonal into thin strips. Dissolve the sugar in the *dashi* and add the soy sauce, *mirin* and salt. In a large skillet or cast iron pot, heat the oil to medium and add the chicken. Sauté for a few minutes until brown. Add the mushrooms, carrot and beans. Sauté a minute more. Add the *dashi* stock and *o-kara*, and cook on a medium heat, covered until all the ingredients are cooked through, and the liquid almost gone. Garnish with finely chopped spring onions, either in small bowls individually or family style in one large bowl. Serve hot, or at room temperature, as a main protein dish. You can be as inventive as you like with this dish, adding different mushrooms and root vegetables according to seasonal availability. *Hijiki* sea vegetable would be a flavoursome addition.

SOY MILK SKIN
YUBA

In Chinese restaurants you may have seen vegetarian 'duck' and other fake meat dishes on offer. They are usually made from a type of *yuba*, soy milk skin, which is chewy and thickly rolled. Dried *yuba* in Japan is usually sold in delicate little cellophane packages, containing small rolls of *yuba*, ready to pop in to the bottom of a lacquer bowl and be re-constituted with a clear or miso soup. Chinese stores abroad sell dried *yuba* but it lacks the delicacy of the Japanese variety, and unfortunately the large sheets are often broken by the time they reach the consumer. In Japan, fresh *yuba* is available in very few places outside Kyoto, but if you're ever lucky enough to visit Kyoto it's well worth trying. If you can see it being made even better. I saw the process in one of the small wooden shops in a cobbled back street, typical of Kyoto, where huge shallow pans of soy milk are left on a low simmer. Dangling from the ceiling are bamboo hangers. After long simmering a skin forms on the milk, which is skillfully scooped up with a bamboo stick and hung up to dry. The sheets of *yuba* suspended in the steam create a scene remarkably like a laundry – but with a smell you want to taste. If you're feeling adventurous – and patient – you can try making *yuba* yourself. It's not something you'd do every day but it's worth it to sample the taste of the real thing. Anyway it's fun! Use the best most concentrated soy milk you can buy, which must be unsweetened. Buy a litre pack and pour the milk into a clean large and shallow pan (like a paella pan, frying pan, or even a baking dish), to a depth of about 3 cm/1 inch – no more. A square or rectangular dish will of course produce straight sided sheets, whereas a round pan will result in rounded sheets. In Japan the pans are placed over simmering water, *bain-marie* style, but if this is difficult just place the pan on a very low flame, using a heat diffuser. The milk needs to heat, but not bubble or boil. After about 15 minutes you'll see the top wrinkle, and a skin will have formed on top. This skin is what you want – *yuba*. Lifting it off though is tricky. Using a knife or chopstick gently free the *yuba* from the edges of the pan, where it will have stuck. Then, even more gently, slide a long cooking chopstick under the *yuba* and lift it off. Hold it above the pan for a few seconds to let any excess milk drain off then lay it on a clean board or cloth. The *yuba* will have stuck to the chopstick so cut along this edge. You now have a semi-circular, or rectangular sheet of *yuba*. Repeat this process until all the milk is gone. You can stack the sheets on top of each other and then roll them up or keep them separate.

FRESH SOY MILK SKIN
NAMA YUBA

When making your *yuba* pile the sheets on top of each other, and when you've finished roll them up. Cut the roll into small pieces about an inch long. Put one or two pieces per person into a small dish and serve with a dash of soy sauce drizzled over and a smidgeon of *wasabi* paste. The evaporating process concentrates the protein and oil in the soy milk, making it quite rich. This is a luxury food, like caviar, not to be eaten in quantity but as a gastronomic experience.

Note: This is a good way of serving fresh *yuba* which may have broken up and become a bit messy, as it doesn't need to be in a neat roll. You can just lift a small mound of it (a couple of tablespoons per person) and pile into a small deep dish.

DEEP FRIED SOY MILK SKIN ROLLS
YUBA MAKI

If you skillfully managed to keep your sheets of *yuba* unbroken you can use them to make the following recipe. They are like a very delicate spring roll skin. When *yuba* is deep fried it puffs up to a delightfully light and crispy texture. I made these for my priest friend, Seiji Kimura and his wife Hitomi in Japan, and they loved them. In fact I think it was the experience of eating these that inspired them to persuade me to teach and demonstrate Japanese cookery. However, if all this *yuba* making is too time consuming and fiddly you can try reconstituting the dried Chinese variety, which is sold in big sheets, or even just use the following filling for spring rolls, using spring roll skins. The result won't be as light and crisp, or with the aura of elegance that *yuba* provides, but it'll be tasty. (If you do use spring roll pastry fry them immediately once they are filled. They go soggy if left sitting around, and fall apart.)

FILLING:	I tablespoon light miso
125 g/ 4oz bean sprouts	4 pieces of fresh or dried *yuba*
I medium carrot, grated on a Western style grater – using the big holes	(reconstituted in water) about 25 cm/10 inches x 20 cm/ 8 inches
4 dried *shiitake* mushrooms, reconstituted in water	pinch seven peppers (*shichimi tōgarashi*) seasoning or ½ teaspoon *yuzu* powder

Plunge the bean sprouts into a saucepan of boiling water for 30 seconds to soften them. Remove with a slotted spoon and put into cold water. Drain. Chop roughly. Dunk the grated carrot in to the same water for I minute to soften. Drain and squeeze excess water out of the carrot. Finely dice the mushroom caps (discard the tough stems).

In a large bowl mix the miso with the vegetables, using a wooden spoon, and a dash of the *shiitake* soaking water to soften the miso if necessary (but not too soft – you want a stiff filling not a slop). Season with the *yuzu* powder or pepper.

Take a generous tablespoon of the mixture and place into the centre of each piece of *yuba* skin. Roll up, tucking in the edges as you go, to make a roll. With luck you'll get a double layer of *yuba* skin, and it'll seal itself with its moisture. Slide into low to medium hot oil (about 155-165C/ 310-330F) to deep fry. You want the *yuba* to sizzle and puff up as soon as it hits the oil, but not to burn. Fry for 2-3 minutes until golden and puffy. Be careful not to fry the rolls for too long or they'll brown – you want them golden. Also, as they puff up and trap air you may find they float, so only one side gets cooked. Keep your eye on them and keep turning them with chopsticks so they cook evenly. Drain well on kitchen paper (they can be greasy). Serve immediately whilst still hot. (As the filling contains miso you don't need any soy sauce dip for these – just eat them as they are, as an unusual starter, or as the deep fried (*age mono*) course in a Japanese meal.)

NATTO YUBA ROLLS

Natto is a disgusting-smelling (but so is Stilton cheese) sticky fermented soybean product which is sold in small polystyrene tubs. Even some Japanese don't like it. But it's delicious, and nutritious too (see the section on *natto* later). When *natto* is cooked it loses its stickiness, so only the nuttiness remains, making it much more palatable. The combination of the crispy *yuba* and nutty *natto* is delectable – it's one of my favourite things. I discovered the combination when trying to think of things to deep fry *natto* in. You'll need 2 packs of *natto*, so you can divide it up evenly amongst the *yuba* skins, depending on their size. Do not over fry – you don't want the *yuba* too browned, or the *natto* burnt.

FILLING:

2 packs *natto* (*hikiwari natto* is best, where the beans are chopped into small pieces)

mustard to flavour (*natto* packs always contain a little sachet of mustard to mix with the *natto*)

4 pieces of *yuba* soy milk skin as before

If using frozen *natto* leave it to thaw. Mix the mustard in (but not the little sachet of soy sauce). Lay a sheet of *yuba* out and place half a pack of *natto* in the centre. Roll up and deep fry as before. Serve with a soy sauce dip.

CRISP FRIED DRIED YUBA
YUBA KARA-AGE

Even a lot of Japanese people won't have tasted fresh *yuba*, so you don't have to feel you are cheating by using the dried version. Besides – it's got its own particular qualities – in this recipe it's deep fried, and puffs up to a crisp, like popadoms or prawn crackers. It's great as an accompaniment to drinks. Be sure to drain well on kitchen paper before serving, to get rid of the greasiness.

4 large sheets dried *yuba*
oil for deep frying

freshly ground sea salt

Cut the dried *yuba* into small pieces about 5 cm x 5 cm/ 2 inches square. Heat the oil to medium (170C/340F). Drop the pieces into the oil and watch them expand. Remove immediately, before they burn, and drain on paper. Sprinkle with salt and serve as an accompaniment to saké or beer, instead of crisps.

Note: Instead of salt you can sprinkle with a dried sea vegetable condiment. In the UK Seagreens produce organic dulse and wild wrack seasonings, to be used in place of salt. In the US Maine Coast Sea Vegetables make and export a range of sea vegetable condiments in table top size drums. Alternatively you can make your own by putting *dulse* or *nori* into a low oven to dry (not burn), and then crushing to a powder in a grinding bowl.

DEEP FRIED DRIED YUBA SIMMERED WITH SHIITAKE MUSHROOMS
AGE YUBA TO SHIITAKE NO NIMONO

This takes the recipe above a stage further. The *yuba* is deep fried, and then simmered in a weak soy based stock. This is not of course anything like a main dish, but a protein side dish which would be part of a Japanese meal, or could be served as a starter.

	SIMMERING LIQUID:
8 small dried *shiitake* mushrooms	300 ml/ ½ pint *shiitake* soaking water
I medium carrot cut into rings and then 12 flower shapes cut from the slices	3 teaspoons light soy sauce
4 sheets dried *yuba* soy milk skin	I teaspoon caster sugar
	2 tablespoons saké

Soak the mushrooms in just over 300 ml /½ pint warm water until soft (about 1-2 hours). Par boil the carrot flowers in a little boiling water for a few minutes until just softened. Remove, drain and cool. Deep fry the *yuba* as before. In a bowl pour boiling water over the *yuba* and leave a few minutes to soften. Strain the *shiitake* soaking water into a small saucepan, and add the soy sauce, sugar and saké. Cut the stems off the mushrooms and cut a decorative cross in the cap, if desired. Add the *yuba*, *shiitake* and carrots to the flavoured simmering liquid and bring to a boil over medium heat. Simmer for a few minutes. Serve a few pieces of *yuba*, two mushrooms and three carrot flowers per person in a small bowl, arranged as artfully as possible. Spoon 2-3 tablespoons of the juice over each dish. Can be served hot or at room temperature.

FERMENTED SOYBEANS
NATTO

Once Japanese people realise I can use chopsticks quite well, and then realise I am interested in Japanese food they almost always ask the same question – "can you eat *natto*?" I take great delight in replying that I love the stuff. Fits of giggles or looks of horror ensue, especially if my inquisitor is from the Kansai region of Japan – *natto* is very much a Tokyo taste and regarded as far too unsophisticated for the refined tastes of Kyoto folk! I have to admit that I too thought it most disgusting when I first tasted it (in 1976 I think) and it's definitely an acquired taste. However, once you decide you like it you can't get enough of it. In the past it was made by leaving cooked soybeans wrapped in rice straw in a warm place (legend has it that the process was discovered by accident in some farmhouse somewhere in the depths of the Japanese countryside). The bacteria (*bacillus natto*) that occured naturally in the straw fermented the beans. The result is smelly and sticky. These days it's commercially produced (in polystyrene pots), the *bacillus natto* is artificially introduced, and the temperature carefully controlled. The rice straw is gone too, although occasionally one can find *natto* packaged in quaint rice straw bundles – purely for the nostalgic effect. Outside of Japan *natto* will only be available frozen – allow to defrost before using. Alternatively you can try making your own in the airing cupboard. Like yoghurt, *natto* needs a warm even temperature to thrive in. The culture, *natto bacillus*, can be obtained by mail order from Future Foods (see appendix).

FERMENTED SOYBEANS WITH RAW TUNA
MAGURO NATTO

Here's a simple *natto* recipe for the adventurous, combining as it does, *natto* and raw fish. Make sure the fish is fresh enough to eat raw (see the section on fish, page 181).

200 g/ 7 oz fresh *sashimi* – quality tuna fillet (*maguro*)	**soy sauce and mustard (usually supplied with the *natto*)**
2 packs *natto* (it's usually sold in packs of two) about 200 g/ 7oz total	

Chop the fresh fish into cubes (*sainome giri* style) about 1 cm/ ⅜ inch in size. Divide between 4 small deep dishes. Divide the *natto* – half a pack per person – and pour into the dish over the tuna. Serve immediately with a drizzle of soy sauce and mustard.

 # NATTO DEEP FRIED IN PERILLA LEAVES
AGE NATTO

This is similar to the *natto* deep fried in fresh soy milk skin (*natto yuba* rolls) but instead of being wrapped in *yuba,* soy milk skin, the sticky beans are encased in a perilla (*shiso*) leaf, and coated in a light tempura batter. If you can't get perilla leaves you can try substituting squares, or triangles, of *nori* sea vegetable.

1 pack *natto*	**125 ml/ 4 fl oz ice cold water**
8 perilla (*shiso*) leaves	**1 egg**
TEMPURA BATTER:	**pinch salt**
75 g/ 3 oz plain flour	**oil for deep frying**

Don't mix the *natto* with the little packets of soy sauce and mustard that come with it, as you want to keep the *natto* stiff and sticky. Take one large teaspoonful of *natto* and place it in the centre of each leaf, on its rough (under) side. Fold over, making sure that the sticky *natto* seals the edges. Heat the oil to 170C/ 340F. Prepare the batter by mixing the egg, flour, salt and water very quickly to a lumpy but fairly thin mix, whilst keeping it as cold as possible. Slide the folded leaves very carefully into the batter, using chopsticks or a spoon. Quickly fry for about 1-2 minutes, until golden. Be careful not to overcook them – burnt *natto* isn't what you want, and it burns easily. If you are a deft worker you can even try this without the leaves, by sliding a spoonful of *natto* into the batter and rolling it in the batter whilst holding it together. Serve hot, with a dipping sauce of soy sauce and mustard (from the packets).

RICE – THE SACRED GRAIN

"When you are hungry, eat rice. When you are weary, sleep."

Zen proverb

When a Japanese housewife wants to call her family together for a meal she'll shout *"Gohan desu yo"* which means "The rice is ready". The rice is ready, means the meal is ready. So important is rice in Japanese life and culture that it is a synonym for food itself. *Gohan* means both rice and meal at one and the same time. Without rice a meal is considered incomplete. In fact it's even more than that: rice is considered the main dish. Unlike the equivalent carbohydrate staples in the West, bread and potatoes, rice is not eaten alongside other things. Other things are eaten alongside rice. All other dishes – even fish and meat – are considered *o-kazu* (side dishes) supporting players to the main actor.

Cooked rice is called *gohan*, and uncooked raw rice is called *kome*. Because of the reverence the Japanese people have for rice, *kome* is always referred to as *o-kome* including the honorific prefix *o*. In other words – Honourable Rice. Incidentally this honorific is commonly used for other foods as well (see reference to *o-kazu* above) and will crop up in this book when I talk about *o-cha* (tea), *o-den* (Hot Pot), *o-sekihan* and *o-zōni* (Rice Cake Soup).

"The Chinese and Japanese enumerate five cereals as the staples to which agricultural labour should be devoted. These are rice, barley, wheat, millet and beans. But rice ranks above all the rest – equal in fact to all the others put together."

Basil Hall Chamberlain, *Things Japanese*

In feudal times the lives of the Japanese people revolved around the yearly cycle of planting and harvesting rice. Because it is so labour intensive and relies so heavily on teamwork, it is sometimes seen by sociologists as the origin of the Japanese tendency to do things in groups. Whether that is the case or not, in Japan rice has enormous social and religious significance. Samurai were paid in rice, and rice was a measure of wealth. Shinto is the animistic 'religion' that co-exists with Buddhism in Japan. It is essentially nature worship, where every natural thing, such as mountains, trees, rivers, rocks, wind and rain (and most importantly, rice) has a god who must be worshipped and respected. One of the most important elements of Shinto ceremony is purification. White rice, along with salt and water, symbolises purity, and thus features heavily in Shinto purification rituals.

In fact rice was more than a symbol of wealth – it was wealth. It was money. Peasants were compelled to pay their masters in rice. This meant that at times many of the peasant farmers, although driven to devote their whole lives to raising rice crops could not actually eat it themselves. They had to make do with barley and millet. This is perhaps another reason why rice is still so revered – there's a collective memory of the time when it was a nobleman's food – collected off the backs of the poor.

By 1879 however, this had evidently changed.

"In the past one could count on one's fingers the days in the year when farming families of the middle class or even above ate rice, but in recent years many farmers have found themselves in a position to afford a daily rice diet."
From *Japanese Life and Culture in the Meiji Era* by S.Keizo, translated by C.S.Terry

It's interesting also to note that in the past, on the rare occasions when the poor were able to eat rice, however small a quantity, they didn't mix it with other grains. To make it stretch they simply made it into a gruel with more water. So precious was it that they wanted to savour its delicate and refined taste. The rich on the other hand, who had rice available to them most of the time, did mix the rice with other cheaper grains, such as millet or barley, or even *daikon* radish – in order to relieve the monotony of rice every day!

In the 1700s white rice was reserved only for ceremony, and the rice that was eaten was whole brown rice. But there was one section of the community that was specially allowed to eat white rice – fishermen. At that time Buddhist precepts against killing living things were still common, so fishermen were taking two risks with their lives when they went out with their boats. Not only were they were risking their physical lives – many boats and men's lives were lost at sea, but they were also risking their spiritual lives by incurring the wrath of the gods – for taking the lives of the fish. To appease the gods and protect the fishermen they were given white rice to take on their fishing trips. This is a perfect example of the way that Buddhism and Shintoism overlap or work together in Japanese traditional culture. It was Buddhist tenets that forbade the killing, but the fishermen overcame it with a Shinto ritual.

Another traditional ceremony, that may still be practised in some rural areas, occurs at the time of childbirth. Grains of white rice are shaken from a bamboo tube over the expectant mother before she gives birth, which is supposed to strengthen her for the delivery and ward off bad energy, or *ki*.

In early autumn, the first rice harvest appears in the shops. This rice is called *Shin mai* (literally 'new rice', *mai* being another pronunciation of *kome*), and is the subject of endless discussion and conversation. All Japanese have an opinion on which variety is best, and where in Japan the best rice comes from – usually from the home town of the speaker! It is still common for country dwellers to send parcels of fresh young rice to their urban relatives as a nostalgic reminder of home – and of nature. Such seasonal gestures are common and serve to remind Japanese of their closeness to nature, even if only in a sentimental way. Every spring the emperor partakes in a public ceremony in which he plants the first rice seedlings of the year. In fact the emperor has his own rice plot, which supplies the rice for the Imperial household. And he's not the only one – one of the most surprising things about the Japanese countryside is the number of tiny rice fields. Each farmer will have his own little rice field, even if his plot is practically the size of a postage stamp. Even on the outskirts of urban areas in Tokyo you can see them, just like allotments in London suburbs.

Although much fuss is made in Japan of the superiority of Japanese rice over foreign rice, the Japanese have in fact been importing rice since the end of the 19th century. Shortages of local rice in Osaka in 1890 drove the rice merchants to import it from China. Although it wasn't popular at first people soon became accustomed to it. Nowadays rice is imported from the United States, but although the canny consumer has reluctantly been persuaded to eat foreign rice, mainly on account of cost, there is still something special about Japanese rice which makes it more than a foodstuff. It's as if it contains the very essence, or soul, of Japan. Rice has a very special place in the hearts of all Japanese.

HOW RICE IS SERVED

In a formal meal rice is served at the end of the meal, together with pickles and soup. Sir Ernest Satow in A Diplomat in Japan 1853-64 describes a typical evening's entertainment for diplomats in Japan at the time.

"After two or three hours of conversation, perhaps enlivened by some music and singing performed by professionals hired for the occasion, and you had had enough liquor, you bowed to your host, and said that you would like some rice. This was the well understood signal."

In Japan, the cooking of rice is considered so important that high class restaurants have a chef whose sole duty it is. In the past rice was cooked in a pot over the fire, but these days it's rare to find a Japanese household that doesn't have a rice cooker. The advantage of rice cookers is that you get perfect rice every time, and you can cook in quantity and keep it warm. With hungry children around it's handy to have a big pot of rice on the go for snacks. My friend's teenage son would regularly break off from his studies, and dive downstairs for something to keep him going – a handful of warm rice and, to hold it together, a fresh crisp sheet of *nori*. Quick, delicious – and nutritious too.

WASHING RICE

Before cooking, rice must be washed, and washed well. My Japanese friends tell me to wash it at least ten times. In the temples, the washing of rice is seen as a kind of meditation. The temple's cook (called the *tenzo*), must focus silently on the washing, letting no distraction enter his or her mind. This of course is the essence of Zen – concentrating the mind on the job in hand – not thinking about any result. Just to be engaged with the process. This is the reasoning behind Japanese *sumi-e* (water colour) painting – once you've put the stroke on the page you can't change it. It's there. So the 'work' is beforehand – in concentrating the mind. It's the same with cooking. Although we can't all be Zen cooks it is good to keep some of their principles in mind when we cook. Indeed much of the basis of the Japanese attitude to food – its preparation and presentation – comes from the Zen Buddhist way of cooking and eating. A Zen cook respects the ingredients he or she is working with, and their preparation becomes an act of love and gratitude to God who provided them. The Zen cook never forgets where the food came from – from God and nature – so an attitude of eternal gratitude is ever present. In the temples, before eating, the monks and nuns recite the 'gokan no ge' the five reflections.

"I reflect on the work that brings this food before me; let me see whence this food comes.

I reflect on my imperfections, on whether I am deserving of this offering of food. Let me hold my mind free from preferences and greed.

I take this food as a medicine to keep my body in good health.

I accept this food so that I will fulfill my task of enlightenment."

Soei Yoneda, The Heart of Zen Cuisine

It's really just the same as the Grace that we were brought up to say before meals, "For what we are about to receive, may the Lord make us truly thankful." So – let's begin, and be thankful.

RICE RECIPES (GOHAN MONO)

PLAIN BOILED WHITE RICE
GOHAN

Japanese rice is the short grained variety, *Oryza sativa japonica*. Short grained rice is easier to eat with chopsticks, as it sticks together. This is completely the opposite of what one aims for in cooking long grain Indian-style rice, where the ideal is separate grains. Don't even think about making Japanese food with anything other than short grained. Luckily, with the increasing popularity of sushi, it's much more widely available now than it used to be, and many of the major supermarkets stock it. In the past, when it wasn't so readily available, I even resorted to pudding rice as a last minute substitute. It's certainly better than using inauthentic long grain rice for Japanese cooking. However, Californian short grain rice is widely available now – some common varieties are *Kokuho* Rose and California Rose. *Koshihikari* and *Nishiki* are popular varieties, but *Akitakomachi*, readily available in Japanese supermarkets, is one of my favourites – really creamy tasting.

How to cook rice: As rice is such an important part of Japanese cooking you find that cooks have different and preferred ways of preparing it. In any case no rice is exactly the same as another. Sometimes it will turn out softer or harder than the previous time you cooked it. Don't worry! For example, rice grown in Asia, in paddy fields, will have a higher moisture content than rice grown in the US or Europe, and to top class Japanese chefs this must also be taken into account when measuring the proportion of water to rice. Shizuo Tsuji in his book, *Japanese Cooking, A Simple Art*, recommends a ratio of 5:6, or 20% more water than rice by volume, for Asian rice, and a ratio of 4:7 or 75% more water by volume for European rice. Actually I usually split the difference, and employ a ratio of 2:3 that is, 50% more water by volume. So if you are using 2 measures of rice, use 3 measures of water. I have included cup measures for the rice recipes, because it is such a convenient way of measuring , and the Japanese always measure their rice by volume.

Measuring method II Alternatively you can calculate the amount of water you need by covering the rice with water to a depth of 2.5 cm, or 1 inch above the rice. My housewife friend Nobuko measures the depth with her knuckles.

Measuring method III Or you can measure your rice dry and then leave it to soak, as some chefs prefer. If you do this then measure the rice again after soaking and add water to just over a 1:1 ratio.

This all may sound very tricky, but it does make sense. If your rice is stickier than you intended just tell your guests you've cooked it tea ceremony style! Finally, although rice cookers are convenient and more or less guarantee perfectly cooked rice, it's not necessary to have a rice cooker in order to cook rice well. I use a heavy bottomed saucepan with a tightly fitting lid. Please note that Japanese chefs don't add salt to rice, as the accompanying foods in a Japanese meal are salty enough.

Allow 125 g / 4 oz of rice per person (or ½ cup by volume)	500 g / 16 oz / 2 cups rice 720 ml/ 22 fl oz/ 3 cups water

Put the rice in a large pot and, in the sink, cover with water. Stir with your fingers and press down with the heel of your hand. Gently pour off the cloudy milky water and cover with fresh water. Stir again and pour off again. Keep rinsing in this way for about 5 minutes, or 10 rinses. The water will become progressively clearer. The grains will also become more tender as they absorb water during this process, so be more gentle with it on the later rinses. If you are frightened of throwing away the rice with the water use a colander to rinse the water away. After washing leave the rice to drain in a colander for 30 minutes. (Incidentally this cloudy water can be kept and used for cooking root vegetables, such as burdock, *daikon* radish, bamboo shoot and lotus root – it's especially good for vegetables with a bitter edge.)

Put the rice in a heavy bottomed pot with a tight lid. The rice will expand during cooking so you need to give it room to do so, but at the same time cooking in too large a pot for the amount of rice you have may give a dry or scorched result (scorched rice however is regarded as a treat, see below).

Bring the rice to a boil over medium heat, with the lid firmly on. When it starts to boil and spill over the sides of the lid turn the flame down to the lowest it'll go, and cook until all the liquid is absorbed by the rice (about 10 -15 minutes). Try not to lift off the cover during cooking – you need the steam in the pan, not in the kitchen. When it's done turn off the flame but leave the pan on the stove for 5 minutes to steam a little more. The grains should cling together without being porridge-like. Before serving 'fluff up' the rice with a wooden rice paddle, using a cutting motion, and transfer to a wooden rice pot to take to the table. A wooden bowl or pot is best as it absorbs moisture and keeps the rice warm without causing condensation. I have two beautiful cypress pots bound with copper especially for the task – one small one for two servings and a large family style one. These copper-bound pots (called *o-hitsu*) are made in Japan in the same style as bath tubs were traditionally made. Sadly, wooden bath tubs are a rarity these days – I've used one only twice – but the fragrance of the cedar or cypress in the heat of a steamy bathroom is unforgettable. A cedar pot full of warm rice replicates the smell – with the aroma of cooked rice as a bonus.

If you do scorch the rice at the bottom of the pan – don't despair. It's practically a delicacy (like cake mixture left in a mixing bowl). In fact it even has a name, *o-koge,* which means 'to scorch', and it's often eaten just as it is, as a snack, or added to *o-chazuke,* Rice Soup, where it imparts a smoky flavour.

Seasonal rice variations

The Japanese like to 'taste' the changing seasons, and rice is therefore often cooked with a vegetable to celebrate the season. In spring, peas, or even cherry blossoms, may be added to the rice; in autumn, mushrooms or chestnut.

There are even different names for types of cooked rice:

Takikomi gohan is rice cooked with something else (in the pot).

Maze gohan is rice where something is mixed in after cooking.

O-kayu is rice gruel, which is explained in more detail later.

Sushi meshi is the rice used in sushi, which is flavoured with sweetened vinegar.

Anyway, here are some seasonal suggestions for your rice, guaranteed to instill an awareness of nature and gratitude to God in your cooking.

Spring:

Pickled cherry blossoms (yes, they really do eat them). These are available in foil wrapped packets preserved in salt. As they are very salty rinse them lightly first. Mix them in after cooking, or just place one flower on top of each bowl.

Bamboo shoots – chopped up bamboo shoots can be mixed in before cooking (*takikomi* style).

Green Peas – par boil separately and add to rice before serving – if you cook them with the rice they will lose their colour.

Summer: do not cook any of these with the rice. Mix them in after (*maze gohan* style)

Perilla leaves (shiso) cut into shreds and lightly coat with salt before mixing in with rice.

Green tea rice – this is a very strange and esoteric way of celebrating the arrival of the fresh young green tea – called *shincha* – on the market. The dried tea, which must be of the highest quality – is chopped up very finely and mixed with salt and sprinkled over the rice after cooking (in the same way you would use *goma shio* – sesame seeds and salt).

Autumn/Winter: (cook with the rice – *takikomi* style).

Mushroom rice – slice any well flavoured mushroom thinly and scatter on top of rice before cooking. Wild mushrooms give this dish extra glamour and seasonal piquancy.

Ginger rice Slivers of fresh ginger give the rice a distinctive oriental taste and can be enjoyed in any season. Slice the ginger into small matchsticks, or mince.

Chestnut Just chop into halves or quarters and scatter on top of the rice before cooking.

HOW TO SERVE RICE ATTRACTIVELY

1. The Japanese way is in proper porcelain or earthenware rice bowls, which shouldn't be too full. Rice is usually served in two paddlefuls – use your judgement so as not to pile up the bowl too much. The more elegant the occasion the smaller the helping.

2. If you don't have Japanese dishes and want to serve your food Western style on one large plate you can still present your food beautifully, and convey the essence of Japanese eating. Instead of heaping the rice in a pile you can mould it. Use a small bowl 5-8 cm/ 2-3 inches in diameter, wet it first to stop the rice sticking, and pack it with rice, pushing well down. Invert the rice on to the plate, and arrange other foods alongside, leaving plenty of space between each one. For extra prettiness you can decorate the rice with a sprinkle of poppy seeds or black sesame seeds, or something seasonal like a mushroom, half a chestnut or a cherry blossom.

3. If you have a triangular *o-nigiri* mould, you can also use it to shape rice for a Western style plate.

BROWN RICE
GENMAI

In spite of its superior nutritional qualities brown rice has for a long while been regarded as undesirable – an unrefined food for unrefined people. Indeed there is only one section of the Japanese populace I've been told who eat it regularly, and that's prisoners. Its image must be bad if it is seen as a punishment. Monks though have been known to exist on brown rice alone for long periods, and it is said that Emperor Hirohito always ate brown rice, grown in his own paddy fields. Unfortunately, however beloved of emperors and macrobiotic hippies in the 1970s, brown rice may never shed its beards and sandal image. For some dishes though it can be a delicious, nutty and of course, nutritious, alternative. When I was in Japan I used to cook both white and brown rice, although the latter was notoriously difficult to get hold of. When I went into the local rice shop, and asked for "*genmai*" the poor rice man would begin to shake his head and suck his teeth, and wonder where on earth it could be – "*genmai ka*... hmmm... we have some somewhere." Usually they'd have to go around the back, or in the basement, or some forgotten place, but they'd get it for me in the end. Luckily things have changed a bit since then and there are more 'health food' stores selling it, but it still hasn't achieved the status that, say, wholewheat bread has in the West. What is more easily available in Japan is *haiga mai* – half refined rice where the husk is removed but the germ is left intact. Unfortunately I haven't seen it out of Japan, which is a shame because it is more nutritious than white rice, and more elegant than brown.

How to cook brown rice

There are two ways of cooking brown rice; with a pressure cooker or without. I usually cook it in a heavy pot with a close fitting lid, as with white rice, but with twice the amount of water to rice, a 1:2 ratio. The other difference is that you don't have to wash brown rice as thoroughly, as you aren't washing away the starch. What you should do is pick it over in its dry state to check for small stones or bad husks, and then wash it through a colander to get rid of any dust or dirt. The other difference is that you add a pinch of salt.

Saucepan method

For 4 people allow 125 g/ 4 oz rice to 240 ml/ 9 fl oz water	960 ml/ 1 pint 14 fl oz/ 4 cups water
500 g / 16 oz / 2 cups short grain brown rice	pinch salt

Wash the rice as described on page 82 and place in a medium heavy bottomed pot, with the water and salt. Bring to a boil then reduce the heat to low (you can use a heat diffuser to distribute the heat if you like). Keep on a very low simmer for about 40 minutes, until all the water has been absorbed and the rice is soft. Do not disturb the rice by stirring during cooking. However, unlike white rice, you can add more water and cook for a little longer if you want a softer rice. After cooking turn off the heat and allow the rice to stand for a few minutes.

Pressure cooker method
This results in a softer rice, as it's cooked under pressure.

For 4 people allow 125 g/ 4 oz rice to 240 ml/ 9 fl oz water	960 ml/ 1 pint 14 fl oz/ 4 cups water
500 g / 16 oz / 2 cups short grain brown rice	pinch salt

In a medium sized pressure cooker, bring the ingredients to full pressure. Turn down the heat and cook under pressure for 35 – 40 minutes. Remove from the heat and leave the pressure to decrease naturally, or hold under cold tap to reduce. Fluff up the rice before serving.

RICE RECIPES

VARIETY RICE
GOMOKU MESHI
Gomoku means 'five things' and there are lots of '*gomoku*' dishes in Japan – dishes which contain a variety of little bits and pieces. This is a bit like a risotto, where the raw ingredients are cooked along with the rice in a big pot – without stirring. It's served hot and would be a good accompaniment to a well flavoured protein dish, such as saké simmered mackerel or *daikon* with miso.

75 g/ 3 oz boneless chicken thighs	**SIMMERING STOCK FOR FLAVOURING:**
1 small carrot	500 ml/ 1 pint *dashi* stock (made up
1 deep fried tofu pouch	with the *shiitake* soaking water if using
(*usu-age* or *abura-age*)	dried mushrooms)
4 large *shiitake* mushrooms	½ teaspoon salt
(dried or fresh)	2 tablespoons *mirin*
75 g/ 3 oz bamboo shoot	4 tablespoons soy sauce
400 g/10 oz short grain white rice	

Cut the chicken into small bite size pieces. Peel the carrot and slice into medium thick rounds, them make flower shapes from the rounds, with a cutter (or dice the carrot into small cubes). Put the tofu into a colander and pour boiling water over it, to get rid of excess oil. Cut crosswise into thin julienne trips. Cut the stems off the *shiitake* and cut the flesh into thick slices (if using dried ones soak first for 30 minutes in warm water, and keep the soaking water for the *dashi*.) Cut the bambo shoot into thick juliennes.

Wash the rice as described on page 82. Place the rice in a large earthenware casserole, heavy bottomed pot with lid, or a rice cooker. Scatter the solid items on top, but mix them in slightly if the layer is too thick. Mix the *dashi* and seasoning ingredients, and pour over the rice without mixing. Bring to a boil over a high heat, with the lid on. Turn down and simmer for about 15 minutes, until all the water is absorbed and the ingredients cooked. Turn off the heat but leave with the lid on for 10 minutes more. Mix in the vegetables and meat carefully before serving.

Note: This is a dish that is suitable for brown rice – making it nuttier and more substantial. In which case use ⅔ more liquid in the stock (830 ml/1½ pints) and cook for longer.

RICE BALLS WITH NORI
O-NIGIRI O-MUSUBI

Once again the importance of rice in Japanese culture is demonstrated by the use of the honorific O. O-musubi is the more romantic (and old fashioned) name for rice balls. To make them you press rice between the palms of your hands. *Musubu* is a verb of Shinto origin, and means the ritual clapping of the hands, performed at visits to Shinto shrines. This clapping is supposed to symbolise the meeting of the male god, Izanagi who resides in your left hand, and the female god Izanami, who resides in your right hand. What profundity in rice balls. No wonder they are honoured with an 'O'.

In the centre of each rice ball is a surprise – a mouthful of salmon, some dried bonito flakes or a spoonful of tinned tuna (sometimes mixed with mayonnaise). *Umeboshi* plum is popular with Japanese but may be a bit of an acquired taste for Westerners. But why not try some of each?

TO MAKE 12 (3 PER PERSON FOR A PICNIC)

1 kg / 2¼ lbs cooked white short grain rice

pinch salt (optional)

FILLINGS:

4 teaspoons cooked salmon fillet, (or smoked salmon, tinned salmon, tinned tuna with mayonnaise)

1 tablespoon *umeboshi* paste

1 tablespoon *katsuo* flakes

COVERING:

3 sheets sushi *nori* (toasted seaweed)

Mix the cooked rice well with the pinch of salt. Have a bowl of water handy to wet your hands. Take a large scoop of rice (about 2 tablespoons worth), in one hand and pack and compress it into shape with the other hand, so it no longer falls apart. Make a spherical shape, and then an indentation in one side. Place a teaspoonful of salmon (or ½ teaspoonful of *umeboshi* paste) into the hollow, and then wrap the rice around it to conceal it. Once you have a sphere again, slightly flatten the ball and push the edges to make a triangular shape. Try not to get the rice too wet. The trick is to press the rice firmly enough so that it holds together, but not so firmly that it becomes a sticky dense mass. Practise will show you how. Cut each sheet of *nori* into four thick strips and wrap one strip around each triangle (or you can wrap the whole thing in *nori*, folding over at the corners so it completely covers).

Repeat using the *umeboshi* paste, and the *katsuo* flakes for the remaining balls. These are the ultimate picnic food, but be aware that when you take them on a picnic and therefore leave them wrapped for a long while before eating them, the *nori* wrapping loses its crispness (not its taste though). The Japanese have devised an elaborate wrapping system to solve this problem. In Japan when you buy ready made *o-nigiri* to take away the *nori* is wrapped in a layer of cellophane separating it from the rice. Like some culinary *origami* the cellophane is folded in such a way that it peels away and the *nori* wraps itself around the rice ball in one easy motion. Crisp or soggy they are still delicious – and can be found in most Japanese school children's lunchboxes.

Note: If you have a plastic rice shaper, this is the time to use it.

STEAMED TURNIP CUP
KABURA NO CHAWAN MUSHI

This unusual recipe is a speciality of Sankō In Temple and was taught to me there by the Abbess Koei Hoshino. It's a vegetarian version of the well known *chawan mushi* Steamed Savoury Custard. Because Zen Buddhists don't eat eggs or meat this is made without either. It's surprisingly delicious. When you mix in the hot sauce with the rice and solids and the *wasabi* the effect is much more than the sum of its parts. Again, it's a good way of using left over rice. If you have proper Japanese *chawan mushi* cups then this is your chance to use them. Alternatively you can use any handleless cup, or even mugs (which are heatproof), and improvise lids with foil or wooden coasters. Chinese stores often sell inexpensive cups with lids which can be used for steaming. You need a capacity of around 250 ml/ 8 fl oz per cup. You'll also need a flat bottomed steamer, big enough to hold the cups.

2 chestnuts (optional)

4 heaped tablespoons cooked rice

4 small white turnips – peeled

4 *shiitake* mushrooms (fresh if you can get them, dried and reconstituted if not)

12 mange tout

12 slices of carrot, cut into maple leaf shapes

12 ginkgo nuts (optional)

½ deep fried tofu pouch (or 2 tablespoons deep fried *yuba* (see page 13) or 1 small piece 10 cm x 10 cm/ 4 in x 4 in)

Deep Fried Gluten (see page 27). This is to add a little protein and oiliness

SAUCE:

2 tablespoons potato starch (or *kuzu*)

2 tablespoons water to dissolve starch in

1⅔ cups *dashi* (if you are making this for non-fish eaters use *kombu* kelp *dashi* only, together with *shiitake* soaking water if you have it. For fish eaters use bonito flakes (*katsuo*) in the *dashi* as well)

½ teaspoon salt

1 tablespoon saké

1 teaspoon soy sauce

1 teaspoon *wasabi* paste to finish

First prepare the chestnuts if you are using them. To shell the chestnuts you can either soak them in warm water for about 2 hours to soften them, or make a little nick in the top of the shells and boil them for 5 minutes. Then peel off the shell and the bitter inner skin carefully with a small knife, trying to keep as much flesh as possible.

Chop the cold rice so the grains are broken up (into thirds). Grate the turnip using a Japanese style grater – to make a mush – not flakes. Use the smallest size on a western style grater if you can't get a Japanese one. Squeeze excess liquid out of the turnip pulp. You need about eight tablespoons of the grated pulp. Mix the rice and turnip together. Discard the stems of the mushrooms, cut each mushroom into three thick slices and place them into the bottom of each cup. Par boil the mange tout and add 3 to each cup. Par boil the carrot 'leaves' and add three to each cup. Break the shell off the ginkgo nuts by placing them on a table and giving them a gentle thump with a small hammer. They should break easily. Place the shelled nuts into a small saucepan of water and bring to a boil. Reduce the heat to medium low and keep them simmering for about five minutes, during which time take a slotted spoon or skimmer and jiggle the nuts about. This should loosen the skin – and underneath you'll see the ginkgo nut turning a beautiful delicate shade of green. Remove from the heat, drain, and place the nuts on a kitchen towel. Rub the skins off with the towel, and place three nuts into the bottom of each cup (which is fast filling up by now). Add the tofu (or *yuba* or gluten), again cut and distributed evenly, and finally pop half a chestnut in each cup.

Once you have assembled the ingredients in the bottom of each cup you need to pack the rice and turnip mixture on top. Divide the mixture evenly between the cups – you should get about 2-3 tablespoons per cup. Press the rice mixture well down inside the cup (it shouldn't be full – only about ⅔ full depending on the size of the cups). Place the cups in a steamer, over boiling water. Place a towel between the cups and the lid to prevent drips falling in, and steam for 10 minutes.

Meanwhile make the sauce. Mix the starch to a thin paste with cold water. Combine the other ingredients in a small saucepan, and bring to a boil. Add the starch slowly, stirring well, and keep stirring for a minute or two until it thickens, and to get rid of any lumps.

Using a cloth, take the cups off the heat and remove the towel (be careful as it will be hot) and spoon the sauce over the top of each cup. Steam for a further 5 minutes, again with the towel under the lid. Before serving place a generous dab of *wasabi* on top of each cup, and put a lid on to keep warm. Serve hot, and mix everything up (with chopsticks or a spoon) before you eat. This would make a very interesting starter to a vegetarian meal and is warm and comforting in cold weather. It's especially appropriate for autumn, as the ginkgo, chestnuts, carrot maple leaves and *shiitake* mushrooms are typical of the season. I do hope you'll try it – it really is a nice surprise dish.

RICE CROQUETTES
GOHAN KORROKE

This is a good way of using left over rice. Other ingredients can be varied according to what is available. Instead of *hijiki* you could use dulse, which is soft and mixes well, and you could add parsley or chopped spring onions. This is not sophisticated food, but basic country cooking. Serve instead of rice alongside vegetables or meat.

2 tablespoons dried *hijiki*	4 tablespoons plain flour
1½ tablespoons miso	pinch salt
550 g / 1¼ lbs cooked white short grain rice	oil for frying

Soak the *hijiki* in warm water to soften. Drain it well and squeeze all the excess moisture out of it. Chop it into small pieces (about 6 mm/ ¼ inch long). Mix the miso, *hijiki*, rice, flour and salt in a large bowl. Make sure it's well mixed, and the mixture not sloppy. If it's too liquid add a little more flour. You can even prepare the mixture the day before if you like and leave it in the fridge to chill. The flavours will mingle, and the mixture stiffen. When you are ready to cook them divide the mixture into eight large, or twelve smaller patties. Just lightly coat the bottom of a frying pan or griddle with oil, and fry each patty on a medium heat for 2-3 minutes until golden.

TOASTED RICE BALLS
YAKIONIGIRI

These are a toasted version of the above, but without the fillings and *nori* wrapping. This is a common way of rounding off an evening's drinking and snacking in an *izakaya* – they're cheap and filling. Again, a triangular plastic rice shaper will make your life a bit easier. Have a bowl of water handy to keep wetting the plastic bits as you go along.

TO MAKE 8 (2 PER PERSON)
800 g/ 1¾ lbs cooked white short
  grain rice

2 tablespoons soy sauce

Shape the rice balls into flattened triangles about 2 cm/ ¾ inch thick, as for *O-nigiri*, pages 88-89. Place them under a hot grill until golden brown on both sides. Brush a little soy sauce on the toasted sides (not too much or they'll fall apart). Grill a few seconds more. Serve immediately.

RICE BALES
TORORO KOMBU NO O-NIGIRI

Tororo kombu is a very finely shredded type of *kombu* (kelp) sea vegetable. It's normally scattered over soups or bowls of noodles. In the packet it looks like shredded linen, or dry hay, but when it's put in hot liquid it disintegrates and becomes somewhat slimy – which sounds awful but tastes nice! In this recipe the *tororo kombu* is used to roll rice croquettes in, and the look of dry hay is what gives it its name. It's another seasonal speciality I learned at Sankō In. It's simple, tasty and makes a change from rice in a bowl. It's especially appropriate for autumn of course, as it celebrates the harvesting of grain or hay. If you want to be really seasonal you can scatter real pieces of straw over when serving, to emphasise the effect, or place them on top of a fallen autumn leaf.

MAKES APPROXIMATELY EIGHT
'BALES'
800 g/ 1¾ lbs freshly cooked white rice

8 tablespoons *tororo kombu*
(shaved kelp)

Place the *kombu* on a dry cutting board and finely chop with a sharp knife (cut or chop straight down *oshi giri* style). Take a handful of rice (about 2 tablespoons) and shape into a cylinder. Roll each cylinder in the chopped *kombu*, so each surface is covered. Serve 3 per person, on a side plate.

GREEN TEA AND RICE SOUP
O-CHAZUKE

The *o-cha* in *o-chazuke* means green tea – and this is exactly what this soup is made with. Originally it was a very quick way of finishing off your rice at the end of a meal, by swilling out the rice bowl with your tea. Over time it has become a standard dish – another good way to finish off an evening's drinking – or a quick lunch using left over rice, and even left over fish. It can be as elaborate or as simple as you wish to make it. The simplest version would be rice, tea and an *umeboshi* plum, but this is a more substantial version – it's still quick and easy though. The recipe says cooked salmon, which is traditional, but any flavoursome and salty fish would be good – such as smoked haddock or trout. You can use smoked salmon scraps too – the hot tea will 'cook' them. (But don't be tempted to use pickled herring or anything with vinegar – it will be yuk.)

450 g / I lb left over cooked rice (it doesn't have to be hot)	1.2 litres/ 2 pints hot green tea
	1 sheet *nori* – cut or tear into strips
200 g/ 7 oz cooked salmon (or other fish)	(or *nori* strips ready made)
	wasabi (optional)

Divide the rice between four deep bowls (larger than a regular rice bowl). Flake the fish, making sure there are no bones, over the top of the rice. Pour the hot green tea over, and garnish with the strips of *nori*, and a small mound of *wasabi*. Mix everything in before eating. Add salt to taste if necessary.

Variations: Pickles such as *takuan,* or *umeboshi* plum can be added or used instead of fish.

RICE GRUEL
O-KAYU

This is a very simple rice 'porridge'. It's the Japanese version of the Jewish mama's chicken soup – good for anyone who's feeling delicate. "Ill-person's rice" is the way my friend Manami first described it to me. Its long cooking and soft texture make it easy to digest, and, depending on how sick or well you are feeling, all sorts of toppings and additional seasonings can be added, just like *O-chazuke* above. In this case *umeboshi* is a particularly suitable flavouring for someone who is sick or whose digestion is playing up, as it is a popular and well known folk remedy for acid stomachs and queasiness. Other quick toppings could be a sprinkling of dried bonito flakes (*hana katsuo*) or strips of *nori* sea vegetable.

Note: The servings here are for one not four as usual, as it is to be hoped you won't need to feed four ill people at once.

I SERVING	½ teaspoon salt
125 g/ 4oz short grain rice	1 *umeboshi* plum
840 ml/ 1 ½ pints water	

Wash the rice as described. Place in a large pot with the water and a lid on. You can increase the amount of water to twice this if you prefer a thinner soup. Bring to a boil over high heat. Reduce the heat and simmer for at least 40 minutes until a thick porridge has formed. Do not stir during cooking, but check that it doesn't catch at the bottom. You can use a heat diffuser to distribute the heat and prevent burning.

Add the salt at the end before serving. Serve in rice bowls with an *umeboshi* plum, or a small spoonful of *umeboshi* paste, on top.

SUSHI RICE
SUMESHI

This section contains the basic technique for making sushi rice, and some simple rice-based sushi dishes. There are more fish-based sushi recipes in the section on fish and sushi.

For health and safety reasons ready prepared and take away sushi sold in the UK is kept in chilled cabinets at low temperatures – this keeps the fish fresh but it renders the rice tasteless. Personally I think chilled rice is an abomination – I'd rather do without. Anyway if you're making it at home you don't need to put the rice in the fridge, because sushi rice contains sugar and vinegar, which act as a kind of preservative, keeping it fresher longer. In fact the origins of sushi are accidental. Centuries ago, fish was packed in rice as a way of preserving it. The rice fermented and this in turn preserved the fish. These days the vinegar and sugar added to the rice serves a similar preservative function, as well as being an attempt to replicate this original taste. In some country areas this 'original' sushi is still made – rice and fish layered in stone jars – where it is called *nare zushi*. In the Osaka region of Japan sushi is made in a similar way, in wooden moulds. Vinegared fish is pressed on top of the rice in rectangular shapes. This type of sushi is called *battera zushi*, and I've included a recipe for it in the section on fish and sushi. Both of these differ from the sushi made in little finger pieces, called *nigiri zushi,* which is a feature of the Tokyo area, and the type which is exported and most widely eaten abroad. *Nigiri* means pressed or clenched, which is what is done to the rice to shape it. In most sushi shops the goings on behind the counter are an essential part of the fun. You can see the sushi master (or *itamae* as he is called – the 'one who stands in front') deftly mould the rice in his fingers, and flip the pieces of fish on top. He'll usually be chatting and joking at the same time, and greeting customers, and keeping a track of everyone's bill!

The making of the sushi rice itself though is the one thing you generally don't see, but which is a great pity. It's practically a theatrical performance – an assistant madly fans the rice with a paper fan (called *uchiwa*) to cool it, whilst the rice chef cuts through the steaming rice with a wooden paddle (called *o-shamoji*).

To make sushi rice yourself cook it in the same way as regular short grain white rice, but use slightly less water. You want the grains to be just a little harder, a little more separate and chewier than soft boiled rice. (You can experiment by making it with hot water instead of cold, as they do in some sushi establishments.) The other key to good sushi rice is quick cooling, which is what the fanning is for. This gives the rice a glossy sheen, and the correct texture. The sugar and vinegar mixture is no bother to mix up yourself, but you can buy ready sweetened vinegar called 'seasoned rice vinegar' which is a useful alternative. Don't even *think* about using any vinegar other than rice vinegar. There is no alternative. Luckily it's widely available these days.

To make about seven cups cooked sushi rice you'll need:

500 g/ 1 lb 2 oz / 2 ½ cups short grain white rice	**SEASONING**
	5 tablespoons rice vinegar
600 ml/1 pint / 2½ cups water	2 tablespoons sugar
1 piece of *kombu* (dried kelp) about 8 cm/ 3 inches long	1 teaspoon salt

Wash the rice well and cook it as described earlier, but placing the *kombu* in with the water. This adds a little flavour and assists the cooking process. Remove the *kombu* as soon as the rice begins to boil and turn down the heat. Replace the lid and continue as before.

Whilst the rice is cooking, prepare the vinegar dressing by dissolving the sugar and salt in the vinegar, in a small pan over a low heat. Cool the mixture by standing the pan in a bowl of cold water.

Using a wooden spoon or rice paddle spread the cooked rice out into a large shallow bowl. A wooden bowl is best. In fact a proper shallow sushi making bowl is the best of all. Called *hangiri* or *sushi oke*, they are made from cedar and bound in copper. The wood absorbs moisture efficiently, and the shallow shape helps cool the rice. If you don't have one use a large plastic or stainless steel bowl – the shallower the better. Start pouring the vinegar mixture over in little dribbles, and at the same time cut through the rice with a rice paddle, using a horizontal motion, to cool it, separate the grains and distribute the vinegar. **At the same time** (this is why an assistant is handy) fan the rice with a Japanese fan (or piece of card) to cool it. Be careful that the rice doesn't become mushy and pudding like, or so wet that it falls apart. Add the vinegar bit by bit as you may not need it all. When the rice is at room temperature, and the grains glossy and separate, the rice is ready.

You can now use this rice to make any of the following dishes, and as the basis of Finger Sushi (*Nigirizushi*), see page 190.

TOFU POUCHES STUFFED WITH RICE
INARIZUSHI

These are the little tofu pouches filled with rice that are found in take away sushi boxes. The tofu pouches are themselves flavoured with sugar and soy sauce which adds richness to a simple food. (In Japanese stores you can buy ready flavoured sushi pouches – I find them rather overpoweringly sweet – but they are useful if you are in a hurry.)

To make about 3½ cups cooked sushi rice you'll need:

250 g/ 9 oz / 1¼ cups short grain white rice	6 deep fried tofu pouches (*usu-age*/ *abura-age*)
300 ml/ ½ pint/ 1¼ cups water	**TO FLAVOUR THE POUCHES:**
1 piece of *kombu* (dried kelp) about 8 cm/ 3 inches long.	2 tablespoons soy sauce
SEASONING FOR RICE:	1 tablespoon caster sugar (or less if you don't want them too sweet)
2½ tablespoons rice vinegar	1 tablespoon *mirin*
1 tablespoon sugar	125 ml/ 4 fl oz water
1 teaspoon salt	

Cook, flavour and cool the rice as described in the recipe for Sushi Rice. Cut each tofu pouch in half widthways, and put into a colander. Pour boiling water over to get rid of excess oil. Put the seasoning ingredients for the tofu into a saucepan and bring to a boil, making sure the sugar is dissolved. Add the tofu pouches and simmer, uncovered, over a low heat, until all the liquid is absorbed, and the pouches sweet and sticky. Leave to cool to room temperature. When cool, stuff each pouch with sushi rice, leaving 1 cm/ ½ inch at the top. Fold one side over the other at the open end and place fold side down on a plate to serve. Alternatively you can secure with a cocktail stick or softened gourd strip (*kanpyō*). These make good party buffet fillers, picnic and packed lunch food.

SCATTERED SUSHI
CHIRASHIZUSHI

This is a popular party style version of sushi rice. Basic cooked sushi rice is topped with a mixture of vegetables. The vegetables are flavoured by simmering in sweet soy sauce. In addition strips (or 'golden strings') of thin omelette are scattered over. It's always served family style in one large bowl, with all the different bits and pieces scattered colourfully on top. Try to get a good mixture of colours and textures. I've included *arame* sea vegetable in this, as the black contrasts beautifully with the yellow omelette strips and white rice.

Note: Although the omelette 'strings' are a typical garnish for *chirashizushi* (and *hiyashi sōmen* later on) if you find the omelette making tiresome then just omit it. It's traditionally made in a special small rectangular pan. Don't worry if you don't have one as any small frying pan will do.

500 g/ 1 lb 2 oz / 2½ cups short grain white rice

600 ml/ 1 pint / 2½ cups water

1 piece of *kombu* (dried kelp) about 8 cm/ 3 inches long.

SEASONING FOR THE RICE:

5 tablespoons rice vinegar

2 tablespoons sugar

1 teaspoon salt

Vegetables to scatter on top of rice tofu pouch (*abura-age*)

1 medium lotus root (*renkon*) (optional)

1 small carrot cut into fine julienne strips (or carrot flowers)

3 *shiitake* mushrooms (if dried reconstitute in warm water)

FLAVOURING FOR THE ABOVE VEGETABLES:

2 tablespoons caster sugar

3 tablespoons soy sauce

2 tablespoons saké

350 ml/ 12 fl oz water (or *shiitake* soaking water)

10 small green beans, cut on the diagonal into thin strips

1 tablespoon dried *arame*, soaked in cold water to reconstitute

FOR THE OMELETTE GARNISH:

2 eggs

2 teaspoons caster sugar

pinch salt

First cook, cool and flavour the rice as instructed in Sushi Rice. Then prepare the topping. In a colander pour boiling water over the tofu pouch to eliminate excess oil. Cut into thin strips widthways. Peel the lotus root and cut into thin rounds. Cut each round into quarters. Place immediately in lightly vinegared water to prevent discoloration. Put the carrot, *shiitake*, lotus root (drained) and tofu into a small saucepan, together with the flavouring ingredients. Bring to a boil and then turn down the flame and simmer for about 10 minutes, until the liquid is absorbed and evaporated. Leave to cool.

You now need to par boil the green beans, by plunging into salted boiling water for two minutes. Remove and place immediately in very cold water to arrest the cooking and retain the colour. Drain well. Drain the *arame* from its soaking water and squeeze out excess water. Put aside.

Now make the omelette garnish: Mix the eggs with the salt and sugar, but do not beat. Strain the egg through a sieve to get rid of the white stringy bits. Grease the bottom of the pan and bring to a medium high heat. Add a small amount of the egg mixture and quickly tip the pan so it covers the entire surface – but very thinly. You want the thinnest omelette you can imagine. When the top surface is dry carefully flip the egg over. Because it is so thin this is easier with a smaller pan than a larger one. Cook for a few more seconds until done. Turn out onto a board and leave to cool. Make more omelettes in the same way until the mixture is used up, but **do not stack them on top of each other** whilst they are hot as they will stick together – thereby destroying all your effort in making individual thin omelettes. When cooled to room temperature roll each omelette up and cut into thin strands.

Carefully mix the seasoned vegetables with the rice and the *arame*. Scatter the green beans and omelette strips on top. Serve accompanied by pickled ginger pieces. **Variation:** add flaked cooked fish, such as salmon, or mackerel at the final stage.

SUSHI ROLLS
MAKIZUSHI OR NORIMAKI

Using avocado in sushi is one of those interesting Japanese hybrids: it was invented by Japanese immigrants in California, then exported back to Japan, where it is now extremely popular and called 'California roll'. I think it's a terrific invention, and I've added to it by using smoked mackerel, which is a cheap and convenient way of making sushi rolls, if you haven't time to go looking for fresh raw fish. Smoked salmon is another convenient filling – nice on its own.

Traditional fillings which are used alone are *takuan* radish, *umeboshi* paste and *natto*, none of which would include *wasabi*. Plain cucumber roll is known as *kappamaki*, and is a traditional way of 'filling' up and cleansing the palate in a sushi bar, after an evening's indulgence in raw fish. A *kappa* is a mythological water creature, who appears often in Japanese folklore, and whose favourite food is said to be cucumber.

SUSHI RICE AS BEFORE
I pack sushi *nori*
FILLINGS:
I small smoked mackerel fillet, cut into boneless strips
quarter of a medium sized avocado
I small cucumber, cut into strips ½ cm/ ⅛ inch thick and 24 cm/ 9 inches long (first score the skin of the cucumber with a fork, pulling down the length of it)
I medium piece of smoked salmon, cut into strips as above
4 pieces of *takuan* radish, ½ cm/ ⅛ inch wide and 24 cm / 9 inches long (the width of a bamboo rolling mat and sheet of *nori*)
wasabi paste

Prepare the following: a bamboo rolling mat (*makisu*) arranged on a chopping board or marble slab; a bowl of water lightly vinegared to wet your hands and knife; a very sharp knife.

Prepare the fillings and lay them out on a large platter: the mackerel cut into ½cm/ ⅛ inch strips, the avocado cut into thin strips end to end and the cucumber cut into thin strips.

If the *nori* is not pre-toasted or if it's gone a bit limp, liven it up by passing it over a gas flame, using a fanning movement. Be careful not to scorch it – it should turn from brown to green and become crispy.

Lay a piece of *nori* onto the bamboo mat, with the shiny side of the *nori* down. Moisten your hand in the vinegar water and take a handful of rice. Spread onto the *nori*, flattening it out with your moistened hand (be careful not to overdo the water – you don't want a

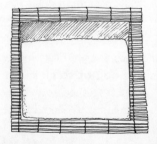

soggy *maki!*) Cover the *nori* except for a 3 cm/ 1 inch border at the top. The amount of rice determines how fat or thin the roll will be. Thinner ones are generally rolled with one single ingredient, whereas rolls with several ingredients tend to be fatter (really fat ones are called, unsurprisingly, *futomaki* – fat rolls). Take a chopstick and press a channel in the rice, about ⅓ the way up the *nori*, from left to right. Spread some *wasabi* (the size of a pea will do) along the channel. Now press a piece of cucumber, strips of mackerel and avocado along the channel, laying them side by side and on top of each other to form a central core. If the strips are too short lay two or three end to end so they reach along the whole width of the *nori* and rice.

Now (this is the tricky bit) with your finger tips keep the filling ingredients in place, and, using your thumbs, turn over the mat so that the nearest edge of *nori* flips over and meets the top edge of the rice. Pull the edge in, tucking it in firmly, but gently. The bamboo mat assists greatly in this, and helps to keep the roll even (and you from losing your nerve). Finally roll the mat all the way around and gently squeeze, (but not too hard or the ingredients will shoot out of the ends. If they do just push them back in again). Hold the whole thing in place for a few seconds so that the *nori* edge seals itself. It should do this naturally with the moisture from the rice, but if it doesn't, and it's still flapping open, seal it with a little water brushed along the edge with your finger.

Now lay it with the sealed edge downwards on a cutting board. Take your sharp knife, wet it in the water and, holding it upright, tap the base of the handle on the table. This distributes water along the length of the blade. Cut the roll in half, and each half into quarters to create eight rolls. Cut with a gentle but firm pulling motion, pulling the knife towards you (*hikigiri*). Do not saw as if you were cutting bread – it will be a messy disaster. Wipe the knife with a clean damp cloth every two to three cuts, to prevent it clogging up with rice. Lay the pieces cut side down so the filling is visible, and a spiral effect evident (if you have rolled it correctly). Do not worry if your filling is not completely central – that is the ideal, but it will come with practice, and in any case the taste will still be good. After making avocado and mackerel rolls try some more simple fillings: *takuan* radish and cucumber; smoked salmon and cucumber. Then use up the leftovers in any other combination you fancy – and have fun. If you want to make these ahead of time leave the rolls intact and wrap the whole thing in cling film. This will keep them fresh for a few hours. Cut them just before serving.

Then you can have even more fun displaying them. This is a great opportunity to use an attractive or unusual platter – a black lacquer or plain wooden tray; a slab of wood, marble or slate; or perhaps a favourite piece of stoneware, to serve them. They are the ultimate finger food for parties, but try not to leave them hanging around for too long, as the *nori* goes soggy and the rice dries up. They are best within a couple of hours. I have to say I have never found this a problem, as they usually disappear within minutes!

Other possible fillings:

natto (fermented soybeans)

umeboshi plum paste

fresh raw tuna (*maguro*) – buy from a reputable fishmonger and make sure it is really fresh

canned tuna and mayonnaise

canned salmon

shiitake strips pre-cooked in soy sauce and sugar (as for Scattered Sushi, *Chirashizushi*)

kampyō (gourd strips) pre-cooked in soy sauce and sugar (as above)

RED RICE
SEKIHAN

This is rice for festive occasions, and for religious offerings. The red colour comes from the (ubiquitous) *azuki* beans, with which the rice is mixed. A plate of this felicitous and colourful rice may be set before the family shrine to honour a dead ancestor, on important birthdays, and even to mark the start of a new school term. My friends in Japan used to make *sekihan* for me on my birthday. It's made with glutinous sticky rice (or sweet white rice, the same rice used for making *mochi* rice cakes) and it is never boiled. It is always pre-soaked and steamed. Because there's a lot of waiting around (leaving things to soak and cool down) in this recipe you need to anticipate when you are making it – but as it's usually made for special occasions it's exactly the type of thing you're likely to be able to plan beforehand anyway.

100 g/ 3½ oz dried *azuki* beans	1 teaspoon salt dissolved in 3 tablespoons water
750 ml/1¼ pints water (to cook beans – keep this water)	toasted black sesame seeds for garnish
450 g /16 oz glutinous rice (sweet white rice)	

First pre-cook the beans. This must be done the day before you want to eat the rice, as the rice needs to soak in the bean cooking water. Soak the beans for two to three hours. Drain and put them in a saucepan in plenty of fresh cold water. Bring to a boil and boil rapidly for 6 minutes. Throw away this water, and rinse the beans. Using the measured water above, put the beans back in the pot and bring to a boil. Boil on a medium heat uncovered for about 40 minutes or until the beans are just cooked – just getting soft but not yet mushy, and the water stained red.

Drain off and keep the red water. Leave both the beans and water to cool down at room temperature (force cooling will make the beans go mushy).

Now prepare the rice. Wash the rice as normal. Put into a large pot with the red water from the beans, and leave to stand overnight. The rice will turn pink, and the next day you can pour off the water.

Line a bamboo steamer with damp cheesecloth. Mix the beans and rice together evenly. Spread the mixture over the cloth. Put the lid on the pot and steam over a high heat for 20 minutes. Lift the lid (be careful, use a cloth or pot holder to avoid scalding yourself with steam) and sprinkle a little salty water over the mixture (salting too early on makes the beans tough). Put the lid back on and continue steaming for about 15 minutes or so, until both the rice and beans are cooked. Serve as a main carbohydrate dish in place of rice.

POUNDED RICE CAKE
MOCHI
THE ESSENCE OF RICE

"February 11th was the Japanese New Year's day, which I passed at Yedo. Rice cakes (mochi) had been prepared and decorated in proper fashion with a Seville orange and fern, and dried fronds had also been hung up in the alcove (tokonoma) in my study. Silk cushions had been provided for a guest and myself to sit on as we ate our zōni. This is a soup in which pieces of fried mochi are soaked."

Sir Ernest Satow A Diplomat in Japan

The Japanese now celebrate New Year on January 1st, but although the date has changed, the celebrations remain the same. Because rice is a symbol of wealth and good fortune, the god of rice, called Inari, is a very important participant in New Year celebrations. Everyone hopes for happiness and prosperity in the coming year so, naturally, it is the rice god they pray to. They do this by offering gifts of rice to Inari himself. At Shinto shrines, gifts of saké, which is made from rice, are offered to the gods (and served to the people in gold kettles by the Shinto priests). At home, in the alcove (called *tokonoma*) which is reserved for seasonal decorations, large white cakes of pounded rice, called *kagami mochi*, are displayed, along with pieces of *kombu* (kelp) seaweed and ferns. To finish the display a tangerine, or satsuma orange, is placed on top of the rice cakes. (One Japanese word for this tangerine is *dai dai* which also means long life, so this food is therefore considered an appropriate food to offer to the gods at New Year.) In addition, the seaweed, ferns and tangerine are products of Japan's mountains and sea, so it's rather like a harvest festival offering. The pounded rice cake is said to contain the essence of rice, or the rice spirit, and is thus sacred. It's made by pounding steamed glutinous rice into a sticky stretchy mass, and at New Year this pounding is a seasonal ritual. In the old days all country people made their own, but sadly this practice is dying out. At Nenogongen, a temple high in the mountains outside Tokyo, they still make *mochi* every winter, in the same way they've been making it for hundreds of years, completely by hand. I went there to film the process. Snow was falling outside, and the huge old wooden kitchen was a mass of steam, as the rice was steamed in huge square wooden steamers, which were lined with cotton and the water was heated over wooden fires, which were stoked by hand with logs. When the rice has finished its steaming it's turned out of its cheesecloth lining and dumped into a wooden tub called an *usu*, ready to be pounded with a huge wooden mallet (*kine*). The *usu* at Nenogongen is over a hundred years old, worn smooth with years of pounding. Traditionally the pounding was done by man and wife, and it became a kind of exercise in trust. The husband, wielding the mallet, pounds the rice into a sticky mass, and in between poundings the wife dives forward and reaches her hand into the tub to turn the rice. Their timing has to be perfect – she has to be well out of the way before the mallet comes crashing down! After much pounding and turning, sweating and grunting, the rice turns into *mochi* – and in fact it's hard to believe it was ever rice. The flavour and texture of freshly pounded *mochi* is unsurpassable, so, if you can't go to Japan to try it (which I recommend) it might be fun to have a go yourself. Remember you need sweet glutinous rice, and it must be steamed, not boiled. I've been told that table top hand driven meat mincers are good for extruding the rice, but I haven't tried it myself. Nor have I tried using the dough hook on a food processor as I don't have one, but I'd be happy to hear from someone who's willing to try. I have only ever tried low-tech methods, that is a large *suribachi* and *surikogi* (pestle and mortar) as I don't happen to have a tub and mallet. It was hard work it has to be said, and the result wasn't as smooth as the real thing, but it wasn't a bad imitation, and just as delicious.

At New Year, as well as being offered to the gods, lumps of *mochi* are eaten in a soup called *o-zōni*, as part of the New Year breakfast. (Later on in January, when the festivities are coming to an end, the rounded *mochi* cakes, which have been sitting in the alcove as an offering, are also eaten. These are seen to be especially enriched, having been received by the god of rice. Although blessed, this sacred food takes some practise to eat! Its glutinous texture means that it tends to stay in one sticky lump. But everyone wants to try it as they want to be personally enriched with the spirit of the rice god to provide them with good fortune in the coming year (anyway it tastes nice). Sadly, at the start of every New Year, Japanese newspapers carry stories reporting the deaths of elderly citizens, who just couldn't manage it, and who choked on their *mochi*. Don't let it put you off – just make sure you chew it well. It's delicious, more than the sum of its parts, and deceptively filling – one lump of *mochi* is equivalent to a bowl of rice. In the shops *mochi* is available in squares, plastic wrapped. It's softened either by grilling or placing directly into hot soup.

NEW YEAR SOUP
O-ZŌNI

This is the soup which is traditionally eaten as part of the first meal of the New Year. There are probably as many recipes as there are families in Japan – there are certainly a myriad of regional variations, but the one thing they all have in common is lumps of *mochi*. Once you get a taste for it you may want to eat it at other times of the year too, and this is perfectly acceptable. In fact I recommend it! I'm suggesting a couple of combinations here, which you you can vary at will. You certainly don't need to include meat – a vegetarian version is perfectly fine.

Pork version

This is my memory of the very first o-zōni I ever ate, made for me twenty years ago, by my boyfriend at the time, Momose, who was a great cook. I hope he'll forgive me if my memory of the recipe isn't quite perfect. The trefoil gives a lovely delicate flavour, but if you can't get it leave it out or use coriander or watercress instead.

I litre/ 1¾ pints dashi	4 pieces mochi
200 g/ 6 oz pork (loin or fillet) cut very thinly into bite size pieces	I tablespoon soy sauce (to taste)
	a few sprigs trefoil (mitsuba)
I carrot, peeled and sliced and cut into flower shapes	seven spice pepper (shichimi togarashi)

In a medium saucepan put the dashi and the slices of pork. Bring to a simmer and cook until the pork is tender, and the stock enriched – about 20 minutes. Add the carrot 'flowers' about 10 minutes before the end. Meanwhile toast the pieces of mochi lightly under a grill. They will puff up and soften, which is what you want, but you don't want a hard crust, so keep an eye on them. Add the soy sauce to the soup. Put a piece of mochi in the bottom of everyone's soup bowl and pour the soup over it, making sure the pork and carrots are evenly distributed. Garnish with a few sprigs of trefoil, cut into 5 cm/ 2 inch pieces. Sprinkle with seven spice pepper to taste.

Instead of grilling the mochi to soften it you can put it directly into the soup and simmer for about 3 minutes. Be careful not to simmer for too long otherwise it will fall apart and just become a goo.

Chicken version

New Year eating is full of symbols of good fortune and felicity. The tortoise is yet another symbol (of longevity again), so here the daikon radish is cut into hexagonal shapes as a reminder of the pattern on the tortoise's back.

200 g/ 7 oz skinless chicken breast (or thigh if you like a fattier taste)	750 ml/ 1½ pints dashi (or combination of dashi and chicken stock)
4 cm/ 1½ inch length of daikon radish, cut into 4 rounds	½ teaspoon salt
	I teaspoon soy sauce
I carrot, peeled, cut into rounds and then into flower shapes	4 pieces mochi
	a little dried yuzu rind or powder
a handful (two sprigs per person) of chrysanthemum leaves (substitute watercress or spinach if unavailable)	½ sheet nori sea vegetable

Slice the chicken diagonally into thin bite-size strips. Bring them to a boil in lightly salted water and simmer for a few minutes until just cooked. Remove. Strain this chicken stock and use for the soup together with dashi, if liked. Shape the rounds of radish into hexagonals. Par boil in lightly salted water for about 20-30 minutes until just tender. You can parboil the carrot flowers at the same time, for about 5 minutes. Parboil the chrysanthemum leaves for 2 minutes until just before tender. Shock in cold water, squeeze out the excess moisture and put aside.

Prepare the *dashi* and bring to a boil. Reduce the flame to keep it on a simmer and add the salt and soy sauce to taste. Add the dried *yuzu* rind at this point if using (but not the powder, that should be added at the end). Add the chicken to the soup to warm through, and the cooked *daikon* radish rounds. Grill the *mochi* until puffed up but not burnt, turning and watching as you go. Place a piece of *mochi*, carrot flowers and chrysanthemum (or other greens) in each bowl. Carefully ladle over the hot soup, distributing the chicken and one piece of *daikon* evenly for each person. Sprinkle *yuzu* powder on top if using, and the *nori* sea vegetable cut into strips or squares.

How to eat o-zōni

These soups should be served in lacquer bowls just like miso soup. Chopsticks are used to retrieve solids, at the same time as the bowl is brought to your mouth to sup the liquid. The *mochi* is held between chopsticks, as the bowl is held under your chin, and pieces bitten off. The rest is left to fall back into the bowl.

GRILLED RICE CAKES WITH NORI
ISOBEMAKI

In the centre of Tokyo, after a night out at the bars, you can usually find someone selling *isobemaki*, which are *mochi* rice cakes, grilled, wrapped in a sheet of *nori* and dipped in soy sauce. As a very quick snack before catching the last train home they are unbeatable. They are also extremely easy to make yourself.

8 pieces *mochi* (2 per person)	**a little unsalted butter**
4 sheets *nori*, cut in half	**soy sauce to dip**

Melt a knob of butter over medium heat in a frying pan. Add the *mochi* pieces and fry gently, turning from time to time, until soft, about 4 minutes each side. Make sure they don't burn, and turn down the heat if they are in danger of doing so. When they are soft right through, remove and wrap a piece of *nori* around each one. Dip in soy sauce and eat hot – with your fingers if you dare!

MOCHI WAFFLES WITH MAPLE SYRUP
CHYĀRI NO WAFURU

Not only is this a wonderful low fat version of a waffle, but it also transforms the *mochi*, making it crisp and chewy. It was shown to me by Charlie Kendall, a dynamic American who makes *natto* and other fermented Japanese foods in the countryside of Massachusetts, so it's not traditional Japanese, but an American adaptation. Serve with maple syrup for an American style flavour. You'll need a waffle iron for this one.

4 pieces *mochi*   **4 tablespoons maple syrup**

Lightly grease the waffle iron and heat up. Put one piece of *mochi* in and close. The heat will soften the *mochi* and it'll spread out and fill the holes. Cook until crisp on the outside and cooked inside. Serve with maple syrup.

See the section on sweets for more sweet cakes made with rice flour. (See page 235).

NOODLES – THE NOURISHING STAPLE

"Everyone lives on it (rice) who can afford to do so, but as a rule the peasantry cannot. Wheat, barley, and especially millet are the real staples throughout the rural districts, rice being there treated as a luxury to be brought out only on high days and holidays, or to be resorted to in case of sickness. We once heard a beldame *in a country village remark to another, with a grave shake of the head, 'What, do you mean to say that it has come to giving her rice?' the unexpressed inference being that the patient's case must be alarming indeed, if the family thought it necessary to resort to so expensive a dainty."*

Basil Hall Chamberlain, *Things Japanese*

Luckily for us the exclusivity of rice meant that the Japanese had to exist on other grains as well, and so they devised many interesting and delicious dishes made from wheat, buckwheat and millet. In some ways these are still regarded as poor relations. Noodles are generally regarded as cheap lunchtime food, rather than banquet fare. But do we care? They are delicious, quick and easy, and nutritious as well. And in Japan even noodles have their aficionados.

WHEAT NOODLES
UDON

Traditionally when wheat was ground into flour in Japan it was not made into bread, but noodles. Originating in China, noodles are now a firm favourite in Japan. It's common to see groups of office workers standing behind a short curtain (*noren*) in station noodle stands slurping a quick bowl of noodles for lunch. Topped with various bits of sea vegetable or tofu, they make a nutritious and cheap snack. Making as much noise as possible as you slurp them down, and taking as little time as possible to eat them, seems to be the point. I've been almost deafened in some small neighbourhood *noodle* shops at lunchtime, with twenty or so hungry salarymen all slurping at once. In typical Japanese fashion there are different and seasonal ways of preparing them. In winter a piping hot bowl of noodles in soup is a welcoming sight. In summer, served cold, they slip down easily when everything else seems too much to contemplate. The most common type of wheat noodle is called *udon*, which is quite thick and can be either round or flat. *Udon* are always eaten hot, and are popular in the Western Kansai region of Japan. Other wheat noodles are *kishimen* which is similar to *udon*, but wider and flatter. *Hiyamugi* and *sōmen* are both thin, delicate noodles and are eaten cold in summer.

BUCKWHEAT NOODLES
SOBA

Buckwheat isn't strictly speaking a grain, but the seed of the herbaceous buckwheat plant (*Fagopyrum esculentum*). Because buckwheat grows well in cooler northern climes (buckwheat groats, called *kasha*, are a staple in Russia) noodles made from buckwheat are a feature of the northern prefectures of Japan such as Nagano and Niigata. They are also more popular in the Tokyo area than wheat noodles (*udon*), (which in turn are favoured by the people of the western Kansai region around Osaka). However, when *soba* noodles are made with 100% buckwheat flour they tend to break up easily, and, although extremely good for you due to the rutin in buckwheat, they are somewhat heavy and dense. Pure buckwheat is also expensive, so buckwheat flour is often mixed with a percentage of wheat flour – usually in a ratio of 40 – 60 %. This makes the noodle lighter, and especially suitable for summer (and also cheaper). Other things are sometimes mixed in too – such as green tea powder to make *cha-soba*, and dried mugwort, to make *yomogi-soba*.

When someone moves to a new house in Japan it's traditional to call on one's new neighbours with gifts of *soba* noodles, a custom called *hikkoshi soba* which literally means 'moving next to you'. The Japanese have many hononyms, and this is one of them. Because *soba* also means 'next to' or close, giving gifts of *soba* is deemed appropriate for good future neighbourly relations. The aficionado's way of eating them, especially delicious in summer, is with virtually nothing except a dipping sauce, and a garnish of *nori*, and served in a basket called a *zaru* (hence *zaru soba*).

There's a tiny little place in a back street of Akasaka that is a real *soba* aficionado's haunt. From the outside it looks poky and downtrodden – the usual traditional wooden building with sliding doors and *noren* curtains. But this place, being in the centre of town, in the government and business area, is frequented by politicians – and *yakuza* (gangsters). I once witnessed a remarkable scene outside this noodle shop. A big black limo drew up, and some personage alighted – I was told it was a politician – to enter the *soba* shop. At the very same moment a white limo drew up to collect a different personage – leaving the *soba* shop – all patent shoes, white socks, curly hair and loud striped suit – the hall marks of a gangster. There ensued the faintest of bows between them before the politician disappeared in to the restaurant for his quick noodle lunch, and the gangster was driven off in his white limo! Noodles then are classless. Everyone eats them, either standing at a station noodle bar or in specialist restaurants like the one in Akasaka.

Another specialist shop is Takeyabu in Chiba, just outside Tokyo, which is reached via a steep climb up a tree lined path. At the top is perched an immaculate little wooden restaurant, with a charming water feature and rocks outside the sliding door at the front. The rustic interior is bedecked with old kitchen implements and noodle-making items. One of the specialities here is *sobagaki*, which is a dumpling. It's nothing more than a lump of buckwheat flour, shaped into a large round ball and slowly steamed or simmered until cooked through. It sounds easy, but it's not. How to get the texture light and puffy (or *fuwa fuwa* as the Japanese so charmingly say) and smooth is something only the cook at Takeyabu knows. So in spite of my enthusiasm for eating *sobagaki* I am unable to tell you how to make it. The recipes that follow however, couldn't be easier.

COOKING NOODLES

Cooking noodles is similar to cooking spaghetti – lots of water brought to a rolling boil – but because Japanese noodles are made with salt it's not necessary to add any to the water. Allow 2½ litres/ 4¼ pints of water to every 250 g/ 8 oz of noodles, in a large deep pot. It's essential to use a deep saucepan — buckwheat (soba) noodles especially, foam up and can boil over very easily. Add the noodles slowly to the boiling water and stir in, taking care that they don't stick together. The more traditional method of cooking them is to 'shock' cook the noodles. Have a cup of cold water ready, and as soon as the noodles boil up to the brim, throw the water in, to stop the boil. You'll have to do this 3 or 4 times before they are cooked – al dente – just like pasta. Alternatively you can just keep them on a medium heat until cooked through. If you've ever wondered (as I did) what the small aluminium cup on a long pole in Japanese kitchen shops are for – here's your answer. It's for ladling cold water into noodles.

Once cooked, drain the noodles (reserving the water if needed – see below) and rinse thoroughly in a bamboo colander under cold running water. The hot soup will warm them up if served in a broth. In fast food noodle bars the noodles are pre-cooked in this way, and each serving is heated up in hot water when needed.

BASIC NOODLE BROTH
KAKE JIRU

This broth can be used with either soba or udon. With soba it is customary to use slightly more dark soy sauce to taste.

1 litre/ 1¾ pints dashi (a strongly flavoured dashi, such as that made with niboshi (sardines) is especially good in this)	3 tablespoons dark soy sauce
	3 tablespoons light soy sauce
	2 tablespoons sugar (or grain syrup)
2 teaspoons salt	2 tablespoons mirin

Bring dashi to boil, add the rest of the ingredients and bring to a boil again. Take off the heat and keep until needed. If used immediately you can keep on a low simmer, or you can cool it and keep it in the fridge for 3 days. It must be very hot when served. Ladle over noodles in large deep bowls.

NOODLE DIPPING SAUCE
TSUKE JIRU

This is a stronger and more concentrated sauce which is served at room temperature in small deep cups to accompany cold soba noodles in summer. It's twice flavoured with bonito (katsuo) as the basic dashi itself can be made with bonito, and then more added specifically to flavour this sauce. The noodles are dipped in the cold sauce to which a variety of condiments (such as sesame seeds, wasabi, grated ginger and chopped spring onion) are added. The cloudy starchy water in which soba noodles are cooked, called soba yu (soba's hot water), is often kept – and then offered to guests in small kettles at the end of the meal for them to add to any left over dipping sauce. Thinned down in this way it makes a delicious soup, and again is considered the aficionado's way of eating.

This makes enough for about 6 people.

600 ml/ 1 pint 2 fl oz *dashi*	1 teaspoon sugar
180 ml/ 6 fl oz plus 1 teaspoon, dark soy sauce	30 g/ 1oz *katsuo* flakes (the coarse bonito flakes can be used here)
4 tablespoons *mirin*	

Put all the ingredients except the bonito into a saucepan and bring to a boil. Add the bonito flakes and take off the heat. Leave the flakes in the liquid for 10-20 seconds until there are no dry flakes left. Strain off and keep the flakes for another use (e.g. to make *dashi* for thick soups or stews). This sauce should be allowed to cool before use. It will keep for several months if covered and refrigerated.

BUCKWHEAT NOODLES IN A BASKET
ZARU SOBA

This was one of the very first Japanese dishes I ever tasted, cooked for me by my very good friend Nobuko Takano when she was a student in London. I thought the simple combination of ginger and soy sauce in the dipping sauce was the very best thing I'd ever tasted. Eating it hastened my resolve to visit Japan as soon as possible.

Once there I further discovered that nothing beats the taste of fresh hand made noodles. I tasted and watched the process in a charming old establishment called Matsuya in Jimbo cho. Although in the centre of Tokyo, the entrance to the shop is decorated with an arrangement of potted trees and stones – the stones watered daily in summer to keep the customers feeling cool. Inside you can see the noodles being rolled out by hand and deftly cut into long strands by the chef, who stands behind a glass screen in the corner of the room.

2 packs *soba* noodles (200 g per pack/ total 400 g/ 14 oz)	1 sheet *nori*, toasted and cut into small strips
2 spring onions	600 ml/ 1 pint noodle dipping sauce
3 cm/1 inch piece fresh ginger	(*tsuke jiru*) page 108

Cook the noodles as directed, either by the shock method or keeping them on a steady simmer. When *al dente* rinse thoroughly in a bamboo colander under cold water, and leave to drain and cool.

Chop the spring onions finely, and place in a small bowl. Peel and grate the ginger, using a Japanese grater (or the fine teeth on a western grater). Place it in a little mound on a small saucer. Divide the noodles into four large handfuls and place them on flat bamboo baskets (called *zaru*). Scatter the strips of *nori* on top of each mound. Serve with a small cup (about 150 ml/ 5 fl oz) of the dipping sauce. Each person should help themselves to some of the ginger and spring onion, which should be added to the individual dipping cups. A mouthful of noodles is then dipped in the sauce, the cup is lifted to the mouth and the noodles slurped out of the cup with as much noise as you care to make! It is *de rigeur* to be noisy when eating noodles. If you sip them silently everyone will think you are not enjoying them. And another thing – don't wear white shirts when slurping them.

BUCKWHEAT NOODLES WITH MATSUTAKE MUSHROOM
MATSUTAKE ZARU SOBA

The aforementioned *soba* shop in Akasaka – haunt of politicians and dodgy characters – is where I first tasted this – buckwheat noodles unadorned, except that it was autumn so I was treated to some *matsutake* – the horrendously expensive wild mushroom that appears in the shops for a brief period every autumn, and signals the start of mushroom madness. I savoured one single slice on top of my *soba*. It emitted an aroma akin to truffle – with the same cachet attached! If you can't get fresh wild mushrooms use dried slices of porcini or cep, reconstituted in water.

---

2 x 200 g packs *soba* noodles
   (400 g/ 14 oz)
1 *matsutake*, or other fragrant wild
   mushroom

600 ml/ 1 pint noodle dipping sauce
   (*tsuke jiru*) page 108

Cook the noodles as directed, by either the shock method or keeping on a steady simmer. Rinse thoroughly in a bamboo colander under cold water, and leave to drain.
   Wipe the mushroom well with a damp cloth, and slice thinly. Wrap the mushroom in a foil package, seal well so that juices cannot escape, but leave some space inside so the mushroom can 'breathe' and steam can be created inside the package. Place under a hot grill, or preferably on hot coals, for a few minutes until the mushrooms are lightly cooked. Place a large handful of the *soba* noodles onto a flat bamboo basket, and lay a few slices of the fragrant mushroom on top. Serve with a small cup (about 150 ml/ 5 fl oz) of the dipping sauce.

COLD BUCKWHEAT NOODLES WITH VEGETABLE TEMPURA
TEN ZARU SOBA

To the west of Tokyo, in a small town called Mitaka, lies Jindai Ji Temple. It was there in 1978 that I first tasted *ten zaru soba*, sitting outside on a warm spring day. (I seem to have a lot of early *soba* noodle memories...) This delicious, and typical temple food, is served at temples and specialist *soba* shops all over Japan in spring and summer. Sitting outside on low tables covered with red cloths, and a paper parasol to shield the sun, you can enjoy these chilled noodles accompanied by crisp light tempura. For this dish the tempura needs to be freshly fried – not left overs. *Ten zaru* means *ten* as in tempura and *zaru* is basket (the same as in *zaru soba*).
   Follow the recipe for *zaru soba*, and serve with a separate dish of hot crispy tempura. The tempura has a special dipping sauce which is mixed with grated *daikon* radish.

2 packs soba noodles
**TEMPURA DIPPING SAUCE
(TENTSUYU):**
250 ml/9 fl oz *dashi*
80 ml/ 3½ fl oz *mirin*
80 ml/ 3½ fl oz soy sauce
4 tablespoons grated *daikon* radish
I tablespoon grated ginger
VEGETABLES TO DEEP FRY:
I medium aubergine (or 2 small)

2 small green peppers
4 thick (½ cm/ ⅛ inch) slices of sweet
    potato (about half a large potato)
4 perilla (*shiso*) leaves
TEMPURA BATTER:
150 g/ 5 oz plain flour
I tablespoon cornflour
I egg
iced water (about 200 ml/ 7 fl oz)
oil for deep frying

Cook the noodles as previously directed, rinse, drain and put aside. Make the dipping sauce by putting the liquid ingredients in a small saucepan, bring to a boil and simmer for a minute. Remove from the heat and leave to cool. Peel then grate the *daikon* finely and squeeze off excess water. Place a mound of *daikon* (pressed into a cone shape) on each person's tray on a little dish. Make the grated ginger into 4 smaller mounds and place this mound on top of the *daikon* mound (like a snow capped mountain).

Prepare the vegetables. Shave the stem end off the aubergine, and cut it into four lengthways, (if using small aubergines just cut each one in half). Make three cuts about a third of the way up the aubergine, so the wide end fans out. Cut the peppers into four, removing seeds and membrane. Assemble the slices of sweet potato (one per person) and four perilla leaves and pat all vegetables dry. Leave to drain on kitchen paper.

Now you need to make the batter. You can put the oil on to heat as you do this, as you need to make the batter immediately before you need to use it. Don't leave it to stand (see page 136, Summer Vegetable Tempura). In a large bowl, just very lightly mix the egg, flour and water together, using chopsticks, and leaving lumps of flour in it. Check the temperature of the oil – it should be medium hot 170C/340F. If you don't have a temperature gauge you can test the oil by flicking in a drop of batter. It should sink and then float to the surface. If it just sinks it's too cool, and if it rises immediately it's too hot.

Dip the vegetables in the batter and deep fry for a few minutes until just cooked and the batter golden. Do not fry too many things at once as this will lower the temperature. Fry the sweet potato first as it will take longer than the aubergine and pepper. The perilla leaves (*shiso*) should be coated in batter on one side only, and this side carefully slid into the batter. Cook only briefly as you don't want the leaf to scorch. Drain the vegetables on absorbent paper and a mesh rack, preferably in a warm place until ready to serve, which should be as soon as you can. Give each person one piece of sweet potato, aubergine, perilla leaf and two pieces of green pepper. Serve the tempura on a separate plate or small basket with paper under (Japanese stores sell squares of white paper especially for holding tempura), the noodles on a flat basket, and the dipping sauce in a small bowl. The condiments should be offered in small dishes separately.

BUCKWHEAT NOODLES IN HOT SOUP
KAKE SOBA

The last item to be eaten on New Year's Eve, before the festivities of the New Year begin, is *soba* – in this case in hot soup as it is winter. Called *toshi-koshi soba* (meaning the year is passing) the length of the noodles is supposed to signify longevity for the coming year. Use the recipe for the Basic Noodle Broth (*kakejiru*), page 108, and use any topping you have handy.

---

2 packs/ 400 g/ 14 oz dried *soba* noodles

1 litre/ 1¾ pints basic noodle broth
  (*kake jiru*) page 108

seven spice pepper (*shichimi tōgarashi*)
  to season

Cook the noodles as before and drain. Place in a large bowl and pour the hot broth over.

Suggestions for toppings:
Wakame soba
Place a handful of chopped and reconstituted dried *wakame* seaweed on top of the bowl of broth.
Natto soba
For the adventurous place a few spoons of *natto* (fermented soybeans) on top of the noodles. It's a challenge trying to eat slippery soybeans in soup with chopsticks!
Kitsune soba
Deep fried tofu pouches (*usu-age* or *abura-age*) (follow the instructions for Fox Noodles page 114).
Tororo soba
Grated *nagaimo* mountain potato, which has a slippery texture similar to *natto*.
Tororo kombu (shredded kelp)
Put a handful of dried shredded *kombu* on top of the noodles. Upon hitting the liquid the shaved *kombu*, which looks like chopped linen, turns slippery and emits a delicious smell of the sea.

BUCKWHEAT NOODLES IN BROTH WITH TEMPURA
TEMPURA SOBA

This is a good way of serving left over deep fried vegetables or fish. Of course freshly fried foods are fine, but because they are doused in soup, they don't have to be freshly fried, as is the case with most other tempura dishes. Very large tiger prawns (*ebi*) are a common and traditional *tempura* in soup. In autumn a few slices of tempura'ed pumpkin (*kabocha*) are delicious, but you can use aubergine, onion, pepper, anything you fancy. In fact the most basic *tempura soba* doesn't have any vegetables at all. Bits of batter, retrieved from the pan, are placed on top of the bowl of hot soup and noodles. See the recipe for Cold Buckwheat Noodles with Vegetable Tempura page 110, or Summer Vegetable Tempura page 136, for detailed instructions on how to prepare tempura.

2 packs 400 g/ 14 oz dried soba noodles	seven spice pepper (shichimi tōgarashi) to season
1 litre/ 1¾ pints basic soup broth (kake jiru) page 108	

Cook the soba noodles as instructed on page 107-108 and rinse and drain. Prepare the Noodle Dipping Sauce, (page 108) as instructed and keep hot on a low flame. Dunk the noodles in hot water to heat up before serving. Place a portion of noodles in a deep soup bowl, place one or two pieces of tempura on top, and pour the hot broth over. Sprinkle with togarashi pepper.

FULL MOON UDON
TSUKIMI UDON

In autumn tsukimi or 'moon-viewing' is another traditional activity, like viewing the cherry blossoms in spring. In the past parties would be held in well known beauty spots for a special view of the full moon on a clear autumn night, where guests would express their rapture and even write poems in appreciation of its beauty. This very simple dish of noodles echoes the sight – the yolk of the egg represents the moon and the white of the egg the clouds swirling around it. Obviously, as this includes raw egg, the fresher the better, (and best avoided by the elderly or pregnant). In any case the hot broth will 'cook' the egg slightly (just as it does in egg drop soup and in sukiyaki).

2 packs (400 g/ 14 oz) wheat (udon) noodles	4 fresh eggs
1 litre/ 1¾ pints basic noodle broth (kake jiru) page 108	2 spring onions, finely chopped, to garnish
8 slices kamaboko fish cake *	seven spice pepper (shichimi tōgarashi) to season

Cook the noodles as described on page 107-108, until just cooked, or al dente. Rinse them well under cold running water (in a colander). Prepare the noodle broth and keep it hot. Before serving heat up the noodles by dunking them in hot water for a few seconds (like they do in fast food stalls). Divide the noodles evenly between four noodle bowls (large and deep are the requirements). Pour broth into each bowl, just covering the noodles. Place a couple of slices of kamaboko on top of the noodles, and then carefully crack the egg in to the centre, making sure the yolk stays whole. Sprinkle the spring onion on top, and serve immediately with the pepper as a condiment.

*kamaboko is a type of processed fish sausage, usually coloured pink. If you don't have kamaboko a couple of slices of cold cooked chicken or pork will do just fine.

FOX NOODLES
KITSUNE UDON

As well as being a messenger of the rice god, the Japanese fox is regarded as as wily as a non-Japanese one, and feared and revered in the same way. Japanese foxes however, unlike their British counterparts, are apparently inordinately fond of deep fried tofu – which is where this dish gets its name. It's just another simple variation on noodles in hot soup – with a different topping.

2 packs (400 g/ 14 oz) wheat (*udon*) noodles	6 tablespoons soy sauce
1 litre/ 1¾ pints basic noodle broth (*kake jiru*) page 108	2 tablespoons *mirin*
2 deep fried tofu pouches (*abura-age*)	2 spring onions, finely chopped, to garnish
FLAVOURING FOR THE TOFU POUCHES:	seven spice pepper (*shichimi tōgarashi*) to taste
8 tablespoons *dashi*	

Cook the noodles as described on page 107-108, until just cooked, or *al dente*. Rinse them well under cold running water (in a colander). Rinse the tofu pouches in boiling water under a colander to get rid of excess oil. Cut each piece in half and put into a saucepan with the flavouring ingredients. Simmer gently until all the liquid is absorbed and the tofu well flavoured. Remove and cut each half into two triangles. Prepare the noodle broth and keep it hot. Before serving heat up the noodles by dunking them in hot water for a few seconds. Divide the noodles evenly between four noodle bowls. Place two pieces of the flavoured tofu pouch on top of the noodles in each bowl and pour the broth over. Garnish with the chopped spring onion and serve immediately. Serve seven spice pepper as a condiment – *shichimi tōgarashi* is the traditional spice for *udon* wheat noodles, not *wasabi*.

NOODLE ONE-POT
NABEYAKI UDON

The fun of this dish is that it is served in individual one person casseroles – called *nabe*. I used to practically live on it when I was working as a film editor in Tokyo – we had it delivered to the work place, at lunchtime. In fact this is an original fast food – on the scene long before home delivery pizza was invented. At first I couldn't imagine how anyone could ride on motor scooters with dishes of hot soup and not spill it. The answer of course is a special carrying box, which is suspended on a spring at the back of the bike, and which keeps the bowls level at all times. Nevertheless it's a terrifying sight watching the cavalier manner in which the young white coated delivery boys set off on their bikes, and scream to a halt at their destination – soup and noodles (and bowl) intact. The soup even arrived hot – always – and that's the way it should be served. It's real comfort food – great on a cold and dull wintery day. You'll need four individual flameproof casseroles for this.

2 packs (400 g/ 14 oz) wheat (*udon*) noodles	half a *kamaboko* fish cake (the pink one)
1 litre/ 1¾ pints basic noodle broth (*kake jiru*) page 108	a handful of trefoil (*mitsuba*, or watercress if you can't get trefoil)
4 large *shiitake* mushrooms, stems trimmed and a cross cut attractively in the centre (preferably fresh)	4 fresh eggs
	2 spring onions, finely chopped
4 large prawns, cleaned, shelled and de-veined (but leave the tails on to be authentic)	seven spice pepper (*shichimi tōgarashi*) to taste

Cook the noodles as directed on page 107-108. Rinse well under cold water. Heat up the broth and keep it on a low simmer. Divide the noodles between the four small *nabe*. Put the mushrooms, prawns, and slices of *kamaboko* on top. Pour the hot broth over until just covered. Put the lids on and place the casseroles on the heat. Simmer gently for 5 minutes until the prawn and mushrooms are cooked. Add the watercress or trefoil. Then, make a small dent or hollow in the soup and crack a fresh egg into it. Cover again and simmer, until the egg is cooked but the yolk still soft. Garnish with chopped spring onion, and add seven spice pepper to taste. Serve immediately for a hearty and filling lunch, and eat making as much slurping noise as you like!

FINE WHEAT NOODLES
SŌMEN

Sōmen are very fine wheat noodles, nearly always served cold. This delicate and elegant version of *udon* noodles is associated with Zen training – this is the food that Buddhist monks are given to mark the completion of their arduous training session and fast every summer. Because *sōmen* are light and easy to digest they are particularly refreshing in hot weather, especially when eaten cold. The cooling effect of cold noodles can be further emphasised by floating the noodles in an icy-cold mountain stream. Yes it really happens. This custom is known as *nagashi sōmen* – flowing noodles, and I visited Ugenta restaurant on the outskirts of Kyoto to witness this outlandish custom. The restaurant is not easily reached. It's a long walk up a wooded hillside, and the restaurant is indeed perched alongside, in fact almost in, a flowing mountain stream. *Tatami* – matted platforms dressed with low tables – are suspended over the water. Little bamboo spouts channel the noodles downstream and within your reach, whereupon chopsticks are wielded to catch a mouthful of icy cold noodles before they disappear for ever! The strike rate is remarkably good – it'd have to be or or they'd be out of business I suppose. Stray noodles are presumably gobbled up by the local fish. You don't need a flowing mountain stream though to enjoy *sōmen* noodles in summer – just humid, enervating weather – and enough energy to chop a few bits of cucumber and ham.

COLD WHEAT NOODLES CHINESE STYLE
HIYASHI SŌMEN

In this dish, fine wheat noodles are served in a little cold broth which is flavoured, Chinese style, with sesame oil. If you like you can serve the cold broth as a dipping sauce in a separate cup (as for *zaru soba*) and the noodles on a basket or plate.

BROTH:

600 ml/ 1 pint *dashi*

5 tablespoons soy sauce (or 4 tablespoons light soy sauce)

1 tablespoon caster sugar

4 tablespoons *mirin*

¼ teaspoon toasted sesame oil

3 eggs (for making a thin omelette)

2 teaspoons caster sugar

400 g/14 oz dried *sōmen* noodles

100 g/ 4 oz cold ham (or you can substitute cooked chicken or pork)

1 small cucumber (or half a large one with seeds removed)

sesame seeds to garnish

2 spring onions, finely chopped

Japanese mustard

First make the broth, as it needs to cool. In a small saucepan bring the broth ingredients to a boil, making sure the sugar is dissolved, and leave to cool. Once cooled, refrigerate to chill. Now, mix together the three eggs and the caster sugar and make a thin omelette as described in the recipe for Scattered Sushi (*chirashi-zushi*) page 96. Cool and cut into fine strips (golden strings). Then cook the noodles according to the instructions for *udon* and *soba* (page 106) – make sure they are not too soft, as they'll cook more quickly being finer. The cold shock method is especially good for *sōmen*. Drain and rinse in cold water. Leave them in cold water to prevent them sticking together. Chop the ham and cucumber into thin strips.

To serve, divide the noodles equally between four dishes – large shallow glass bowls are ideal. Place two or three ice cubes around each pile. Place the ham, cucumber and omelette side by side (covering a third of a circle, 120 degrees each, radiating from the centre outwards) on the top. Pour the cold broth gently over each mound of noodles. Sprinkle with sesame seeds and chopped spring onion, and a blob of Japanese mustard to taste. Eat with chopsticks.

NOODLE ROLLS
SŌMEN NORIMAKI

This simple but tricky dish was shown to me at Sankō In Temple by the abbess, Koei Hoshino, when we filmed her for my documentary. Thin *sōmen* noodles are wrapped, sushi style, in sheets of crisp green *nori* seaweed. It's important that the noodles are well drained, so the *nori* doesn't get too wet, and that the rolls are eaten soon after making them, again to stop them becoming too soggy. Rolling wet noodles in *nori* sheets requires a measure of dexterity, so it may be a good idea to hone your technique on sushi rolls, using rice, first. It seems to be especially difficult when you are being watched. When we were filming the abbess (bless her heart) making these, she just couldn't get it right – and ended up going through about ten packets of noodles before she met with success. Tip – don't try this in front of a film crew!

400 g/ 14 oz *sōmen* noodles or 4 bundles (and a piece of cotton or fine string)	4 sheets *nori* seaweed *wasabi* soy sauce to dip

The main trick here is to keep the noodles in a neat bundle as you cook them, by tying them together at one end. You may find when you take your noodles out of the packet that they are already tied together with a strip of paper into bundles, in which case keep it in place while you tie them, then remove before cooking. Otherwise, divide the noodles into four and, using light string or cotton, tie each bunch together, about half an inch from one end. Place in boiling water, but do not agitate – you want the noodles to stay in a neat bundle. Once cooked (after about 2 – 3 minutes) drain well and cool. Now carefully, keeping the noodles in a neat bundle, cut off and discard the uncooked end piece where the tie was. Lay a piece of *nori* seaweed, with the shiny side down, on a rolling mat (*sudare*). The bamboo strips should be horizontal, as you face them. Lay a bundle of noodles on top of the *nori*, and spread them out, leaving a small gap at the front, and a bigger gap (about 4 cm/ 1½ inches) at the top edge. Carefully roll the bundle away from you and towards you, tucking the front edge under, and pulling tightly to keep it taut. The top edge of *nori* should stick to the damp *nori* along the length of the roll. Using a very sharp and dampened knife carefully cut the roll in half, and each half into half and half again, creating eight small rolls. Use a careful pulling motion, so as not to tear the *nori* wrapping. Lay the pieces cut side down in an attractive manner on a plain plate. You can even use a slab of wood, marble or slate. Serve with a dipping sauce of soy sauce and *wasabi* paste, and eat as soon as possible.

SAVOURY PANCAKES
O-KONOMIYAKI

These savoury pancakes are originally from Hiroshima and the Kansai region of Japan (around Osaka), but nowadays chains of *O-konomiyaki* restaurants can be found all over the country. The fun of this dish is cooking it yourself, at a table which has a hot plate or griddle embedded in it. *O-konomiyaki* means 'cook as you like it' so the point is in the cooking itself. It's a fun meal for sharing with friends – definitely not suitable for a romantic meal or a business lunch, as there are too many cooking fumes around. In restaurants you choose a selection of solid ingredients – seafood or meat for example, which is then brought to your table in a small bowl, mixed (but not cooked) with egg, flour and chopped cabbage. (This is another one of those foods which have a *gomoku* [5 things] variety version.) At home you can use a griddle or a heavy based frying pan. Because they are quite thick these pancakes must be cooked fairly slowly, so check that the ingredients are cooked through before serving. The cooked pancake is traditionally served with a generous sprinkling of green *nori* flakes (called *ao nori*) and a thick sweet soy sauce – which is halfway between soy sauce and Worcestershire sauce. Japanese shops sell ready-made *o-konomiyaki* sauce. You can substitute *ton katsu* sauce, Worcestershire sauce, or make your own, following this recipe here. Pickled shredded ginger is also served alongside.

Variations: You can vary the meat and fish ingredients in any way you want – use fresh prawns instead of dried shrimp, chicken instead of pork etc. Adding *katsuo* flakes (dried bonito) to the mixture makes it even more Japanese and fishy tasting.

SAUCE:	8 eggs
125 ml/ 4 fl oz *tamari* soy sauce	200 g/ 7 oz roast pork cut into small
125 ml/ 4 fl oz saké	strips
60 ml/ 2 fl oz *mirin*	100 g/ 4 oz fresh squid – cut into rings
1 tablespoon caster sugar	or strips
1 teaspoon rice wine vinegar	1 small packet *katsuobushi* (dried
	bonito flakes – the fine one)
75 g/ 3 oz plain wheat flour	6 *shiitake* mushrooms, sliced finely
(commercially prepared flour	½ small white cabbage, shredded into
especially for *o-konomiyaki* is also	fine strips
available – it's usually got dried shrimp	pinch salt
and dried *jinenjo* (*yamaimo*) starch	vegetable oil for the griddle
added)	

If you are not using a commercially prepared sauce first make your own. Combine all the ingredients in a small saucepan, bring to a boil and simmer for 10 minutes until it starts to thicken and become a little viscous. Leave to cool. When you are ready to eat, in a large bowl mix the flour, eggs, pork, squid, *katsuo* flakes, *shiitake* mushrooms and shredded cabbage, and add the salt. Mix well but carefully, so as not to damage the solid ingredients. You need a thick smooth batter. Heat a little oil on the griddle or skillet, until fairly hot. Pour the mixture in four separate spoonsful to make small pancakes, or, if you want one large one, pour it out all at once. Cook for about 5 minutes one side, until the mixture hardens and bubbles form. Flip over and cook for a few more minutes – making sure the batter is not soggy, the cabbage is soft, and the fish cooked through. Ladle the sauce thickly on top and sprinkle generously with the *nori* flakes. Serve individually or cut into thick slices (like a pizza). This makes a casual lunch or supper.

WHEAT GLUTEN – MONKS' MEAT

FU AND NAMA BU

Wheat gluten almost always appears in a standard Japanese meal as a type of garnish. It's usually made into little flower or leaf shapes, reflecting the seasons – orange maple leaves in autumn, and green bamboo leaves in spring. In this fashion it appears in soups, or in simmered dishes. The texture is a little chewy, and the taste resembles bread. It also resembles bread nutritionally, being high in protein, calcium and niacin: that's because it's made from the same thing, wheat flour. The decorative type of gluten is sold dried in little sealed bags. Other varieties are square flat cakes, which look like crackers, or round 'crackers' with a hole in the middle called *kuruma* (meaning wheel) *fu*. Both of these products are suitable for putting in soups or simmered dishes. They absorb flavour well, and soften when added to the pot. This dried gluten is known as *fu*. Because gluten is high in protein it has become an important ingredient in the strictly vegetarian diet of the Buddhist temples (a cuisine called *shōjin ryōri*). Kyoto in western Japan has the highest concentration of temples, and is well known as a place to sample *shōjin ryōri* or temple cuisine. It is here that you will find fresh gluten, known as *nama bu* (*nama* means raw or fresh, and *fu* becomes *bu* when preceded by another word). Together with *yuba* (fresh soy milk 'skin') fresh gluten has become associated with Kyoto. I was taken to Uji restaurant in the grounds of Nanpukuji Temple in Kyoto, to sample a complete lunch of fresh gluten dishes, cooked in a variety of ways.

The fresh variety is extremely hard to get hold of outside Kyoto. It's the kind of thing you buy at the souvenir shops in Kyoto station (a Japanese friend of mine always used to bring me some to Tokyo when she visited from Kyoto). Although not dried, the 'fresh' product is still lightly steamed. If you want completely raw fresh gluten (which is delicious deep fried) then you have to make it yourself. Luckily it's not at all complicated, but it does take effort: like making bread it requires kneading. Fu Ka is the oldest shop making *fu* in Kyoto, and here the process is partly mechanised. The kneading and extruding is done by small machines, but the shaping, finishing and flavouring is still done by hand. I was shown around by a truly eccentric and charming gentleman, Josef Justice, who I believe has since returned to the US to set up his own gluten making business. At that time he was possibly the only non-Japanese to have worked alongside the natives at Fu Ka, and in true innovative Japanese fashion they encouraged him to experiment with non-Japanese flavours. Josef added chilli, garlic and herbs to his gluten, which is most un-temple like. Here though, follows the basic unflavoured method. This amount of strong bread flour will yield about 200 g/ 7 oz of raw gluten. If you make it with plain flour the gluten yield will be less – about 150 g/ 5 oz from 450 g/ 1 lb flour.

BASIC GLUTEN RECIPE
NAMA BU

450 g/ 1 lb strong white bread flour	a large bowl to mix, and colander to
250 ml/ 9 fl oz water to mix	drain

Mix the flour with water to make a very firm dough. Knead the dough for about 15 minutes to activate the gluten and make it smooth. If it's too tiring you can knead for five minutes then rest for five and knead again. Leaving the dough to rest helps activate the gluten. When it's nice and smooth and well kneaded cover it with a damp cloth to stop it drying out, and leave for at least 30 minutes (longer is OK). The next stage is the interesting bit, where you wash the starch out of the dough, until you are left with pure gluten. I usually do this in the sink. In a large bowl knead the dough under cold (or warm) running water. Turn off the tap and knead the dough well, under water. The starch will begin to come away, and the water turn milky. Pour away this water. Keep kneading and rinsing alternately, until the water you throw away is almost clear, meaning that most of the starch is gone. (After a few minutes the dough will begin to break up and the stringy structure of the gluten will become apparent. Don't panic if it looks as if it's going to fall apart – but do use a colander to rinse it and prevent pieces of gluten going down the sink.) It should soon start to hold together again. It'll now be much smaller – about half the size, and quite stretchy and rubbery. You can now do several things with your raw gluten.

1. Leave it in the fridge overnight, just as it is. The next day it will be very smooth, and perfect for deep frying (see below).

2. Knead it so it becomes smoother, and use it straight away (for example for deep frying).

3. If you want to steam your gluten, or have a firmer textured result, you can knead some glutinous rice flour into this raw dough. You'll need about 1 tablespoon for each 100 g/ ¼ lb of gluten. This is not easy, as the dough is wet and the flour dry, so it takes some time to knead out the lumps. Commercially produced fresh gluten (which is bought pre-steamed) contains rice flour, but I confess that I don't always bother to put it in. I almost always deep fry it, and it works out just fine without.

All this may seem like a lot of bother, but it can be great fun, and fascinating to observe the changes in the dough. Also, it can be put in the freezer. In its deep fried or raw state it freezes very satisfactorily, so it's worthwhile making a lot in one go. When I'm having a gluten-making session I usually double these quantities (using a whole bag of flour), have a big deep frying session and put some away for emergencies. Pieces of deep fried gluten can be taken from the freezer and added to soups and stews. The following recipe is from Sankō In, and is surprisingly delicious for such a simple food.

DEEP FRIED GLUTEN
RŌBAI

I first tasted this deep fried raw gluten at Sankō In Temple, where they call it *rōbai*, and I loved it immediately (especially the mustard in the simmering stock). This method of deep frying gluten is also popular among macrobiotic cooks, who use gluten a lot, as it's a good source of non-animal and non-dairy protein. Macrobiotic cooks call both deep fried and simmered gluten *seitan*.

vegetable oil for deep frying	light soy sauce for dipping
650 g/ 1½ lb raw gluten	*wasabi* to taste

Heat the oil to about 170C /340F, medium temperature.

Cut the gluten into pieces about 5-7 cm /2-3 inches in diameter. Stretch the gluten by pulling around its edge with your fingers and turning as you go to create a circle. The aim is get a piece the size of a saucer which is fairly thin and even. Holes may

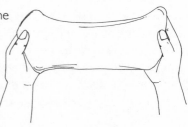

appear but this doesn't matter. Immediately place the gluten into the hot oil. It will puff up (like making prawn crackers). Now you have to work quite quickly. Using chopsticks (one in each hand) keep pulling the gluten apart, stretching it, to maintain the large round shape. After about 40 seconds of frying, when it's golden brown, turn it over and briefly cook the other side. Remove from the pan and drain on paper. The result should be crispy and golden. If the gluten was too thick it will need longer cooking, or may not be cooked through. This is not a major problem if you are going to cook it again by simmering, but if you are going to eat it now it shouldn't be raw in the middle. I can never resist tasting some just as it is, dipped into soy sauce, with a dab of *wasabi*. When it's hot and crispy it's heaven. If you don't eat it all you can now proceed with this recipe.

  Note: this can be made with wholewheat flour, although the result is slightly heavier, and not quite as attractive. It's more nutritious though, and just as yummy.

STEAMED GLUTEN
MUSHI BU

This gives a heavier consistency, like a chewy bread, and is similar to the 'fresh gluten' you'd buy in Japan.

---

225 g/ 8 oz raw gluten

2 tablespoons glutinous rice flour
  (*shiratamako*)

clingfilm to wrap steamer

If the rice flour is lumpy, you need to first crush it into a fine powder. You can do this either by putting it into a paper bag and crushing with a rolling pin (the old fashioned way), milling it in a food mill, or grinding it in a pestle and mortar (the Zen Buddhist way). Then, on a marble or plastic board, knead the rice flour into the raw gluten, folding and mixing well to make a smooth dough. Form into cylinders about 10-15 cm/ 4-6 inches inches long and 4 cm/ 1½ inches thick. Wrap each piece in clingfilm and place in a bamboo steamer. Steam for about 20 minutes until cooked. The result will be chewier and more thickly textured than the deep fried version. It can now be cut into slices or shapes and added to soups or stews. You could use it in *o-den* as a vegetarian alternative to fish and sausage for example.

DEEP FRIED GLUTEN, SIMMERED IN BROTH
RŌBAI NO KARASHI NI

---

2 -3 pieces of deep fried gluten (*rōbai*)

600 ml/ 1 pint *dashi*

6 tablespoons soy sauce

2 tablespoons *mirin*

1 teaspoon Japanese mustard

Cut the rounds of deep fried gluten into thick strips about 3 cm/ 1 inch wide. Put the simmering ingredients (except mustard) in a small pan. Add the gluten and simmer on a medium heat for about 2 minutes until heated through, and the flavours have mingled. Do not boil or overcook as the gluten will fall apart. Serve a few pieces in individual bowls with a good blob of mustard mixed in with the broth. This should be served as part of a Japanese style meal, in particular a vegetarian one.

BROCCOLI, MUSHROOM AND GLUTEN SALAD WITH PLUM DRESSING
BURROKORI TO RŌBAI NO UME DORESHINGU

In this recipe small pieces of deep fried gluten are incorporated into a cooked salad, and dressed with an *umeboshi* flavoured dressing. The *umeboshi* plum is ubiquitous in Japan. The unripe fruit (technically not a plum, but an apricot) is pickled in salt and is very tart. The mashed up flesh of the plum, called *bainiku* or *umeboshi* paste, is sold separately in jars. This recipe is adapted from Barbara and Lenny Jacobs' book, *The Book of Seitan,* and uses the paste to make a tasty and unique salad dressing. It's fondly remembered by everyone I've introduced it to, and seems to suit the Western palate. The creaminess of the soy milk mitigates the tartness of the plum.

FOR THE DRESSING:	1 medium head broccoli, broken into small florets
1 heaped tablespoon *umeboshi* paste	
150 ml/ 5 fl oz unsweetened soy milk	1 large piece deep fried gluten
½ teaspoon toasted sesame oil	15 g/ ½ oz dried *arame*
½ teaspoon vegetable oil	125 g/ 4 oz small white button mushrooms
½ teaspoon rice vinegar	

Make the dressing by slowly adding the soy milk to the *umeboshi* paste, mixing constantly to get a smooth paste (use chopstocks or a miniature wire whisk). Drizzle in the oils and vinegar, and shake or whisk well. This keeps a few days in the fridge.

Rehydrate the *arame* in cold water. Cut the crisp deep fried gluten (*robai*) into small bite size pieces. Wipe the mushrooms and slice them (not too thickly and not too thinly). Dunk them in a saucepan of boiling water for 30 seconds to soften them. Remove with a slotted spoon and drain on kitchen paper. Par boil the broccoli (you can use the same water, but add a pinch of salt) for about 3 minutes, until just beginning to soften, but still with a bite. Drain and plunge into cold water immediately to arrest the cooking. Drain well, squeezing out any excess water carefully. Drain the *arame* which should have softened by now. Gently combine the broccoli, mushrooms and *arame*. Scatter the *robai* pieces on top and drizzle the dressing over. Serve soon after you've mixed the dressing in.

STEAMED GLUTEN WRAPPED IN NORI AND DEEP FRIED
FU NO ISOBE AGE

This is inspired by the Zen Buddhist delicacy, millet *fu*, which is a feature of Kyoto temple life. I first ate the millet version at Sankō In Temple, and then again at Uji, the gluten restarant in Kyoto, where I was taken by Josef Justice, the American gluten experimentalist. This is a simpler all-wheat version.

225 g/8 oz steamed gluten (see page 121)	oil for deep frying
1 sheet *nori* seaweed	1 teaspoon ginger juice from freshly grated ginger

Cut each length of gluten into slices about 2 cm/ ¾ inch thick. Cut the *nori* into strips about 1 cm/ ⅜ inch by 7 cm/ 2¾ inches – in other words long enough to wrap around each piece of gluten, with room to spare. Wrap one piece of *nori* around the middle of each gluten piece and moisten the ends so it holds together. *Nori* shrinks when it is deep fried so wrap it very loosely at this stage – it'll tighten when it cooks. Drop each piece into medium hot oil (about 170C/340F) and deep fry until golden – about 2 minutes. Serve hot with a dip of soy sauce and ginger juice. This could be served as the deep fried element of a Japanese meal, or as a starter in a Western style meal (an alternative to deep fried Camembert perhaps?).

MILLET AND DULSE CROQUETTES
AWA NO KORROKE

Millet is a delicious and much neglected grain – in the West it's used mainly as bird seed. In the past it was commonly used by Japanese country people instead of the more expensive rice. These days in Japan it's used to make *awa mochi* a kind of millet rice cake, and *awabu* – a millet based gluten. This recipe uses millet grain to make croquettes, which are then deep fried. Because millet goes hard and sticky when cooked it's good for croquettes as they hold together well. Dulse is a North European or North Atlantic sea vegetable, not known in Japan, but this recipe is in the spirit of Japanese country cooking, and a favourite amongst macrobiotic devotees. The best ones I ever tasted were cooked by Setsuko Dawson, wife of Christopher Dawson who has been so instrumental in distributing traditionally made quality Japanese foods into the West, through the macrobiotic companies Mito Ku and Clearspring.

150 g/ 5 oz millet	15 g/ ½oz (or a small handful) dried dulse
1 litre/ 1¾ pints water	1 tablespoon chopped parsley
pinch salt	oil for deep frying
1 tablespoon miso	

Wash the millet and place in a large pan with the water and salt. Bring to a boil, reduce the heat and simmer until cooked (about 20 minutes). Millet has a tendency to stick to the bottom of the pan, so placing a heat diffuser under the pan helps to distribute the heat. Leave it to cool – it will go hard as it cools. Put the dulse in water and soften – it only takes a couple of minutes. Drain and pick through the dulse for stones or bits of hard shell and remove them, then chop it finely. Mix the millet and dulse well with the miso and finely chopped parsley, distributing the ingredients well. You can use your fingers for this if you like. (If the mixture doesn't hold together well you can add a little plain flour). Take two tablespoonsful of the mixture and press it into a compact ball. Then roll it into a thick sausage or croquette shape. Deep fry in medium hot oil (170C/340F) for a few minutes until golden. Serve hot, either as a substitute for rice or with a miso or mushroom sauce.

VEGETABLES – FRUITS OF THE LAND

"Buddhism has left its impress here, as on everything in Japan. To Buddhism was due the abandonment of a meat diet, now over a thousand years ago. The permission to eat fish, though that too entailed the taking of life, which is contrary to strict Buddhist tenets, seems to have been a concession to human frailty."

Basil Hall Chamberlain, *Things Japanese*

Vegetarianism in Japan is almost exclusively a religious concept – the result of the Buddhist prohibition on killing living things – or 'sentient beings' as they are more usually referred to. At times this was interpreted as meaning four legged creatures, but to the more devout embraced any living thing – including fish and fowl. The Buddhist scriptures state that *"he who does not follow the path of vegetarianism will be re born as cattle in a later life"* (quoted in *The Heart of Zen Cuisine*). This means that, although there is a long tradition of vegetarianism in Japan, it has always been associated with the temples and monasteries, and has been a religious, not secular or sentimental, interpretation. This explanation notwithstanding, such influence has meant that Japanese cuisine has many delicious ways of cooking vegetables and vegetable products. This chapter therefore deals with the many interesting and unusual ways of serving vegetables which are now an established part of family and *izakaya* cooking. It also includes some temple specialities, features of Zen Buddhist cuisine which I was privileged to learn at Sankō In Temple. Some of these recipes are good as main dishes in a vegetarian spread. Others are new ways of serving up well known vegetables – spinach in a sesame dressing, broad beans with *wakame* sea vegetable, for instance.

The most important point is that the vegetables used should be fresh and of good quality. Japanese cooking emphasises the natural taste of the ingredients, and usually also the natural appearance. You can tell what you are eating by looking at it. Vegetables tend to retain their shape and their colour. Cooking serves only to bring out and enhance the natural taste and texture. Vegetables do not usually become a mush, cooked out of recognition. Green peppers for example, are either grilled or deep fried, retaining their crispness and colour – they are never boiled or stewed. Very often ingredients are cooked and flavoured separately and then combined (artfully of course). Parboiling – cooking rapidly in boiling water for a very short time, then plunging into cold water – a technique called *yugaku*, is second nature to Japanese cooks, preserving, as it does, the colours and shapes of each individual ingredient, essential for leafy green vegetables (*yu* means hot water as mentioned in the section on tea ceremony). Root vegetables, if sliced, can also be plunged into ready boiling water, but large pieces should be immersed in cold water, and brought slowly to a simmer – the same as in Western cooking.

The cooking styles of vegetables follow the main patterns of cooking, *nimono* – simmered, *yakimono* – grilled, *mushimono* – steamed, *agemono* – deep fried, and *itame mono* – sautéed. Vegetable salads are not composed of raw vegetables, but will most likely, in Japanese cuisine, be *aemono* – 'dressed things', where the vegetable is cooked or salted and combined with a dressing, such as tofu, miso or sesame; or they will be *sunonmono* – 'vinegared things' served with a slightly sweet vinegar dressing. At their most basic, vegetable 'salads' are simply salted and pressed.

Notes on flavouring vegetables

In general root vegetables such as potatoes and carrots are suited to longer cooking in a sweet and rich seasoning (such as *nikujaga*, and *o-den*). Root vegetables are also suitable for sautéeing – burdock, lotus root, carrot are all examples of root type vegetables which are commonly cooked in this way. Green leafy vegetables are cooked barely at all – parboiled – and subjected to the *irodashi* technique – colour giving – whereby they are plunged into cold water after quick boiling. They can be eaten either *ohitashi* style, with a simple adornment of soy sauce or sesame, or added (at the last minute) to one-pot dishes such as *sukiyaki*, *shabu shabu*, and *chirinabe*.

A meal would normally combine one of each of these cooking styles, but not necessarily all of them, unless it is a fairly grand affair. The greater the array of dishes the grander the meal. If you are out drinking in an *izakaya* (rather than at a banquet) you are free to order whatever you like – you can have ten deep fried dishes if you can stomach them. But as a general rule common sense prevails, and you would most likely want to eat several dishes each prepared in different cooking styles.

Because the best vegetables are fresh it follows that they will be eaten in season. In Japan certain foods are still very much a harbinger of the season and are eaten in celebration, a practice which is being lost in western industrialised urban areas. A great fuss is still made of the arrival of bamboo shoots in spring, and mushrooms in autumn. The best example of this seasonal fever is the appearance of the *matsutake* mushroom, which bursts into the shops for only a few weeks in autumn, and heralds the start of mushroom madness. *Matsutake* only grows wild in pine forests, and is accordingly extortionately expensive. One single mushroom (admittedly a pretty large one) can sell for as much as thirty to forty pounds. *Matsutake* are never dried, so their season is short. Like the cherry blossom, its brief appearance makes it all the more precious, and its presence is accordingly celebrated. This mushrooming of mushrooms everywhere means that department stores make up special autumn lunch boxes (or *bento*) where a few slices of the treasured *matsutake* are scattered on top of a bed of rice. For the less extravagant who still want to celebrate autumn's arrival chestnut lunch boxes are an alternative seasonal treat. If you walk around a large department store's food department during this period you will be bombarded with the shouts of food vendors, entreating you to buy the latest seasonal delicacy, "*Irrashai mase, matsutake gohan igaka desu ka? Irrashai mase, kuri gohan ikaga desu ka? Irrashai mase!*" (Welcome, how about *matsutake* rice, or chestnut rice? Welcome!). It's all great fun.

In spring, country people go foraging for all manner of wild foods. I have a very fond memory of walking home through the woods in Nagano in spring with the Momose family, and stopping to pick huge buds off the trees. They were *taranome* (sometimes translated as angelica tree buds). With our baskets full we rushed home to make tempura out of them. This fondness for wild foods, gathered from the forest and hedgerows inevitably reinforces seasonality, and an appreciation of where food comes from. There is thus a spiritual awareness, and a child-like thrill in the appreciation of nature's abundance, in the preparation and eating of such foods. It's akin to the gathering of brambles in autumn or elderflowers in summer – a thrill I hope I'll never grow out of.

This section then is divided into four seasons, to emphasise the seasonality of vegetables. As seasonality is a variable thing, some vegetables may appear in one season when they could be in two, so just think of the divisions as a guide and inspiration rather than a rule. I've included some distinctive Buddhist recipes from Sankō In Temple, which I hope will help to re-awaken a gratitude for the gifts of nature, and perhaps inspire you to go foraging for wild foods when available. So to begin our vegetable cooking section we'll start with spring, and some typical Japanese spring foods.

SPRING

BAMBOO SHOOT
TAKENOKO

Takenoko means 'baby bamboo' or, as my friend Naho once described it 'child of bamboo'. How sweet. Less poetically, they are referred to as bamboo shoots and that is indeed what they are. Bamboo shoots, along with the cherry blossom, are *the* indicators of the passing of winter, and the emergence of spring, and in the old days families would go out into local bamboo groves to harvest the shoots themselves, at their first appearance. The small shoots start to show around the roots of the established trees, and grow at an alarming rate – about ten centimetres, or one foot, a day. You may be able to find fresh bamboo in Chinese markets, so if you can, here's how to prepare it.

How to prepare fresh bamboo shoots
After harvesting, the shoots are covered in layers of rough brown husks. The tender edible part is beneath this (like a sweet corn). Don't remove the husks straight away – you must boil the whole thing, husks and all, for one to one and a half hours, to remove bitterness. Drain and cool then remove the layers of husks. Then cut in half down the centre and remove the stringy bits from the inside.

Pre-packed shoots
If using canned, or water packed shoots, you'll find a white residue in the centre of the shoot (which is a result of the canning process). Remove it by washing thoroughly, or lightly scraping.

BAMBOO SHOOT DUMPLINGS
TAKENOKO DANGO

This is a speciality of Sankō In Temple, and a dish to celebrate spring.

Grated bamboo shoots are mixed with flour and formed into small balls. These are deep fried and then simmered, to soften them, in a soy based stock.

I medium bamboo shoot	**FOR SIMMERING:**
4 tablespoons plain flour	480 ml/ 17 fl oz *dashi*
oil for deep frying	I tablespoon saké
	I teaspoon soy sauce
	pinch salt

Prepare the bamboo shoot as described on page 127. Grate on a fine Japanese style grater, so you have a pulp. In a large bowl combine with the flour and salt to make a fairly stiff paste. Take a tablespoonful of the mixture and, with your hands, form into small balls, about 1½ cm/ ¾ inch in diameter. Heat the oil to about 160C/320F, and deep fry the balls until golden. Drain on kitchen paper. Combine the simmering ingredients in a medium size saucepan, and bring to a boil. Add the dumplings and simmer for 5 minutes, until the dumplings are slightly softened, but not falling apart. Serve hot – three pieces per person in medium size deep bowls.

BAMBOO SHOOT TEMPURA
TAKENOKO TEMPURA

The bamboo shoot here is separately flavoured by simmering in a light soy sauce based broth before it's dipped in the batter and deep fried. It's another temple speciality.

I large bamboo shoot	**TEMPURA BATTER:**
FLAVOURING FOR BAMBOO:	175 g/ 6 oz plain flour (sift first)
250 ml/9 fl oz *dashi*	250 ml/ 9 fl oz iced water
I tablespoon light soy sauce	I egg
I tablespoon *mirin*	oil for deep frying
	fresh sea salt crystals to serve

Cut the bamboo shoot into thick slices (about ½ cm/ ⅛ inch) and then into quarters.

Combine the simmering ingredients in a small pan, and add the bamboo shoots. Bring to a boil and simmer, uncovered for 5 minutes. Remove from heat.

Now make the batter by quickly combining the flour, egg and water, (or follow the instructions for Summer Vegetable Tempura page 136). If you want authentic Zen temple-style batter don't include the egg. Mix your batter whilst you are bringing the oil to temperature – 170C / 340F. If you don't have a temperature gauge you can test the oil by flicking in a drop of batter. It should sink and then rise to the surface. If it just

sinks it's too cool, and if it rises immediately it's too hot. Mix the batter quickly and roughly leaving lumps of dry flour, and keeping the batter cold. Dip the pieces of bamboo into the batter and then into the oil, being careful not to splash. Deep fry for about 3 minutes until golden. Serve hot with freshly ground, or crystals of, sea salt.

BAMBOO SHOOT AND GREEN PEA SUSHI RICE
TAKENOKO NO CHIRASHI

Another temple speciality from Sankō In, this is a double celebration of spring, using bamboo shoots and early green peas. The rice is flavoured with vinegar and sugar as described in the section on sushi rice. Again the bamboo shoot is separately flavoured.

100 g/4 oz bamboo shoot, cut into ½ cm/ ⅛ inch thick rectangles, (*tanzaku giri*)	1 tablespoon saké ½ teaspoon sugar pinch salt
FLAVOURING FOR BAMBOO: 250 ml/ 9 fl oz water	50 g/ 2 oz young green peas 300 g/12 oz prepared sushi rice page 94

Simmer the prepared bamboo shoot in the water, sugar and saké mixture for 5 minutes, until flavoured. Drain and leave to cool. Par boil the green peas and drain. (Do not put the peas into cold water to cool because the skins will wrinkle.) With all the ingredients at room temperature mix the peas and bamboo shoot together gently with the rice, combining well. Serve as a salad style rice dish, with raw fish, or with a salty vegetable dish like Aubergine and Pepper in Miso (*Nasu no miso itame*, page 56) or Braised *Hijiki* and Deep Fried Tofu (*Hijiki no nimono*, page 168).

BAMBOO SHOOT WITH VINEGAR MISO DRESSING
TAKENOKO NO SUMISO AE

This very simple side dish shows off the mild, earthy, taste and crunchy texture of bamboo shoots. You can use the water packed variety or even canned. This is an example of an *ae mono* dish, where the vegetable is 'dressed' or tossed in a thick dressing – in this case a miso-based one.

1 small bamboo shoot, either water packed, fresh or canned **DRESSING:** 1 tablespoon sweet white (*saikyō*) miso	1 tablespoon light/yellow (*shinshu*) miso 2 tablespoons saké 2 tablespoons rice vinegar a sprinkle of *yuzu* powder (or fresh peel finely grated)

If using fresh bamboo follow the instructions for preparation at the beginning of this section. If using canned or water packed shoots, rinse well to remove the white residue. Slice the bamboo shoot thinly into half moons. Now make the dressing. In a medium size bowl blend the miso and slowly add the saké and vinegar, mixing with a wooden spoon, to a smooth paste as you go. Add the bamboo shoot and gently toss, coating all the pieces with the dressing. Sprinkle *yuzu* powder on top, sparingly. Serve at room temperature as a side dish.

BAMBOO SHOOTS SAUTÉED WITH CARROT
TAKENOKO TO NINJIN NO ITAMEMONO

200 g/ 7 oz bamboo shoots	2 tablespoons soy sauce
2 medium carrots	2 tablespoons *mirin*
15 g/ ½ oz dried *arame*	75 ml/ 3 fl oz *dashi*
2 teaspoons toasted sesame oil	1 red chilli, seeds removed and cut into
1 tablespoon vegetable oil	thin rings

Cut the bamboo into large juliennes (*sengiri*) about 3 cm/ 1 inch long, not too thinly. Peel the carrot and cut into thin slices. Using a flower cutter (preferably cherry blossom shape to emphasise spring) cut the carrot into shapes. (You can use the left over carrot bits for some other dish where you need minced carrot, for a filling or croquettes.)

Soak the *arame* in cold water until soft and drain well. Heat the oils in a large heavy bottomed pan and add the bamboo shoot, carrot and *arame*. Sauté for 3 to 4 minutes, then add the liquid and flavouring ingredients, including the chilli. Simmer gently uncovered until some of the liquid has gone and the vegetables soft. Turn off the heat and leave it to cool to room temperature in the liquid, which will continue to give flavour to the vegetables, like a marinade. Serve at room temperature with a little of the liquid.

BAMBOO SHOOTS SAUTÉED WITH MANGE TOUT AND ARAME
TAKENOKO TO SAYAENDŌ NO ITAMEMONO

This is a colourful dish to celebrate spring, and extremely quick and easy to prepare.

200 g/ 7 oz bamboo shoots, cleaned and	1 tablespoon rapeseed oil
cooked (or canned)	1 tablespoon soy sauce
125 g/ 4 oz mange tout	1 tablespoon saké
15 g/ ½ oz dried *arame*	

Cut the bamboo into thin rounds and then quarters. Wash the mange tout.

Soak the *arame* in cold water until soft and drain well. Heat the oil in a heavy bottomed pan and add the bamboo shoot and mange tout. Stir fry for 2-3 minutes then add the *arame*. Sauté for a few minutes, then add the soy sauce and saké. Quickly put on a lid as it sizzles. Leave for one minute then take off heat. Serve hot or at room temperature.

SAKÉ BRAISED MANGE TOUT
OR SUGAR SNAP PEAS
SAYAENDŌ NO SAKAMUSHI

This very simple temple side dish makes the most of crisp and juicy mange tout. When sugar snap peas are in season use them to elevate this dish to classic and simple elegance. The saké seems to accentuate the delicate taste of the peas.

200 g/ 7 oz mange tout (about 40)	I teaspoon vegetable oil
2 tablespoons saké	½ teaspoon light soy sauce
pinch salt	

Wash the peas, top and tail, and put into a saucepan with the saké, oil, salt and soy sauce. Simmer for about 3 minutes with a lid on (important, as there is so little liquid in the pan). Check that the liquid is enough and they don't burn – add a little water if necessary. They should be slightly crisp, with a bite. Serve immediately as they will discolour if left.

PAK CHOI, BEAN SPROUT AND GLUTEN STIR FRY
YASAI TO RŌBAI NO ITAMEMONO

This was inspired by a similar dish I learned at Sankō In. It's quick, easy and light.

2 medium heads pak choi	(shichimi togarashi)
I large piece of deep fried gluten (robai – see page 120)	pinch salt
	I teaspoon soy sauce
150 g/ 5 oz bean sprouts	I teaspoon vegetable oil
	½ teaspoon toasted sesame oil
dash of seven spice pepper	

Wash the pak choi, and cut the leafy bit off the stem. Cut the stem into 3 cm/ I inch lengths. Cut the gluten into small squares about I cm/ ⅜ inch square. Rinse and drain the bean sprouts. Heat the oil in a wok and quickly throw in the gluten, stems and leaf of the pak choi, and finally the bean sprouts. Keep everything moving and cooking for about 2 minutes, until the bean sprouts are just cooked, the pak choi wilted and everything hot. Season with the salt, a dash of soy sauce and the pepper. Serve at once as a protein enhanced vegetable dish.

SPRING GREENS WITH RADISHES, ARAME
AND PLUM DRESSING
YASAI TO ARAME NO BAINIKU ZU

In this salad the greens are par boiled, but the two radishes are pressed, with salt. This is a very common technique in Japanese cooking, whereby root vegetables are salted, and pressed under heavy weights. It's a sort of quick pickling technique, and removes excess water from the vegetables, making them limp, but still crunchy. I decided to use two types of radish here for the colour, and the use of spring greens gives it a Western twist. Why not? The white and the red look lovely with the deep green cabbage and black *arame*, and the taste of *umeboshi* plum complements cabbage well. The quantities here make more dressing than you need (you don't want to drown the vegetables), but any excess will keep in the fridge for a week or so.

7 cm/ 3 inch length *daikon*	**PLUM DRESSING:**
6 red radishes	2 tablespoons *umeboshi* plum paste
½ teaspoon salt	(*bainiku*)
I medium head spring greens	I tablespoon rice vinegar
20 g/ ¾ oz dried *arame*	2 teaspoons *mirin*
	4 tablespoons *dashi*

First press the radishes. Peel the *daikon* and cut into wafer thin slices. Cut into half moons. Top and tail the red radishes and slice as thinly as possible. Mix together in a large bowl and add half a teaspoon salt. Mix well with your fingers. Place a small plate on top, which should cover the vegetables but not touch the sides of the bowl. If you have a wooden pickle lid you can use it here. Place a heavy weight on top – a 2lb or kilo weight, or cans of food. Leave for at least half hour. Meanwhile, wash the greens and chop into long strips, I cm/ ⅜ inch wide. Par boil for 2 minutes in boiling salted water until just cooked, then drain, plunge into cold water and drain again. Squeeze excess water out by hand. Put the *arame* into cold water and leave to soften (about 10 minutes). Drain well. Remove the plate and weights from the radishes. Pour off the water that has been liberated from the vegetables, and in your hands squeeze the radishes well to get rid of excess moisture. Taste the radish here – if it's too salty give it a light rinse, and squeeze again. Combine the dressing ingredients, adding the liquids to the plum paste bit by bit, to make a smooth paste. If it's too salty either add more *dashi* to dilute it, or add a little soy milk to make it creamier. Toss the salad in 2 or 3 tablespoons of dressing (to taste), and serve as a vinegared salad course.

CARROT AND ALFALFA SALAD WITH SESAME DRESSING
NINJIN TO MOYASHI NO GOMA AE

Although not a traditional Japanese dish, this salad encompasses the spirit of Japanese cuisine. I came up with it whilst cooking Japanese style macrobiotic lunches in London. Mung bean sprouts are more authentically oriental than alfalfa, but I like the delicate crispiness of alfalfa. The sesame dressing would traditionally be made with freshly ground sesame seeds, but again I've 'Westernised' it by using tahini, sesame paste.

6 medium carrots, grated roughly (on a Western grater)	2 tablespoons light tahini
	water to mix (about 125 ml/ 4 fl oz) depending on how thick or thin you want the dressing
1 pack alfalfa sprouts (or if making your own about 2 large handfuls)	
2 tablespoons toasted sunflower seeds	1 tablespoon light soy sauce

Bring some water to boil in a saucepan, and dunk the grated carrot in for 10 seconds to soften. Drain and press out excess water. Mix the carrot and sprouts together in a large bowl, using your fingers or chopsticks to prise the alfalfa apart and distribute evenly. Mix in the sunflower seeds. In a separate bowl add the water slowly to the tahini to make a creamy paste. Add the soy sauce. Test for seasoning, and add more soy sauce or water if desired. Combine the dressing and salad. This is quite rich, so only small portions are needed.

SUMMER

DEEP FRIED AUBERGINE WITH FRESH BROAD BEANS
NASU NO SORAMAME AE

This is another Sankō In Temple dish which, I think, is more than the sum of its parts. It's a dish for early summer, when broad beans appear in the markets. In Japan they are not sold in their pods as they are in Britain, but shelled. Little round baskets, the size of a small dinner plate, are piled with the ready shelled beans and offered for sale. I never found out who shelled them, but I was grateful all the same. In this recipe any previous work is welcome, as it involves some more fiddly work in preparation. It's worth it though. The cooked beans are pressed one by one out of their skins, and the pulp is mashed. If you can find someone to help then it's more fun, although personally I love squeezing the pulp out of the bean skin – it squeezes out easily, and is a beautiful vibrant green – nothing like the grey mush we usually associate with beans. The green contrasts beautifully with the purple, and the flouriness of the beans complements the oiliness of the aubergine. Do try to use small aubergines if you can, as they are fried skin side down to reduce the absorption of oil. If you fry large areas of cut flesh the dish will be too greasy.

36 large broad beans	4 small aubergines (or 2 larger ones) stalks removed, and cut in half, lengthwise
2 teaspoons *mirin*	
pinch salt	
vegetable oil for deep frying	

Cook the beans in lightly salted boiling water, for a few minutes until tender, (about 5 minutes will do). Drain and rinse in cold water. Make a little nick at the top of each bean and squeeze the pulp out into a grinding bowl. Discard the skins. Crush with a pestle (or fork). Mix in the *mirin* and salt. The mash should be slightly lumpy, not too smooth. Now you need to fry the aubergines. Heat the vegetable oil to 170C/ 340F on a medium heat. Place the aubergines skin side down and fry for about 3 minutes (longer if using bigger ones), until they begin to soften. Turn over and fry for a further minute, flesh side down, until just soft all the way through.

Drain well on kitchen paper. Cut diagonally into thick 2 cm/ ¾ inch slices.

Combine carefully with the mashed bean mixture, and serve in individual dishes, as a side dish. This could also make an interesting starter in a Western meal.

SIMMERED BROAD BEANS AND WAKAME
SORAMAME TO WAKAME NO NIMONO

Wakame is a very versatile sea vegetable, and ready dried and cut *wakame* is also very convenient. It's a quick and easy way of incorporating the goodness of sea vegetables into your diet. *Wakame* is also reputed to have anti-blood clotting properties, so, as well as being delicious, it's one of those things that helps guard against heart disease. This recipe celebrates summer, using fresh broad beans (never use canned). If you have time you can take the beans out of their skins once boiled (as in the previous recipe) and the colour will be even more attractively green.

25 g/1 oz dried *wakame*	500 ml/18 fl oz water
40 fresh broad beans	pinch salt
2 teaspoons caster sugar	1 teaspoon light soy sauce
4 tablespoons saké	

Soak the *wakame* in warm water to re-hydrate. When soft (about 5 minutes) drain and squeeze out excess water. Cook the beans in salted water and simmer for about 4 minutes until just cooked (not too soft). Cool and then either leave them in their skins or peel them. Dissolve the sugar in a saucepan with the saké, water, salt and soy sauce. (If you do have light soy sauce use it, as it will discolour the dish less, but it's not critical.) Add the *wakame* and beans, taking care not to break up the beans. Simmer lightly for about 5 minutes, until the flavours are absorbed. This can be served in individual bowls as a side dish, or family style in one bowl so people can help themselves. Left overs will keep a couple of days in the fridge, although the *wakame* may become a bit slimy. If you don't fancy that then you'd better eat it straight away!

AUBERGINE WITH MISO TOPPING
NASU DENGAKU

Small Japanese style aubergines are best for this dish. You'll also need two skewers for each piece (if you are being authentic). Alternatively you can simply pop them under the grill.

4 small aubergines (or 2 large ones)	I tablespoon vegetable oil
Dengaku miso toppings (see the recipe for Tofu with Miso Topping, *Tōfu Dengaku* page 62)	skewers (optional)

Wash the aubergines and remove some of the stem and calyx, but keep a little to retain the shape. Cut them in half lengthwise. Score the cut edge with a criss cross of cuts about 2 mm depth (this helps absorb the topping). If you are using very large aubergines it's best to cut them into thick round slices abut 2 cm / ¾ inch thick (again score on one side). Lightly brush with vegetable oil (this stops them from becoming dry and tough). Holding the aubergine horizontally, put two skewers into it side by side vertically, making a slight V shape as the width between them increases towards the top (like a fan shape). Heat the grill to medium hot.

Grill each side for a few minutes until soft. Apply the miso topping thickly to the scored side, and grill a few seconds more. Serve at once, whilst hot.

GRILLED AUBERGINE WITH BONITO FLAKES
YAKI NASU

A classic dish to accompany drinking in an *izakaya* in summer. The spiciness of the ginger, and richness of the bonito flakes (*katsuo*) makes a hearty tasting dish from a fairly bland vegetable. And it couldn't be easier. This would make a good starter in a Western style meal, or the grilled (*yaki mono*) dish in a Japanese one.

2 large or 4 small aubergines	2 tablespoons soy sauce
4 tablespoons fine bonito flakes (*hana katsuo*)	2 teaspoons freshly grated ginger

If using small aubergines you can grill them whole. If large ones cut them in half lengthways. Place them under a grill (or over a charcoal brazier) and grill slowly until the skin separates from the flesh. Turn them from time to time during this process.

Then peel the skin away (you may find it easier to do this under water), but leave the stem end on to keep them intact. Cut whole aubergines in half and make three long cuts along the length of each piece, to about half way up. Lay on a plate (2 pieces per person) so these pieces fan out (it makes them easier to eat with chopsticks, and anyway they look nice). Sprinkle a spoonful of the bonito flakes (*katsuo*) on top, and a small mound of ginger. Serve with a drizzle of soy sauce over. Eat hot.

SUMMER VEGETABLE TEMPURA
YASAI TEMPURA

Tempura is one of the classics of Japanese cuisine, its light crispy batter (called *koromo*) being renowned all over the world. In fact this method of deep frying is not truly Japanese in origin at all, but was almost certainly introduced by the Portuguese, who visited Japan as missionaries, in the sixteenth century. Being devout Christians, they ate deep fried fish on their holy days, or *tempora* days. The Japanese adapted it, and *tempora* became *tempura*. These days it's not only fish that's 'tempura'ed', although it is very popular (particularly the large Tiger prawn called *ebi*). Vegetables are also a firm favourite, and can simply be adjusted to suit the season. Tempura is usually served with freshly grated raw *daikon* radish, and there's a very good reason for it. Just as the British eat fish and chips with vinegar, the *daikon* helps to cut the oiliness of deep fried food, and make it more digestible.

The secret of making crispy light tempura is to make the batter immediately before you need to use it (unlike making pancakes) and don't beat the batter too much. Just lightly mix the ingredients together, using chopsticks, and leave lumps of flour in it. (Some chefs don't even mix the batter at all, but have separate bowls of flour, and egg and water mixture. The food is dipped into the egg/water, then the flour, then the egg/water again and finally the flour.) This results in the light lacy effect which is a hallmark of good tempura. The water used *must* be ice cold – you can even add ice cubes to the batter, and the fat must be hot. When the ice cold batter hits the hot oil it puffs up and creates air and steam between the coating and the food inside. Because of all these requirements the very best tempura in Japan is served at specialist tempura restaurants, where dedicated chefs churn out freshly cooked tempura, from freshly mixed batter, for each individual order. Like sushi bars, the customer sits watching the chef as he prepares each morsel, which is placed before you to be eaten immediately.

Traditionally, a wife at home would never expect to eat tempura with her husband and guests – she'd be too busy slaving away in the kitchen, making sure everything was freshly fried. The crispy hot morsels are dipped into a light broth, called *tentsuyu*, and into which each diner mixes grated *daikon* and ginger. Sometimes instead of the broth, tempura is served simply with crushed salt.

The quality and freshness of the oil is also crucial to the taste. Tired oil ruins it. In fact the most exclusive tempura restaurants in Japan use their oil only once. It is then passed on (sold) to lesser establishments, who will use it a few times more.

You can use almost any vegetable you like, but the following are typical. Do not use dense root vegetables (such as *daikon*) that require long cooking (unless you par boil them first) as they will burn before they cook. Fresh *shiitake* are preferable to dried here. In fact in one exclusive tempura joint I was served fresh *shiitake* stems, coated in batter and deep fried, and they were delicious.

DIPPING SAUCE (*TENTSUYU*):
250 ml/9 fl oz *dashi*
80 ml/ 3½ fl oz *mirin*
80 ml/ 3½ fl oz soy sauce (or use light soy sauce and omit the salt)
½ teaspoon salt

A variety of seasonal vegetables, cut into large bite-size pieces which are easy to hold with chopsticks:
2 small green peppers, de-seeded and cut into four
2 small courgettes, cut into diagonal slices (or juliennes)
2 small aubergines, halved and cut into fan shapes (see drawing) or
1 aubergine cut into rounds
4 fresh *shiitake* mushrooms, stems separated from cap

4 perilla (*shiso*) leaves
20 small green beans, arranged in bunches of 5 (parboil first)
2 large carrots, cut into medium juliennes about 5 cm/ 2 inches long

BATTER:
250 g /9 oz plain flour (sift first)
375 ml/ 13 fl oz iced water (a thin batter gives a lighter coating)
1 egg
extra flour (to dip the ingredients in before coating with batter)

½ medium *daikon* radish, peeled and grated on a fine grater
2 teaspoons grated ginger
rapeseed (or other vegetable) oil for deep frying

Prepare the dipping sauce by combining the ingredients in a small pan and bringing to a boil. Divide between four individual dipping bowls. Divide the grated *daikon* and ginger into four, and place a mound for each person on a side dish (or you can be creative and use a small shell, or a leaf). After washing and cutting the vegetables as instructed dry them well on kitchen paper. Line up your vegetables, flour on a plate and batter, so the vegetables are 1) dipped in flour, 2) dipped in batter and 3) placed into the hot oil. Then, on the other side of the deep fryer, have a wire draining basket and kitchen paper. In addition you'll need a mesh spoon for scooping off bits of stray batter from the oil, and long chopsticks (or tongs) to retrieve the morsels from the oil. Japanese tempura chefs use thick wooden chopsticks to mix the batter, and dip the ingredients, then fine metal chopsticks to fish them out of the oil. Both of these are a bit tricky to use, and take a bit of practise, so wooden cooking chopsticks will do for both. Long chopsticks are essential though to avoid splashing yourself with hot fat, but don't ever use lacquered ones – the lacquer melts in the hot oil!

Mix your batter whilst you are bringing the oil to temperature, 170C/340F.

If you don't have a temperature gauge you can test the oil by flicking in a drop of batter. It should sink and then float to the surface. If it just sinks it's too cool, and if it rises immediately it's too hot. Quickly and lightly mix the egg, water and flour, leaving lumps of dry flour, and keeping the batter cool. (You can put ice cubes in the batter itself and also stand the batter bowl in a larger bowl of iced wate.) Dip the vegetables in the flour (by hand if you like) and shake off any excess, then into the batter and then into the oil, being careful not to splash. Cooking time depends on the ingredient – but around 3 minutes is average. You want a fairly light golden coating. Be careful not to fry too many pieces at once as it will lower the temperature of the oil. The perilla (shiso) leaves should not be coated in flour, and only one side of the leaf is coated in batter. (Use your fingers to do this.) (The same goes for pieces of nori, when you tempura them.) The carrots and the bean juliennes are held together with your chopsticks in a little bundle. This bundle is coated in the batter, and slid carefully into the oil, whilst still holding them together. The batter encases them as it cooks, stopping them falling apart.

If possible serve immediately, passing pieces to the diners as you go. Crisp tempura is so much nicer than soggy. If you can't do this then keep the tempura hot, but don't allow pieces to touch each other, as the batter will stick together. The dipping sauce is served in small individual bowls, and the daikon and ginger mixed in, for each diner to dip as they like.

TOFU AND FENNEL WITH SESAME AND MISO
TŌFU TO AMAUIKYO NO GOMA MISO AE

I invented this one day when pondering what to do with a fennel bulb at the macrobiotic lunch club where I was cooking. Fennel has a lovely crisp texture and distinctive taste which lifts tofu out of the ordinary.

I pack cotton (firm) tofu	4 tablespoons water
DRESSING:	½ teaspoon toasted sesame oil
I tablespoon tahini (sesame paste)	2 teaspoons vegetable oil
I tablespoon sweet white miso	I small fennel bulb, cut into thin slices,
I teaspoon soy sauce	and then into thirds

Drain the tofu in a cloth and under weights for 30 minutes, to get rid of excess moisture. In a small bowl mix the tahini, miso and soy sauce, adding the water slowly and mixing well to avoid lumps. The tahini will thicken, and then become thin again as you add more water. Cut the tofu into small cubes about 2 cm/ ¾ inch. Heat the oils in a wok or heavy bottomed pan. Sauté the fennel for 2 minutes then add the tofu. Keep the mixture moving to avoid the tofu sticking, but try not to break up the tofu, and sauté for another minute. Lower the heat, add the dressing ingredients, mix carefully, and remove immediately. Serve hot.

COURGETTE WITH SESAME AND MISO DRESSING
ZUKINI NO GOMA MISO AE

Courgettes are another summer vegetable that tend to come in gluts. Here's another simple way of serving them. The sesame dressing makes this into a rich dish, so keep servings small, as a side dish.

2 tablespoons sesame seeds, toasted	2 medium courgettes
2 tablespoons sweet white miso	I tablespoon oil for frying
2 tablespoons saké	

Toast the sesame seeds until just beginning to pop. Remove, and grind in a pestle and mortar (*suribachi*). Add the miso and saké, blending well to remove lumps from the mixture (bits of sesame seed are fine though).

Cut the courgettes into thick 2 cm/ ¾ inch diagonal slices. Heat the oil in a wok or frying pan. Fry the courgette slices until just beginning to get soft. They should not be mushy but still slightly crisp. Remove from the heat and combine with the sesame paste (use a rubber spatula to mix the slices in the *suribachi* if possible). Serve hot. This goes soggy if it's left to stand too long, as the water from the courgettes leaches into the dressing.

COURGETTES IN THICK SOUP
ZUKINI NO ANKAKE

Another simple but refined way of serving courgettes which retains the shape and colour of the vegetable. This can also be served chilled, but I think the thick soup may be more appealing to non-Japanese if hot. Again it would make an unusual starter, or can be served as a side dish in a Japanese meal.

4 small courgettes	I tablespoon *mirin*
I tablespoon *kuzu* (or *katakuriko*)	2 teaspoon ginger juice (squeezed from
600 ml/ I pint *dashi*	freshly grated ginger)
I tablespoon soy sauce	

Cut the courgettes into thick (I cm/ ⅜ inch) slices diagonally, and then into juliennes, so each piece has green on either end. Parboil in salted boiling water for about 30 seconds until just beginning to soften. Remove from the heat and drain. Mix the *kuzu* (or potato) starch with a little cold water to a thin paste. In a saucepan add to the *dashi* and other ingredients (except ginger juice). Bring to a gentle boil over a medium heat, and keep stirring whilst the mixture thickens. Take off the heat and add the courgette pieces. Divide between four bowls, and pour ½ teaspoon of the ginger juice over each bowl. Serve hot.

GREEN BEANS WITH MISO DRESSING
SAYAINGEN NO MISO AE

Green beans in Japanese are *ingen* – named after the monk who is supposed to have brought them over to Japan from China three hundred years ago. The young bean is *saya ingen*. This is a simple miso dressing, using the sweet white miso which is a hall mark of Zen temple food. You can also try this miso dressing with brussels sprouts – just make sure they are not overcooked, and still slightly crisp, and green.

DRESSING:	½ teaspoon Japanese mustard
3 tablespoons sweet white miso	
I teaspoon medium miso	*yuzu* peel or powder
I tablespoon sake	250 g/ 9 oz green beans, washed and
I tablespoon water	trimmed

Mix the dressing, adding the saké and water to the miso slowly, and mixing to a smooth paste. Add the mustard. Parboil the beans in plenty of salted boiling water for about 3 minutes, until just beginning to cook, so they are crisp but not raw. Drain and plunge immediately into cold water to arrest the cooking and retain the colour. Drain well. Chop the beans into four and mix gently with the dressing. Sprinkle the *yuzu* powder (or a squeeze of lime juice) on top, and serve at room temperature. This makes a good side dish or buffet dish.

WAKAME AND CUCUMBER SALAD
KYŪRI TO WAKAME NO SUNOMONO

This is an easy way of incorporating sea vegetables (and the accompanying calcium and fibre) into your diet. This salad can be used as a side dish in a Western style meal or as part of a full Japanese spread. The sweetish vinegar dressing makes it very refreshing in summer. The trick here is to slice the cucumber very thinly, so, after letting it stand in the salt for a while, it loses its shape, but not its crunchiness. Salting vegetables so they lose some of their water is a typical Japanese way of serving and preparing salads – the Japanese don't go in for Cranks' style chunky salads with raw vegetables. Don't let the salad stand in the dressing too long before serving or it will become watery.

25 g/ I oz dried *wakame*	2 tablespoons caster sugar
(cut *wakame* is even easier)	½ teaspoon soy sauce
2 small cucumbers (or ½ large one)	3 cm/ I inch piece of fresh ginger (for
⅓ teaspoon salt	garnish)
5 tablespoons rice vinegar	
(plus a bit extra)	

Soak the *wakame* in cold water for 10 minutes to soften. Rinse in cold water and squeeze. Sprinkle I tablespoon vinegar over it. If you use large pieces of *wakame* you will have to cut off the hard spine, and then chop it into 3 cm/ 1 inch lengths.

Score the skin of each cucumber by running the tines of a fork down the length of it. If using a large one, then spilt it in half and scoop the seeds out. Slice the cucumber as finely as you can (wafer thin) using a thrusting cut (*tsuki giri*), and sprinkle the salt over the slices. Let stand for 5 minutes until soft and watery, and then rinse off the salt and squeeze thoroughly. Mix the vinegar, soy sauce and sugar, making sure the sugar is dissolved. Chop the ginger into fine matchsticks (*mijin giri*). Combine the *wakame*, cucumber and dressing and garnish with the ginger.

Optional extras
You can also add tiny dried shrimps or *shirasuboshi* (tiny baby sardines, sold dried) for extra flavour.

 ## SPINACH WITH SESAME DRESSING
HŌRENSŌ NO GOMA AE

This is a real classic – served at home, in temples, *izakaya* and restaurants in Japan and abroad. The simple ground sesame dressing is a favourite with spinach, but can be used with other vegetables such as mange tout, green beans, watercress, chrysanthemum leaves – even burdock root – anything that is fresh and available.

Cook the spinach lightly. You don't want a pulp – but to be able to discern the leaf shape. Sesame is rich in calcium and vitamin E, so be generous with it.

1 large bunch fresh spinach (350 g/12 oz)	1 teaspoon caster sugar (or *mirin*)
3 tablespoons white sesame seeds	1 tablespoon soy sauce

Wash the spinach well. Plunge it into an inch of salted boiling water (it doesn't need submerging). Cook for 20 seconds, then remove and plunge immediately into cold water. This arrests the cooking and retains the vivid green colour. Drain and squeeze out excess water (don't be fainthearted about this – you don't want it watery). You can use a bamboo rolling mat (*makisu*) to help you do this, if you like. Cut the spinach into large (about 3 cm/ 1 inch) pieces. In a small jug dissolve the sugar in the soy sauce.

Toast the sesame seeds in a heavy skillet or sesame roaster, moving them around to prevent them from burning. When they start to pop remove from the heat. Put into a large *suribachi* (grinding bowl) and grind with a heavy circular movement until they are fine, but not a paste – little bits of rough seeds mixed in with them is OK. This is an extremely pleasant task – I love it. If you sit on a chair and steady the bowl between your legs it is not hard work, and quite meditative. The grinding also releases a wonderful aroma. The bits of sesame that get stuck in between the grooves in the bowl can be scraped out with a fork or pointed chopstick. I have a wonderful little brush made from split bamboo, which I got in Japan, and is exactly the right tool for this job, but a chopstick will do fine. Next add the soy sauce mixture, and then combine with the spinach (use chopsticks or your fingers to combine). Serve a small mound of the salad in small deep bowls, individually, as a side dish.

Variation: Walnut dressing

An interesting variation on this can be made with ground walnuts, instead of sesame seeds. The nuns at Sankō In Temple were great improvisers, and were always on the look out for ways to use up what they had, rather than going out and buying expensive ingredients. They were regularly given large quantities of walnuts by one of the local people, and this is one of the ways they devised to use them. It was an inspired idea as walnuts are rich in alpha-linolenic acid, one of the fatty acids our bodies need to stay healthy, and which has been suggested as one of the ways to help prevent heart disease. I think this is a great way of incorporating walnuts into a healthy diet – better than eating large quantities of walnut cake, which is probably somewhat self-defeating.

To make the walnut version follow the instructions exactly but substitute 3 tablespoons of chopped walnuts for the sesame seeds, toast and grind them in the same way.

BOILED SPINACH WITH BONITO FLAKES
O-HITASHI

This is a quicker version of the classic dish, O-hitashi, where spinach is soused in chilled and seasoned dashi, and served with a simple topping of katsuo – dried bonito flakes. The katsuo is rich in protein, and full of flavour, so don't be stingy – pile it on!

For this dish the spinach is formed into a roll and cut into 3 cm/ 1 inch lengths which are placed cut side down on to a small plate.

FLAVOURING:	salt
2 tablespoons soy sauce (light if possible)	1 large bunch/ 350 g / 12 oz spinach, with roots attached
4 tablespoons dashi stock	4 tablespoons finely shredded bonito flakes (katsuobushi)
1 teaspoon mirin	

First combine the flavouring ingredients in a small saucepan. Bring to a boil and remove from heat. Leave to cool, or force cool by transferring to a bowl and standing in iced water.

Wash the spinach well, but keep the roots on. (This will help you keep the spinach in a tidy bunch.) Plunge it into an inch of salted boiling water (it doesn't need covering). After 20 seconds remove and plunge immediately into cold water. This arrests the cooking and retains the vivid green colour. Drain and squeeze out excess water as in previous recipe. Chop off the roots (you can serve these separately if you like, as they do in the temples. Just be sure they are clean). Cut the 'roll' into 3cm/ 1 inch lengths and place one or two pieces, cut side down (like sushi rolls), on a small side plate.

Drizzle the flavouring liquid lightly over the spinach rounds. Sprinkle the bonito flakes generously on top of each.

This is good with any tender leafy green vegetable. Instead of spinach you can use watercress or chrysanthemum leaves, and it's equally good with green beans or bean sprouts. Be sure to serve chilled.

CUCUMBER WITH SESAME AND MUSTARD DRESSING
KYŪRI NO GOMA KARASHI AE

This is a refined and elegant dish from Sankō In Temple, light and rich at the same time. It's also extremely easy. If you can use Japanese style 'baby' cucumbers then do so – they are less watery because they have fewer seeds. This recipe again incorporates the typical Japanese technique of salting vegetables. This rids them of excess water, but still retains crispness.

2 small cucumbers, or one large one	I tablespoon rice vinegar
½ teaspoon salt	I teaspoon soy sauce
2 tablespoons white sesame seeds	½ teaspoon Japanese mustard (*karashi*)
½ teaspoon caster sugar	

Score the skin of each cucumber by running the prongs of a fork down the length of it. If using a large one, then spilt it in half and scoop the seeds out. Slice the cucumber as finely as you can (wafer thin) using a thrusting cut (*tsuki giri*). Place the slices in a large bowl and sprinkle with the salt. Mix with fingers to coat well. Place a saucer, small plate or pickle lid on top and weigh down with weights or cans, making sure the saucer doesn't touch the rim of the bowl – you need the whole weight on top of the cucumbers to press the water out. Leave for at least 30 minutes. Meanwhile mix the dressing – toast the sesame seeds until they start to pop. Remove from heat and grind in a *suribachi*, leaving bits of seed (you don't want sesame butter). Dissolve the sugar in the vinegar and add the mustard. Add to the ground sesame. Rinse the cucumber lightly under running water, and squeeze out remaining moisture. Combine with the dressing, gently mixing with fingers, chopsticks or rubber spatula. Serve as a side salad.

 ## CORN ON THE COB WITH NORI
NORI TOMOROKOSHI

Corn on the cob is a popular food at summer festivals in the grounds of Shinto shrines. It's grilled over charcoal braziers until just scorched and tender, and served either just as it is or with a drizzle of soy sauce. No wonder the Japanese are healthy; instead of candy floss, Japanese kids scream for '*tomorokoshi*' (corn on the cob).

This is an enhanced version, inspired by Shibuya-San, an elegant and entertaining 'mama-san' who used to run a little bar called Lamp many years ago in Koenji in Tokyo. This was where I first ate sweet corn with *nori* (and melted butter). I was instantly converted to the combination of *nori* and corn. As butter is not an indigenous Japanese ingredient I have re-converted Shibuya-San's recipe to a more authentic (and healthier) Japanese style by using soy sauce instead. So – if you love sweet corn, but don't want melted butter, this is the answer.

2 large corn on the cob	2 tablespoons green laver (*nori*) flakes
salt	(*ao nori*)
	I tablespoon soy sauce

Cook the corn by plunging into ample boiling and salted water. Boil for 10 minutes until cooked and bright yellow. Remove and chop into two halves. Place one on each plate, and sprinkle with the *ao nori* flakes. Drizzle soy sauce over.

If you like you can grill or barbecue the corn instead, in which case brush it with a little soy sauce during cooking.

Variation: In Japanese shops you can find something called *edomurasaki*. It's a paste, sold in a jar, made from mashed up *nori* and soy sauce. It's supposed to be eaten with hot rice, but I think it's wonderful spread on corn on the cob. You can try it spread on cheese on toast too!

YAM CAKE NOODLES AND BEAN SPROUT SALAD WITH VINEGAR MUSTARD DRESSING
SHIRATAKI TO MOYASHI NO KARASHI ZU

When *konnyaku* is made into noodles instead of blocks, it's called *shirataki*. You can buy it water packed in Japanese shops, and occasionally dried, which you have to re-hydrate.

200 g/7 oz bean sprouts	3 tablespoons rice vinegar
200 g/7 oz *shirataki* noodles	I teaspoon vegetable oil (such as
DRESSING:	rapeseed)
I teaspoon ready mixed Japanese	I teaspoon sweet white miso
mustard	(*Saikyō* miso)
3 teaspoons *mirin*	I teaspoon soy sauce

Immerse the bean sprouts in a pan of boiling water for 30 seconds then remove with a slotted spoon and drain. Add the *shirataki* noodles and boil for 5 minutes. Remove, place in cold water to cool and drain. Chop into 3 cm/ I inch lengths. Combine the dressing ingredients and mix to a smooth paste. Squeeze out any excess water from the sprouts and noodles and combine with the dressing. Serve immediately at room temperature.

WATERCRESS WITH TOFU, MISO AND PLUM DRESSING
KURESON NO MISO SHIRA AE

½ block firm tofu	2 teaspoons saké
200 g/7 oz watercress	2 tablespoons sweet white miso
2 teaspoons white sesame seeds,	(*Saikyō* miso)
toasted	I teaspoon *umeboshi* (pickled plum)
I teaspoon caster sugar	paste (*bainiku*)

Drain the tofu in a cloth under weights for 30 minutes to remove moisture (as described in the section on tofu, page 58). Par boil the watercress for 30 seconds in boiling salted water. Remove, and plunge into cold water to arrest cooking. Drain and squeeze out excess moisture. Chop roughly. In a *suribachi* grind the sesame seeds. Add the tofu and grind further until the tofu is fairly well mashed up. In a separate bowl dissolve the sugar in the saké, and add the miso and *ume* paste. Mix to a smooth paste. Add to the tofu and sesame in the *suribachi* and mix well. Combine with the chopped watercress, and serve as a protein-rich side salad.

CAULIFLOWER, CARROTS, BROCCOLI AND ARAME WITH BONITO
KARIFURAWA TO ARAME NO OKAKA AE

The combination of colours in this cooked salad is very appealing – orange, white, green and black. This is fine prepared in advance and served at room temperature.

200 g/7 oz cauliflower	3 tablespoons *katsuobushi*
200 g/ 7 oz broccoli	(fine dried bonito) flakes
I large carrot, cut into thin slices, and	2 tablespoons soy sauce
then flowers (or juliennes)	2 teaspoons grated ginger
20 g/ ¾ oz dried *arame*, reconstituted	
in water	

Tear the broccoli and cauliflower into bite size florets and parboil in boiling salted water for about 3 minutes until just cooked, but still with a bite. Remove, plunge into cold water and drain. Parboil the carrots in the same water for 30 seconds until just softened. Remove and drain. Drain the *arame* when softened. Mix the bonito, soy sauce and grated ginger, and combine with the vegetables.

GREEN BEANS AND ENOKITAKE IN WALNUT DRESSING
INGEN TO ENOKI NO KURUMI AE

Enokitake mushrooms are the small white stringy ones which have recently appeared in British shops. They've been a favourite in Japan for a long while. This is a interesting way to serve them. The walnut dressing is quite rich.

200 g/ 7 oz green beans	2 tablespoons *mirin*
125 g/ 4 oz *enokitake* mushrooms, the	I tablespoon soy sauce
mycelium 'root' removed	I tablespoon sake
DRESSING:	
75 g/ 3 oz walnuts	

Parboil the beans, ends trimmed, in boiling salted water for about 3 minutes until just beginning to cook. Remove with slotted spoon and plunge into cold iced water. Drain well. In the same water parboil the mushrooms – dunking them for only 30 seconds until just not raw. Cool in cold water and then leave to drain. In a skillet or frying pan lightly roast the walnuts. Remove and place in a *suribachi*, grind roughly so bits of walnut still remain. Use a small bamboo 'scraper' if you have one to remove the bits of walnut from the grooves, and 'sweep' them to the centre of the bowl (or use pointed chopsticks). Combine the liquid ingredients, then add to the walnut and combine to make a paste. Squeeze excess moisture from the beans and mushrooms and gently combine with the dressing.

TOFU AND ASPARAGUS IN AGAR AGAR JELLY
TŌFU TO ASUPARA NO KANTEN

Square metal moulds with a removable lining for easier turning out are the authentic way of making this, but you can experiment with other moulds. For maximum beauty you also really need a flower shaped cutter to cut the tofu into large blossom or leaf shapes. The resulting 'white blossom' tofu and the green asparagus spears look lovely glistening through the amber coloured agar agar (*kanten*) jelly – the Japanese (and vegetarian) version of aspic. *Kanten* doesn't melt as readily as gelatine so it's ideal for hot weather – it sets quickly and looks cooling. You'll need a mould that holds at least 850 ml/1½ pints. If you have a square metal Japanese *nagashibako*, so much the better. The inside lifts out to help you turn it out neatly.

14 g/ ½ oz agar agar flakes	block)
700 ml/ 1¼ pints *dashi* (well strained), page 49	2-3 spears asparagus
	4 tablespoons soy sauce
½ block 'silk' soft tofu (or 1 long life	½ teaspoon ginger juice

Put the agar agar into the *dashi* in a saucepan and leave to soak for 10 minutes, to soften. Cut the tofu into flower shapes, or squares or triangles if you don't have a cutter. Take your mould (square if possible) and wet it inside. Then stand it in a larger dish or tray (later you will pour cold water into this to force cool the mould). Place 2 or 3 shapes of tofu into the wetted square mould, or deep dish. Parboil the asparagus until cooked, plunge immediately into ice cold water to keep the colour, and cut off the hard end stems. Arrange 2 or 3 spears asymmetrically alongside the tofu flowers.

Put the agar agar and *dashi* on to the heat and bring to a boil. Simmer until the flakes are completely dissolved. Add the soy sauce and ginger juice and carefully pour over the tofu and asparagus. Now take a jug of iced water and pour it carefully into the larger dish, around the mould, thereby cooling it. Stop before the mould begins to float. When cool, put into fridge to chill, and turn out onto a glass plate to serve. Cut into four when ready to eat and serve as a side dish in summer. It would also make an elegant and light starter, or could be part of a summer buffet, Western style.

Variation: Your imagination is the limit here, as you can add anything you fancy instead of the tofu and asparagus. *Soba* buckwheat noodles and finely chopped spring onion are another good combination, both visually and taste wise. Just cook 115 g/ 4 oz *soba* noodles, cool, and chop 1 tablespoon chopped spring onion, and put into the mould instead of the tofu and asparagus.

AUTUMN

I used to think that pumpkins were overrated, rather watery and tasteless. That was before I went to Japan and discovered *kabocha*. Otherwise known as Hokkaido pumpkin, *kabocha* has a creamy, dense, yellow flesh, which is very sweet. Butternut squash and Turk's cap are similar and can be used instead. When I left Japan I was so keen to have Japanese *kabocha* that I kept seeds and brought them to England for my father to grow. He can grow almost anything, but he's especially famous for his pumpkins. Pretty soon we were harvesting our own *kabocha*, in Herefordshire, thousands of miles from Japan, and taking seed from them for the following year. He's been growing them every year since, and I've been cooking, and eating, them. Since those early days they have become much more available in the shops, but of course there's nothing like the thrill of harvesting your own.

SIMMERED PUMPKIN
KABOCHA NO NIMONO

This classic and very simple way of cooking *kabocha* brings out the sweet and delicious flavour. It also looks very pretty, with the mottled skin. You can add fresh *shiitake* mushrooms if you like.

---

350 g/ 12 oz *kabocha* (or similar) pumpkin	1 tablespoon *mirin*
350 ml/ 12 fl oz *dashi* (page 49)	1 tablespoon light soy sauce

---

Wash the *kabocha* well. Now, using a pushing cut (*oshi giri*) and a very sharp knife, and holding your hands on top of the knife, cut it in half. Then remove the seeds and fibrous insides (you can keep these for next year's crop if you fancy having a go at growing your own). Next you want to remove some, but not all, of its skin. You want a mottled effect of bits of green and yellow. This stops the flesh from falling apart, allows flavour to be absorbed, and looks attractive. Using the same cutting technique, and keeping your fingers well out of the way, chop the pumpkin into large irregular pieces, about 5 cm/ 2 inches a piece, and then trim bits of skin away, to create the mottled effect.

Put the *dashi*, *mirin* and salt into a large saucepan and add the cut pumpkin. Bring to a boil, lower the heat and put a lid on (drop lid if you have one). Simmer slowly for about 15 to 20 minutes, until the flesh is tender. Serve either family style in a large bowl or in small dishes with an extra drizzle of soy sauce if desired.

PUMPKIN AND AZUKI BEANS
KABOCHA TO AZUKI NO NIMONO

Kabocha and *azuki* beans is a classic autumn combination, and a classic colour combination too. The deep yellow pumpkin looks beautiful with the dark red of the beans. This is practically a meal in itself – in fact served with rice, soup and pickles it would be a handsome country style repast.

150 g/ 5 oz (dry weight) *azuki* beans
1x 8 cm/ 3 inch piece *kombu* (kelp)
450 g/ 1 lb *kabocha* or similar pumpkin
pinch salt

yuzu zest (or powder)
soy sauce to taste

Soak the *azuki* beans in cold water overnight. The next day throw away this water, then, in a large saucepan place the *azuki* beans and the *kombu*, and plenty of fresh water. Bring to a boil, and boil rapidly for 5 minutes. Drain and throw this water away, but keep the *kombu*. Place the beans in a large pot with 1.4 litres/ 2½ pints fresh water and the *kombu*. Bring to a boil, reduce the heat and simmer, covered, until cooked but not mushy (should be about 40 minutes, but may be longer). They will only be cooked for another 20 minutes or so after this, so they need to be pretty much done at this stage. If they are not, keep simmering, and adding more water until they are. Meanwhile, cut the *kabocha* in half and remove the seeds and fibrous insides (you can keep these for next year's crop if you fancy having a go at growing your own). Wash the pumpkin well, and remove all the skin. Using a very sharp knife, and holding your hands on top of the knife, chop the pumpkin into large irregular pieces, about 4 cm/ 1½ inches a piece. When the beans are almost cooked remove the *kombu* and place the pieces of pumpkin on top (if the water has dried up, add a little more, but not too much. The water should cover the beans but not the pumpkin, reaching about a third of the way up the pumpkin, so it half steams, half simmers). Add a pinch of salt, 1 teaspoon soy sauce, the *yuzu* zest (or powder), cover and simmer gently until the pumpkin is soft, and the beans cooked (it doesn't matter if they are a bit mushy). Serve in individual bowls, or family style heaped in one large bowl in the centre of the table. This can be served hot or at room temperature.

PUMPKIN AND LOTUS ROOT DUMPLINGS SIMMERED IN BROTH
KABOCHA TO RENKON DANGO

200 g/7 oz Hokkaido pumpkin, peeled
　and de-seeded
2 medium (about 12 cm/5 inches) lotus
　roots (canned is not suitable)
2-3 tablespoons rice flour
salt
oil for deep frying

FOR SIMMERING:
400 ml/ 14 fl oz *dashi* (page 49)
1 tablespoon saké
1 teaspoon soy sauce
pinch salt
Japanese mustard to serve

Cut the pumpkin into 2 cm/ ¾ inch chunks. Place in a steamer of boiling water and steam until soft – about 10-15 minutes. Peel the lotus root and grate on a fine Japanese style grater, so you have a pulp. (It will slightly discolour but don't worry.)

Squeeze out excess water. In a large bowl or *suribachi* mash the cooked pumpkin and the lotus root together. Add the salt, then the flour, bit by bit, until you have a fairly stiff paste. Take a tablespoonful of the mixture and with your hands form into small balls, about 2 cm/ ¾ inch in diameter. Heat the oil to medium high (about 160C/320F) and deep fry the balls until golden. Drain on kitchen paper. Combine the simmering ingredients in a medium size saucepan, and bring to a boil. Add the dumplings and simmer for 5 minutes, until the dumplings are slightly softened, but not falling apart (you can use a drop lid here if you have one). Serve hot – 3 pieces per person in medium size deep bowls, with a dab of mustard to taste.

PUMPKIN 'CHESTNUTS'
KABOCHA NO KURI

This dish employs one of the fancy decorative techniques used in tea ceremony cuisine. I first saw it being done at Kaisaku – an elegant (and expensive) restaurant in the centre of Tokyo in Akasaka, where the chefs, in perfect harmony, and incredibly cramped conditions turned out the most gorgeous looking dishes. This dish resembles chestnuts – in their prickly outer coating. It's all artifice – done with noodles. The basic mixture is the same as in the previous recipe, but before deep frying you roll each ball in chopped up lengths of dried noodles. Because these are not simmered after deep frying less flour is used to make a softer mixture. This makes them tricky to handle, and although the result can be stunning it is a bit fiddly. This is one for the adventurous.

200 g/7 oz Hokkaido pumpkin, peeled and de-seeded	salt
2 medium (about 12 cm/5 inches) lotus roots (canned is not suitable)	½ pack *sōmen* noodles, broken into small strands 1 cm/ ⅜ inch long
1 tablespoon rice flour	plain flour to coat the balls before frying
	oil for deep frying

Prepare the basic pumpkin and lotus root mixture as in the previous recipe, using less flour in the mixture. Scatter the broken noodles onto a flat plate. Put some sifted plain flour on another plate. Form small balls of mixture and roll them first in the flour, to seal, and then in the noodles. You may need to stick some of the noodles individually into the balls as well as roll them, as you want 'spikes' of noodle sticking out, and you don't want them to fall off. The idea is that it resembles the prickly outer coating of a chestnut. Carefully slide the coated balls into the hot oil and deep fry for about 3 minutes, until the inside is cooked, and the 'thorns' golden. Serve hot.

FRESH SHIITAKE IN BUTTER AND LEMON JUICE
SHIITAKE NO BATAA YAKI

I am very happy that fresh *shiitake* are now more readily available outside Japan, but I still regard them as a little bit of a delicacy. One of the big thrills of living in Togoshi Ginza, in Tokyo, on the street of one of the best vegetable markets in the city, was being able to completely indulge myself in fresh *shiitake*. I could buy a plateful for the equivalent of fifty pence and fry them up for breakfast. I have a memorable photograph of myself holding two huge *shiitake* specimens – one in each hand and bigger than either of them. Because they have such a rich flavour and meaty texture I like to eat them just as they are. Sautéed in butter with a little lemon juice and black pepper, and served on a stoneware plate to reflect their earthy origins, they make a delectable side dish or starter. Again this is a typical *izakaya* dish.

12 large (they don't have to be hand size!) *shiitake* mushrooms	freshly ground black pepper
large knob of unsalted butter	squeeze of lemon juice from half a lemon
pinch salt	

Cut the stalks off the mushrooms. In a heavy bottom skillet or frying pan melt the butter. Place the *shiitake*, cap side down and sauté for a minute. Turn over and sprinkle with the salt and lemon juice and cover. Turn down the heat to very low and leave them to sweat for 2-3 minutes. Serve with freshly ground black pepper, cap side uppermost. Serve 3 mushrooms per person.

SHIITAKE AND KOMBU CONDIMENT
KOMBU TO SHIITAKE NO TSUKUDANI

This is a rich dish, to be served as a condiment with rice, in small quantities, as you would a pickle. It's a good way of using up *kombu* previously used for making *dashi* or cooking beans. *Tsukudani* is the process of simmering in soy sauce and sugar or *mirin*, resulting in a sweet, sticky and salty condiment, and it is also a popular technique for preserving small fish and beans.

10 small *shiitake* mushrooms	150 ml/ 5 fl oz *dashi* (page 49)
1 large piece of *kombu* sea vegetable (approx 12 x 7 cm/ 5 x 3 inch, left over from making *dashi*)	4 tablespoons soy sauce
	2 tablespoons saké
	3 tablespoons caster sugar

Slice the *shiitake* mushroom very thinly. Cut the *kombu* into thin matchstick slivers, about 2 cm/ ¾ inches long. Put into a small cooking pot with the flavouring ingredients and simmer, uncovered, over a low heat until the liquid is absorbed and the mushroom and *kombu* sticky.

SIMMERED SWEET POTATO WITH SHIITAKE
SATSUMAIMO TO SHIITAKE NO MISO NI

450 g/ 1 lb sweet potato	2 tablespoons light miso
8 *shiitake* mushrooms	2 spring onions, chopped finely
1 litre / 1¾ pints *dashi* (page 49)	

Peel the sweet potato and cut with a rolling cut (*ran giri*) to creat 16 irregular shaped pieces. Wipe the *shiitake* and cut off the stems. Place the sweet potato pieces in a large cooking pot with the *dashi*, and put the mushrooms on top. Bring to a boil, cover and simmer until the potato is soft (10-15 minutes). Dissolve the miso in a little of the cooking liquid. Add to the pot and take off the heat. Serve four pieces of potato and two mushrooms per person, in small deep dishes, and garnish with chopped spring onion.

SANKŌ IN AUTUMN TEMPURA (CHESTNUT, GINKGO AND PERSIMMON)
KURI TO GINNAN TO KAKI NO TEMPURA

This is a dish to celebrate autumn, and a speciality of Sankō In Temple, which is where I was first enraptured by it. The three ingredients are evocative of the season, and the use of persimmon is an unusual and inspired idea. This is best with firm persimmons, not the very soft fruits that are sometimes to be found on market stalls (often called sharon fruit in this country). To make the batter follow the instructions as for Summer Vegetable Tempura (page 136). I have used an egg in the batter although in the temples they would never do so. You can omit it if you wish.

Instead of serving your tempura on paper or a basket, as is usual, you can display it on an autumn leaf which is changing colour. I filmed the abbess doing exactly this. She had picked a handful of persimmon leaves from the tree in the temple grounds, for presentation; some were green, some completely red, and some changing colour. She was hesitating about which one to use for her display, then suddenly she chose – the only one with a hole in it! She then proceeded to cover the hole with the tempura! "How very Japanese" I thought – when the tempura is eaten, the hole in the leaf is revealed – a reminder of nature's capriciousness.

8 chestnuts	240 ml/ 8½ fl oz iced water (a thinner
24 ginkgo nuts	batter will give a thinner and lighter
2 large firm persimmons	coating)
	1 egg
FOR THE BATTER :	extra flour (to dip the ingredients in
150 g/ 6 oz plain flour (sift first)	before coating with batter)

First prepare the chestnuts. Make a small cut in the top of the shell of each chestnut, and boil in a small saucepan for 5 minutes. Remove the hard skin. With a small, sharp, paring knife peel away the stubborn, thin inner skin. Dry on kitchen paper. Now turn your hand to the ginkgo nuts. Remove the hard shell from the outside of the ginkgo nuts by gently whacking with a hammer. It should come away easily. Underneath this there is still a thin inner skin, which must be removed. You can do this by boiling the nuts in a little water for a few minutes, and jiggling them around at the same time, with a mesh skimmer. The skin should slide off. Remove from the water, rub off any remaining skin, and pat dry. Thread 3 nuts apiece onto toothpicks (two sticks per person). Peel the persimmon and slice into half, then each half into three (three pieces per person). Make the batter according to the instructions, working quickly and keeping everything cool. Heat the oil to 170 C/340F. Fry the chestnuts first – dip them in the flour, shake off the excess and then coat lightly in batter and fry until golden – about 1-2 minutes. Fry the persimmons next, and the ginkgo nuts last. Drain well on paper, then arrange attractively on the plate or leaf. Eat whilst hot. This is not served with a dipping sauce, but may be accompanied by a little freshly ground salt (or a salt and seaweed condiment).

Decoration variation: Another typical autumnal decoration, commonly used in high class 'kaiseki' style establishments, is the pine needle. An edible version of this is easily made by taking two pieces of soba or somen noodle, about 5 cm / 2 inches long, and binding them together with a small strip of nori at the base. Deep fry for 30 seconds, until the noodle is golden and resembles a pine needle. Use several as a garnish.

Variation I
Fresh Ginger Tempura (Shōga no tempura)
Fresh ginger makes a sparkling addition to an autumnal or winter tempura presentation. Peel fresh root ginger and cut into long thin matchsticks. Bunch about a tablespoonful of matchsticks together and, holding them carefully, dip them in flour, and then batter. Deep fry briefly. Simple and spicy, this is a delightful finish to a tempura feast and cleanses the palate wonderfully.

Variation II
Yam Cake Tempura (Konnyaku no tempura)
Konnyaku is a hard jelly like cake, made from the starch obtained from the root of the devil's tongue plant. It's rich in dietary fibre, so although it looks weird it's actually good for you, and the taste is not at all objectionable. Boil it briefly before use, to reduce any odour and make it firmer.

1 cake konnyaku (white or unrefined)	flour to dip as before
salt	2 teaspoons ginger juice
batter and oil as before	soy sauce

Boil the konnyaku in plenty of unsalted water for 5 minutes. Drain. Place into a heavy bottomed cooking pot over a high flame, with no water, and wobble it about for a minute or so. Water will come out and sizzle, then take it off the heat. Cut into thick ½ cm/ ¼ inch slices. Dip briefly in flour, then into batter and deep fry. Serve with a soy sauce and ginger juice dipping sauce.

TARO POTATO NORI ROLLS
SATOIMO NO NORIMAKI

The Sankō In version of this dish uses *yamaimo* – the ginseng-shaped tuber which I think is indigenous to Japan. I have therefore substituted taro potato which has a similar gooey texture. Be careful when peeling the thick skins off the potatoes, as it can cause itching on your hands. (Use rubber gloves if you find you are affected.) Although this dish is very simple it's somehow more than the sum of its parts – maybe it's the *wasabi*. You will need a *makisu* bamboo rolling mat for this, the one used to make sushi rolls.

350 g / 14 oz taro potato	2 sheets *nori*
1 teaspoon salt	*wasabi* paste

Peel the taro thickly, and immerse immediately into cold water. Be careful to remove any black bits lurking amongst the knobbles! Cut into large chunks (about 2 cm/ ¾ inch) and place in a saucepan with water just covering. Bring to a boil and simmer until tender. This will take about 10-15 minutes. (Test with a bamboo skewer.) Pour off the water and replace pan onto the heat, but keep shaking the pan around, so any excess water evaporates, but the potato doesn't stick or burn. Remove and mash whilst still hot. (If your potato looks too wet – it should be quite dry – you can keep it on a low heat to mash it.) Once mashed, leave it to cool. Add the salt, mix well and prepare your bamboo rolling mat. Lay a piece of *nori*, shiny side down on your mat. Spread half the potato mixture over the *nori*, covering about ⅔ of it, and leaving a small margin along the top. Take a chopstick and press it into the potato layer to make a channel across, left to right. Squirt some *wasabi* into it and spread it out (not too much – the size of a small pea will be more than enough). Now, holding the mat underneath with your thumbs, and keeping the edge tucked in with your fingers, roll the mat away from you, using the mat to keep the *nori* tight. Don't worry if it's a bit wobbly – the mat will keep firming it up. You'll soon get the knack – and even if you don't, it means you can eat it all to yourself in the kitchen before the guests arrive! However, presuming you've succeeded, now take a very sharp knife and slice in half with a slow and firm pulling motion towards you. Don't use a blunt knife or you'll have a disaster. *Nori* doesn't like blunt knives one little bit. Cut each half into four, and wipe your knife in between cuts. Place cut side down on an attractive plate or piece of slate, wood or marble. This goes soggy if you keep it too long so serve within 3 hours or so – the sooner the better.

TURNIP CHRYSANTHEMUMS
KIKU KABU

I'm not sure whether this shouldn't be in the pickle section. In fact pressed salads, where vegetables are mixed with salt and pressed under weights, or marinated in a vinegar dressing, almost overlap with 'instant' pickles. This is half way between a pickle and a decoration. It's a classic method of preparing fresh young white turnips, where they are cut to resemble chrysanthemums – the national flower of Japan. It's also indicative of autumn – something you can do quite simply for a special occasion, although it does require some dexterity with a knife.

4 small white turnips	1 tablespoon caster sugar
1 teaspoon salt	pinch salt
DRESSING:	pinch red pepper or paprika
3 tablespoons rice vinegar	

Peel the turnips thinly. Cut a thin slice from the top end (where the leaves would be) and place on a cutting board, so it stands firmly. Place two chopsticks either side of the turnip, adjacent to the direction in which you are going to cut. This is to stop your knife slicing all the way through the turnip. Now, with a very sharp knife, and a downward thrusting slicing motion (*tsuki giri*), make very thin slices across the turnip, as finely as you can, but keeping the turnip intact. Do not slice all the way through. It should still be joined at the bottom. Then, holding these slices together, turn the turnip 90 degrees and slice carefully the other way – at right angles to the previous cuts. You will now effectively have julienne pieces which are joined together at the base of the turnip. This is your 'chrysanthemum'. Place into a bowl and sprinkle with a little salt. Leave for 10 minutes. Make the sweet vinegar dressing, making sure the sugar is dissolved. Rinse the salt off the turnips and pour the dressing gently over, making sure it covers the 'petals' thoroughly. You will find that you can pick them up by the base and 'rinse' them in the dressing. Leave them to marinade in the dressing for another 10 minutes. Serve one turnip per person, with a sprinkle of pepper in the middle to represent the centre of the flower. The petals should flop around a bit, now they are limp, and resemble a flower. If you are using it as a decoration only, and don't need it quite as well pickled, you can simply place the cut turnip into salted water as soon as you finish the cutting, and it will 'open up' and float in the water. Leave it there for a while and then gently squeeze out before arranging. A green leaf around its edge will enhance the flower effect.

POTATO WITH PLUM DRESSING
JAGAIMO NO BAINIKU AE

Use a waxy firm potato for this dish, such as the type you'd use for salads. The taste of floury ones is OK but they tend to fall apart a bit, especially when 'dressed'.

300 g/11 oz potato	1½ tablespoons pickled plum
3 teaspoons caster sugar	(*umeboshi*) paste (*bainiku*)
2 teaspoons saké	

Peel the potato and dice into 2 cm / ¾ inch cubes. Place in a saucepan, just covered with lightly salted water. Bring to a boil and simmer until just cooked. Watch them carefully – you don't want a mush. Drain, rinse in cold water, and drain again. For the dressing, dissolve the sugar in the saké, then slowly add to the plum paste, mixing well as you go, to avoid lumps. Taste the dressing and add a little more sugar, saké or even water if you think it's too strong. It should of course be salty with a distinctive *ume* plum taste. Gently toss the potato in the dressing, and serve as an interesting potato salad, in small Japanese-style portions.

SAKÉ BRAISED ENOKITAKE MUSHROOMS
ENOKITAKE NO SAKA IRI

Enokitake are the small stringy mushrooms (that look like bunches of floppy matchsticks) which have recently appeared in the UK. In Japan they are a familiar ingredient in soups and one-pot dishes. To prepare them, cut off the mycelium end and rinse briefly in a colander under water. This simple way of cooking them is influenced by temple cooking. Although the devout may shun fish and meat they are not as pious about alcohol (I suppose they have to have some fun) so simmering in saké is a common cooking technique.

2 bunches *enokitake* mushrooms	½ teaspoon sugar
2 tablespoons saké	½ teaspoon soy sauce
½ teaspoon salt	

Chop the spongy root off the bottom of the mushrooms and rinse. Pat dry, then add them to the flavouring ingredients in a small saucepan. Bring to a boil and then simmer, covered, for 2 minutes until cooked. Serve hot as a vegetable accompaniment to rice and a grilled or fried dish.

BAKED MUSHROOM PARCELS
ENOKITAKE NO MUSHIYAKI

Mushiyaki means steam grilling, and was originally done in an earthenware sealed pot. These days foil takes the place of old fashioned pots, and, wrapped carefully, does a good job of sealing in juices and creating steam for the food to cook in. Charcoal is the favoured heat source for this, so again its something for the barbecue or a sophisticated bonfire night party. Alternatively you can just stick them on the gas on a wire mesh or griddle. At Daitō In temple they are cooked by Hitomi, the priest's wife, on her wood burning stove in the corner of the living room. Steam grilling is particularly suited to fragrant foods such as mushrooms in autumn. The uniquely aromatic *matsutake* mushroom is another suitable candidate for the foil parcel.

2 bunches *enokitake*	slice lemon (or a squeeze of *sudachi* juice)
large piece of foil (about a foot square)	piece of *yuzu* rind or a sprinkle of *yuzu* powder
knob butter	

Cut the spongy mycelium off the root of the mushrooms and rinse lightly. Drain well. Put the mushroom in the foil with a knob of butter and slice of lemon (or squeeze of *sudachi* juice if you have it) and a piece of *yuzu* rind or few grains *yuzu* powder. Wrap the parcel securely but loosely (you need to leave air inside for the steam that will be created), tucking in the edges so juice can't run out. Bake on a hot fire (or in the oven at 240C/ 500F/ gas 9) for about 5 minutes. Open the foil carefully, making sure you don't burn yourself with steam, and serve family style in the open foil. Hitomi used to make little individual packets, which is more work but more fun – then everyone has a little treasure package to open. And the fun is extended if you add more things to the parcel – a medley of wild mushrooms would be good. (See the section on fish for more *mushiyaki* steam grilling recipes.)

Matsutake mushrooms

Many of the *matsutake* found in Tokyo stores are imported from Korea, but the most favoured and most expensive are still gathered in Japan. Not that I know exactly where – their location is a closely guarded secret. When I wanted to film a mushroom gathering scene in Nagano for my documentary years ago, it was a simple matter to find some friendly locals to take us on a mushroom hunt. But take us to where the *matsutake* mushrooms were? No chance. When you consider that some of the larger most-prized specimens were selling then for around 10,000 yen (forty pounds at the time) a piece, you can understand why these country folk wanted to keep the location of such bounty to themselves. If you are lucky enough to find any, or rich enough to buy some, here's a classic way to prepare them.

MUSHROOM SIMMERED IN A TEAPOT
MATSUTAKE NO DOBINMUSHI

A *dobin* is a small teapot, and it is used almost exclusively for this dish – which in itself is served for only a few weeks every year – during the short *matsutake* mushroom season. The earthy aroma of the *matsutake* is captured in the fine broth in the pot in which it is cooked. If you can't get *matsutake* use another aromatic wild mushroom – or even dried *shiitake*, which have a concentrated flavour (soften in water first). Use small deep earthenware casseroles, with lids, which can be put on a flame, if you don't have a *dobin*. Or improvise. The pot should have a lid to retain the aroma of the mushroom and the citrus.

2 large *matsutake* (or 4 large *shiitake* or other wild mushroom)	**BROTH:**
	800 ml/ 28 fl oz primary *dashi* (page 49)
4 large tiger prawns	1 tablespoon saké
1 skinless chicken breast, cut into small pieces	2 teaspoons light soy sauce (*usu kuchi*)
	few slivers of *sudachi* (or *yuzu* or lime)
pinch salt	citrus zest
small bunch trefoil (*mitsuba*)	

Lightly rinse, or wipe the mushrooms. Cut off the stems and slice, not too thinly, not too thickly. Cut the heads off the prawns, remove the shell and de-vein. Cut the chicken into thin shreds, about two pieces per person. Sprinkle with salt and, in a colander, pour boiling water over. Chill in cold water (the *shimofuri* technique). Cut the trefoil (*mitsuba*) into 3 cm/ 1 inch lengths. Combine the ingredients for the broth. Divide the solid ingredients (except *mitsuba* and citrus) evenly between the pots (or into one pot if are going to cook it communally) and pour the broth over. Place on a medium heat and bring to a boil. Skim off any scum, place a few pieces of the *mitsuba* and citrus zest on top, replace lid and simmer for a few seconds more until cooked. Serve hot immediately, placing each pot in front of each diner, so when the lid is lifted the fragrance will envelop their nostrils. (You can serve in lacquer bowls from a communal pot if you don't have a *dobin*).

WINTER

BURDOCK
GOBŌ

If you remember dandelion and burdock 'pop' from your childhood then you know *gobō* – it's the Japanese name for burdock. Although burdock grows wild in Britain it is not cultivated for consumption as it is in Japan, where it is a popular ingredient in salads and side dishes. Some health food stores and organic suppliers are beginning to get wise to its deliciousness, and it can occasionally be found. Ready prepared cut burdock (*kiri gobō*) can be found in the freezer section in Japanese food stores. Salsify and scorzonera, both long, woody roots, are from a related family and are suitable alternatives. I have also discovered that Jerusalem artichokes have a similar earthy flavour, although the texture is softer. If you can get burdock I recommend you try it. It has a delicious earthy flavour, which combines well in a sautéed sesame and soy sauce dressing. Burdock turns black once it's peeled so it's best to plunge it immediately into a bowl of water containing a little vinegar or lemon juice. Some people like to soak the burdock in water for half an hour before using, to lessen its distinctive taste – but I like it.

Cutting burdock: A common way to prepare burdock is to shave it, as if you are sharpening a pencil, turning the root around as you go. This is called *sasagaki*, and can be done making small thin shavings, or thick wedgy ones, depending on how many cuts you make. Alternatively, for thick wedges you can cut using the *ran giri*-technique (*ran* means chaos – remember the Kurosawa film of the same name a few years ago?). Uneven chunks are made by making a diagonal slice on the root, turning it a quarter turn and making another diagonal cut. This creates attractive, uneven, shapes with a large cut area, for fast cooking, and is used for simmered dishes containing carrots, burdock and chunky root vegetables. Alternatively you can cut burdock into long rectangles, a technique called 'clapper cut' or *hyōshigi giri* (see the section on cutting styles pages 37-39).

BURDOCK SAUTÉED IN SESAME
KIMPIRA GOBŌ

Kimpira is probably the most common and popular way of cooking burdock, cut into juliennes, or thin shavings (*sasagaki*). The dish is named *kimpira* after one of Japan's heroes of mythology. It's a very a traditional side dish, cooked in the *itamemono*, or sautéed style. You can serve it alongside a Japanese meal with rice, pickles and a protein dish, such as fish or tofu. It's best served at room temperature, giving the flavours a chance to mingle. It could be an interesting addition to a buffet style party spread, and is good in lunch boxes.

1 medium burdock root (about 150 g/ 5 oz) (or ready cut frozen)	½ tablespoon *mirin*
	2 tablespoons soy sauce
1 medium carrot	3 tablespoons *dashi* (page 49)
1 tablespoon white untoasted sesame seeds	1 dried red chilli pepper
	1 tablespoon toasted sesame oil
1 tablespoon sugar	

First of all, don't peel the burdock, but scrub well with a hard brush. Lightly scrape off the skin with the back of a knife. The flavour is just under this thin skin, which is why you want to keep it. Cut it into thin shavings or fine julienne strips, about 3 cm/ 1 inch long. Have a large bowl of cold water ready with a drop of rice vinegar in, as the next important thing is to immerse the cut burdock into this, to stop it discolouring. Prepare the carrot, after peeling thinly, into the same shape as the burdock. Roast the sesame seeds in a dry pan (or sesame roaster) and when they begin to pop, take off the heat. This roasting deepens the flavour, but keep them moving so they don't burn. Combine the sugar, *mirin*, soy sauce and *dashi* in a bowl or cup. Soak the red chilli in water for a few minutes to soften it, and then remove the seeds. (Be sure to do this under water – seeds are hot.) Chop the flesh into fine rings. Strain the burdock, rinse in clean water and strain again, and pat it dry.

In a saucepan or sauté pan heat the sesame oil (it burns quickly so be careful) and add the burdock and carrots. Sauté over medium heat for a few minutes, until starting to soften. Then add the liquid ingredients and turn down the heat. Simmer slowly, uncovered, until all the liquid is absorbed, and the burdock is cooked – it should be slightly crunchy – not mushy – (about 20 minutes). Take off the heat and add the pepper and sesame seeds. After standing, serve at room temperature in small side bowls, as a salad, or buffet style in a larger bowl. This keeps well, so it's good for picnics and lunchboxes.

BURDOCK WITH SESAME DRESSING
GOBŌ NO GOMA AE

In this dish the burdock is simmered instead of sautéed, and tossed in a richer dressing of crushed sesame seeds. Cut the burdock in a more chunky fashion – either rolling wedges (*ran-giri*) or thick rectangles (*hyōshigi-giri*). Again it's good party or buffet food.

I burdock root scraped or scrubbed clean (about 250 g/9 oz)	4 teaspoons soy sauce
4 tablespoons toasted sesame seeds	I teaspoon saké

Scrape the burdock and shave it into uneven chunks, turning the root as you go (or cut into rectangles). Place it immediately into cold water. Put on the stove on a high heat and bring to a boil. Turn the heat down and simmer until the burdock is done, soft but not mushy, about 20 minutes. Drain and cool.

For the dressing grind the sesame seeds, either in a coffee grinder, or in the traditional way, in a serrated pestle and mortar (*suribachi*). Add the soy sauce and saké to form a runny paste. At this stage you can also add a pinch of ground pepper or chilli (or mustard) to add spiciness if you like. Toss the cooked burdock in the sesame paste, and serve, either individually as a side dish, or piled family style in one bowl. The flavour improves if this stands for an hour or two, and it will also keep for a couple of days in the fridge.

BURDOCK WRAPPED IN GLUTEN
GOBŌ NO FUMAKI AGE

This is a very rich dish, which would constitute a main protein dish in a vegetarian style meal. Chunks of burdock are wrapped in gluten (*nama bu* – see the section on wheat products, page 119), deep fried, and then simmered in a soy based stock.

8 pieces of burdock about 5 cm/ 2 inches long and ½ cm/ ¼ inch wide	**SIMMERING STOCK:**
	250 ml/9 fl oz *dashi* (page 49)
4 rounds of raw gluten, about 8 cm/ 3 inches diameter	I tablespoon soy sauce
	I tablespoon sake
oil for deep frying	I teaspoon Japanese mustard (to be added at the end)

Plunge the (scraped) burdock into cold water and leave for 30 minutes. Drain and put into fresh water, and put on the stove. Par boil for 10 minutes until almost tender (check with a bamboo skewer). Remove, drain and pat dry.

Take a round piece of raw gluten and stretch it out pulling the edges and turning as you go. It needs to be thin. Lay it on a damp cutting board or marble, keeping it stretched. Lay two pieces of the burdock in the middle and wrap the gluten over, sealing the edges with the burdock inside (don't worry – it will easily stick to itself. In fact raw gluten will stick to just about anything – for ever!)

Heat the oil to 170C/340F and deep fry the gluten and burdock rolls for about 2-3 minutes each side. They will puff up and become crispy. Drain on kitchen paper. Put the simmering ingredients in a heavy bottomed pan with a wide base. Add the fried gluten parcels and bring to a boil. Simmer gently for 5 minutes, making sure the gluten doesn't fall apart. Check though that the gluten is cooked through (if your pieces were not stretched enough initially, and are thick, they need longer cooking). Serve one piece per person with some of the simmering liquid, and a dollop of mustard in medium size deep bowls.

BRAISED YAM CAKE AND BURDOCK
KONNYAKU TO GOBŌ NO NIMONO

This is real country food, using traditional ingredients. It's a million miles from elegant sushi bars, but delicious all the same. The *konnyaku* is the thick noodle type, called *ito konnyaku*, which is then shredded, and the burdock is shaved into very small shreds (you can even grate it on a cheese grater). This is a rich and healthy simmered (*nimono*) side dish in a Japanese meal. It's also good as a snack with beer.

115 g/ 4 oz shaved burdock	2 tablespoon *dashi* or water
vinegared water	2 tablespoons *mirin*
1 pack (250 g/ 9 oz) *ito konnyaku* noodles	1 tablespoon saké
1 tablespoon toasted sesame oil	1 tablespoon sesame seeds, toasted
1 teaspoon caster sugar	*shichimi tōgarashi* (seven spice pepper)
2 tablespoons soy sauce (preferably light)	or half a red chilli, chopped into thin rings

Place the burdock shavings (or gratings) into vinegared water and leave for 30 minutes. Put the *konnyaku* noodles into a saucepan with cold water to cover. Bring to a boil, boil for a few seconds then remove, and drain. Chop them into 3 cm/1 inch lengths. Drain the burdock and parboil for 5 minutes in boiling water. Drain. Heat the sesame oil in a heavy bottomed frying pan or skillet, and sauté the burdock for 5 minutes. Add the chopped *konnyaku* noodles and sauté a further 5 minutes, keeping everything moving. Dissolve the sugar with the liquid ingredients and add to the sauté pan. Bring to a boil, turn down the flame and simmer, uncovered, until all the liquid is absorbed and the burdock cooked. (If the liquid evaporates before the food is tender add water or *dashi* to keep it going.) Sprinkle with white sesame seeds and the pepper (or chilli) before serving.

YAM CAKE WITH WHITE MISO
KONNYAKU NO SHIROMISO AE

This is the first dish that was supposed to have been served to Buddha after he attained enlightenment. It is now traditionally served in Buddhist temples in observance of the anniversary of that event each year on December 8th, which

is one of the important Buddhist festivals (although not a public holiday) in Japan.

1 cake white *konnyaku* (200 g/ 7 oz)	1 tablespoon *mirin*
1 teaspoon salt	2 teaspoons ginger juice, squeezed
DRESSING:	from freshly grated ginger
3 tablespoons sweet white miso	pinch salt

Vigorously rub the teaspoon of salt into the surface of the *konnyaku* yam cake. Rinse it and then par-boil in plenty of boiling water for 5 minutes. Drain and cool, either by plunging into cold water or leaving to cool naturally. Pat dry. Cut the *konnyaku* into ½ cm/ ⅛ inch slices. Make a slit down the middle of each piece, leaving each end intact.

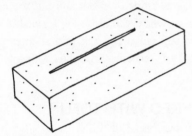 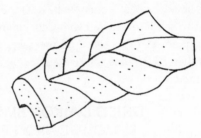

Then, carefully, turn each piece inside out – that is, tuck one end through the slit and pull gently, being careful not to split it. It should become a 'twist'.

In a separate bowl mix the miso, *mirin*, pinch of salt and ginger juice, until carefully blended. Toss the *konnyaku* pieces in the dressing and serve at room temperature, as a starter or a 'dressed' side dish (*aemono*).

 ## SIMMERED DAIKON
KARAMONO

This is a simple and classic dish which enhances the delicate flavour of *daikon* radish. You must use firm, juicy, fresh radishes – if you use shrivelled or old specimens the taste will be lost, and the texture will be ruined. *Daikon* turn dry and woody with age. You can use fresh or dried *shiitake*. This can be served as a starter or as the simmered dish in a Japanese meal. The remaining liquid can be used to cook other vegetables, for example it can be used to flavour *Unohana*, made with *o-kara* soy bean pulp (page 74).

4 large *shiitake* mushrooms	1.7 litres/ 3 pints water (or water made
(dried or fresh)	up with the *shiitake* soaking liquid)
1 medium (fat if you can get it) *daikon* –	6 tablespoons sake
or half a large one (you will need 8	2 tablespoons *mirin*
thick slices, 3 cm/ 1 inch thick)	2 teaspoons salt
10 cm/ 4 inch piece *kombu*, wiped	2 tablespoons light soy sauce

If using dried *shiitake* soak them in warm water for 30 minutes. Peel the *daikon* and cut into 8 thick, 3 cm/ 1 inch slices (2 per person). Then carefully (with a small knife if you prefer) bevel the edges slightly, to prevent the edges crumbling on cooking. When you've done this, use a small knife to cut a cross into the centre of each round, being careful not to cut it in half. This helps the *daikon* to cook through evenly and, when cooked, makes it easier to eat with chopsticks.

In a large pot put the *daikon* rounds and cover with the water (make sure there is ample) and place the piece of *kombu* in with it. Use the mushroom soaking water here if you have it, but strain it first, to ensure you capture any bits of dirt. Cut the stems off the mushrooms, and cut a cross into the cap of each one. If using dried mushrooms you can add them to the pot now (if you're using fresh ones – wait). Bring to a boil and simmer using a drop lid to place on top of the *daikon*. This stops the vegetables from rolling around and also concentrates the heat and distributes the liquid evenly. Simmer gently until the *daikon* is tender – about an hour. You can test to see if it's cooked with a thin bamboo skewer. If you are using fresh *shiitake* add them at this stage. Add the saké, sugar, soy sauce and salt, and simmer for another 20 minutes, so flavours will be absorbed. Serve hot in dishes with a little of the cooking liquid.

DRIED DAIKON SIMMERED WITH TOFU
KIRIBOSHI DAIKON TO TŌFU NO NIMONO

Another simple simmered (*nimono*) dish, which is eaten as a side dish. Dried shredded *daikon* is readily available in Oriental stores and through mail order health food suppliers. Obviously the dried product is not juicy and crunchy like a fresh vegetable, but it has an interesting, chewy, texture of its own, and the flavour becomes more intense with the drying. This would be served as a side dish, together with rice and a protein dish, or as a snack to accompany drinking.

50 g/ 2 oz dried *daikon* radish	3 tablespoons *mirin*
1 deep fried tofu pouch (*usu-age* or *abura-age*)	4 tablespoons soy sauce
	3 tablespoons finely shaved bonito flakes (*katsuobushi*)
400 ml/ 16 fl oz *dashi*	
2 tablespoons saké	

Rinse the dried *daikon*, and then soak in cold water until soft. Meanwhile, pour boiling water over the tofu to get rid of any excess oil, squeeze it dry and then cut it crosswise into thin strands.

Drain the softened *daikon* and put into a saucepan with the tofu strips and *dashi*. Bring to a boil, uncovered, and simmer for 2 to 3 minutes. Add the saké and *mirin* and cook for a further 4 minutes, until the *daikon* is soft and the liquid is reduced. Add the soy sauce, simmer for 2 minutes more, then take off the heat and mix in the bonito flakes. This is best served at room temperature. Serve in small dishes.

LILY OR LOTUS ROOT IN PLUM DRESSING
RENKON NO BAINIKU AE

"There were lotus ponds too, in which the glorious lily, Nelumbo nucifera, *is being grown for the sacrilegious purpose of being eaten!"*

Isabella Bird, *Unbeaten Tracks in Japan*

This is an adaptation of a classic dressing for lily root (*yurine*). If you can get lily root then by all means try that instead. As this recipe doesn't specially make a feature of the lotus root shape you can use the ends of the links (where they join) and slice them haphazardly, but thinly. Incidentally it is believed that the part where the links join is the most nutritious part of the root – so why waste it? This dish is also splendid with regular Western potato, but the flouriness of potato means it doesn't look quite so pretty.

115 g/4 oz lotus root (*renkon*) (frozen is fine for this)	2 teaspoons caster sugar
bowl of water with 1 teaspoon rice vinegar in	3 tablespoons rice vinegar
	1 tablespoon pickled plum paste (*bainiku/ umeboshi* paste)
350 ml/14 fl oz water	1 teaspoon sake

Peel the lotus root. Cut in half lengthwise, and slice thinly to make half moons. Immediately plunge into vinegared water to keep from darkening. Put the water and 3 tablespoons vinegar into a saucepan, and bring to a boil. Add the lotus root and simmer for about 5 minutes. The lotus root should be cooked, but still crisp to the bite. Drain and allow to cool. Dissolve the sugar and saké together, adding another teaspoon of water to help the sugar dissolve if necessary. Then combine the plum paste, sugar and saké in a bowl and mix well. When well mixed, combine the lotus root with this dressing using a wooden or ceramic spoon or chopsticks. If the dressing is a bit sharp you can make it more mellow and creamy by adding a tablespoon of soy milk. This is quite salty, so bear this in mind, and serve in small quantities, almost like a pickle, and avoid serving it with other vinegared dishes.

TARO AND MUSHROOM CROQUETTES
SATOIMO NO KORROKE

At Sankō In Temple these delicious croquettes are made with mountain yam, *yamaimo* (if you are in Japan then certainly use *yamaimo*). I've adapted it using taro potatoes, which have a similar gluey texture. The crunchy coating is made from finely grated freeze-dried tofu (*koyadōfu*). If you can't get the dried tofu then do use some sort of coating otherwise the potatoes are liable to fall apart in the oil – plain flour will do, or breadcrumbs. The *shiitake* is separately flavoured and the result is delicious. It's another one of those 'more than the sum of its parts' recipes.

2 large dried *shiitake* mushrooms

450 g/ 1 lb small taro potaoes, peeled
  thickly (if using larger ones cut them
  in half to boil)

pinch salt

FOR FLAVOURING THE *SHIITAKE*:

2 teaspoons sesame oil

4 tablespoons water from soaking the
  shiitake mushrooms (*shiitake dashi*)

2 teaspoons caster sugar

1 tablespoon sake

2 teaspoons soy sauce

FOR COATING:

2 tablespoons plain flour, sifted

4 tablespoons water

1 piece of freeze-dried tofu (*koya dōfu*)
  grated on a fine grater to make a
  powder

oil for deep frying

Soak the *shiitake* in warm water for an hour until soft. Peel the taro thickly and place in a large saucepan of cold water. Bring to a boil and simmer until cooked (see recipe for Taro Potato Nori Rolls – page 153). Pour off the water and replace the pan on a low heat. Jiggle the pan around to allow excess water to evaporate (just a few seconds), but do not scorch the potatoes. Mash them in the pan whilst hot with a wooden pestle (*surikogi*) or masher, adding a pinch of salt as you go. Remove the stems from the *shiitake*, and chop the flesh very finely – mince it in fact (*mijin giru*). Keep the soaking water for later. In a small frying pan heat the sesame oil and add the minced *shiitake*. Sauté for a minute then add the soaking water, sugar, saké and soy sauce. Simmer on a low heat, uncovered, until all the liquid is absorbed and the *shiitake* sticky. Mix the *shiitake* with the mashed potato, distributing it evenly (use your fingers if you like). Form the mixture into 8 small balls, then roll them on a board to make a croquette shape (cylindrical). Put the sifted flour on a plate and roll the croquettes in it. Then put the remaining flour in a bowl and mix with the water. Dip the floured croquettes in this simple batter, and then in the grated tofu powder (or breadcrumbs if using).

Bring the oil to hot (180C/ 360F) and slide the croquettes in carefully, using a slotted spoon or chopsticks. Deep fry until golden – the tofu coating burns easily, and the ingredients don't need cooking through, so 2 or 3 minutes will be enough. Serve two per person. Best eaten hot, but still delicious cold.

 ## CRISP TURNIP WITH SESAME MISO DRESSING
KABU NO GOMA MISO AE

This is another dressed salad, and an original recipe from Sankō In Temple which is where I first tasted it and learned how easy it was to make. The turnips are salted and pressed, not cooked, as is so often the case in Japanese salad recipes. If you can't get small white turnips you can substitute *daikon* radish. The secret is using the sweet white miso, which really is sweet, and looks pretty.

3 small white turnips (or half a medium *daikon* radish)	1½ tablespoons sweet white miso
	1 tablespoon saké
1 teaspoon salt	½ teaspoon Japanese mustard (*karashi*)
DRESSING:	
3 tablespoons white sesame seeds	

Peel the turnips and cut into fine julienne strips. Sprinkle with the salt, toss to mix, and put in a large bowl. Place a small plate on top, resting on the turnip, with a heavy weight on top of it. Leave to press for about 20 minutes.

Meanwhile, in a heavy bottom frying pan or skillet (or sesame roaster if you have one) toast the sesame seeds until they start to pop. Keep them moving and make sure they don't burn. You only want them lightly toasted. In a *suribachi* (grinding bowl) grind the toasted seeds to a paste. Add the miso, saké and mustard and mix well. Remove the pressed turnip and rinse lightly in a colander under running water to remove salt. Squeeze them well, removing excess water. They should be a little floppy by now, which is exactly what you want. Add them to the sesame dressing and toss well to coat the turnip evenly with the dressing. Serve in small portions (it's quite rich) in small dishes. Eat within a few hours, as it can turn watery if left for too long, although it will still taste fine. The dressing on its own keeps for a few days in the fridge, covered, and can be used with other vegetables in any experimental way you fancy. It's good with cooked greens, burdock and also *konnyaku*.

DAIKON AND APRICOT SALAD
DAIKON TO ANZU NO SUNOMONO

Another example of colour combining, in this case the orange colour of the apricot represents red which, together with white, is a festive combination. The use of apricot in a vinegared salad was shown to me by the abbess at Sankō In, and jolly nice it is too. If you can get dried persimmons (which are a seasonal delicacy at New Year in Japan, like figs and dates at Christmas) they are even more authentically Japanese.

6 dried apricots	**DRESSING:**
1 tablespoon saké	2 tablespoons rice vinegar
½ medium size *daikon* radish	1 teaspoon sugar
½ teaspoon salt	

Chop the apricot into thin julienne strips. Put in a bowl with the saké and leave to soak.

Peel the *daikon* and slice thinly. Then stack the slices and cut across to make julienne strips. Sprinkle with ½ teaspoon salt, and leave to stand for 10 minutes. Dissolve the sugar in the vinegar (or you can use the ready-sweetened sushi vinegar which is now widely available), and add a pinch of salt. Rinse the salted *daikon* radish and squeeze out excess water. Drain the juice off the apricots, squeezing the apricots as you go, and pour it into the dressing. Combine the *daikon* and apricot strips and mix with the dressing. This will keep a few days – the flavours mingling over time. Serve in small quantities as a side salad or as the *sunomono*, vinegared, dish in a Japanese meal. It's especially appropriate at Christmas or New Year.

LOTUS ROOT STUFFED WITH BEAN PASTE
RENKON NO AZUKI ZUME

The Japanese are never ones to miss an opportunity to arouse the visual senses – the arresting pattern of the lotus root must have been made for them. Although it's another of the vegetables that came from China, the Japanese have not been slow to exploit its visual appeal. Those holes were just made for stuffing! This paste made with sweetened *azuki* beans is ubiquitous in Japanese confectionery, so much so that you can buy cans of it ready made (called *an* or *anko*). If you want to save time, and can get hold of some, by all means use it.

1 medium size lotus root, about 12 cm/ 5 inches long	**FILLING:**
600 ml/ 1 pint water	125 g/4 oz cooked *azuki* beans
4 tablespoons rice vinegar	4 tablespoons caster sugar
4 tablespoons *mirin*	pinch salt
2 teaspoons salt	

First of all the lotus root must be cooked, and it's cooked in sweetened vinegar to give it a sweet and sour flavour. Peel the root thinly and chop off the ends. Put into a medium saucepan with the water, vinegar, *mirin* and salt. Bring to a boil, then simmer, uncovered, until the root is cooked through. It should take about 20 minutes.

Whilst the root is cooking you can make the filling. Put the cooked beans into a food processor or blender and whizz to a purée (or you can do it the low-tech way by hand). You need a smooth purée, so if it's not smooth enough and still has bits of skin it, then push through a sieve. Transfer the purée to a deep saucepan and add the sugar and salt. Put on a low heat and keep stirring to prevent it sticking. You need a thick paste, so cook for 5-10 minutes until the water in the beans has gone and the mixture is thick and glossy. Leave to cool. Leave the cooked lotus root in the pan of liquid to cool. Then put the bean paste in a deep bowl, and press the lotus root into it, cut side down, so that the paste fills the holes. Make sure the holes are well filled, then wipe the ends and sides clean. Cut into 8 slices, and serve two per person as a sweet snack with tea, or a final course in a meal.

Note: Japanese cuisine, like other Asian cuisines, mixes sweet and savoury much more than we do in the West. But if you don't fancy sweet bean paste, and want to serve this as a 'savoury' dish then make the bean paste without adding the sugar. The texture will be slightly different.

TRI-COLOUR LOTUS ROOT

I have also made this with mashed up *kabocha* pumpkin, and you could try sweet potato, for a different colour combination. How about this original colourful dish using red, yellow and green fillings?

I large lotus root, cooked as in the previous recipe and cooled	50 g/ 2 oz cooked broad beans, skins removed
50 g/ 2 oz cooked and puréed *kabocha* pumpkin (or sweet potato)	50 g/ 2 oz cooked and puréed *azuki* beans

Put the puréed pumpkin in a small saucepan and stir well over a very low heat, to get rid of water, and make a stiff paste. Add a pinch of salt (or if you like a sweet taste, caster sugar to taste). Do the same with the broad beans and the *azuki* beans, being careful not to scorch them. Cut the lotus root into three equal lengths, and press one into the *azuki* mixture, one into the pumpkin mixture, and the third into the broad bean mixture. Clean the edges and make sure the holes are properly filled. Cut into thick slices and arrange attractively on a large plate.

SEA VEGETABLES - FRUITS OF THE SEA

Sea vegetables (*kaisō*) are also a very important part of the Japanese diet, and are rich in minerals. They contain ten to twenty times the mineral content of land vegetables, and are good sources of calcium, potassium, magnesium, iron and zinc. They also contain small amounts of vitamin B12, which is not normally found in vegetable products. Kelp (*kombu*) is particularly rich in iodine, which is not easily found in other foods. The glutamic acid in *kombu* is a natural food tenderiser, which is why it is good added to beans, as it speeds up the cooking process and makes them more digestible. Glutamic acid is the naturally occurring form of monosodium glutamate, which enhances flavour, and this is why *kombu* is such an essential component of the basic stock *dashi* which gives Japanese cooking its flavour.

Like miso, sea vegetables seem to have an ability to remove pollutants from the body – the alginic acid in sea vegetables binds with any toxins present and eliminates them.

Macrobiotics is the health food movement which was popular with brown-rice eating hippies and students in the late sixties and seventies. In fact it began many years earlier, exported to America and the West by various Japanese teachers. Very briefly, macrobiotics is based on a philosophy of yin and yang, whereby all foods are more or less one or the other. A balanced diet therefore would be neither too yang or too yin, depending on where you live. For example if you live in a tropical climate (which is yang – warming, male energy) you should eat yin food to compensate. Tropical fruits such as pineapples and papaya are examples of yin (cooling, female, energy) foods – in other words exactly the type of food you need. Foods which are neither too yang nor too yin, and therefore suitable for temperate climates (like Europe and Japan) are whole grains, beans and locally grown vegetables and sea vegetables. You don't need to follow all this though in order to enjoy eating macrobiotic food, as it is based on traditional Japanese cooking. In fact it's thanks to many dedicated followers of macrobiotics that so many traditional Japanese foods (sea vegetables being a large part of that), are now available in the West. Americans and Europeans who have studied traditional Japanese food production in Japan have returned home with their knowledge and set up production outside of Japan. There are many good quality misos made in the United States, and a few in France and Britain. Sea vegetables are harvested off the Atlantic coast of Maine, and exported worldwide. In the small sea port of Franklin, Shep Erhart and Carl Karush, helped by their families, harvest a wide variety of sea vegetables from the wild Atlantic coast around them. It is one of the most wild and beautiful places I have ever visited. I filmed them as they waded into the sea and cut *kombu*, by hand, from its roots, and pulled dulse off coastal rocks around the shore line where it gathers. Back at the drying shed the freshly gathered bounty was left to dry naturally, and finally it was processed and packaged, entirely by hand, in a traditional way.

In Japanese cooking sea vegetables are cooked with other vegetables, with soy products like tofu, and in sushi the crisp, dark green *nori* wrapping is essential to *makizushi*, so different types of sea vegetables crop up in all the sections of this book. Because they are most usually dried they are non-seasonal, and you can have some handy at any time of the year. You can chuck them in salads, stir fries, stews and soups. You can use them as garnishes, or to make mineral-rich dishes in themselves.

BRAISED HIJIKI AND DEEP FRIED TOFU
HIJIKI NO NIMONO

Dried *hijiki* keeps well and is chock full of minerals, especially calcium and potassium – both especially important for those whose diet contains no meat or dairy products (such as Buddhist monks, nuns, and macrobiotic devotees). Apart from that, it is delicious, with a firm nutty texture. In this recipe the rich black colour contrasts well with the orange of carrots, lending visual appeal to your food as well as taste, texture and nutrition. This is a classic combination, and method of cooking it. A substantial protein-rich dish, good with rice and other vegetables in a vegetarian meal, as part of a 'bento' lunch box, or even party buffet food.

30 g/ 1 oz dried *hijiki*	3 tablespoons soy sauce
1 deep fried tofu pouch (*usu-age abura-age*, page 58)	1 tablespoon sesame oil
1 tablespoon sugar	1 medium carrot, peeled and cut into juliennes
2 tablespoons *mirin*	1 teaspoon grated ginger
250 ml/ 9 fl oz water	1 tablespoon white sesame seeds

Soak the *hijiki* in water for about 30 minutes, to soften. Discard this water. In a sieve pour boiling water over the deep fried tofu to remove some of the oil. Cut into thin strips. Mix the flavouring ingredients – soy sauce, *mirin* and sugar with the water, making sure the sugar is dissolved. In a deep frying pan heat the sesame oil and add the drained *hijiki* and carrots and ginger. Sauté for a few minutes on a medium heat, but keep the contents moving to prevent the ginger sticking to the bottom of the pan. Add the sliced tofu pouch, and the seasoning liquid. Keep on a simmer, without a lid, for about 10 minutes, or until most of the liquid has disappeared. Serve as a side dish, either warm or at room temperature. Garnish with the sesame seeds sprinkled over.

HIJIKI, CORN AND BEAN SPROUT SALAD
HIJIKI TO MOYASHI NO KARASHI ZU

This recipe is adapted from Monte Bradford's macrobiotic book *Cooking with Sea Vegetables*. Here I've used sweetened rice vinegar, which is sold for use in making sushi rice, but as it contains sugar macrobiotic devotees would never use it. Regular Japanese cooking though uses quite a bit of sugar – as desserts aren't a big deal in Japan sugar is incorporated into savoury dishes – although I have reduced the quantities to cater for Western tastes.

50 g/ 2 oz dried *hijiki*	**DRESSING:**
1 tablespoon soy sauce	3 tablespoons toasted and ground
pinch salt	sesame seeds
80 g/ 3-4 oz fresh peas, parboiled	2 tablespoons sweetened rice vinegar
100 g/ 4 oz sweet corn, taken from a	2 tablespoons water
cob, or frozen	1 teaspoon light (*usu kuchi*) soy sauce
50 g / 2 oz bean sprouts	1 teaspoon Japanese mustard (*karashi*)
3 carrots, grated roughly,	
Western style	

Soak the *hijiki* in tepid water, until softened, as in the previous recipe. If the pieces are long chop them into 2 cm/ ¾ inch lengths. Using half this soaking water, and topping up with fresh water to just cover the *hijiki*, bring the *hijiki* to boil and simmer on a low flame, uncovered, for 20 minutes until soft, adding the tablespoon of soy sauce half way through. The *hijiki* should cook until dry and the water absorbed. Parboil the peas in boiling salted water for 2-3 minutes. Drain, and leave to cool (the 'immediately immerse in cold water to keep the colour' rule, doesn't apply to peas, as it wrinkles the skin). If using corn on the cob, boil it whole in salted water, until cooked, about 10 minutes, then cut off the kernels. Dunk the bean sprouts into the same boiling water for 30 seconds, then remove with a slotted spoon. Do the same with the grated carrot – this is just to soften the vegetables slightly, and take the rawness away. Leave all these vegetables to cool at room temperature. Meanwhile make the dressing.

   Toast the sesame seeds, and grind in a *suribachi*, grinding bowl, until almost a paste, and add the vinegar, water, and soy sauce. It will slightly curdle, but don't worry – just keep mixing it. Mix the mustard in a separate bowl with a little of the dressing, and then put all together.

Combine the cooled *hijiki* and vegetables, and pour over the dressing. Serve at room temperature.

HIJIKI AND TOFU 'TREASURE BALLS'
HIJIKI NO GANMODOKI

This is similar to *Ganmodoki*, the deep fried tofu 'treasure balls', which are sold in all traditional tofu shops in Japan. This version, adapted from Monte Bradford's book, uses only *hijiki* and sesame seeds with the tofu – a great and classic combination. The *hijiki* is pre-cooked, chopped finely, then mixed with mashed up tofu and deep fried. For a visually pleasing presentation serve on a plate lined with maple leaves.

I block firm tofu	I tablespoon white sesame seeds
20 g/ ¾ oz *hijiki*	a little plain flour to help bind the
½ tablespoon toasted sesame oil	ingredients together, if necessary
I tablespoon soy sauce	oil for deep frying
2 tablespoons *mirin*	

Wrap the tofu in a clean cloth and place on a draining board with a weight on top. Leave for 30 minutes to allow excess water to drain away. Meanwhile soak the *hijiki* in warm water for about 20 minutes until soft (keep this soaking water). Mince the *hijiki* finely (*mijin giri*). In a skillet heat the ½ tablespoon sesame oil. Add the *hijiki* and sauté briefly. Then add 250 ml/ 9 fl oz of the *hijiki* soaking water, the soy sauce and *mirin*, and simmer for 20-30 minutes until soft and the water absorbed. Take off the flame and leave to cool. Remove the tofu from the cloth, and crumble it into a large bowl (a *suribachi* is perfect). Mash with a wooden spoon or *surikogi*, to make a thick paste. Add the chopped and cooked *hijiki* and the sesame seeds, and mix well, with your hands, until everything is evenly distributed and the mixture holds together well. Form little balls about 3 cm/ I inch diameter (if the mixture doesn't hold together easily add a little plain flour to help bind it). In a deep frying pan or wok heat some vegetable oil to 170C/ 340F (adding a tablespoonful of toasted sesame oil here if you like – it will give a nice flavour – but be careful because sesame oil has a low smoking point, so keep your eye on it). Slide the balls into the hot oil and deep fry until just golden – don't overcook them so they become hard and crunchy, and don't let the sesame seeds burn. Serve family style on a large plate or two to three per person on individual plates. Serve with a dipping sauce of soy sauce and ginger juice, and serve hot.

HIJIKI AND SOYBEANS
HIJIKI TO DAIZU NO NIMONO

This is one of the few times that soybeans are eaten as whole beans. They take a lot of cooking, and foam up rather rapidly, so they are a bit tiresome to cook. It's probably just as well to cook a large quantity if you are going to go to the bother, and save some in the freezer for future use. Or you could cheat and use canned beans.

250 g/ 9 oz soybeans

10 cm/ 4 inch piece of *kombu*

25 g/ 1 oz *hijiki*

1 deep fried tofu pouch

5 dried *shiitake* mushrooms

1 tablespoon rapeseed (or other vegetable) oil

1 tablespoon toasted sesame oil

350 ml/ 12 fl oz mushroom soaking water (or made up with *dashi*)

4 tablespoons soy sauce

1 tablespoon caster sugar

2 tablespoons *mirin*

Soak the soybeans overnight in at least 850 ml/ 1½ pints of cold water. The next day drain them, and place in a large, deep cooking pot with 3 times their volume of water. Add the piece of *kombu*, wiped with a damp cloth, and bring to a boil. Simmer, uncovered, until just cooked. This will take a long time – maybe 3 or 4 hours. You'll need to keep checking that they haven't boiled over (soybeans foam up rapidly) and skim off any scum that appears. Top up with water if they boil dry before cooking through. (Or you can use previously cooked, and frozen, or canned beans.) When cooked drain and leave to cool. Soak the *hijiki* in tepid water for about 15 minutes, until softened. Drain well and rinse in clean water. Soak the *shiitake* mushrooms in warm water for at least 30 minutes, or until soft. Keep this soaking water but strain it through a fine sieve to get rid of any dirt that may remain. Cut the *shiitake* into thin strips. In a colander, pour boiling water over the deep fried tofu to get rid of excess oil. Cut it in half lengthways and then into thin strips. In a skillet or heavy bottomed pan heat the oils to medium, and add the *hijiki*. Sauté for a few minutes, then add the sliced *shiitake* mushroom and sauté a couple more minutes. Dissolve the sugar, soy sauce, *mirin* and mushroom soaking water (or *dashi*) in a jug. Add the cooked beans to the *hijiki* pan, then add the liquid, and simmer, uncovered, for about 15 minutes, until the *hijiki* is soft and the liquid evaporated. Serve in reasonable quantities as a main protein dish, or in smaller quantities as a side dish.

RED RADISH, BEANS AND ARAME SALAD
RADISHU TO ARAME NO SARADA

Arame looks similar to *hijiki*, but its texture is different – more like *kombu* or *wakame*. It's previously processed by long cooking, and then cut into thin strips and dried before packaging, so it re-hydrates quickly. Simmering enhances its taste and brings out its sweetness, although it's not necessary. Small red radishes are a relatively recent introduction to Japanese cuisine, but are a welcome addition because of their beautiful colour. The radishes are barely cooked.

225 g/ 8 oz white beans (such as cannellini)

10 cm/ 4 inch piece *kombu*

20 g/ ¾ oz dried *arame*

2 tablespoons vegetable oil

200 ml/ 7 fl oz *dashi*

3 tablespoons light soy sauce

2 tablespoons *mirin*

8 red radishes

Soak the beans overnight in plenty of water. The next day rinse them, put into a large pot with water to cover and bring to a rapid boil. Boil for 10 minutes then take off the heat and drain. Put them back into the saucepan with 3 times their volume of water, the piece of *kombu*, and bring to a boil. Simmer, covered, until cooked (but not mushy).

Drain and leave to cool. Soak the *arame* in cold water until soft and then drain. Heat the oil in a skillet or frying pan. Add the *arame* and sauté for a few minutes. Then add the soy sauce, *dashi* and *mirin*, and simmer, covered 10 minutes. There should still be liquid left when you've finished. Meanwhile, slice the radishes thinly, and immerse into a saucepan of boiling water for 30 seconds. Remove and drain. Put the cooked beans into the cooked *arame* with its juices and combine. Simmer 5 minutes more. Take off the heat and add the radish, mixing carefully. Serve at room temperature as a protein-rich side dish.

 ## ASPARAGUS AND ARAME IN PLUM DRESSING
ASUPARA TO ARAME NO UME SHIRA AE

25 g/ 1 oz dried *arame*

225 g /8 oz asparagus

1 tablespoon *umeboshi* plum paste (*bainiku*)

2 tablespoons soft tofu (or 125 ml/ 4 fl oz unsweetened soy milk)

Soak the *arame* in cold water until soft. Drain well. Immerse in boiling water for a few minutes until just cooked. Remove and plunge into iced water to arrest cooking. Cut off the hard stems of the asparagus (about ⅓ way up), and then cut the spears into long diagonals (about 3 per piece). Put the drained *arame* into the same water and bring to a boil. Take off after 30 seconds and drain. Now make the dressing. In a *suribachi* or medium size bowl, mix the *ume* plum paste with the tofu (or soy milk) until well combined. Mix well to a smooth paste. Toss the *arame* with the asparagus, and carefully add the dressing, mixing until evenly distributed without breaking up the asparagus. Serve as a side dish.

 ## DAIKON RIBBONS AND WAKAME SALAD
WITH WASABI DRESSING
DAIKON TO WAKAME NO WASABI ZU

I had this (or something similar) in a small bar in Ebisu in Tokyo, and was instantly converted to the *wasabi* dressing. This is my approximation of the dish from memory.

I *daikon* radish	4 tablespoons rice vinegar
I teaspoon salt	I tablespoons *mirin*
25 g/ I oz dried *wakame*	6 tablespoons *dashi*
DRESSING:	I teaspoon *wasabi* paste
I tablespoon light soy sauce	

Peel the *daikon* radish. You now want long thin ribbons of *daikon*, about 1-2 cm/ ⅜-¾ inch wide. If you have mastered the *itamae*'s technique of peeling a *daikon* into one long thin paper thin sheet, all in one go with a large knife (*katsura-maki*) then by all means do it like that! Chances are you'll be happier using a peeler to shred long thin strips along the length of the radish. In any case cut the whole thing into long strands, or ribbons, and stand in a large bowl. Sprinkle with salt and leave for 30 minutes (or longer, an hour or two is OK). Reconstitute the *wakame* in cold water until soft and rinse. Cut off any hard spine, and cut the *wakame* fronds into long ribbons (like the *daikon*). Rinse the *daikon* under cold water to get rid of the salt, and pat dry. In this case try *not* to scrunch the radish up too much, as you want to retain the ribbon effect. Mix up the dressing, tasting as you go and altering if you desire, to make it more or less vinegary or spicy. Combine the *wakame* and *daikon* carefully and arrange a mound in a large deep bowl. Pour the dressing over and serve. This goes watery if you leave it too long, so mix up just before serving.

ROASTED SEA VEGETABLE CONDIMENT
KAISŌ NO FURIKAKE

You can make your own dried sea vegetable 'sprinkle', which you can use as an alternative to salt, or to sprinkle on rice (it's nice in non-Japanese dishes too).

Simply put a large handful of dried sea vegetable, such as dulse, *wakame* or *kombu* (*tororo kombu* is fine as well) on a baking tray and pop into a low oven (190C/ 375F). Leave to roast until dry and crisp but not burnt. Remove and grind to a powder, either in a *suribachi* or mill. You can also add toasted sesame seeds, pumpkin seeds and coarsely ground sea salt for extra flavour.

PICKLES
TSUKEMONO

Pickles are an essential part of the traditional Japanese diet. In the same way that the cheeseboard signals the end of a meal in the West, in Japan it's the call for rice and pickles that completes a formal repast. Just about every vegetable you can think of is pickled one way or another. Japanese pickles though are crunchy. This was important in the old days before refrigeration, especially in the cold northern areas, where fresh vegetables were unavailable for months, so the closest to fresh that the pickles tasted the better. Western pickles are preserved in vinegar, which adds moisture to them, rendering them limp and soft. Japanese pickles on the other hand, are mainly salted. This removes moisture from them, which leaves them still crisp and crunchy, and fresh tasting. Even though these days pickling is no longer a necessity in the same way as it was in the past, the people in the north of Japan, especially, remain prodigious pickle eaters, chomping them at every opportunity. Apart from salting, other methods of pickling involve some type of fermentation, such as pickling in rice bran, in miso, or in saké lees. It was not only the cold weather but also the long, hot, humid, summers which made food preservation, in one way or another, a necessity. As well as vegetables, fish, and even meat, are preserved in miso, to stop them from spoiling. The simplest preservation method of all is of course drying, and this is used for fish, mushrooms, persimmons, seaweeds, gourds, *daikon*, lotus root – just about anything you can think of.

Traditionally pickles are made in wooden tubs (called *tsukedaru* or *oké*) made from cedar which are bound with braided bamboo called *taga*. This *taga* holds the tub together, and has given rise to a saying. If control is lost in an organisation or group it is said that 'the *taga* is loose'! Wooden lids which fit inside the tubs were weighted down with rocks, and this is still an effective and common way of making pickles in the country or indeed at home. Modern devices have now been created though, and small plastic tubs, with a screw lid with a spring attached, which presses down on the pickles, are very effective, and useful for making small amounts.

Like miso, pickles have an aura of nostalgia and homeliness about them. Because there are so many regional variations everyone has a favourite from 'back home'. Even in these days of modern, urban, living, when Tokyo has expanded to be a city of 12 million people, you will find that these modern city dwellers don't think of themselves as Tokyoites – they still see themselves as country people – from Akita, or Gifu or Kyushu or wherever. I remember when I was an art student, and I used to watch a lot of Japanese movies, both contemporary and old. I was amazed at the frequency of the same storyline – young boy comes to big city and yearns for home (and *Mama*, and her miso soup). It seemed so un-modern to me at the time, but then when I went to live in Japan I began to understand it. It seems to me that a yearning for pickles is just another symptom of that child-like 'homesickness' which seems to be a feature of the Japanese psyche, and which can be quite charming. Regional variations of pickles are endless, and every small town, prefecture and even villages have their own specialities, which are packaged as souvenirs. Station concourses almost always have an array of stalls set out selling local produce for visitors to take back to Tokyo (or wherever) with them. There's a huge choice of dried foods, sweet bean cakes and of course pickles for sale. This is because whenever anyone travels anywhere in Japan it is *de-rigeur* to take back gifts, for colleagues, friends and family. These gifts, called *o-miyage* are invariably food items, so locally produced pickles fit the bill perfectly.

In a formal meal pickles are eaten at the end of the meal, with rice, but in a less formal meal, such as that served at home, or at a lunchtime set meal (*teishoku*) they are served with the rice and soup along with the main dish, which could be something like tempura, grilled fish or a meat dish. In the afternoons, especially in northern areas of Japan where pickle eating is a big habit as I have said, they are eaten in the afternoons as a snack, with coarse brown *bancha* tea. (Green tea is not eaten with pickles but is usually accompanied by sweet things, to complement its bitterness. There is more about this in the section on tea.)

These days most pickles are store bought, although country people often make their own. I recommend that you try out different pickles from a Japanese store if you have one near you, then experiment with making some at home. Japanese kitchenware departments and some health food stores sell small plastic tubs with a spring loaded lid for the purpose. They are hygienic, as the lid is sealed, but it's just as easy to put a plate on top of the pickles and weigh it down with a large stone, or weights from your scales. If you can get a wooden tub so much the better for authenticity. Just be sure that there is a little space between the side of the tub or bowl and plate, so the vegetables are fully pressed.

Some of the most popular and commonly pickled vegetables are *daikon*, cucumber, aubergine, turnip, Chinese cabbage, *rakkyō* (small onions like shallots), *umeboshi*, and burdock (tiny baby burdock roots are delicious). Thin shreds of *kombu*, bonito flakes, ginger and chilli are sometimes added too.

Generally pickles are categorised according to how long they are left, and what they are pickled in. Salt is the quickest and simplest pickling method (called *shio zuke*) and the very quickest salt pickles, so-called instant pickles, are ready in as little as an hour. Below I give recipes for four types:

1. Instant pickles pickled in their own liquid. These are an example of *shio zuke* – salt pickles.

INSTANT SALT-PICKLED TURNIP
KABU NO SHIO ZUKE

This instant pickle is ready for eating in only an hour – it's more of a pressed salad than a pickle, but it will keep a few days in the fridge. Use small, white, tender turnips. In Japan fresh turnips are nearly always sold with the greens attached – if you can get them like this here (for example if you grow them) use them too – wash them well, drain and cut finely.

6 medium size turnips	small piece of lemon rind
2 tablespoons salt	(or *yuzu* citron)
5 cm/ 2 inch piece of *kombu*	

Peel the turnips and slice thinly, into rounds. Stack these rounds and chop crosswise to make fine julienne strips. In a large bowl sprinkle the salt over the turnip, and knead with your hands, mixing the salt in. Do this for about a minute and then pour off the water which is produced, but don't rinse. Add the piece of citron rind and place the piece of *kombu* on top. Put a plate or pickle lid over, touching the vegetables, and place a weight on top. Leave it like this at room temperature, for an hour. To serve, remove pieces and shake off the liquid. If it's too salty rinse lightly. Serve small amounts in individual pickle dishes.

Variation: Add *Daikon* radish, cut into thin rounds or small round slivers of dried red chilli (without seeds).

DAIKON AND CARROT INSTANT PICKLE
DAIKON TO NINJIN NO SOKUZEKI ZUKE

This colour combination of red and white is a felicitous one, used at celebrations especially New Year. This pickle uses less salt, but is marinaded in vinegar and soy sauce.

I *daikon* radish	**DRESSING:**
I medium carrot	I tablespoon caster sugar
½ teaspoon salt	3 tablespoons rice vinegar
I dried red chilli, de-seeded	I tablespoon light soy sauce

Peel the *daikon* and slice finely in rounds. Peel the carrot, slice finely and then cut into matchsticks. Cut the chilli (with scissors is easy) into thin rings. Put the radish and carrot in a large bowl, sprinkle with the salt and knead with your hands. Add the chilli and mix. Place a plate or pickle lid on top and weigh down. Leave for an hour. Meanwhile mix the sugar, soy sauce and vinegar, making sure the sugar is dissolved. Drain off the water which will have been released from the vegetables, and taste. If it's too salty for your taste lightly rinse and squeeze. Then mix the dressing with the pickled vegetables. This will become more limp the longer you leave it in the dressing, but will keep a few days in the fridge.

You can use your imagination here. Matchsticks of ginger can be added instead of chilli. Slivers of *shiitake* mushroom can be added. Cucumber and aubergine pickle more quickly, as they are not dense. *Daikon*, carrot, turnip, red radishes, cabbage, red cabbage and celery can all be experimented with in different combinations. Do not however pickle potatoes, or yams (*cassava*), which are poisonous eaten raw and must be cooked.

2. Overnight pickles are ready in 24 hours. They are not meant to be kept longer, so make them in small quantities to be eaten immediately.

PICKLED BROCCOLI
BURROKORI NO ICHIYA ZUKE
In this unusual pickle the broccoli is briefly parboiled before pickling with salt.

I medium head of broccoli	I large carrot, cut into thin matchsticks
a pinch of salt (for parboiling)	I tablespoon salt
3 cm/ I inch square piece of *kombu* left over from making *dashi* (softened)	½ lemon or lime, sliced

Wash the broccoli and break into small florets. (Do this by turning the broccoli head side down, making a slit in the stalk and pulling it apart. This keeps the florets intact.) Slice the stem into thin (but not wafer thin) slices. Immerse both stem and florets into boiling, lightly salted, water for I minute until just not raw. Remove and immerse into ice cold water. Drain well, and dry further by standing on kitchen paper.

Cut the *kombu* into matchstick slivers. Combine the broccoli and carrots, and fold in the *kombu*. Sprinkle with the salt and mix, being careful not to break up the broccoli too much. Place the lemon on top, put a plate on, touching the vegetables, and weigh down with a heavy weight. Leave overnight (or for several hours). To serve, pour off the liquid, and retrieve the pieces of broccoli, carrot and *kombu*. Do not serve the lemon unless desired.

TURNIP AND CUCUMBER OVERNIGHT PICKLE
KABU TO KYŪRI NO ICHIYA ZUKE

350 g/ 12 oz small white turnips	4 cm / 1½ inch square piece of used
1 medium cucumber, washed well, cut in	*kombu* (left over from making *dashi*)
half lengthwise and seeds removed	1 dried chilli, seeds removed
	1 tablespoon salt

Peel the turnips and slice thinly, but not wafer thin. Cut the cucumber into thick 1 cm/ ⅜ inch wedges. Cut the *kombu* into matchsticks and, using scissors, cut the chilli into thin rings. Combine all in a large bowl and mix in the salt. Cover with a saucer or pickle lid and weigh down, as in the previous recipes. Leave overnight. The next day there should be a fair amount of liquid which can be poured off before eating.

3. Short term pickles The following recipes are examples of short term pickles, which take 2-3 days to ripen and will keep.

CHINESE CABBAGE AND CUCUMBER PICKLE
HAKUSAI TO KYŪRI NO SHIO ZUKE

This is made in larger quantities as it keeps a couple of months. It's a good way to use large quantities of bargain vegetables that are often sold off at the end of the day in street markets. You'll need a big bucket or crock for this and a cool dark place (like a cellar) to keep it in.

2.5 kg/ 5 lbs Chinese cabbage	1 kg/ 2 lbs sea salt
2.5 kg/ 5 lbs cucumber	

Split the cabbages in half lengthwise, by cutting the stem end and pulling apart. Wash well and pat dry. Wash the cucumbers, cut in half lengthwise, and remove the seeds.

Lay the cabbage halves cut side up and rub a generous amount of salt into the leaves, but don't use it up. Sprinkle salt over the cut edges of the cucumber too. Put a layer of cabbage into the bottom of the crock, cut side down, and sprinkle a handful of salt over. Then lay a few cucumbers on top, cut side down and sprinkle more salt. Continue in this way, salting generously and evenly, until all the salt, cabbage and cucumber are gone, making sure that the top is covered with a layer of salt. Put a pickle lid, drop lid or large plate on top, leaving a gap between the side of the bucket. Weigh down with a heavy stone or clean weights, the heavier the better. Leave for 3 to 4 days, by which time much water will have been released and it will have risen above the level of vegetables. (This is why a clean stone is the best weight. Metal weights, especially old rusting ones, are not such a good idea because of the risk of them coming into contact with the pickling liquid.) After this time you may remove the amount you want to eat (probably one cabbage half and one cucumber), rinse well, chop roughly and serve.

MISO PICKLED VEGETABLES
YASAI NO MISO ZUKE

The pickling medium here is miso, so this isn't as economical a pickling method as salt pickling, but it's fun to try, and tasty. The pickles will be ready in one or two days. The softer vegetables, the cucumber and aubergine, will be ready after 24 hours, the denser ones, a couple of days. They can then be kept a further few weeks if they are refrigerated. This does not need to be weighted down.

I medium cucumber, or 2 small ones	500 g/ I lb 2 oz dark red miso
2 small aubergines	125 ml / 4 fl oz *mirin*
I medium carrot	I dried red chilli, seeds removed
½ small *daikon* radish	

Wash and dry the vegetables. Cut the cucumber in half lengthways, and scoop out the seeds, as they are too watery. Cut in half again the opposite way. Cut the hard stem off the aubergine and cut in half lengthways. Cut into four from the bulbous end about two thirds of the way up towards the stem end, so that it's still one piece but fanned out. Cut the carrot into thin slices. Cut the *daikon* in half lengthwise then into thick ½ cm/ ⅛ inch half moons. Leave them all out on a clean towel for a couple of hours until they are dry and a bit limp.

Meanwhile, mix the miso and *mirin* for the pickle marinade and add the chillies, cut into thin rings. Immerse the vegetables in the miso mixture, making sure they are all covered (the vegetables should measure no more than half the volume of the marinade, so if there too many leave some out, and pickle them differently). Place a lid or plate on top of the surface of the miso and leave in a cool dark place for two days. Rinse the vegetables lightly before serving and cut them into bite size pieces.

KOREAN GARLIC PICKLED CHINESE CABBAGE
HAKUSAI NO KIMCHEE

This is not a Japanese pickle at all, but Korean. It is however delicious and easy to make, so I have taken the liberty of including it, especially as I've used it in the recipe for Tofu with Kimchee Dressing (page 68). This recipe was given to me by my Korean friend Suk, who got it from her mother. Most families in Korea still make their own kimchee, so the variations are endless. You can add apple, ginger, turnip – use your imagination. The important elements are that the cabbage is well salted and lots of garlic and chilli are used.

I large Chinese cabbage (*hakusai*)

120 g/ 5 oz rock salt

2 tablespoons medium hot (Korean if you can get it) chilli powder (or 3 dried chillis, de-seeded and I tablespoon paprika, for colour)

3 cloves garlic, peeled and finely chopped

I tablespoon caster sugar

5 spring onions chopped into thin strips, about 10 cm/ 3 inches long

I carrot, peeled and cut into matchsticks

600 ml/I pint cold boiled water

Cut the cabbage in half, down its length, then crossways into large bite size pieces. (If you were making large quantities you would leave the cabbages cut in half to pickle them, and that is how they can often be purchased – a whole half of a cabbage. You may graduate to making such quantities after you've acquired a taste for it). Put the cabbage into a large, deep bowl and toss with the rock salt. Lightly mix so all the cabbage is covered, and make sure the top layer is well salted. Place a large plate on top (or a proper wooden pickle lid if you have one) and weigh down, with a clean large stone or brick (or weight). The plate should sit on top of the cabbage without touching the sides of the bowl. Leave this in a cool place for 5 days. After this time much water will have been given off. Pour this off and lightly rinse the cabbage under cold water. Squeeze out excess water. Mix the chilli (and paprika if using) powders with the garlic, I tablespoon caster sugar and mix to paste with a little hot water. Add the spring onion and carrot to the cabbage and then the paste and mix well. Spoon into a large sterilised jar and pour the cold water on top. Leave in the fridge for a further 3 or 4 days before eating. Eat as an accompaniment to rice or to add piquancy (just a bit!) to any dish you fancy.

KIMCHEE 2

In this variation the vegetables are immersed in a large quantity of boiled salted water. Ready in four days, they will keep for at least a week in the fridge (but be warned – you may not like the strong smell of garlic in your refrigerator).

30 ml/ 2 tablespoons salt

600 ml/ I pint boiled water

350 g / 12 oz Chinese cabbage leaves, washed, patted dry and cut into 5 cm/ 2 inch pieces

125 g/ 4 oz carrots, cut into juliennes

50 g/ 2 oz turnip, diced

3 fresh chillies, de-seeded and finely chopped

5 cm/ 2 inch piece of ginger, cut into matchsticks

2 cloves garlic, crushed and minced

3 spring onions, finely chopped or shredded

Put the boiled water in a large glass or plastic bowl and add the salt. Add the chopped chillies, minced garlic, ginger slivers and chopped spring onion. Then add the cabbage, turnip and carrot. Stir well. Put a small plate or pickle lid on top so the vegetables stay under the water, cover the bowl and leave for 2 or 3 days until the pickle is just beginning to taste sour. Then put in the fridge and leave another two days, when it will be ready to eat.

4. Long term pickles (*Hokon zuke*) for long storage can only be made with dried vegetables as too much water in fresh ones ruins the mixture. They are kept to ripen for a minimum of one month. These **long term pickles** should be kept in a cool dark place, such as a cellar.

RICE BRAN PICKLES
NUKA ZUKE

The most complicated method of pickling with rice bran combines the rice bran with beer as a fermenting agent, and is really only for the dedicated pickle maker, as the mixture requires daily attention and agitation, over a period of about 10 days. Once they are ready to be eaten they will last only a month (although the mash can be used again and again) so, unless one intends to make (and eat) large quantities of pickles regularly it is probably not worth the effort. A second, somewhat simpler method is to pickle in dry rice bran, in which case the pickles will take about 30 days to complete, undisturbed. Here is one recipe for the simpler dry bran method, for those of you who want to experience the taste of home made pickle.

CABBAGE IN RICE BRAN
DAIKON NO NUKA ZUKE

This method is used in Japan to make the ubiquitous *takuan* – the strong smelling crunchy yellow pickle that appears at almost every meal. *Takuan* is made with *daikon* radish, which is hung outside in the autumn sun to dry for several weeks. In country areas you can still see rows of white radishes hung under the eaves of farmers' houses. British weather is usually far too damp for such a practice, but you can try leaving root vegetables to dry for 2 weeks indoors. This recipe uses cabbage (any type will do) whilst you leave it. You can also try this with *daikon* radish, or both. You'll need a small plastic bucket, or wooden pickle crock with a lid that drops inside, and a large stone to weigh it down.

I large head cabbage	3 dried red peppers, seeds removed
1.75 kg/ 4 lbs sea salt or rock salt (crushed)	piece of dried *kombu* about 10 cm/ 4 inches long
1.75 kg/ 4 lbs rice bran	

Cut the hard end off the cabbage and wash the leaves, then dry them by resting on kitchen paper or a clean towel. Put a layer of cabbage into the bottom of the bowl or crock, cover with a layer of salt, and then rice bran. Repeat this process layer upon layer, adding the red peppers here and there. Put in the piece of *kombu*. Make your final layer rice bran. Place the pickle lid or small plate on top, and weigh it down with a clean stone or rock. Leave it in a cool dark place for a month, without disturbing it. At the end of this time much water will have been released. Remove pieces of cabbage as you need them, and rinse before serving. Serve cut into smaller pieces. The remaining pickle should keep a further couple of months in cooler weather.

FISH – LIFE FROM THE SEA

"I went to the fish and fruit market and there saw many new fish. These in themselves would be quite a study. I noticed among them the large prawn of Ceylon and a smaller kind; grey mullet and red; sea perch and snappers of many varieties, diminuitive fish no larger than whitebait, a kind of small sea crayfish and a curious blue crab. ...of delicacies in fact there is no lack and I had a most excellent luncheon."

Richard Gordon Smith, *Japan Diaries*

As a small island nation, which has very little cultivable land, and certainly very little for grazing animals, fish (*sakana*) has been an important source of protein in the Japanese diet for centuries. Although fish was never eaten in the temples or by devout Buddhists, whose diet was completely vegetarian, it has always been eaten by coastal people. Fatty fish especially is high in omega 3 fatty acids, which are said to help prevent cholesterol build up – so the inclusion of plenty of fish in the diet may have contributed to Japan's traditionally low rate of heart disease.

A must for any food lover who is lucky enough to visit Japan is a trip to the fish market in Tokyo – the biggest in the world. The Central Wholesale Market (as it is properly called) is located in Tsukiji, in the old, working class, eastern side of Tokyo, and is popularly known as Tsukiji Market. It certainly feels like the biggest market in the world as you tramp around from one block to another. It's huge. The market backs on to the edge of the Sumida River (the main river that flows through Tokyo) and it's here, by the river's edge, that the tuna (both fresh and frozen) auctions are held. At four in the morning the sight of rows upon rows of solidly frozen tuna, emitting clouds of cold vapour, and weak tungsten light bulbs shining through the mist, is truly memorable. The buyers walk around inspecting the fish one by one, row upon row. Their tools of inspection are a small torch and a little probe, with which they poke around into the flesh of the fish, scrutinising its quality. Each fish has a number, which is an important part of the auction, beginning a little later around five o'clock. The auction is what every foreign visitor goes to the fish market to see. Standing on makeshift upturned boxes, in a space just seven metres square, the auctioneers babble like demented hyenas with hiccups (if you've been there you'll know what I mean). Arms flail around in response to some barely noticeable but essential order – and within minutes the fish is sold. Then the next auctioneer takes his position.

Here is every kind of living creature from the sea: eels writhe about in tanks, blithely unaware that any moment soon they will be yanked out of their temporary prison, pinned to a board by their head, and skinned alive. I am not a particularly squeamish person, but I did find this gruesome when I first saw it. Most fish are kept alive though, in blue plastic tanks full of water, until they are sold, and many are taken back to the restaurants of central Tokyo still living. Nearly every fish that's ever eaten in Tokyo, and a third of all the fish eaten in Japan, will have passed through here. Quite a thought.

Around seven o'clock, when you are tired and satiated with the sights, sounds and smells of fish trading, you want something to eat – breakfast in fact. What better breakfast can you think of than fish? After all, if you insist on freshness for your sushi where better to experience it than the fish market itself? And indeed there's plenty of choice. All around the edges of the market are small, crowded and definitely authentic sushi bars. There is something almost decadent about eating sushi at seven in the morning, in the atmosphere of a working men's caff. Surrounded by men in gumboots there's nothing sophisticated here, except of course the taste.

Although the types of fish that live in Japanese coastal waters are not always the same as the fish in the UK and Europe, you can still cook in the spirit of Japanese cooking, by using what is fresh, in season and available. Rather than pay a fortune for imported and frozen giant prawns, sea bream or yellowtail for example, talk to your fishmonger and find out which fish is local and therefore the freshest. Yellowtail (*buri*) is my favourite fish, but something to look forward to and savour on visits to Japan only. As Shizuo Tsuji says in his classic book, *Japanese Cooking: a Simple Art*, 'Good fish is not good because it is expensive. It is good because it is in season.'

Even cheap and plentiful mackerel is delicious when it's fresh and not overcooked. It's also extremely good for you, bursting with omega 3 fatty acids – which is something we are currently being advised to eat several times a week to stay healthy. It also contains a good deal of iodine and vitamin D. I have therefore included several mackerel recipes, in an effort to encourage people to eat it. In Japan *saba* (as it is known) is a very popular everyday fish, either grilled or simmered. If you are grilling it, it's advisable to have a good extractor fan going when you cook it. Alternatively you can keep grilling for barbecues outdoors, and for indoors cooking either simmer or bake in foil.

Choosing fresh fish

The most important aspect of preparing fish is choosing fresh specimens. This is paramount as any cook book will tell you. It's especially important in Japanese cuisine when choosing fish to be eaten raw. Fresh fish has firm flesh which springs back when you touch it, and which is shiny. The scales of the fish should be intact (they start to fall off as the fish ages) and not slimy. The eyes should be bright and clear and bulging. Flat dull and cloudy eyes indicate that the fish has been a long time dead. The gills should be bright red, but not blood soaked, and not whitish. Finally, if the fish smells fishy, leave it in the shop. Fresh fish smells of the ocean, not of fish. Luckily the high street fishmonger is making a re-appearance in the UK, and he is your best source of advice and information. Of course if you live near the coast you can either catch your own or get someone else to catch it for you. And if you live near a river, then freshwater fish is an excellent local choice.

Another distinction to be made is between fish from day boats and fish from deep sea trawlers. The latter is less fresh as it takes the boat time to get to shore, and although the fish is of course kept iced, specimens from day boats, which are caught closer to shore, will be fresher. Fish from day boats have paler skin, as they are exposed to more light from being closer to the surface of the water.

How to prepare fish

Once you have found your fresh fish you need to take it home and prepare it. Whether you are cooking it, or having it as *sashimi* (raw) you will need to de-scale and gut it, using plenty of running water. Japanese cooks often serve their fish whole, and simply grilled. It's essential that the fish keeps its shape though, so in order to keep the fish intact and attractive to the eye, the gutting is done either through the mouth (if the fish is small) or through the gill opening. If the fish is gutted Western style, with a cut along its belly, it twists and distorts during cooking. For simmering though, you can use fish which has been gutted and filleted Western style.

1ST STAGE OF FILLETING

To gut fish: without damaging the body, take the fish in one hand, holding its head to the right, and stomach towards you. With a sharp small knife make a cut through the gill opening. Cut the membrane inside, and then hook the stomach onto the back of the knife and pull everything out through the hole. Cut away the gills on both sides, and wash the fish well. Run water through the whole thing to ensure it's perfectly clean. Japan is a country with plenty of water, and this is reflected in their food preparations. They use lots of it. Make sure there is nothing left inside, and all traces of blood are gone.

To gut flatfish: if you want to keep the shape of the fish gut it behind the gills as described above. If you are making fillets then you can cut the head off and press the insides out.

Filleting

There is nothing difficult about the way fish is filleted in Japan. Fillets are named after the number of pieces a fish is cut into. Thus, the *nimai oroshi* technique is two pieces. The fish is separated into two fillets, one with bones, the other without. The *sanmai oroshi* technique is in three parts, two boneless fillets from either side, and the

NIMAI OROSHI

centre bone with some flesh attached (which would be used for stock or flavouring). The *gomai oroshi* (five pieces) technique is

GOMAI OROSHI

used for large flat fish, and is basically the same as the *sanmai oroshi*, but the boneless side fillets are each cut into two, creating four boneless fillets. The fifth piece is the central skeleton with some flesh attached. To do this make a slightly diagonal cut at below the head, and a straight cut below the tail. Make a cut down the centre, and then curved around the fins, from head to tail. Pull the fillet up starting from the head end at the centre (the firmest part) pulling the fish away from the bone, out towards the sides.

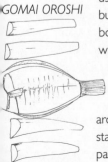

Salting

Japanese cooks often salt fish, whether it is to be eaten cooked or raw, to remove excess moisture, and odour. Fatty fish, which have the strongest odour, such as mackerel, need heavy salting. Fish which is to be eaten raw either as *sashimi* or sushi is salted only lightly, and washed off before eating.

Take a small handful of salt and sprinkle half of it from a distance over the cutting board; place the fish on the board and sprinkle the remaining salt over. Leave it for 30 minutes to an hour, depending on the fattiness of the fish, and whether it's going to be eaten raw or cooked. Wash off excess salt before cooking. If you are concerned about your salt intake you don't have to salt raw fish for *sashimi*, but for grilled whole fish it's essential. In fact for *shio yaki*, salt grilled fish, it's best to leave some salt on the skin. Salt makes the skin crispy and delectable.

Alternatively fish can be 'freshened' by pouring boiling water over it in a colander, and then immersing in a bowl of cold water. This technique is called *shimofuri* (which means 'hoar frosting') and is also used for chicken and liver, to get rid of any odour.

Freshwater fish is additionally washed after slicing, to get rid of the muddy taste which is a feature of river fish. After slicing the fillets wash in fresh water and then plunge them into iced water. Leave a few seconds to chill, and then drain. Do not leave fish sitting in water for any length of time. This is called the *arai* (meaning, wash) technique.

Sushi and sashimi

The astonishing increase in the popularity and availability of sushi in Britain in the last two or three years is a mixed blessing. On the one hand, it's great that it's more readily available. But whenever I mention Japanese cookery, the most common reaction is "oh, sushi". It is a shame that sushi's popularity eclipses all the other interesting Japanese foods available. Another downside to its popularity is that a lot of the sushi that's on the market really isn't very nice, partly because the rice is too cold and the freshness of the fish can't be guaranteed. It worries me that people may try it, not be impressed, and be put off Japanese food forever. The best sushi is freshly made, in front of your eyes, with chilled fresh fish, and freshly cooked, almost warm, rice.

Nothing can beat the experience of eating sushi in a real old fashioned sushi bar with scrubbed cedar counters, glass cabinets glistening with ocean fresh fish, and the friendly smile and welcome of the *itamae* (head chef) to greet you, as you duck under the *'noren'* half curtain and head inside. "*Irrashai mase, Irrashai mase*" cry the chef and his assistants as you slide the door open. "Come in, welcome." Perhaps there is even a tank with live fish swimming around, waiting to be netted and made into *sashimi* for someone's supper. Behind the counter the head chef is deftly making *o-nigiri,* shaping the rice into small finger fulls, and slapping a thick sliver of fresh fish on top. Although it looks easy, the shaping of the *nigiri* takes a great deal of skill, so don't expect to make perfect sushi-bar-style sushis the first time yourself. In fact a professionally made piece of sushi is said to have all the grains of rice facing the same way!

As you sit down at the bar you will be brought a hot towel, chopsticks, a little plate of pickled ginger and soy sauce. But here, soy sauce isn't *shōyu* – it's *murasaki*, meaning purple. Sushi shops have their own vocabulary. The pickled ginger served to cleanse the palate in between bites is called *gari*, *wasabi* (horseradish) is simply *sabi*, and when you ask for your tea at the conclusion of the meal you ask, not for *o-cha* but for *agari* – (being careful not to mistakenly order another pile of pickled ginger!). Although it sounds confusing, it's all part of the fun.

The best time to eat sushi, as any connoisseur knows, is actually lunchtime – the sooner after the fish arrives in the shop the better. Although sushi is associated with late night eating, it stands to reason that earlier in the day is a better time to eat it. The lower end of the sushi market serves fish that has been frozen, so it hardly matters, but if you're going for the top end of the market, lunchtime is best. The other way of ensuring freshness is to have the fish alive in a tank in the shop – the shorter time dead the better.

However, an aficionado knows that the first thing he should order in a sushi bar is not fish at all, but *tamagoyaki*, the egg roll that sits atop a wad of rice – so that he may better judge the quality of the rice. Only then will he proceed to order. Of course he may want to try the fish alone, and before ordering sushi proper may try a selection of raw fish (*sashimi*) accompanied by saké. When the sushi arrives he'll stop drinking saké, as saké is never drunk at the same time as eating rice. Because saké is made from rice it is felt that the flavours do not enhance one another.

All this talk about sushi shops is for a reason: sushi is hardly ever made at home in Japan. If it's eaten at home it is sent out for, and is delivered to your home in a beautiful laquered tray, laid out with exquisite artistry (the tray will be picked up later by the shop's delivery boy). The Japanese housewife is canny enough to know that it's not worth struggling to replicate what it takes a sushi chef years to master. Pressed sushi however is relatively easy to make at home, and the result can be very professional looking. *Makizushi*, rolled sushi (*maki* means roll) is also easy to do at home, and doesn't even need to contain raw fish. Rolled sushi without fish is essentially a rice dish, so follow the recipe for *norimaki* in the section on rice.

Cutting fish for sushi and sashimi

Freshwater fish such as salmon is not generally used for *sashimi* in Japan. However, it is widely used in Britain and the United States. If you do use freshwater fish make sure it is very fresh (i.e. you've just caught it) and give it the *arai* (washing) treatment – after slicing the fillets, wash in fresh water and then plunge them into iced water. Leave a few seconds to chill, and then drain.

Sea bream, sea bass and snapper (temperate water fish with pale flesh) and bonito is often treated with hot water (the *shimofuri* treatment) before serving raw. To do this gently pour over boiling water on the skin side of the fish, holding it over the sink in a colander. Do it gently so that the fish does not break up. Then plunge into iced water to chill. Remove and pat dry. Serve with the skin on.

Additionally mackerel (*saba*) sardines (*iwashi*) (including gizzard shad, *kohada*, a type of large sardine) and herring (*nishin*), which are scavenging fish, are marinaded before eating raw. These fish are referred to as *hikari mono* – things that shine, because of their silvery skin. The skin is not removed, but is usually slashed, to reveal the contrast between the silver and the flesh underneath.

To marinate mackerel, gizzard shad (konoshiro) and other hikari mono:
First salt the fish generously, and leave them for at least two hours. Bigger fish, such as mackerel can be left for four hours or more. Wash off the salt before the next step, which is putting them in a marinade, made by dissolving sugar in vinegar at a ratio of 2 tablespoons caster sugar to 225 ml/ 8 fl oz rice vinegar. Leave in the marinade for an hour. Smaller fish such as gizzard shad and sardines (*kohada*) can be marinated for less time – half an hour will do. The longer you marinate the safer it is, so if it's not absolutely fresh (i.e. just caught) marinate for longer.

Cutting methods

The most common method of cutting raw fish, which will be eaten either as *sashimi* – just simply sliced – or as sushi atop a finger of rice, is to cut straight down across the grain, drawing the knife towards you. This is called *hira giri* or *hira zukuri*. Start from the right of the fillet, and, beginning with the heel of the knife, draw it down and towards you as it cuts through the fish. Use the tip of the knife to push the cut slice to the right. Stack the cut slices on the right, in a row, as you proceed. The slices should be fairly thick, about ½ cm/ ¼ inch. This is suitable for most types of fish.

A second cut, when you want paper thin slices, is called *usu zukuri*. For this the slices are cut diagonally, at an angle, from the top of the fillet, and from the left, not the right. Again draw the knife towards your body, but slice right to left, not straight down. This is often used for delicate white fish, such as striped bass, sea bass and flounder (and for the paper thin slices of potentially poisonous *fugu* – blow fish or puffer fish – which can only be prepared by a chef who is specially licensed to do so).

A third cut, called *kaku giri* is used when you want chunkier pieces. This cube cut is used almost exclusively for soft, thick and firm fleshed fish such as bonito (it's used to prepare *katsuo tataki* – seared bonito) and tuna (*maguro*), used when tuna is served mixed with *natto* (fermented soy beans) or grated mountain yam (*tororo*), and when it's simmered in a soy based stock.

A fourth cut, called *ito zukuri*, is used for squid and *aji* (horse mackerel) and some other firm white-meat fish. Make thick slices as in the *hira giri* cut, then simply cut each slice into thin strips. These are then piled into little mounds. It's especially successful with squid, as it is dense with no grain.

ASSORTED RAW FISH
SASHIMI MORIAWASE

Sashimi **is** served at home, but again the Japanese housewife will normally go to the local fishmonger and buy it ready prepared, that is, sliced, presented on a bed of shredded *daikon* radish, and garnished with perilla (*shiso*) leaves. Alternatively she may buy a fresh fillet or steak and slice it herself. If you are going to do this be absolutely sure that the fish is fresh – either by catching it yourself or buying from a reputable fishmonger – preferably one who supplies Japanese restaurants.

A SELECTION OF FRESH FISH FILLETS, (DEPENDING ON SEASON AND LOCATION)

salmon – apply *arai* washing technique

squid

tuna

trout – apply *arai* washing technique

sea bass – can be served with the skin on – apply *shimofuri* washing technique

flounder

Garnishes: *daikon* radish, *shiso* (perilla) leaves, pickled ginger slivers

---

Follow the methods described for cleaning, salting and slicing the fish. Keep very cold in the fridge, until just ready to serve. Now prepare the garnishes: peel the *daikon* radish. You want long thin shreds of *daikon* – so if your cutting skills are good you can try doing it the way the *itamae* (head chef) does it, using the *katsura-muki* technique. Hold the radish in your left hand and at right angles to your body. With the knife in your right hand (if you're right handed) and held along the length of the radish, peel off a paper thin slice along its length – and keep cutting, so that you get a continuous paper thin sheet. You don't actually move the knife, but hold it, and gently push the radish under the blade. Use your thumbs to hold the radish in place above the blade. Once you have your thin sheet, roll it up and cut across into very thin strands. You can short cut all this if you can get one of the Japanese cutters which makes strands for you, and Japanese fishmongers (in Britain) also sell ready-cut *daikon* radish. Alternatively you can grate the *daikon* to a pulp, as for tempura dipping sauce, and make 'maple leaf radish' (*momiji oroshi*).

Arrange the slices of raw fish alongside the *daikon* shreds, with a couple of perilla leaves to garnish. Serve with *wasabi* paste and a dipping sauce – either plain soy sauce or the *tosa* sauce below, which is especially good with raw fish.

Notes: Flat fish such as flounder, halibut and plaice can be lightly marinated in lemon and vinegar, or *ponzu* sauce for 15 minutes before serving. Because it is caught so far away tuna is often frozen before being used for *sashimi*. Tuna is also cooked and eaten as an appetizer.

TŌSA DIPPING SAUCE FOR RAW FISH
TŌSA JOYU

Most sushi shops have their own secret recipe for the dipping sauce that accompanies *sashimi*. At home you can use plain soy sauce, but here is a classic recipe which is slightly sweetened and flavoured with bonito, which is where it gets its name, as Tōsa is an area in Shikoku island which is famous for bonito. This recipe is adapted from Shizuo Tsuji's excellent book, *Japanese Cooking, A Simple Art,* and is the best I've found.

Although it can be used the day after making it is ideally supposed to be aged – a month is considered the optimum period, but it will keep for up to 3 years !

5 teaspoons saké	3 tablespoons *tamari*
3 tablespoons *mirin*	4 tablespoons dried bonito flakes
5 cm/ 2 inch piece of kelp (*kombu*)	(*katsuobushi*)
225 ml/ 8 fl oz soy sauce	

In a small saucepan combine the saké and *mirin*, and burn off the alcohol by bringing to a boil. Wipe the *kombu* with a damp cloth and place in a bowl with the saké and *mirin* and all the other ingredients. Leave it to stand for a day, then strain it (leaving behind the *kombu* and *katsuo* flakes). Put into a bottle or plastic container and leave it for a month to mature. Keep it in a cool dark place. After this you can refrigerate it, and use as needed.

INSTANT TŌSA DIPPING SAUCE

3 tablespoons soy sauce	2 tablespoons bonito flakes
3 teaspoons saké	(*katsuobushi*)

Put all the ingredients in a small saucepan and bring to a boil. Strain through muslin or a sieve, leave to cool and use the same day.

MAPLE LEAF RADISH CONDIMENT
MOMIJI OROSHI

This is a delightful spicy accompaniment to raw fish. Grated *daikon* radish is mixed with dried red chillies, from where it gets its rather romantic name, *momiji*, after red maple leaves.

1 *daikon* radish	3-4 dried red chillies

Peel the *daikon* thinly. Remove the seeds from the chillies but keep them whole. With a chopstick make three or four holes in the end of *daikon*, up through the length of it. Into each hole insert a chilli, tucking it in well. Grate the *daikon* as normal on a fine Japanese style grater, grating the chilli in with it as you go. Squeeze out some of the water, either by pressing with a spoon against the side of the dish, or wrapping in cheesecloth. The spicy red coloured radish can now be used to flavour your dipping sauces. This can also be used as an accompaniment to tempura, to tofu, hot or cold (*hiya yakko* or *yudōfu*) and other deep fried dishes and fish.

Ponzu sauce is also good with raw fish, and especially if you feel squeamish about the possible presence of parasites, as the vinegar in it is supposed to help to kill them.

EGG ROLL
TAMAGOYAKI

This is the sweetened egg roll which is served in sushi bars. Because it's not raw fish my Japanese friends always assume that it is the first thing I would go for (being a foreigner). Actually they are wrong, as I am not a lover of omelette of any description I'm afraid. But if you are (and I know many people are) then this will definitely appeal. It's made by building up lots of thin omelettes into one rectangular wedge – and it's all done in the pan. You'll need a rectangular pan especially for the task if you want straight sided rolls, but you could improvise with a round one. You could then use any oddly shaped trimmings for Scattered Sushi (*chirashizushi*, page 96). You'll also need a brush to oil the pan in between.

BROTH:	½ teaspoon salt
I teaspoon caster sugar	vegetable oil for frying
4 tablespoons *dashi* (page 49)	½ sheet of *nori* (cut into thick strips
2 teaspoons soy sauce	about 1.5 cm/ ½ inch wide and 8 cm/ 3
I tablespoon *mirin*	inches long, for fastening around the
6 eggs	middle of each piece)

Dissolve the sugar in the *dashi*, soy sauce and *mirin* to make the broth. Mix the eggs lightly, but don't beat (you don't want a fluffy omelette). With the broth at room temperature, pour in the beaten egg and lightly combine. Heat the omelette pan until quite hot then brush lightly with the oil. You will now be cooking the omelette in three stages to make one roll. If you have a small omelette pan you will get two rolls from this mixture – if it's a large one you'll get one roll. So pour one third (or a sixth) of the mixture into the pan and tilt back and forward until you have a very thin layer of egg just covering the base. The egg should immediately sizzle around the edges. Cook over this medium high heat until the egg is 70% cooked – cooked around the edge but soft and runny on top. Then, using chopsticks if you are nifty with them, or a spatula if you aren't, roll the cooked omelette, and push to one end of the pan, tilting it away from you as you do so. Take the oily brush and brush the empty base of the pan. Push the roll away and brush underneath it. Push it back, all the time keeping the pan on the heat. Pour another third of the mixture onto the empty part and tilt the pan and lift the cooked roll so the liquid egg flows underneath. Cook until almost done as before. Then again roll this section up, but using the original 'waiting' roll as its core. Repeat the process, rolling each new omelette around the previously cooked one, until the mixture (or half of it) is used up. A minimum is three layers to the roll, but you can do more if you like. Tip the cooked egg from the pan and leave to cool. Cut into 5 cm/ 2 inch pieces and serve either alone or on top of a wad of sushi rice. It is usual to secure the egg to the rice with a thin strip of *nori* wrapped around the middle.

Variation: If you become quite deft at this and really want to show off you can put a sheet of *nori* in between one of the layers, as you cook. Once rolled and then cut through it will reveal an impressive spiral effect – plus the delightful taste of *nori*.

FINGER SUSHI
NIGIRIZUSHI

As I have said, sushi is almost never made at home in Japan, but I know some readers will want to try it. Plastic sushi making moulds are now on the market to cater for those who want to attempt it, and they can make the task easier. Nothing is as good as sushi made by a master though.

A SELECTION OF FRESH FISH SUCH AS:	marinated mackerel, herring, sardines, gizzard shad
raw salmon fillet	prepared sushi rice (preferably still
raw tuna steak	slightly warm) see the section on
raw flounder fillet	sushi rice, page 94
cooked large prawns, cut down the middle and opened out, tail still on	wasabi

Cut the fish (except prawns) into thin slices across the diagonal, so that each piece is about 5 cm/ 2 inches by 3 cm/ 1 inch. Take the piece of fish in your left hand and dab a blob of wasabi in the middle on the underside. Then take about a tablespoonful of rice and press it onto the wasabi and fish, using the thumb on your left hand to make a dent in the rice. Shape the rice into an oblong with your right hand, shaping the fish around it. Keep pressing and squeezing the rice to compact it under the fish, changing hands as you do so, and working quickly. (The more you handle the fish the less appetising it will be, as the warmth of your hands will spoil it.) Serve with the fish uppermost, concealing the rice 'bale' or 'finger' underneath. Two pieces side by side is a standard serving of one fish. To eat, dip the sushi, fish side only, into soy sauce or other dipping sauce. Do not dip the rice into soy sauce, as it will fall apart.

PRESSED SUSHI
BATTERA ZUSHI

You'll need a wooden sushi pressing box (called oshiwaku) or a small loaf tin, and wax or greaseproof paper, or a banana leaf, to line the mould. Mackerel, with the skin left on and marinated is a classic ingredient, but other strong tasting fish such as herring, or sea bass would be good, as is smoked salmon, for a more Western style sushi. A battera zushi mould is an oblong box with a removable wooden base and lid. The lid presses down on the rice and compacts it. In order to stop the fish at the bottom sticking to the wood the box must be lined with something waxy – traditionally, aspidistra leaves are used (honestly) but a banana leaf, or wax paper will do as well. Obviously a banana leaf is more striking than paper and can also be used to serve it on. Battera zushi is quicker and easier to make than finger sushi as each block makes about six pieces, and there is no hand shaping.

MAKES 12 PIECES OF SUSHI	225 ml/ 8 fl oz rice vinegar
1 medium size mackerel, cut into two fillets	300 g/ 11 oz cooked, prepared sushi rice
MARINADE:	*wasabi*
2 tablespoons caster sugar	

First prepare the mackerel for the marinade. Salt the fish fillets generously, and leave them for at least two hours. Meanwhile dissolve the sugar in the vinegar. Wash the salt off the fish and put in the marinade, making sure it's well covered. Leave for an hour then remove and pull off the thin membrane covering the skin (but leave the skin itself on). Trace around the wooden box onto the wax paper or leaf, and cut out to fit the bottom of the mould. Alternatively you can lay banana leaves crosswise so they go up the sides as well. If you are using a small loaf tin, or some other terrine-style mould, this would be a suitable method.

Lay the fillet with its skin side down and cut through horizontally, making two thin fillets from one thick one. You now want to line the mould with these. Cut each piece on the diagonal so you have pieces which are half the width of the mould. These will lay side by side on the bottom. Put one piece skin side down in the bottom, and another without skin next to it. Lay more in the same way if they are not long enough to cover the base. Spread some *wasabi* over (about the size of two peas) and then fill the mould with the cooked sushi rice. Use your fingers, moistened in vinegared water to prevent sticking, to press the rice down. When the box is full, moisten the lid of the box with the water and press down firmly to compact the rice. Use your thumbs to press down, and your other fingers to steady the box underneath, then carefully flip it over as you press the lid all the way through. You should have a wad of rice with the fish embedded on top. Peel off the paper or leaf, and cut it carefully into thick slices. Again, use a sharp wet knife, so the rice doesn't stick, and use a pulling motion for cutting it. This type of sushi is good for transporting – you can make it at home then cut it into slices at your destination. It's therefore good for picnics and outside catering and also makes a charming and unusual gift.

ROLLED SUSHI
MAKIZUSHI

The technique for rolled sushi is described in detail in the rice section, page 98. *Maki* means roll, and so this is also sometimes called *norimaki* – meaning *nori* roll.

For those who are squeamish about raw fish you can try fillings of:
Non-raw fish
smoked mackerel – cut into thin strips
smoked salmon – you can use scraps or cut sheets of it into thin strips
tuna mayonnaise – mash tinned tuna with mayonnaise
avocado – cut into strips and use with crab sticks or smoked mackerel
crab stick – cut into strips and use with avocado and cucumber

Cooked fillings: chicken breast, flavoured *teriyaki* style with soy sauce and ginger
salmon or trout *teriyaki* style

Traditional vegetable fillings
takuan, pickled radish, cut into thick strips
pickled plum (*umeboshi*) paste (don't use too much – one teaspoonful spread along
the centre is enough)
simmered and flavoured gourd strip (*kanpyō*)
shiitake mushrooms

To prepare gourd (kanpyō) strips and shiitake filling

4-5 pieces gourd strip about 30 cm/ 1
   foot long
4 large *shiitake* mushrooms, softened if
   dried, and cut into thick strips
1 tablespoon salt

FLAVOURING BROTH:
225 ml/ 8 fl oz *dashi* (page 49)

1 tablespoon sugar
2 teaspoons soy sauce

PLUS (TO SIMMER *SHIITAKE*):
1 tablespoon sugar
1 teaspoon *mirin*
1 tablespoon soy sauce

Wash the gourd strips in water and then rub in the salt, to help break down the fibres.
Soak in water for 2-3 hours until soft. Rinse. Combine the broth ingredients in a small
saucepan. Add the gourd strips and simmer for 10 minutes. Remove and leave to cool.
Meanwhile, use the left over broth to simmer the *shiitake* and flavour them. Add the
extra simmering ingredients to the broth, with the sliced *shiitake* mushroom, and
simmer until well coated and the liquid almost gone.

   Cut the cooked and cooled gourd strips to exactly the length of a width of *nori*
seaweed (reserve the end bits to use for another purpose – add to cooked rice when
making scattered sushi for example). Place one strip of gourd and two or three slices
of *shiitake* mushroom end to end along the centre of the roll. Roll up as described in
norimaki in the rice section, page 98.

COOKING FISH
The first important rule for fish cookery is: use the freshest fish you can find. The
Japanese housewife (like her French counterpart) expects to shop daily for fresh
ingredients such as fish, vegetables and meat. Frozen food has never made much
impact in Japan, where texture and flavour are paramount.

   The second rule is: don't overcook it. For whole fish you'll need a less intense heat
than for fillets, as you need to make sure the inside is cooked. Cook until the flesh loses
its transparency, and then stop. 10 minutes per 3 cm/ 1 inch (measured at the thickest
part of the fish) is plenty. 5 minutes each side is a good guide for an average size fish

for one person. As varieties of fish differ in the UK from Japan, some improvisation will be needed, but be guided by what is fresh and available, and consult the list of ingredients at the beginning of the book.

Cooking methods

Cooking fish follows the same five cooking methods as other Japanese foods:

Grilling (yakimono) is good for fatty fish such as mackerel, salmon, and swordfish. Also trout, sea bass, dab, herring, red mullet, and sole. Sprats and squid can be grilled whole, squid first being brushed with oil or a soy marinade.

Shio-yaki is salt-grilled – and a classic Japanese technique for cooking whole fish. Use for mackerel, salmon, sweetfish (ayu), halfbeak (sayori) and trout. Flounder, shrimp and squid are frequently salt-grilled too.

Simmering and poaching is used for any delicately flavoured fish (usually fillets) and fish that would otherwise be dry, as it cooks in its own juices. Cook quickly over a high heat, and spoon some of the lightly flavoured simmering liquid over to serve. Freshwater fish is usually simmered for a little longer to reduce odour.

Mackerel and other strongly flavoured fish can also be simmered, but usually in a heavily flavoured stock containing miso or saké, which reduces odour. Simmer over a medium heat.

Steam grilling (mushiyaki) Steaming in foil (or banana leaves) is another very good technique for fish. It's quick, clean and retains juiciness and flavour in delicately flavoured or dry fish. Less suitable for oily fish.

Deep frying (agemono) Suitable for white fish, such as filleted plaice, dab, monkfish, sole fillets and squid. The fish can be first coated in a batter or simply sprinkled with flour. Deep fried fish is often accompanied by grated daikon radish, to help digestion of oil.

Note: Octopus (tako) is not eaten raw. As it is not easy to guage the freshness of octopus, marinating, vinegaring or some cooking method is always used.

GRILLED RECIPES
YAKIMONO

Skewering fish helps retain its shape, and is imperative in Japan where food is grilled over charcoal. If you use a Western style grill, the fish is supported under the heat source so skewering isn't necessary, but because skewering is also a part of the finished appearace of some kinds of grilled fish, especially those grilled whole, I have included a brief guide to how to do it. Ideally no trace of the skewers should remain on the cooked fish as it is presented to the diner, although when we did our photograph we left them in, both to show how it is done and because we thought it aesthetically pleasing. Fish is always presented with the head facing left, so in order to skewer, place the fish on a cutting board with the head facing right. You'll need two sharp skewers. (Dull skewers will tear the flesh and ruin the appearance.) Insert the first one above the eye, bringing it out again about a third way along its length, then push in again and out over the tail. Two things: the skewers should not go all the way through the fish and out the other side. The idea is to keep the other side (the top as it's served) unblemished; and the skewers should be inserted at a slight diagonal, towards the tail. Thus, when you've inserted your second one, starting under the gill, the skewers touch or cross at the tail.

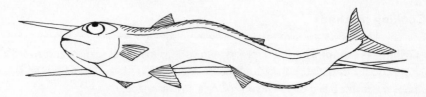

This makes the skewers easier to hold, and turn. This method is good for whole round fish (such as mackerel, trout, snapper, sea bass, sea bream, etc.). Like I said, this method is the ideal. If you find yourself skewering all the way through the flesh, don't worry. The point of this is for the fish to cook into a curved S shape, which imitates the action of a fish still swimming (a technique called *uneri gushi*.) As far as flavour is concerned, just putting it under the grill is fine!

Another trick (which is easy) is to cover the tail with a small piece of foil, which stops it from scorching and preserves the appearance.

SIDE SKEWERING

In Japan, because foods are grilled **over** charcoal, rather than **under** a grill, skewering is also used for fish steaks. Put the skewers at right angles to the grain of the fish (two side by side) so the pieces don't flake off. This is called *hiragushi* – flat skewering. Again, if you are using a Western style grill then skewering isn't strictly necessary.

Another method, for smaller fish, is to thread several fish on to three skewers, in which case the skewers are pushed at right angles to the fish, from edge to edge. Again the two skewers should slightly fan, creating a 'handle' to grip. This is called *yoko gushi*, or side skewering, or fan skewering.

HIRAGUSHI

YELLOWTAIL OR SALMON TERIYAKI
BURI / SAKE NO TERIYAKI

This is delicious with yellowtail (*buri*) fillets, so if you can get them, especially during the winter when they are fatty and tender, use them. Because of its oiliness yellowtail is a fish that freezes well, so it could be worth trying it even if you can only get frozen imported yellowtail. However, *teriyaki* is equally delicious with fresh salmon steaks or fillets, and also with swordfish. The fish is first marinated and then grilled or pan fried. A separate similar, but lighter, sauce is poured over to serve.

4 yellowtail or salmon fillets (or 2 salmon steaks, cut in half with the centre bone removed)	I tablespoon sugar 2 teaspoons ginger juice (squeezed from freshly grated ginger root)
MARINADE:	**SAUCE:**
4 tablespoons soy sauce	2 tablespoons light soy sauce
2 tablespoons *mirin*	I tablespoon *mirin*
2 tablespoons saké	I tablespoon saké

Mix the ingredients for the marinade. Apply the *shimofuri* washing technique to the fish, then lay the fillets in a flat shallow dish and pour over the marinade. Leave for at least 30 minutes, but preferably longer (2 hours if you can) in a cool place. Remove from the marinade (reserve the left over marinade) and place under a hot grill. Depending on the thickness of the fish, grill either side for about 3 minutes, until just done, so the flesh is opaque and no longer translucent. Tertia Goodwin at the Authentic Ethnic Cookery School swears by her rule of 10 minutes per 3 cm/ 1 inch, for any fish cookery from any country. Whilst the fish is cooking, put the sauce ingredients, and any left over marinade (strain it first) into a saucepan and bring to a boil. When the fish is cooked, place one fillet attractively on each diner's plate, and spoon a little of the sauce over. Garnish with a sprig of fresh ginger, spring onion or small mound of grated *daikon* radish. For a more elaborate presentation garnish with a turnip chrysanthemum (*kiku kabu*). Serve hot, with a bowl of rice, miso soup, pickles and a simmered vegetable dish (*nimono*) or dressed salad (*aemono*).

Variations: this is good with any boneless fish steak, such as swordfish, salmon, tuna, prawns and scallops. It is also good with octopus or squid. Cut into bite size pieces before marinating, and pan fry instead of grilling.

SALT-GRILLED WHOLEFISH
SAKANA NO SHIO YAKI

My first experience of simple salt-grilled fish was at a bustling and noisy bar called Okajyoki in Nakano in Tokyo, when I was first in Japan, about twenty odd years ago. Having been brought up on soggy British fish and chips, the taste was a revelation. The fish was cooked over a big charcoal fire, which was surrounded by a huge circular counter, at which the diners sat, and watched the fish being cooked. The salt makes the skin crispy and the flesh juicy and flavoursome. The trick is not to overcook it. Grill until the flesh is just opaque. This technique can be used for many different kinds of fish, such as trout, sea bream, red mullet, herring, sardines or, in Japan, sweetfish (*ayu*).

4 small red mullet or herring (or other fish) cleaned, but heads left on	½ *daikon* radish, peeled
3 tablespoons salt	I teaspoon poppy seeds to garnish 8 metal skewers

This is simplicity itself. Wash the prepared fish and pat dry. Sprinkle half the salt over a board and lay fish over. Sprinkle remainder over the fish and leave for 30 minutes. Meanwhile prepare the garnish, peel and grate the *daikon* on a fine or Japanese grater until you have a pulp. Squeeze out excess moisture. Arrange into four little mounds, one for each person. Sprinkle a few poppy seeds on top for visual effect (or make *momiji oroshi* with chillies). Wipe the fish with a kitchen towel to remove any moisture that has been extracted. Now carefully skewer the fish from end to end as described in the section on skewering. Rub a little more salt into the skin, especially the tail. (Half way through the grilling you can also place a small piece of foil over the tail to prevent it burning. This is simply for aesthetics, but a well preserved tail is nicer than a charred one!) Grill under a medium hot grill (or over charcoal) turning once only. Remember that you will be serving the fish with the head facing left, so try to make sure that the side which will be uppermost is attractive, with no torn skin. When cooked, remove the skewers carefully, trying not to break the flesh, and serve on oblong fish plates, with the mound of *daikon* in one corner. Serve hot with rice, soup and pickles. The skin should be crispy and the flesh tender and juicy.

SALT-GRILLED SEA BASS FILLETS
SUZUKI NO SHIO YAKI

4 fillets of sea bass (or sea bream)	1 lemon cut into wedges
2 teaspoons sea salt	

Cut each fillet into two, crosswise. Take a handful of salt and sprinkle half on a marble (or cutting) board. Place the fish skin side down and sprinkle the remainder over. Leave for 30 minutes. Rinse lightly and pat dry. Skewer the fish (if using) with two skewers going from side to side, two pieces on each pair (flat skewering *hira gushi*). Under a hot grill, or over a charcoal burner, grill the skin side first until about 60 percent done, that is until the flesh starts to sweat, it should be crisp but not completely blackened. Then turn and finish the other side – it will only need a minute or two. Twiddle the skewer inside the fish to stop it sticking. Serve without skewers, arranged attractively on a plate, with the lemon garnish. The skin should be crisp and the flesh juicy.

SEARED BONITO
KATSUO TATAKI

Although in the section of grilled recipes, this belongs partly in the raw fish section, as the fish is barely cooked. *Tataki* actually means pounded, and in this case refers to the pounding of the ingredients which are kneaded into the skin to flavour it.

MARINADE:

½ large *daikon* radish

2 spring onions

4 cm/ 1½ inch piece of fresh ginger

1 clove garlic (optional)

1 teaspoon crushed, but not fine, sea
   salt

400 g/ 14 oz fillet of fresh bonito

1 teaspoon finely ground sea salt

1 lemon to serve

soy sauce to serve

First prepare the marinade. Peel the *daikon* and grate to a pulp, then squeeze some of the excess moisture out. Wash the spring onions and chop finely. Peel the ginger and grate to a pulp. Put aside half of the grated *daikon*, ginger and onions – these will be used as garnish later. Now crush the garlic, and mix with the remaining half of the grated *daikon*, ginger and onions, and the sea salt. Put aside. This is your marinade.

On a board sprinkle the teaspoon of ground salt. Roll the bonito fillet in the salt, put in the fridge for 20 minutes, remove, then wash off under cold water. Pat dry. Now place the whole fillet under a grill (or skewer and place over hot charcoal). Grill each side for 1-2 minutes, no more. The fish should still be mostly raw. Plunge into iced water to chill, then pat dry.

On a board spread a large piece of cling film, or foil. Spread the marinade mixture over, and then place the bonito fillet on top. Using the end of a knife, pound the bonito lightly into the marinade, making sure it is well covered, and the flavours absorbed. Then wrap it up firmly and put in the fridge for an hour.

When you are ready to eat, take it from the fridge and cut into thick slices (*hira giri* or *kaku giri* technique) discarding the marinade. Place in a deep dish to serve, and sprinkle the reserved condiments (*daikon*, ginger and onion) generously over the top. Eat with a dip of soy sauce and a squeeze of lemon.

EEL
UNAGI

Eel are at their best during the summer in Japan, when they are consumed in huge amounts, as they are supposed to give stamina and revive bodies wilting from the enervating humidity. The most popular days for eating eel are the 'days of The Ox', which are determined by the ending of the rainy season, and the beginning of the long humid summer.

*"Eels are eaten on any day of the bull (doyō no ushi) that may occur during this
period of greatest heat."*

Basil Hall Chamberlain, *Things Japanese*

This probably makes more sense than at first appears, as eel is high in protein. Donald Richie in his fascinating book *A Taste of Japan*, also points out that eels are rich in vitamins A and E, and associated with improving one's love life! They are usually served grilled with a soy sauce marinade, and placed on top of a bed of rice. Served on top of rice in a box the dish is called *unajyū* (*jyū bako* means box) and on top of rice in a bowl it's called *unadon* (*donburi* means bowl).

GRILLED EEL
UNAGI NO KABAYAKI

Try to get eel which is already filleted, but if you want to prepare it yourself you'll have to strip the bone and remove the guts and head. Slice along one edge to open it up so that it is flat. Cut into four decent size fillets. Apply the *shimofuri* technique by sluicing with hot water and then cold. The rich sweet sauce complements the oiliness of the eel beautifully.

5 tablespoons soy sauce	I large eel
125 ml / 4 fl oz *mirin*	

Put the soy sauce and *mirin* in a small pan and bring to a boil over a medium heat.
Simmer slowly for about 5 minutes, so that some of the liquid is reduced. Take off heat. Put the eel under a hot grill (or skewer *yoko gushi* style and put over hot coals). Grill for about 5 minutes each side, then brush with the soy sauce marinade. Grill a minute more. Repeat once more on the first side and repeat the procedure for the other side, until the eel is cooked and the surface sticky and glossy. Serve as it is, with some of the left over marinade poured over (boil it up first). You can use eel cooked in this way in *Chawan mushi* (Steamed Egg Custard, page 226) or in *Tamago kaiyaki* (Egg and Fish in a Shell, page 205). Cut into smaller pieces it is a popular topping for finger sushi, when it is held in place on top of the rice with a thin strip of *nori* wrapped around its middle. A quick and easy way or serving it as a full meal is to serve it on top of a bed of rice as below.

GRILLED EEL ON A BOWL OF RICE
UNAGI DONBURI OR UNADON

This is said to have originated in the Edo era as a quick snack intended for eating in between performances at the Kabuki theatre, where it would have been served in laquered boxes (not bowls), and called *Unajū* (a *jubako* is a tiered food box, usually highly decorative, and a big feature of New Year food). *Sanshō* pepper is a traditional accompaniment to greasy foods.

SAUCE:	4 large bowls hot cooked rice
4 tablespoons *mirin*	eel (about 350 g/ 12 oz) cooked as in
4 tablespoons soy sauce	previous recipe
4 tablespoons *dashi*	*sansho* pepper (prickly ash) to garnish
I tablespoon caster sugar	

Combine the sauce ingredients and bring to a boil. If you have other left over marinade use that too and bring to a boil together. Lay the pieces of eel on top of the rice in a large *donburi* bowl, and pour over the hot sauce, dividing equally between the four bowls. Serve at once, sprinkled with *sansho* pepper.

This is a very rich dish, as the fish is full of protein and the sauce sweet and salty. It is extremely popular in the summer in Japan, where it is usually prepared by specialist eel shops.

SALMON AND RICE BURGER
RAISU BAAGA

A Japanese burger chain sells a healthy Japanese style burger made with rice instead of bread, and salmon instead of beef. The result is fabulous, so I've tried to replicate the taste here. You'll need to shape the rice into 'bun' or pattie shapes with your hands. The salmon is flavoured *teriyaki* style and placed in between two layers of compressed rice 'buns'. If you have left over salmon, from a poached whole fish, you could use it here instead of the fillets, and although it would be without the *teriyaki* flavouring it will still be good. This is fun, not elegant, food.

4 small salmon fillets, cooked *teriyaki* style

4 bowls fresh hot cooked rice (see section on rice, page 83)

4 slices cheese (the burger chain uses processed, but you can use mild cheddar, edam or mozarella if you prefer)

1 sheet *nori*, cut into four squares

Cook the salmon fillets *teriyaki* style according to the instructions for Salmon *Teriyaki*, page 194 or for a milder flavour you can simply grill them. Divide each bowl of rice into two and shape into two pattie shapes. Do this by compacting the rice into a large ball with your hands, and then flattening it out slightly. Be careful it doesn't fall apart. Put the salmon on top of one rice pattie, lay a slice of cheese on top, then a piece of *nori*, and put the second rice pattie on top. Wrap in foil and warm up under a low grill or in the oven. Serve hot.

GRILLED SQUID WITH TOFU AND WALNUT STUFFING
IKA NO TSUMEYAKI

This was inspired by one of Gaku Homma's recipes, in *Japanese Country Cooking*, but as it's quite rich I lightened it by adding tofu to the walnut and miso stuffing. Serve with plenty of rice and a light vegetable dish, such as Simmered *Daikon*, page 160, or a vinegared salad (*sunomono*).

STUFFING:

I block firm (cotton) tofu

2 *shiitake* mushrooms, dried or fresh

2 spring onions

3 tablespoons chopped walnuts

I tablespoon medium or yellow miso
  (*Shinshu* or *awase*miso)

I tablespoon sweet white miso

I tablespoon *mirin*

4 medium to large cleaned whole squid
  (each about 20 cm/ 8 inches long)

TO BASTE:

I tablespoon soy sauce

I teapoon *mirin*

First press the tofu between a clean cloth and under a weight to get rid of excess moisture, as described in the tofu section on page 58.

If using dried *shiitake*, soak them in warm water until soft.

While you are waiting, prepare the squid and other stuffing ingredients. Make sure the squid is clean with no head or tentacles, and the inner soft bone removed (it's easier to ask your fishmonger to do this for you). Score the outside of the skin with a criss cross of fine cuts – this prevents the squid curling up when cooking and keeps it tender.

Clean the spring onions and chop finely. Finely mince the *shiitake* mushrooms. Toast the walnuts briefly in a skillet, shaking them about, until just beginning to brown, then grind them into small pieces in a *suribachi*, pestle and mortar. Add the drained tofu and grind to a thick chunky paste. In a separate bowl mix the miso and *mirin* until blended to a smooth paste. Add to the tofu mixture and combine well. Finally add the chopped spring onion and *shiitake* mushroom.

Divide the mixture into four and stuff inside the cavity of each squid. Do not fill the squid – it shouldn't be any more than half full, as it will shrink considerably when cooked. Fasten the end with a cocktail stick. Brush each squid with a little of the soy sauce and *mirin* basting liquid, and place under a hot grill. Turn frequently whilst cooking. The squid will shrink to about half its size, and will be cooked in about 10-15 minutes. Serve hot.

SIMMERED DISHES
NIMONO

Simmering fish, especially in saké or miso, reduces any fishy odour, so it's a quick and clean way to prepare a meal. Saké is used to tenderize as well as lessen odour. Miso is usually added later, as its goodness is destroyed by long cooking.

MISO SIMMERED MACKEREL
SABA NO MISO NI

Quick, easy and nutritious – it's also cheap. This is a better choice than grilling if you are cooking mackerel in a confined space, as it is less smelly. The saké, miso and ginger all help to reduce the fishy odour.

4 fillets of mackerel (total weight about 400 g/ 14 oz)	4 tablespoons medium (*shinshu* or *awase*) miso
water to just cover the fish (225 ml/ 8 fl oz)	2 tablespoons caster sugar
125 ml/ 4 fl oz saké	2 tablespoons *mirin*
1 teaspoon fresh ginger juice	a few matchsticks of fresh ginger to garnish

Practise the *shimofuri* technique with the mackerel fillets – place them in a colander and pour boiling water over them, to reduce odour and firm them up. Put them in a wide saucepan (so they can sit side by side) with the water, saké and ginger juice. Bring to a boil and simmer for 5 minutes – the fish should be about half cooked – that is, still transparent inside. Using a couple of spoonsful of the juices from the pan mix the miso, sugar and *mirin* to a thin paste in a small bowl. Add to the pan, being careful not to break up the fish as you mix. Simmer on a low heat for about 5 minutes (more or less depending on the thickness of the fish), until just cooked and still tender. Serve attractively on rectangular plates, and spoon a little of the liquid over. Sprinkle a few shreds of ginger on top. If you prefer a milder ginger taste add the ginger juice later, just before serving, and use only ½ a teaspoon. Serve with rice, pickles and a vegetable dish.

SARDINES SIMMERED IN PLUM DRESSING
SANMA NO UMEBOSHI NI

This is inspired both by a dish I had in a little bar in Tokyo and by Gaku Homma's charming book *Japanese Country Cooking*. *Sanma* (Pacific saury) is a long thin fish from the northern waters of Japan. It is oily, and cheap, like mackerel, so it is a common fish for serving at home, either salt grilled or, as here, simmered. I have substituted sardines, but you can try it with mackerel or herring instead. Of course if you can get *sanma*, then use it. Cooking oily fish in saké reduces the fishiness, and the grated *daikon* helps to cut through oiliness. Remember though that this is healthy oiliness – fatty fish such as mackerel and sardines are a good source of Omega 3 fatty acids – and therefore excellent for the heart.

3 cm / 1 inch piece of fresh ginger	4 large sardines, cleaned and heads removed
½ *daikon* radish, grated finely	225 ml/ 8 fl oz *bancha* (coarse brown) tea
2 tablespoons sugar	
2 tablespoons saké	1 tablespoon *umeboshi* paste (*bainiku*)
5 tablespoons soy sauce	
2 tablespoons *mirin*	

Peel and chop the ginger, and cut into fine juliennes. Peel the *daikon* and grate to a pulp on a Japanese grater. Squeeze out excess water and put aside in a small dish.

Dissolve the sugar with the saké, soy sauce and *mirin*, and pour into a shallow pan (such as a frying pan) big enough to hold all four fish in a single layer. Add the fish and bring to a simmer, covered, over medium heat. In a separate cup mix the *umeboshi* paste with a little of the hot liquid, to make a thin paste, then add the tea. Pour over the fish and simmer, uncovered, over a low heat for 10 minutes, until liquid is reduced and the fish cooked. Serve one fish per person (be careful not to break it up when serving). Spoon a little of the cooking liquid over, garnish with a few strands of the ginger, and serve with a small mound of grated *daikon*.

CLEAR SOUP WITH SEA BASS
BOTAN WAN

This is more of a substantial soup than a main dish. The fish is lightly poached in saké, not simmered in a flavoured stock. This is elegant guest food, not family fare. *Botan* is a peony, which the fish is fancifully said to resemble, as it sits at the bottom of the bowl in the clear soup.

2 thick fillet steaks of sea bass (about 450 g/ 1 lb in total)
½ teaspoon salt (to poach fish)
2 tablespoons saké
CLEAR SOUP:
800 ml/ 1½ pints primary *dashi* (page 49)

1 tablespoon soy sauce
1 teaspoon saké
½ teaspoon salt
½ sheet *nori*, cut into thin strips

Apply the *shimofuri* washing technique to the fish, then poach the steaks in lightly salted water, with 2 tablespoons saké added, until cooked – about 7 minutes depending on size. Cut in half and place one piece in the bottom of each lacquer soup bowl. In a saucepan bring the *dashi* to a boil, and add the salt, saké and soy sauce. Taste it and adjust seasoning if required. Take off the heat and ladle carefully into each bowl, being careful not to break up the fish. Sprinkle the *nori* strips on top to garnish. Place a lid on and serve at once.

FISH CAKE BALLS
SURIMI DANGO

Although these are not strictly speaking *kamaboko* (fish paste cake), they can be used if you can't get commercially made *kamaboko* for one-pot dishes such as *o-den* (see page 206). They are also good in soups.

450 g/ 1 lb white fish fillet (coley is fine, as appearance is not important)

3 tablespoons plain flour (sifted)

1 tablespoon *mirin*

½ teaspoon salt

pinch chilli powder (optional – if you want spicy ones)

2 egg whites

50 g/ 2 oz potato flour (*katakuriko*) for dusting

oil for deep frying

Apply the *shimofuri* washing technique to the fish. Skin the fish fillets, remove any bones and chop finely. If you have a food processor put the fish in and blend to a smooth purée. If you haven't got a processor then use a pestle and mortar (*suribachi* and *surikogi*) to grind the fish to a smooth paste. Add the plain flour, *mirin*, salt and chilli powder if using, and mix well. You should have a very stiff paste. Now beat the egg whites to a stiff foam and mix in. The mixture should still be fairly stiff but lighter than it was. If it's too sloppy add more flour to bind it, as you now need to shape it into small balls or croquette shapes. Dust the croquettes lightly with the potato flour. Deep fry in medium hot oil (170C/340F) for about 5 minutes until cooked inside and firm on the outside. Drain and serve either as they are, or as part of a one-pot meal, such as *o-den*, in which case they will be simmered further in stock.

DEEP FRIED AND SIMMERED PLAICE WITH GRATED DAIKON
KAREI NO AGEMONO

4 plaice fillets (or other flat fish such as halibut or flounder *karei*)

flour for coating

pinch salt

oil for deep frying

SIMMERING SAUCE:

4 tablespoons *mirin*

4 tablespoons soy sauce

125 ml/ 4 fl oz *dashi* (page 49)

TO GARNISH:

1 small or ½ large *daikon* radish, peeled and finely grated

3 spring onions, finely chopped

Wash the fish in cold water and pat dry. Salt the flour and sprinkle on a plate, then coat the fish pieces well. In a deep frying pan bring the oil to a high heat (175C/ 350F). Slide the coated fish pieces carefully into the hot oil, using a spatula (or chopsticks if you're nifty with them!). Fry for about 5-6 minutes until golden brown and just cooked.

Put the simmering ingredients together in a large but shallow saucepan (so the fish can sit side by side). Bring to a boil, then carefully add the fried fish, and scatter the grated *daikon* on top. Simmer very gently for 3 minutes more until cooked through and hot (but don't cook for so long that the fish falls apart). Be very careful when removing the fish as they will be quite soft by now. Use a fish slice to slide underneath and get good support. Serve on shallow rectangular dishes and spoon plenty of the simmering liquid and *daikon* on top. Garnish with the chopped spring onion. Serve with rice and a dressed salad or vegetable side dish.

COD AND TOFU ONE-POT
CHIRINABE

This warming one-pot dish is cooked at the table, on a portable gas ring, and is similar to chicken *mizutaki*, with fish in place of chicken. Delicate white fish such as cod is suitable for this dish, but you can use a combination of cod and salmon if you like, as we did for our photograph. In the cold northern island of Hokkaido, where salmon is plentiful, this is routinely made with only salmon, where it is called *ishikari nabe*.

4 large cod fillets (about 900 g/ 2 lb)

2 small bunches of chrysanthemum leaves (or watercress) about 200 g/ 7 oz

4 large Chinese cabbage leaves

pinch salt

8 large *shiitake* mushrooms (preferably fresh)

4 Japanese *negi* – long onions (or 2 small leeks or 8 large spring onions)

1 block grilled tofu (*yakidofu*) or firm cotton tofu

water to fill casserole

10 cm/ 4 inch piece of *kombu*

CONDIMENTS:

grated *daikon* with chilli (see *momiji oroshi*, page 188)

ponzu sauce (see page 216)

Cut the fish fillets crosswise into thick 3 cm/ 1 inch slices. Apply the *shimofuri* technique by placing in a colander and pouring boiling water over. Rinse in cold water and pat dry. Keep cool.

Prepare the vegetables as follows: parboil the watercress or chrysanthemum, by plunging into boiling water for 30 seconds. Remove, plunge into iced water and then squeeze out excess water vigorously. A bamboo rolling mat will assist you in this. Put aside. Then parboil the Chinese cabbage leaves for 2 minutes until tender, but be careful not to tear them, as you need them whole. Drain and pat dry, then lightly salt them. You are now going to make attractive cabbage and chrysanthemum rolls. On a bamboo rolling mat, place two leaves end to end (the leafy bits overlapping and the stems furthest away from each other) horizontally. Place half the spinach in a roll along the cabbage about ⅓ the way up the mat. Then, holding the edges carefully with your thumbs, roll up the cabbage, using the mat to keep everything packed tightly together, and squeezing out excess water as you go. Give a few more squeezes to firm up the roll. Remove and cut the roll into 4 thick rounds. Place cut side up on a large platter, so that the green centre is visible.

Cut a cross in the centre of the *shiitake* mushrooms and cut off the stems. Arrange alongside the cabbage rolls.

Cut the *negi* (or leeks or spring onions), diagonally into 1.5 cm/ ½ inch pieces, and the grilled tofu into 8 pieces. Arrange with the other items. Place the pieces of fish alongside the vegetables.

Prepare a table top burner (gas, electric or charcoal) and place the casserole, containing water and the piece of *kombu*, on top. Bring to a simmer. (You can do this at your cooker if you like and bring to the table once it has started to boil.) Begin by adding pieces of fish to the stock – this will give it flavour. Then add the vegetables and tofu. Simmer for a few minutes until the fish is cooked. Do not put in everything at once and overload the casserole. Each person can add their own items and retrieve what they fancy with a small slotted spoon.

Eat the morsels accompanied by a small dish containing the *ponzu* dipping sauce, and adding the spicy grated radish to taste. Serve with hot rice, which makes a complete meal.

EGG AND FISH IN A SHELL
TAMAGO KAIYAKI

This is an adaptation of a recipe discovered in a wonderful book about the *Edo* era (1603-1868) cooking, called *Edo Ryori*, which was given to me by a girl friend in Japan. The translation isn't exact, as it's one of those recipes which are flexible (quite a lot of Japanese cooking is like that). For example I've substituted scallop for abalone, as it's more easily available. The ingredients are similar to those for Steamed Egg Custard (*Chawan mushi*, page 226), but instead of being steamed this is cooked over a flame. It's served in a half scallop (or abalone) shell, and traditionally would be cooked in the shell too, over charcoal on a table top burner. You can try cooking it like this it at the barbecue, or you can pop the filled shells under the grill to set if you want the egg less runny. The recipe can be adapted with different ingredients and would make an interesting starter – a sort of oriental Coquille St. Jacques! You'll need 4 large abalone or scallop shells.

4 medium *shiitake* mushrooms (dried or fresh)	**TO FLAVOUR *SHIITAKE*:**
1 large piece of Jew's ear (*kikurage*)	4 tablespoons *dashi* or mushroom soaking water
100 g/ 3½ oz fresh prawns (or 2 per person if using the larger Tiger prawns)	½ teaspoon soy sauce
	1 teaspoon caster sugar
	4 eggs
4 water chestnuts (canned are fine)	pinch salt
4 scallops (without the orange roe)	1 tablespoon soy sauce
	4 tablespoons saké
	4 sprigs trefoil (*mitsuba*) or watercress

Soak the *shiitake* in warm water for 30 minutes, and the *kikurage* separately in warm water until soft and expanded (it will expand quite a lot so don't soak too big an amount – one piece will do). Remove the shell from the prawns, de-vein, and, if large, cut into two. If using fresh water chestnuts peel and boil for 10 minutes until cooked. If using canned, just drain, and slice thickly. Cut the scallops in half (two halves per person).

Then in a small saucepan combine the 4 tablespoons *dashi* or mushroom soaking water, sugar and soy sauce. Slice the *shiitake* mushrooms thickly and add to the pan, bringing it to a boil. Simmer on a low heat, uncovered, until the liquid has disappeared, and the *shiitake* flavoured.

Parboil the watercress (if using) and plunge into cold water. Cut into 3 cm/1 inch lengths and drain. If using trefoil (*mitsuba*) just chop into 3 cm/1 inch lengths. Drain the *kikurage* and cut into thick slices, removing any very hard bits (it does have a hard chewy consistency anyway though).

In a colander pour boiling water over the scallops and prawns. Refresh in cold water and drain.

Check that the shells are clean and without holes. Whisk the eggs well with a pinch of salt. Put the prawns, scallops, water chestnuts, Jew's ear and *shiitake* in a medium size saucepan, with the saké and 1 tablespoon soy sauce. Bring to a boil, lower the flame, then carefully add the beaten egg. Mix lightly over the heat until just set. If you mix too much you'll get scrambled egg, and if you don't mix at all you'll get an omelette consistency. Actually you want something in between, which is still a little bit runny. Don't overcook, or the egg will scramble and the shellfish will become rubbery. If the egg mixture is too hard or dry add a tablespoon or more of *dashi* or *shiitake* soaking water to soften it.

Take off the heat and lightly mix in the chopped trefoil (*mitsuba*) or watercress. Now, whilst the egg is still a bit runny, but cooked, divide equally between the four scallop shells, making sure everyone has equal portions of fish and mushroom. You can now put the shells over a charcoal burner, or under the grill, to set the egg a little more. Serve hot.

HOT POT

O-DEN

"When we stopped at wayside tea-houses, the runners bathed their feet, rinsed their mouths, and ate rice, pickles, salt fish and 'broth of abominable things', after which they smoked their tiny pipes..."

Isabella Bird

It's possible that the broth Isabella Bird refers to here is *o-den*. I had a similar reaction at first, but now I love it. In fact the contents of this broth are not in the least abominable! It's simply a combination of vegetables, tofu and different types of fish 'cake' (*kamaboko*) simmered together for a long time, so that the flavours mingle and are absorbed.

I first tasted it at the popular seaside resort of Enoshima, just outside Tokyo, where it was being served by the *yatai*, or street vendors, in this case little old ladies, who sat around their portable burners, shielded from the sun behind split bamboo blinds.

Ducking under the blinds I discovered huge shallow pans containing rounds of succulent *daikon* radish, chunks of chewy fish cakes, cubes of deep fried tofu, creamy taro potatoes and and stuffed tofu pouches, steaming and bubbling away in a rich soy-based stock with a faint aroma of the sea. The aroma, in fact, of *kombu* seaweed and bonito which, I very soon came to learn, are the ingredients of all good *dashi* stock, and the basis of all Japanese cooking.

After this first encounter I eventually became very fond of o-den, and would order a bowl at any opportunity – such as at the local noodle shop on a Saturday lunchtime or from a street vendor on my way home from work. Best of all was the temporary stall (again shielded by bamboo blinds) which appeared late at night right next to a highway, on a busy street junction in Meguro in the centre of Tokyo. In those days it was quite unusual for a foreign woman to venture into such places on her own, but although I got stared at, I was always safe. I just couldn't resist the tempting smell – especially on a winter's night, when fragrant clouds of steam curl into the cold night air, and, behind the bamboo curtain, you know there'll be plenty of hot saké to drink too!

The basic principle of making o-den is: balance items that give flavour (such as the fish paste cake [kamaboko], and shiitake mushrooms) with items that absorb flavour (such as tofu and daikon radish). The longer the cooking the better the absorption of flavours. At least an hour (two is better) is required for the best taste. (A regional variation, from Kyoto in western Japan, cooks ingredients separately, but we won't bother with that here. As o-den originated in the Tokyo area we'll stick to the Tokyo way of doing things.) O-den is sometimes served with the items skewered onto bamboo sticks, and this is where it gets its name. It has the same etymology as dengaku, which refers to things on sticks. In this case dengaku was shortened to den and the honorific prefix, o, added.

8 dried shiitake mushrooms

I block konnyaku yam cake

I daikon radish

12 small taro potatoes (satoimo) or
  small new potatoes

3 large carrots

I pack grilled or deep fried tofu

4 hard boiled eggs

4 sticks of chikuwa (a type of fish
  sausage)

I cake hanpen (a fluffy white 'cake'
  made of fish paste)

2 cakes kamaboko fish paste cake

6 small hot dogs (optional)

I large piece of softened kombu, left
  over from making dashi

SIMMERING STOCK:

2 litres/ 3½ pints of secondary dashi or
  I litre/ 1¾ pints secondary dashi and I
  litre/ 1¾ pints fresh chicken stock

180 ml/ 6 fl oz soy sauce

180 ml/ 6 fl oz mirin

2 teaspoons salt

Japanese mustard (or powdered English
  mustard made up with water) to
  serve

Soak the shiitake mushrooms in warm water and leave to soften.

Take a tablespoonful of salt and, on a board, rub it into the surface of the konnyaku, kneading it as you go. Leave it salted for five minutes, then rinse off. Now plunge the whole konnyaku into a saucepan of boiling water and simmer for five minutes. Remove and rinse in cold water. Now you can either cut it into eight triangles, or make twists (see instructions at the end of the recipe). Put aside.

Peel the daikon radish and cut into thick 2 cm/ ¾ inch rounds. Using a sharp knife bevel the edges – this stops the pieces crumbling during the long cooking. Then, using a small knife cut a cross into the centre of each round, being careful not to cut it in half. This helps the *daikon* (which is quite dense) to cook through evenly and makes it easier to prise apart with chopsticks.

Peel the taro potatoes thickly, and put them into cold water. (If you find your hands become itchy when you peel these tubers, use rubber gloves to protect them. Rubbing a little vinegar into the skin helps alleviate the itching.)

Peel the carrots and, using a rolling cut (*ran giri*), cut them into large uneven chunks.

Put the deep fried tofu in a colander and rinse under boiling water to get rid of excess oil. Cut into large cubes (Chinese shops sell deep fried cubes, so you don't have to cut them).

Peel the hard boiled eggs and keep whole.

Prepare the fish paste items – the *chikuwa* and *kamaboko* – by cutting into thick (2 cm/ ¾ inch) slices.

Cut the *hampen* into triangles.

Cut the softened *kombu* into thick strips (about 2 cm/ ¾ inch wide and 10 cm/ 4 inches long). Tie each piece into a loose knot.

Remove the softened *shiitake* and cut off the stems. Strain the soaking water to get rid of any dirt particles and add it to the *dashi* stock.

Combine the soy sauce, *mirin* and salt with the *dashi* and chicken stock, if using.

Place all the solid ingredients into a large, shallow pan, and pour over the flavoured stock. The pieces should be floating in the stock at this stage. The liquid will reduce as it cooks, and be absorbed by the cooking morsels. Simmer over a very low heat for one to two hours (or even longer) making sure the liquid doesn't reduce to less than half.

Check that the potatoes and *daikon* are cooked and the *kombu* softened before serving.

Serve generous portions in medium size or large bowls with a good dab of mustard (this is very important) and some of the juice.

How to make konnyaku twists (see diagram page 160)

Cut the block of *konnyaku* into thin slices across the narrow width of the block. Make a slit in the centre of each piece along its length, but keeping the top and bottom edges intact (don't slice it in half). Then carefully fold the top edge into the slit, and gently pull it through. The *konnyaku* will form a pretty twist. Be careful not to cut too close to the ends or they will split, and if the slices are too thick it will be difficult to turn them inside out.

Note: Chinese-style processed fish cakes can be used in place of Japanese *kamaboko*, or you can make your own (see *surimi dango*, page 202).

ESCABECHE
NANBAN-ZUKE

This is deep fried fish pickled in vinegar. It was almost certainly introduced by the Portuguese in the 16th century, who were referred to by the Japanese as *nanban-jin*, meaning southern barbarians. The use of the word *nanban* always denotes a cooking style or ingredient which is not indigenous to Japan, such as the use of chilli or black pepper. Meat dishes are often styled *nanban*, and *nanban gashi* are Western style sweets. Variations on this spicy pickled fish are to be found all over south east Asia, indeed all over the world. I have even been given a South African recipe which originated with the Cape Malay people, Asians who settled in Cape Town.

4 large fillets of white fish, such as plaice, flounder or cod	2 dried red chilli peppers
plain flour to coat fish	1½ tablespoons *mirin*
vegetable oil for deep frying	1 tablespoon caster sugar
	125 ml/ 4 fl oz rice vinegar
	2 tablespoons soy sauce
MARINADE:	4 tablespoons *dashi* (page 49)
4 large spring onions	

Lightly salt the fish and leave for 30 minutes. Grill the onions over a flame or under a grill, until limp and slightly charred, then slice into thin slices with a diagonal cut. In a bowl of water, or under a running tap, de-seed the chilli peppers. If you like spicy tastes you can now slice the peppers into thin rings, but if not leave them whole (so you can fish them out later). Add the peppers and onion to the other ingredients in a saucepan and bring to a boil. Take off the heat. Rinse the salt off the fish by immersing in hot water. Rinse and pat dry. Dip in the flour, coating both sides and immerse into medium hot oil (170C / 340F) until golden brown and cooked through. Drain on kitchen paper, then place in a shallow bowl. Re-heat the marinade and pour over the fish whilst both are hot. Marinade for at least 30 minutes before serving, but, once cooled, you can marinate for up to 3 days in the refrigerator. If you've kept the chillies whole remove them before serving. This can be served at room temperature or chilled.

You can use any fish you like for this – if you like using whole small fish then whitebait (*shirauo*) or smelt (*wakasagi*) are good. The bones will soften the longer you marinate them and you'll get the added bonus of the calcium.

Note: This is the only instance in Japanese cooking where a vinegar dressing is added to warm food. The usual rule is that vinegared foods are served cold.

STEAMING AND STEAM GRILLING
MUSHIMONO/ MUSHIYAKI

This technique is similar to the French *en papillote*, where food is wrapped in a parcel and then grilled. Traditionally leaves or paper were used, but these days foil has replaced both of them. The ingredients steam inside the foil, and aromas are trapped inside, which is why it's a popular technique for wild mushrooms in autumn. It's also a gentle way of cooking, so good for delicate food like fish.

 ## FISH STEAMED WITH VEGETABLES
HIRAME NO MUSHIYAKI

In this attractively presented dish, the fish fillets are scattered with juliennes of vegetable and mushroom, and carrot 'maple leaves', to represent fallen leaves in an autumn forest. Wrap each parcel separately in foil, so that each person can open up their own. You can cook the bundles any way you like – over a fire, under the grill, in the oven or steam them in a steamer. Any non-oily white fish is suitable, such as sea bass, cod or monkfish.

---

4 fillets of flounder or other flat fish	1 pack *enokitake* mushrooms
3 tablespoons salt	12 small green beans
1 medium carrot, peeled and cut into thin slices	12 ginkgo nuts, shelled and peeled (see page 151, Sankō In Autumn Tempura)
4 fresh *shiitake* mushrooms	3 cm/ 1 inch piece of fresh ginger root
4 oyster mushrooms	4 thin slices of lemon (optional)

Salt the fish fillets lightly and leave for an hour in a cool place. Meanwhile prepare the vegetables. From the carrot slices cut maple leaf shapes with a cutter (or juliennes if you don't have a cutter). You want at least three leaves per person. Parboil in boiling water for 1 minute to soften. Wipe the *shiitake* and oyster mushrooms, cut the hard stems off the *shiitake*, and slice all the caps into long thin slices. Chop the mycelium off the *enokitake* mushrooms and discard, then rinse the mushrooms lightly. Pat dry. Top and tail the green beans, cut on a long diagonal into thin strips and parboil in salted water for 30 seconds. Drain and plunge into cold water. Drain again and pat dry. Peel the ginger root and cut into very fine small juliennes or matchsticks.

Wash the fish well but gently, then take off the skin. If you are going to steam over water, now prepare a large steamer with boiling water. To make the parcels take four large squares of foil, big enough to hold the fish and vegetables, with room to spare. Divide the mushrooms and vegetables into 4 portions. In the centre of each piece of foil scatter half the beans and mushrooms. Place a fillet of fish on top and scatter the remaining vegetables, ginkgo nuts, carrot 'leaves' and ginger matchsticks on top. Sprinkle with a little salt, and place the slice of lemon on top. Wrap up each bundle securely, bringing the sides well up to seal so that juices will not escape. Leave space inside for steam to expand. Place the bundles side by side in the steamer, or on the fire, in the oven, or under a hot grill. Let the contents steam inside the bundles for about 15 minutes until the fish is cooked and the vegetables tender. Serve with *ponzu* sauce (page 216) if desired. Serve as a main course with rice, a salad and soup, or with *chirashizushi*, buffet style (page 96).

MONKFISH STEAMED WITH CHESTNUTS
ANKO TO KURI NO MUSHI YAKI

Although the fish itself is exceptionally ugly, monk fish is very tasty, with soft boneless meat, similar in texture to lobster. In this dish it's steamed in heatproof bowls or cups, such as *chawan mushi* cups, and a thick hot sauce ladled on top before serving.

4 small fillets of monkfish (about 150 g/ 5 oz each)	**THICK SAUCE:**
12 chestnuts	450 ml/ 16 fl oz *dashi* (made up with the *shiitake* soaking water)
4 ginkgo nuts	1 tablespoon light soy sauce
12 carrot 'maple leaves' (shaped from thin carrot rounds)	2 tablespoons *mirin*
4 dried *shiitake* mushrooms, re-hydrated in warm water	pinch salt
	2 teaspoons *kuzu* starch, mixed to a thin paste with a little cold water
4 x 2 cm/ ¾ inch pieces of kombu, wiped with a damp cloth	1 teaspoon *wasabi* paste
4 small sprigs of watercress, parboiled	steamer, big enough to take 4 bowls
4 tablespoons saké	4 deep bowls, which will withstand heat

Apply the *shimofuri* treatment to the fish fillets by placing in a colander and pouring boiling water over. Put into iced water to chill. Drain and pat dry.

Shell and peel the chestnuts and ginkgo nuts as described in the recipe for Sankō In Autumn Tempura (page 151), then slice the chestnuts thinly. Leave the ginkgo nuts whole. Parboil the carrot 'maple leaves' in boiling water for 1 minute. Remove with a slotted spoon and pat dry.

Remove the mushrooms when softened from the soaking water. Strain this soaking water through muslin so it is nice and clear, and put aside to use in the *dashi* for the sauce. Cut the stems off the mushrooms and cut a decorative cross in the cap.

Now assemble the items in the bowls. First of all place a piece of *kombu* in the bottom of each cup (this will not be eaten) to impart flavour during steaming. Put a piece of fish on top, then a layer of chestnut slices. Add the sprig of watercress, a mushroom, one ginkgo nut, and the carrot maple leaves.

Finally, pour a tablespoon of saké over everything to moisten. Cover the cups with foil or plastic wrap, making sure they are well sealed. Place in a steamer (which is already steaming) and steam over a high heat for 15 minutes.

Whilst they are steaming you can make the sauce. Put the *dashi* (made up with the mushroom soaking water), *mirin* and soy sauce in a small saucepan. Bring to a boil, and then lower the flame to a simmer. Taste and adjust seasoning if required. Whilst it is simmering carefully add the *kuzu* starch (dissolved in water) in a thin stream, and stir well. Let it thicken, stirring, for a minute or two, then take off the heat.

Remove the cups from the steamer, take off the foil and ladle about four tablespoonsful of the sauce over the contents of each cup. Place a small dab of *wasabi* in the centre of each and serve immediately whilst hot. Serve as a starter or a steamed course (*mushimono*) in a Japanese meal, accompanied by rice and vegetable side dishes. It would go nicely with *Chirashizushi* (Scattered Sushi, page 96).

TROUT IN FOIL
MASU NO MUSHIYAKI

This can be made with either freshwater trout, rainbow trout or sea trout. In fact it's such a basic recipe that it will suit any pale or lean fish. The steaming keeps the juices in and the fish moist so it's good for non-oily fish. You can substitute mullet, sea bass, red snapper or whitefish.

4 small freshwater trout fillets	I tablespoon light soy sauce
MARINADE:	8 spring onions
2 tablespoons sweet white miso	I teaspoon vegetable oil
(*Saikyō* miso)	4 teaspoons fresh lime juice
4 tablespoons saké	

Apply the *arai* technique to the trout – wash in cold water, drain and then place in iced water for 2 minutes. Drain and pat dry. This gets rid of any muddy taste which sometimes lingers on freshwater fish. (If using saltwater fish apply the *shimofuri* technique instead.) Mix the miso, soy sauce and saké for the marinade. Smear over the fish and leave to marinate for 20 minutes.

Wash the spring onions and slice into thin diagonal slices. Take four large squares of foil, and lightly grease the inside (non shiny side) with butter or vegetable oil. Remove the fish from the marinade (leaving a little coating the fish) and place one piece of the fish on each square of foil. Scatter spring onion on top, and sprinkle the lime juice over. Wrap up well, sealing the sides.

Place under a hot grill, or over a charcoal fire, for about 15 minutes (or in a medium hot oven for 20 minutes). When it's just cooked through, remove from the heat, and serve immediately. Let each diner unwrap their own, the better to appreciate the fragrant aroma which will envelop their nostrils as the foil is pierced open.

MEAT – FOOD OF THE HAIRY BARBARIANS

As recently as 1869, on the island of Hachijojima south of Tokyo,

"10 persons were banished, 10 others fired and 3 others scolded for the crime of killing and eating an ox as 'an unclean crime of this sort was thought to invite misfortune upon the whole community.' As a general rule meat was not considered proper food."

Japanese Life and Culture in The Meiji Era by S. Keizo, trans.C.S.Terry

For two hundred years, from the 17th century to the 19th, Japan was closed to outsiders, with no contact with the West. Then, in 1853, Commodore Perry from America sailed in to Japan with his infamous Black Ships, and persuaded the Emperor of the time, Meiji, to open Japan's doors to trade. Change didn't happen overnight though, and at first the big strange foreigners with their long noses and hairy faces were distrusted. The fact that they ate meat didn't help either, and for a while they were referred to as hairy barbarians. Eventually though, as often happens, attitudes softened. People became curious. The Japanese saw how enterprising these foreigners were, so treaties were signed and trade officially begun. In addition the Japanese were impressed by the physical size of these foreigners – the Japanese at that time were tiny – and it was officially decided that eating meat was no longer taboo, and was indeed something to be desired and encouraged. In fact, in a complete reversal of attitude from the previous Buddhist influence, the people were practically ordered to eat meat. Local authorities issued edicts similar to the following issued in 1872 by Tsuruga Prefectural Office.

"Meat is a nourishing food that helps keep people in good spirits and strengthens the blood, but some people bound by conservatism, not only refuse to eat it themselves, but over that it is unclean, and that people who eat it cannot appear before the gods...This is sheer bigotry."

This was at the start of what was called the Meiji Restoration, named after the Emperor, Meiji. All things Western suddenly became fashionable, and it wasn't long before meat eating was one of them. However, luckily for the health of the Japanese, although meat eating was no longer forbidden, meat, especially beef, still wasn't readily available. There was very little land to spare for grazing cattle, and no history of animal husbandry, so meat was eaten sensibly, in small quantities, and never usurped the sacred grain, rice as the main dish in a meal. Certainly it hadn't done so by the time Basil Hall Chamberlain wrote the following passage, and it still hasn't.

"Of course no actual prohibition against eating flesh, such as existed under the old regime, obtains now. But the custom of abstaining from it remains pretty general."

Basil Hall Chamberlain, *Things Japanese*

 SUKIYAKI

Although one of the most famous Japanese dishes, *sukiyaki* was only invented around 150 years ago. Whilst people were being encouraged to eat meat they really didn't know what to do with it. Lacking ovens and any tradition of long cooking techniques such as roasting, the meat was finely sliced and cooked in a hot skillet with some vegetables chucked in – and inevitably a soy sauce based stock was added. (Even today you won't find meat on sale in Japan in huge joints for roasting. It is always sliced or cut up in some way.) The resulting dish, named *sukiyaki*, somehow caught on, and is still regarded with some awe by most Japanese. In addition it is almost always one of the dishes offered to a visiting foreigner – both because it appeals to the Western palate, and because it is expensive. Because of this, going out to eat *sukiyaki* in Japan is a big deal, even more so if you go to the oldest *sukiyaki* restaurant in Tokyo, owned by the Miyamoto family, which was established over a hundred years ago. They are still serving *sukiyaki* on the same premises, (albeit re-furbished) and going there is like visiting a geisha house. Waitresses trip around in beautiful kimono, sliding open paper screens noiselessly, as they carry in lacquered trays of drinks and food. When you serve it at home you can do so with appropriate fanfare – it's special, and the better the beef the more special it is. The best beef is supposed to be that which is produced in the area around Kobe, where the cows are fed on beer and massaged daily. The result is a finely marbled beef with a high but even fat content – said to be the most tender and delicious (I've had it only once, and actually it is). You don't have to go all the way to Kobe for your beef for this dish – topside or rump will do. However, in order to get the very thin slices that are required, put the meat first in your freezer, but don't freeze it completely. It needs to be about half frozen. It's then quite easy to cut thinly if you use a very sharp knife, and cut across the grain. The slices need to be thin – thinner than escalopes, or even bacon slices if you can. The way of eating this is one of its attractions – the wide shallow *sukiyaki* pan is placed on a portable gas ring in the middle of the table, and people cook their own portions. Each diner has a small bowl in which to crack a raw egg, and the cooked hot morsels of beef are swished in the egg before eating. It may sound strange, but as the hot juices mingle with the egg, the whole thing becomes remarkably palatable. Delicious in fact. However, if you're squeamish about raw eggs then just eat it without, as it's still good.

You'll need a cast iron skillet, preferably without a long handle, and a table top burner for this. Perhaps you'll even feel inspired to don a kimono...

750 g/ 1½ lb rump steak or topside, sliced finely

3 Japanese *negi* or 3 small leeks or 6 large spring onions

12 fresh *shiitake* mushrooms

2 packs *shirataki* noodles (about 300 g)

1 pack grilled tofu (or if you can't get it then use firm tofu, press it and grill it or pan fry it yourself until golden brown)

1 large bunch chrysanthemum leaves (*shungiku*) or watercress

SWEET SOY SAUCE FLAVOURING:

5 tablespoons soy sauce

3 tablespoons saké

3 tablespoons *mirin*

250 ml/ 9 fl oz *dashi*

4 tablespoons caster sugar

piece of lard or beef fat to begin frying with 4 very fresh eggs – one for each person

Slice the beef thinly and arrange attractively in overlapping slices on a large platter. Wash the leeks and slice on a steep diagonal into fairly thick slices (about 1 cm/ ½ inch). Cut the stems off the *shiitake* mushrooms and cut a decorative cross in the centre of each one. (To do this, hold a sharp knife at an angle and make a thin cut just the right of the centre, sloping towards the centre. Then do another cut on the other side of the centre, and pull away the thin slice you've cut out. Turn the mushroom 90 degrees and do the same again, creating a white cross in the centre of the brown cap.)

Arrange both mushrooms and leeks attractively in a large flat basket (*zaru*), grouping the same ingredients together. Drain the *shirataki* noodles from their water and plunge into boiling water for 2 minutes. Rinse in cold water and drain well. Cut the tofu into eight pieces, and arrange on the basket with the *shirataki*. Wash the chrysanthemum leaves or watercress, cut off any hard root section, and put on the basket along with everything else. Mix the ingredients for the sauce together, making sure the sugar is dissolved, and take to the table in an attractive small jug.

You are now ready to begin the meal – so bring the platter, basket and cast iron pan to the table, where the diners are already seated (perhaps drinking sake while they wait!).

Light the gas ring and put the skillet on to a medium heat. Take a chunk of beef fat or tablespoon of lard, and coat the bottom of the pan. When it's nice and hot add some leek or onions and slices of beef, and mushrooms. Keep moving them about using cooking chopsticks, over a fairly high heat, and when the meat starts to brown add a couple of tablespoons of the sauce. Add more meat and vegetables as the first bits cook (and get eaten). Proceed in this way with everyone taking morsels as they are cooked, dipping in the egg and eating. Keep two long pairs of chopsticks on the table – one for stir frying and one for picking up the uncooked foods. Keep adding more sauce – but not so that the ingredients are swimming. The broth needs to just cover the pan and ingredients – about 1.5 cm/ ½ inch. *Sukiyaki* is usually served with a bowl of plain rice, and pickles.

SHABU SHABU

This is another cook-at-the-table meal of which the Japanese seem so inordinately fond. I think it appeals to their need to be part of a group and doing something together. In this case the pot is an earthenware *donabe* (deep casserole) and the food is cooked in a good depth of thin broth. The wafer-thin slices of meat are merely swished in the hot liquid (held by chopsticks) for the briefest of moments, and this is where the dish gets its name. *Shabu shabu* is the onomatopoeic word for the swishing sound the beef is supposed to make. The vegetable ingredients are dropped into the soup and left there to cook for a few minutes. The broth itself is not highly flavoured, but the dish is accompanied by two strongly flavoured, and contrasting, dipping sauces, a creamy sesame sauce and an acidic soy-based sauce called *ponzu*. *Ponzu* sauce is flavoured with *yuzu* or *sudachi*, Japanese citrus fruits, but you can substitute lemon or lime quite happily. *Ponzu* is excellent with fish and poultry, for example with chicken *mizutani*, and with any fish one-pot. It's also good with *sashimi* (raw fish), especially lean white fish. It needs to be made at least the day before you want to use it.

PONZU **DIPPING SAUCE:**

2 tablespoons lemon juice and 2 tablespoons lime juice (or 4 tablespoons *sudachi* or *yuzu* juice if available)

2 tablespoons rice vinegar

6 tablespoons soy sauce

2 tablespoons *tamari*

4 tablespoons *mirin*

10 cm/ 4 inch piece *kombu*

1 small packet (small handful) *hana katsuo* bonito flakes

SESAME DIPPING SAUCE:

85 g/3 oz white sesame seeds

180 ml/ 9 fl oz *dashi* (page 49)

6 tablespoons soy sauce

2 tablespoons *mirin*

2 teaspoons caster sugar

2 tablespoons saké

750 g/ 1½ lbs top quality marbled beef, such as sirloin

1 medium to small head Chinese cabbage (*hakusai*)

1 Japanese *negi*, or leek or 2 large spring onions

8 large fresh *shiitake* mushrooms

1 block firm (cotton) tofu

1 large bunch of chrysanthemum leaves, or large bunch watercress or baby spinach (about 300 g/ 11 oz)

50 g / 2 oz dried fine rice vermicelli (*harusame*)

2 litres/ 4 pints *dashi*

CONDIMENTS:

4 spring onions, chopped finely

maple leaf radish (*momiji oroshi*)

Begin the day before by making the *ponzu* sauce. Put all the ingredients together in a jug and leave for 24 hours. The next day strain the sauce through muslin (you can use the *kombu* for another purpose, such as *kombu tsukudani*). This will keep for several weeks in the refrigerator.

Now make the sesame sauce. Dissolve the sugar with the other liquid ingredients. In a dry frying pan or sesame roaster, toast the sesame seeds until golden. Keep shaking them around to stop them burning, and take them off the heat as they begin to jump. In a *suribachi* (Japanese grinding bowl) grind the seeds to a paste. Add the remaining liquid ingredients, and blend well, using a wooden spoon or rubber spatula. This doesn't keep much longer than a few days. Both sauces are available commercially, which is convenient when you are either a beginner or in a hurry, but it's just as well to know how to make the real thing.

Prepare the ingredients for the meal by first of all putting the beef in the freezer to half freeze (as in the previous recipe for *sukiyaki*) and then slice it as thinly as possible. Try to get the slices almost transparent if you can. Arrange on a large plate, the slices overlapping attractively. Wash the Chinese cabbage and cut lengthways down the spine then across into large pieces (about 4 cm/ 1½ inches wide). Arrange on a second large plate. Wash the leeks and slice with a diagonal cut into 5 cm/ 2 inch lengths. Wipe the mushrooms, cut the stems off and make a decorative cross in the centre of each one. (Hold a sharp knife at an angle and make a thin cut just the right of the centre, sloping towards the centre. Then do another cut on the other side of the centre, and pull away the thin slice you've cut out. Turn the mushroom 90 degrees and do the same again, creating a white cross in the centre of the brown cap.) Cut the tofu into eight pieces, and arrange attractively on the vegetable plate with the mushrooms and leeks. Wash the chrysanthemum leaves (or watercress or spinach) cut off any hard root section, and put on the basket along with everything else. Put the rice noodles (*harusame*) in a bowl with hot water to soften them (it'll only take a few minutes). Rinse in cold water and disentangle them, drain and put on the platter along with everything else (if you haven't got a big enough plate divide the ingredients evenly between two plates, but keep the meat separate).

You can start the broth on the stove and take it to the table when it's heated. In an earthenware pot or *nabe*, bring the *dashi* to a boil, and then carefully transfer it to the table top burner, and keep on a simmer. The vegetables are dropped in the broth, a few pieces at a time, to cook for a few minutes, but the meat is merely suspended in the liquid – just swished back and forth until it changes colour – the inside should still be pink. Give each diner a small bowl, in which to put a generous amount of the dipping sauce of their choice (about 6 tablespoons). The cooked morsels are dipped and then transferred to the mouth – all with chopsticks. Small amounts of grated radish or onion can be added to the dipping sauce as well.

MEAT AND POTATOES
NIKUJAGA

Nikujaga means meat and potatoes – which is what it is. *Niku* is meat, and *jaga* is a shortened form of *jagaimo* which is the Western potato. It gets its name from Jakarta in Indonesia (*Jagatara* in Japanese), as this is where it came from, having been introduced into Japan in the sixteenth century by the Dutch traders. *Nikujaga* is a kind of meat stew – meat and potatoes are cooked together in the ubiquitous soy sauce based stock, sweetened with sugar. The practise of eating meat and sugar is relatively recent, as even until the late 1880s sugar was regarded as a rare commodity and treated like a medicine.

Nowadays though it's used in nearly all Japanese dishes. If you're not keen on using sugar you can substitute a grain syrup as a healthier alternative, or simply just leave it out altogether. Using it though does give your food an authentic Japanese flavour (like the food you eat in Japan). Again, the beef is very finely sliced, as in *sukiyaki*, and doesn't 'stew' at all, but cooks quickly. The meat does not constitute a large proportion of the dish (very sensible). Thinly siced pork can be used instead of beef.

2 tablespoons vegetable oil	1 large onion, thickly chopped
few drops toasted sesame oil	6 tablespoons soy sauce
225 g/ ½ lb beef, finely sliced	1½ tablespoons caster sugar
450 g/ 1lb potatoes, cut into chunks	1 tablespoon *mirin*
225 g/ ½ lb carrots, cut into chunks	1 tablespoon saké

In a heavy bottomed saucepan heat the oil and add the beef. Over a medium heat brown the beef, then add the vegetables and sauté a few minutes more. Cover with water and bring to a boil and simmer for a few minutes. Scum should rise to the surface now, so scoop it off. Add the rest of the flavouring ingredients and simmer for 15 to 20 minutes or until the potatoes and carrots are soft. Check seasoning and add salt and pepper if desired. This can be served as a main dish, with an additional side dish of green vegetable for balance. It's a typical *izakaya* dish, and is sometimes served in a little cast iron cooking pot.

BEEF OVER RICE
GYŪDON

A well known chain of eateries in Japan which specialises in this dish advertises its wares as *Yasui! Oishii! Hayai!* 'Cheap! Tasty! Fast!'. It's a quick filling lunch, popular with students and workmen, designed, like noodles, to be eaten hastily, not lingered over. At home however you can serve it more elegantly, with vegetable side dishes, but it is still basically a filling 'main dish'. A *donburi* is a deep pottery bowl, similar to, but about twice the size of, a rice bowl and it comes with a lid. It's used to serve rice with a variety of hot toppings, and thus gives its name to the dish itself, albeit shortened to '*don*'.

2 Japanese *negi*, small leeks, or 1 medium mild onion	4 tablespoons *mirin*
	2 teaspoons ginger juice, squeezed from freshly grated ginger
250 g/ 9 oz beef, very thinly sliced (as for *sukiyaki*)	
3 tablespoons vegetable oil	6 rice bowls full of cooked hot rice
TOPPING SAUCE:	(each *donburi* bowl should hold about
250 ml/ 9 fl oz water	1½ rice bowls full)
4 tablespoons soy sauce	

Cut the long onion on the diagonal into slices about 1.5 cm/ ½ inch thick. If using a round onion slice into half and then crescents, along the length of the onion. Cut the thinly sliced beef into strips. Heat the oil in a skillet or frying pan to a high heat. Add the onions and stir fry a further minute (then add beef and stir fry for a further minute). Combine the sauce ingredients and add to the beef, keeping the contents moving, for another 3-4 minutes. Put 1½ bowls of rice into each *donburi* bowl, and divide the beef topping evenly between them, spreading the beef and onions over the rice to cover it, and then pour some of the juices over. Put the warmed lid on to keep the heat in, and serve immediately (to hungry teenagers for example).

CHICKEN
TORI NIKU

I used to love walking home from Togoshi Ginza station, in the heart of Tokyo, down the *shotengai*, the busy shopping street where I lived. Early evening in summer, when it was still warm, but already dark, was the most magical time of all. On either side of the road were shops of all kinds displaying their wares, which spilled out into the street. Tungsten bulbs strung over the stalls glowed warmly, illuminating piles of juicy satsumas, shiny red apples, plump white *daikon* radish, or fresh fish glistening atop mounds of ice. Housewives deftly wove their bicycles through the crowds of shoppers, their baskets on the front piled high with fresh food. Stall holders shout inducements to shoppers to buy, '*Irrashai, irrashai*'. Loudspeakers, installed at intervals along the street, played an assortment of jingles and adverts for the local shops, and, at festival time, traditional folk songs. But in addition to the visual and aural delights were olfactory ones. The smell of chicken being grilled over charcoal – *yakitori*. One waft before my nose and I'd be right there, placing my order and waiting patiently whilst the man dipped and grilled each little skewer. *Yakitori* is bite sized pieces of chicken grilled over charcoal. It's street food, par excellence, cooked over portable charcoal braziers. My local vendor in Togoshi sold *yakitori* so you could eat it right there and then, standing in the street, or to rush home in containers, but many other street traders cook *yakitori* as part of a street café. Right in the moneyed centre of Tokyo, bang next door to the elegant Imperial Hotel and the sophisticated Ginza Shopping area (the Bond Street of Japan) is Yurakuchō. Here the *shinkansen* bullet train passes through the city on raised tracks built on a massive concrete bridge, and the space underneath the tracks is a popular drinking area. Benches and tables are jammed together, and the air is thick with the smell of charcoal grilling. In one establishment the smoke is wafted away by a middle-aged Japanese woman in a frilly white pinny, using a traditional paper fan, whilst the trains rumble overhead. Office workers, taking a quick break after work, before the long journey home, sit and talk and laugh, in the open air, drinking glasses of cold sake and beer, and line their stomachs with a tempting array of things on skewers.

The dipping sauce called *tare* is the secret of good *yakitori*. The raw meat is not marinated in the sauce, but the almost-cooked morsels are dipped in it, then grilled a little longer, then dipped again. With proper care (such as boiling and straining after each use) the sauce can be used again and again, and is simply topped up from time to time. In fact some *yakitori* establishments pride themselves on the age and 'maturity' of their sauce, the taste getting richer and fuller over time. I was told of one old established *yakitori* place in Tokyo which has kept its sauce going for decades. So precious was it that, during the war (World War II) stone crocks containing the sauce were taken up to the mountains and buried, to protect them from the bombs, and preserve them for use when peacetime eventually came. If you've been to Tokyo you may even have tasted it! My recipe here however is for a quick and simple sauce to be used once only. I think chicken thigh is the best cut for *yakitori* – it's juicier than breast – and chicken liver is delicious. Minced chicken balls, called *tsukune*, are another popular *yakitori*, and vegetables such as *shiitake* mushroom, green peppers and leeks are also included.

CHICKEN GRILLED ON SKEWERS
YAKITORI

A selection of the following – the quantities are simply a guide, to feed four, but of course use your judgement. If you are doing this for a barbecue party increase the amounts.

DIPPING SAUCE (*TARE*):
7 tablespoons saké
180 ml/ 9 fl oz soy sauce
7 tablespoons *mirin*
2 tablespoons caster sugar
6 chicken thighs
2 Japanese *negi* or small leeks (alternate with pieces of chicken on one skewer)

12 small fresh *shiitake* mushrooms (skewer alone)
225 g/ 8 oz chicken livers
4 small green peppers (thin skinned if you can get them) or *shishitō* (skewer alone)
small bamboo skewers (18 cm/ 7 inches long) soaked in water

First make the dipping sauce: mix the ingredients together in a small saucepan, and bring to a boil to dissolve the sugar and get rid of the alcohol. Take off the heat and put into a tall and narrow jug, which is the correct size to dip a small bamboo skewer in.

Prepare the ingredients to be grilled. Cut the chicken thigh into bite size pieces – i.e. quite small, about 2 cm/ ¾ inch. You can remove the skin or leave it on, depending on your desire to eat more or less healthily, or you can grill the pieces of skin separately. Cut the leek into 2 cm/ ¾ inch slices. Wipe the mushrooms and cut off the stems. In a colander pour boiling water over the livers, to eliminate odour, then plunge into cold water and drain. Wash and de-seed the peppers and cut into bite size pieces.

Thread the ingredients onto the skewers: about five small pieces of chicken on one skewer; three pieces of chicken alternated with two pieces of leek; three *shiitake* on another. Put green peppers on another, and the liver separately. The items are mostly cooked separately because the grilling times will vary for each ingredient.

Grill either over charcoal or under a grill. (See the notes on grilling and the hazards of burning bamboo skewers in the section on skewering, page 36.) Grill for about 5 minutes (depending on ingredient and size) until 80% cooked. Dip into the sauce and return to the grill for about 3 minutes more, until the chicken is just cooked through. You may have to test the first one to get the timing correct – you don't want to serve under done chicken, but nor do you want it dried out or completely blackened. A little charring is fine – attractive and desirable. Dip once more into the sauce before serving, and allow any excess to drip back into the pot. Serve with beer or saké, and plenty of conviviality! To fill up you could serve toasted rice balls (*yaki onigiri*) afterwards, and get the feeling of being in a Japanese *izakaya*. Although most delicious hot, these can be eaten at room temperature, particularly if taken on picnics or as part of a *bentō* – lunch box.

All yakitori is not what it seems!

If exploring in Japan, beware, not all *yakitori* is as palatable as the above. One drunken evening, a group of friends and I, the worse for wear probably, stumbled across what looked like a *yakitori* bar in the suburbs of Tokyo. It was charming – old wooden sliding door, *noren* hanging curtain etc. and we were hungry. So we all trooped in. Ominously there was no-one there at all apart from the *mama-san* behind the counter. Undeterred we ordered. Unfortunately, rather than selecting our kebabs, we just asked for a selection. The first mouthful was tough and chewy, but the second was even worse – sinewy. We soldiered on for a bit longer, enjoying it less and less, and eventually got into conversation with the rather dour looking *mama-san*. It turned out we weren't eating chicken at all. It wasn't a *yaki TORI* place, but *yaki TON*. Meaning pig. In fact we'd been chewing our way through pigs ears, throats, noses, testicles and god knows what else! I was then informed that this 'stamina' food is supposed to enhance a man's virility, so I probably shouldn't even have been in there in the first place!

CHICKEN MEAT BALLS
TSUKUNE

These tasty little balls of ground chicken are a common item in *yakitori*, threaded onto skewers and grilled. You can also add them to *o-den*, or pop them into miso soup.

250 g/ 9 oz minced chicken	3 teaspoons soy sauce
1 teaspoon freshly grated ginger	2 tablespoons corn starch or potato starch (*katakuriko*)
3 tablespoons *dashi*	
1 tablespoon *mirin*	

Mix all the above ingredients throroughly in a bowl or *suribachi* (pestle and mortar), pounding well until the mixture is stiff and sticky. Take tablespoons of the mixture and form into balls. Drop the balls into a large saucepan of boiling water and simmer on a low heat until the balls rise to the surface, and they are cooked through. Remove and drain. You can now thread them onto bamboo skewers, two or three at a time and grill them *yakitori* style.

CHICKEN ONE-POT
MIZUTAKI

This is a one-pot dish, popular for cool autumn and winter evenings, when everyone wants to huddle around the cooking pot and generally be convivial. The chicken is pre-cooked before taking to the pot, and the whole thing is eaten with a soy sauce-based dip, usually *ponzu* sauce, which is flavoured with *sudachi*, a Japanese citrus. You can buy *ponzu* sauce ready made, or you can make your own (see *Ponzu* Sauce page 216) but note that it needs to be made the day before you want to use it.

900 g/ 2 lb chicken thighs	1 large bunch (200 g/7 oz)
10 cm/ 4 inch piece *kombu* (kelp)	chrysanthemum leaves (or watercress)
6 leaves Chinese cabbage	**CONDIMENTS:**
200 g / 7 oz *harusame* noodles	*Ponzu* dipping sauce
12 fresh *shiitake* mushrooms	*momiji daikon* radish (page 188)
2 Japanese *negi* or small leeks	5 cm/ 2 inch piece ginger, peeled and
(or 4 large spring onions)	grated to a pulp
1 block grilled tofu	2 tablespoons toasted sesame seeds
1 carrot (cut into flower shapes)	

Put the chicken thighs into a large pot with the *kombu* and plenty of water to cover. Bring to a boil and simmer until the chicken is tender. Use a fine mesh ladle to keep skimming off scum as it appears. When the chicken is cooked take the pot off the heat and remove the *kombu*. Strain the broth to remove any bits of bone or gristle. Transfer the stock and chicken to an earthenware casserole (or Japanese *nabe* if you have one). This is what you will serve the dish in at the table.

Prepare the other ingredients thus: parboil the Chinese cabbage for 2 minutes. Drain, lightly salt, and roll them up in twos in a bamboo mat, squeezing out excess water as you go. (Lay them widthways across the mat with the leaves overlapping in the middle.). Roll tightly then cut into 5 cm/ 2 inch pieces. Arrange attractively on a large platter, cut side down. Soak the *harusame* noodles in warm water until softened. Rinse in cold water, drain well and arrange on plate. Cut a decorative cross in the centre of the *shiitake* mushrooms and cut off the stems. Arrange alongside the cabbage. Cut the Japanese *negi* (or small leeks, or large spring onions), diagonally into 1.5 cm/ ½ inch pieces, and the grilled tofu into 8 pieces. Arrange on plate. Parboil the carrot flowers for 2 minutes in boiling water to soften them. Remove and cool. Arrange attractively on the plate alongside the other ingredients. Wash the chrysanthemum leaves and lay alongside the other vegetables.

Put the three condiments onto small dishes, and place in centre of table. Prepare a table top burner (gas, electric or charcoal) and place the casserole, containing the chicken and broth, on top. Bring to a simmer. Add some of the vegetables from the plate and cook until tender. Each person can do this for themselves, and retrieve what they want with a small slotted spoon.

Eat the morsels accompanied by the dipping sauce, and spicy condiments to taste. **Variation:** If you are handy with the rolling mat, you can make the cabbage rolls even more attractive. Parboil the chrysanthemum (or watercress) after the cabbage, giving them the *irodashi* cold water treatment. Squeeze out excess moisture so that the bunch becomes a roll. Lay this in the centre of the cabbage leaves before you roll them up. Cut into short sections as before. The cabbage roll will now have a nice green centre.

CHICKEN BREAST WITH VINEGAR, MUSTARD AND MISO DRESSING
SASAMI NO KARASHI ZU

This is an elegant dressed 'meat salad' if you like, which could be served to guests, as a starter, as part of a Japanese meal, or buffet, or even just with sake or beer.

4 skinless chicken breasts
MARINADE FOR CHICKEN:
2 tablespoons soy sauce
1 tablespoon *mirin*
225 g/ 8 oz large spring onions
VINEGAR MUSTARD DRESSING:
3 tablespoons yellow miso (such as Shinshu)
1 tablespoon red *akadashi* miso

1 tablespoon *mirin*
2 tablespoons caster sugar
225 ml/ 8 fl oz *dashi* stock (or chicken stock)
1 tablespoon saké
1 tablespoon Japanese mustard (*karashi*)
2 tablespoons rice vinegar

Boil the chicken breasts in water for 7-10 minutes until cooked but tender. Take out and shred the flesh by pulling apart roughly (you can keep the cooking water to use as stock for the dressing). Combine the soy sauce and *mirin* and marinate the cooked chicken in this for 5 minutes. Remove. Cut the spring onions diagonally into 5 cm/ 2 inch pieces, and plunge into boiling water to soften for 30 seconds. Drain and put aside.

Combine the dressing ingredients by adding a little liquid at a time to the miso, to make a smooth paste and avoid lumps. You can use the chicken cooking water here in addition to a little *dashi* if you like. In a saucepan put the mixture on a low heat and stir until it thickens. Add the mustard and vinegar. Mix the marinated chicken with the onion and combine with the dressing. Serve warm or at room temperature.

WARM CHICKEN WITH PLUM AND PERILLA DRESSING
SASAMI NO UMESHISO ZU

This is my version of a delicious dish eaten in a little jazz bar in Ebisu in Tokyo in 1996. Perilla (*shiso*) leaves are sometimes available in Japanese stores, but you can also try growing them yourself, as it's not difficult, and they really do add to the flavour.

DRESSING:	3 perilla (*shiso*) leaves, shredded
I tablespoon *ume* plum paste	(or dried *shiso*)
½ teaspoon rapeseed oil	2 large chicken breast fillets
I tablespoon rice vinegar	½ teaspoon toasted sesame oil
120 ml/ 5 fl oz *dashi* stock	I tablespoon vegetable oil

First make the dressing. In a bowl put the plum paste and add the *dashi* little by little, mixing well with a wooden spoon, until it's well combined and you have a smooth paste. Add the oil and vinegar and continue mixing. Put aside. Cut the chicken breasts in half lengthwise with the grain, then pop them into boiling water and boil for 3-5 minutes until not quite cooked. Remove and shred into long pieces by pulling apart along the grain. It should be slightly pink in the middle. Heat the oils in a skillet and sauté the chicken on a medium heat for about a minute until the pink is gone. Add the plum dressing and toss well, keeping on the heat until it's heated through. Remove from the heat and serve with the perilla leaves cut into thin strands and scattered over the top. Serve at once, as a main protein dish, with rice and a side vegetable dish, or as a snack to accompany drinking. If you can't get perilla you could try coriander or basil, which are completely different tastes, but like perilla strongly aromatic.

Note: seeds for many of the Japanese herbs and vegetables mentioned can be obtained by mail order from Future Foods – see the directory at the end of the book.

LIVER TERIYAKI
REBĀ TERIYAKI

The secret of tender juicy liver is of course not to overcook it. I was brought up on great slabs of the stuff, which after God knows how long simmering usually ended up like old shoe leather. So when I first had liver like this it was a revelation. Using chicken livers makes it doubly tender and delicious. The *teriyaki* sauce adds sweetness and flavour, the liver is a good source of iron, and it's quick.

250 g / 9 oz calves' or lambs' liver	3 tablespoons *mirin*
***TERIYAKI* SAUCE:**	I teaspoon ginger juice, squeezed from
I teaspoon caster sugar	freshly grated ginger
3 tablespoons soy sauce	flour for dusting
3 tablespoons saké	I tablespoon vegetable oil for pan frying

Put the liver in a colander and, over the sink, pour boiling water over (or immerse in a bowl of boiling water for 30 seconds). Rinse in cold water, drain and pat dry. Combine the *teriyaki* sauce ingredients, making sure the sugar is dissolved. Cut the liver into thick strips (or if using chicken liver, just bite size pieces) and remove any tough membrane. Sprinkle the flour on a plate and lightly dust the strips (or you can put the

flour in a plastic bag, add the liver and shake it about - a perfect job for children who want to help). Heat the oil in a frying pan and add the liver. Sauté, on quite a high heat, moving it around so it doesn't stick, for about 5 minutes, until it's browned and not quite cooked through. Add the *teriyaki* sauce and sauté a minute more, with the heat turned down, until cooked through, and the pieces nicely coated with the sauce. Serve with hot rice and a side vegetable dish.

CHICKEN TERIYAKI
CHIKIN TERIYAKI

The meat can be either cut into bite size pieces, marinated and cooked, or it can be marinated and pan fried as whole breast fillets, then cut into bite-size pieces to serve.

2 large chicken breast fillets (skinless) each cut into 2	I teaspoon ginger juice, squeezed from freshly grated ginger
MARINADE:	***TERIYAKI* SAUCE TO POUR OVER:**
3 tablespoons soy sauce	I tablespoon *mirin*
3 tablespoons sake	I tablespoon soy sauce
I teaspoon caster sugar	2 tablespoons saké
3 tablespoons *mirin*	I tablespoon vegetable oil for sautéeing

Apply the *shimofuri* technique to the chicken by pouring boiling water over it in a colander. Rinse in cold water. Remove any tough membrane or fat. Combine the marinade ingredients, making sure the sugar is dissolved, and pour over the chicken fillets in a flat dish. Leave for 30 minutes. Meanwhile make the *teriyaki* sauce by combining the ingredients in a small saucepan, bring to the boil and take off the heat. Heat the oil to medium high in a frying pan and add the chicken pieces, removed from the marinade. Pan fry, on a medium heat, for about 7 minutes each side (or less if cut into small pieces – about 3 minutes each side) until just cooked through. Add the left over marinade and sauté a minute more, with the heat slightly higher, until cooked through, and the pieces nicely coated. Heat the *teriyaki* sauce separately. Place one piece of chicken, cut diagonally into slices on each plate, and pour over a little of the hot sauce. Serve with hot rice and a side vegetable dish.

CHICKEN OVER RICE WITH EGG
OYAKO DONBURI

This is the chicken version of *gyudon*, with the addition of egg. Half-cooked egg is put on top of hot rice, the heat of which finishes off the 'cooking'. The soft egg mixture mingles with the sweet salty sauce and the result is quite delightful – delivering more than it promises to at first sight. However, this is everyday lunch food, or family food. It's not elegant party food. *Oyako donburi* means 'parent and child bowl', and when this dish is made with beef and eggs it's called *itoko donburi* – meaning 'cousin bowl'. You can even make it with pork in which case it becomes a 'stranger-bowl' *tanin donburi*. The simplest version uses only egg and onion, which has a simpler name – *tamago don* – 'egg bowl'.

2 Japanese *negi*, or 1 medium mild onion

SAUCE:

350 ml/ 12 fl oz *dashi* (page 49)

3 tablespoons caster sugar

4 tablespoons dark soy sauce

250 g/ 9 oz chicken thigh or breast

5 eggs, lightly mixed

6 rice bowls full of hot cooked rice

1 sheet *nori*, cut into thin strands to garnish

Warm four *donburi* or large deep bowls. Cut the long onion on a diagonal into slices about 1.5 cm/ ½ inch thick. If using a round onion, slice into half and then crescents, along the length of the onion. Cut the chicken into small bite size pieces. (You can leave on or remove skin, whichever you prefer.) Combine the sauce ingredients in a shallow but wide saucepan or skillet, and bring to a boil. Pop the pieces of chicken in and simmer, uncovered, for 5 minutes, or until scum rises to the surface. Scoop it off then add the onions and simmer for a further 3 minutes. Do not cover. Scoop off any further scum with a fine skimmer.

Check the flavour and add more soy sauce or sugar if needed. Now – this is the important bit – keeping the heat at medium, pour the lightly beaten egg slowly into the pan, evenly covering the chicken and onion mixture. Do not move the mixture about – you want a gooey sort of omelette mixture, not scrambled egg. When the egg is about ¾ set (with a few runny bits) stir lightly and remove from heat . Do not let the egg go hard. The mixture itself should be quite wet, but not a soup. Put 1½ bowls of hot rice into each of the four *donburi* bowls and then divide the chicken and egg mixture into four and place on top of each bowl of hot rice. The wet topping will seep into the rice, making it sweet and moist. Sprinkle with the *nori* strips. In Japan each portion is made individually, using a special *donburi* pan, which is like a small, deep, pancake pan. If you have something similar then by all means use it.

STEAMED EGG CUSTARD
CHAWAN MUSHI

"...each person received a bowl containing a sort of pudding made of eggs, loach and the large seeds of the maidenhair tree."

Sir Ernest Satow *A Diplomat in Japan* 1853-64

Eggs were a popular protein food during the Edo period (1600-1853) before the country was opened up to the West and meat eating became acceptable. There were many subtly different ways of cooking them, and it's likely that the Japanese have been eating this dish for two or three hundred years. As in any egg custard the trick is not to curdle it and to get it to set properly, so the proportion of egg to stock and temperature is important. The custard is cooked in a china cup, and served with a lid, but any heatproof cup will do. A Japanese steamer, which is square with a flat bottom, perfectly accommodates four cups, but you can improvise by standing cups in water in a large saucepan, or even baking them in the oven. The items at the bottom of the cup can be altered to suit the season. Fish can be substituted for chicken. Mange tout beans can be used. A vegetarian version could contain a little *aburu-age* (deep fried tofu pouch, previously simmered in a sweet soy sauce-based broth) or a few pieces of *rōbai* (fried wheat gluten). Use your imagination.

75 g/ 3 oz chicken breast, without skin	4 sprigs of trefoil (*mitsuba*)
MARINADE:	12 ginkgo nuts
2 teaspoons of soy sauce	
1 teaspoon saké	**FOR THE CUSTARD:**
1 teaspoon *mirin*	4 medium eggs
¼ teaspoon ginger juice	600 ml/ 1 pint *dashi* (you can make the *dashi* up with the *shiitake* soaking water and good quality light chicken stock if it's convenient, but have the *dashi* at room temperature)
4 dried *shiitake* mushrooms	
½ medium carrot (fat enough to fit a cutter inside the circumference)	
4 medium shrimp or prawns, shelled and peeled, and de-veined	1 tablespoon *mirin*
	1 tablespoon light soy sauce

Prepare the solid ingredients as follows: cut the chicken into 12 small pieces – about 3 per person and leave in the marinade for half an hour. Soak the *shiitake* mushrooms in warm water, until soft. Peel the carrot and cut into thin slices, then, using a flower shaped metal cutter, make seasonally appropriate flower shapes from each slice (making one or two flowers per person). Parboil for 20 seconds then drain. Apply the *shimofuri* technique to the shrimp – plunge into boiling water for 30 seconds then remove and chill in cold water. Cut the trefoil (or coriander) into short 1 cm/ ⅜ inch pieces. Remove the *shiitake* from the soaking water, and cut off the stems. Strain the soaking water and put into a measuring jug ready to make the *dashi*. Shell and peel the ginkgo nuts according to the recipe for Sankō In Autumn Tempura.

Now – beat the eggs (quite well) in a measuring jug. This is so you can measure the volume, as you want the seasoned stock to be three times the volume of the eggs. So add the *mirin*, soy sauce and salt to the *shiitake* soaking water, and top up with *dashi* (or chicken stock) to the correct volume in a separate measuring jug. Slowly pour the stock into the beaten egg and mix gently – you don't want it to foam up.

Arrange the solid items (except the trefoil) in the bottom of each of 4 cups, divided evenly. Pour the egg mixture on top, but don't fill the cups. There should be at least 1.5 cm/ ½ inch space at the top, maybe more depending on the size of the cups. Sprinkle the trefoil on top of each. Place the cups in a steamer and place a clean cloth under the lid to absorb steam, and stop it dripping in the cups (or cover each cup with plastic wrap if using an oven style steamer). Steam for 20 minutes over a medium heat, until the custard is set. Test it by inserting a fine bamboo skewer or wooden toothpick – it should be clean. Although set it should still be quite soft. Serve hot, as an alternative to a soup course, or as the first course in an elegant Japanese meal. This is one of the few dishes in Japanese cuisine that is eaten with a spoon – a teaspoon will do, although chopsticks are used as well, to retrieve the solid items from the bottom.

PORK
BUTA NIKU

PORK AND GINGER SAUTÉ
BUTA NO SHŌGA YAKI

One of my earliest memories of eating in Japan was this dish, which was made for me by my dear friend, and then flatmate, Nobuko. It's quick and easy. The ginger and soy combination gives it a basic Japanese taste, so it's a good beginner's dish. You can use *shiitake* mushrooms, sliced thickly, instead of green peppers, or a combination of both to accompany.

---

4 thin pork loin pieces or escalopes or 675 g / 1½ lb pork loin or fillet, sliced very thinly

4 small thin skinned green peppers (or 2 large ones)

½ tablespoon toasted sesame oil

½ tablespoon vegetable oil

SEASONING :

2 tablespoons saké

1 tablespoon *mirin*

1 tablespoon soy sauce

3 cm / 1 inch piece of ginger, finely grated

Cut the pork across the grain into thick shreds – about 1.5 cm/ ½ inch wide. Cut the peppers in half and de-seed, then into thick strips. Heat the oils in a frying pan or skillet and add the pork. Sauté quickly, keeping the meat moving to prevent it sticking, until half cooked (about 4 minutes). Now add the green peppers and sauté for about 4 minutes more. Finally add the combined seasoning ingredients and cook on a medium high heat for another minute, until almost dry. Serve on a flat plate, accompanied by rice, pickles and miso soup. For a more substantial meal you can also serve a vegetable side dish, either a dressed salad, a vinegared salad or a boiled vegetable.

DEEP FRIED PORK CUTLET
TON KATSU

This is a popular lunchtime dish, and varies from a cheap and cheerful set menu lunch served at small, family run, establishments to a more up market version served at specialist *ton katsu* restaurants, where a variety of different meat cuts are used. The best is fillet (*hire* in Japanese) tender and juicy, with no fat. It's always accompanied by grated raw cabbage and rice, and the ubiquitous *ton katsu* sauce, which is like a thick Worcester sauce, or English Bulldog sauce. Because meat eating gained popularity in the Meiji era when all things Western were fashionable, then I assume that this sauce was another of the imported Western foods doing the rounds at the time, and somehow the two became inseparable.

This sauce is available in Japanese stores, but if you can't get it use either Worcester sauce, which is thinner, or brown sauce, which is the correct consistency but less spicy.

half a medium white cabbage	4 pork fillets or thick pork steaks
I large egg	(without bone) about 150 g/ 5 oz
3 tablespoons plain flour	each and 1.5 cm/ ½ inch thick
salt and pepper to season	oil for deep frying
8 tablespoons breadcrumbs (do not	*ton katsu* or Worcestershire sauce to
use Western style proprietary brand	serve
fine breadcrumbs. If you can't get	I tablespoon mustard (Japanese or
Japanese style breadcrumbs, make	English)
your own from stale bread)	

Wash the cabbage and shred finely. Beat the egg. Season the flour with salt and pepper and sprinkle onto a large plate. Trim fat from the pork (if there is any). Now you need to heat the oil for deep frying and get a little production line in place for the pork fillets. The oil needs to be medium hot, 170C/ 340F. Side by side place the plate of flour, beaten egg and breadcrumbs. Dip each fillet first into the flour, coating all over. Shake off any excess, dip into the beaten egg, into the breadcrumbs, and then into the hot oil. Fry for about 5 minutes each side, until golden brown, making sure the pork is properly cooked, with no pink in the middle. Drain on kitchen paper. To serve, cut each piece into diagonal slices and place on a large round plate (lay the pieces side by side as if they were uncut) with a mound of finely shredded cabbage alongside. Sauce should be dribbled over both the pork cutlet and cabbage. A large dollop of mustard goes extremely well with this, and fresh hot rice and miso soup completes a very satisfying lunch.

PORK RICE BOWL
KATSUDON

This is the pork equivalent of *gyūdon*, using deep fried pork fillet to put on top of a bowl of rice. Left over *ton katsu* can be used, or freshly cooked pork pieces, cooked as above.

4 pork fillets, coated in breadcrumbs,	I tablespoon caster sugar
and deep fried, as for *ton katsu*	4 tablespoons *mirin*
I large onion or 2 Japanese long onions	4 eggs, lightly beaten
SAUCE:	4 large bowls of hot cooked rice (keep
240 ml/ 10 fl oz *dashi* (page 49)	hot whilst preparing the rest of the
5 tablespoons soy sauce	dish)

Cut the deep fried pork cutlets into thick slices. Peel and slice the onion thinly. Combine the sauce ingredients in a medium size saucepan and bring to a boil. Add the sliced onion and simmer gently for 2 minutes until the onion is soft. Add the pork pieces, sliced thickly. Simmer for a further minute until the coating is soggy and some of the broth absorbed. Add the beaten egg, and stir lightly (do not scramble). Cook for about half a minute until the egg is almost but not quite set. Remove a quarter of this mixture and place on top of one of the bowls of hot rice, then repeat with the other portions. Be careful to divide the pork pieces evenly, and distribute any remaining sauce over each bowl. This is a popular quick and easy lunch or supper, for children or hungry family members, filling and unpretentious. There's not much fancy presentation in this dish, so it's not considered guest food.

MINCED PORK DUMPLINGS
GYŌZA

These are not, strictly speaking, Japanese at all but an import from China. But, like bowls of *rāmen* noodles, they are such a part of Japanese daily eating, and so nice when they are home-made that I had to include them. (The use of garlic tells you that they are another foreign import, like *kimchee*, the only two recipes that include garlic in this book.) I used to enjoy eating *gyōza* in a particular *rāmen* bar in Koenji years ago, and then my friend Nobuko showed me how to make them, so now I don't have to go all the way to Koenji. Because each little dumpling is hand filled and formed they are time consuming to make, but it's the type of task you can share with your children, or friends, as you chat around the kitchen table. The results are worth the effort. An important part of the experience is the hot chilli oil and vinegar which is added to the soy sauce dip. This is casual family or party food, and must be served hot.

200 g/ 7 oz minced pork

½ Chinese cabbage, very finely shredded and minced

3 cm/ 1 inch piece of ginger, peeled and grated

4 spring onions, finely chopped

2 cloves garlic, peeled and crushed

½ teaspoon salt

1 pack *gyōza* skins (small round wheat flour skins, which can be bought ready made in Chinese and Japanese shops)

2 teaspoons toasted sesame oil, for frying

TO SERVE:

a few drops chilli oil

2 tablespoons rice vinegar

In a large bowl mix together the minced pork, chopped cabbage, ginger, spring onion, salt and garlic. Mix well. Have the *gyōza* skins ready and a small bowl of water handy. Take a teaspoon of the mixture and place in the centre of one round skin. Fold over the pastry to make a half moon, moistening one edge with water. Carefully seal the edge by pleating or overlapping along the curved edge, so that you make a crescent shape. Repeat until all the mixture, or skins, is used up. (Freeze any left overs if not previously frozen.)

Heat the toasted sesame oil in a large frying pan. Place the *gyōza*, side by side in rows (the crescent shapes will fit together neatly) and fry over a fairly high heat for about a minute until browned. Now take a kettle of boiling water, have a large lid ready which fits the pan, and splash about 4 tablespoons of water into the pan. Immediately place the lid on top to trap the steam (there'll be lots of it). Turn the heat down to medium and leave to steam for 3 or 4 minutes until cooked through. To serve, slide a long metal spatula underneath, and place a row of six on one plate (they'll be stuck together so be careful not to break them). Each person has a small saucer of soy sauce into which they pour a few drops of chilli oil and rice vinegar. The gyōza are dipped, one by one, into this before eating. Serve as a starter before a bowl of noodles.

PORK SIMMERED WITH VEGETABLES
BUTANIKU NO NITSUKE

4 large dried *shiitake* mushrooms	**SIMMERING INGREDIENTS:**
I pack *konnyaku*	3 cm/ I inch piece fresh ginger root, peeled and minced
3 large taro potatoes (*satoimo*) or ordinary waxy potatoes	4 tablespoons soy sauce
2 medium carrots	I ½ tablespoons caster sugar
100 g/ 4 oz bamboo shoots (canned is OK for this dish)	160 ml/ 8 fl oz *dashi*, made up with the mushroom soaking water
400 g/ 14 oz pork	3 tablespoons saké
	pinch salt
	12 mange tout (snow peas)

Soak the *shiitake* in 160 ml/ 8 fl oz of warm water. Boil the *konnyaku* in clean water for 2 minutes, then remove and cool in cold water. Cut into small triangles (or spirals, as described in the recipe for o-den, page 206). Peel the taro potatoes thickly (using rubber gloves if you are susceptible to itchy hands). Cut into thick bite size chunks, of uneven shapes. Peel the carrots and cut, with a rolling wedge (*han giri*) into thick bite size chunks. Cut the bamboo shoots in a similar fashion, removing any outer skin that's fibrous, and any white residue. Cut the pork into bite size pieces. When the *shiitake* mushrooms have softened remove them, and strain the soaking water through fine mesh or a cheesecloth. Use this water to make up the simmering ingredients, then put the seasoned liquid into a medium size saucepan, and add the pork. On a medium heat bring to the boil and simmer for 10 minutes. Remove scum with a mesh skimmer as it rises to the surface. Remove the pork with a slotted spoon and put aside.

Put the vegetables (except the mange tout) and *konnyaku* into the hot liquid and simmer for 10-15 minutes, until just tender, but not mushy. Meanwhile parboil the mange tout peas in salted boiling water for I minute. Drain and give them a cold water shock to chill. Pat dry.

Make sure the pan hasn't scorched during simmering, but equally you don't want the ingredients swimming in liquid (just add a little more water if it gets too dry before the vegetables are cooked). By the end of their cooking period there should be very little liquid left (about ½ cm or ¼ inch) in the bottom of the pan. When the vegetables are ready add the pork and heat through – making sure the pork is thoroughly heated. Arrange the vegetables in an attractive mound in deep bowls, and arrange three mange tout per person, in a fan shape propped up in between the pieces of pork and vegetable.

SWEETS, BEVERAGES AND SPECIALITIES

"I thought that I might get some fresh milk, but the idea of anything but a calf milking a cow was so new to the people that there was a universal laugh, and Ito told me that they thought it 'most disgusting', and that the Japanese think it 'most disgusting' in foreigners to put anything 'with such a strong smell and taste in to their tea!'"

Isabella Bird, *Unbeaten Tracks in Japan*

Such an aversion to milk was the norm only a hundred years ago, and can still be seen in older country folk today, who often won't touch the stuff. Although milk is now an acceptable item in Japanese homes it is not associated with tea, but either drunk as it is (often by teenage boys) or used in Western style cooking. Dairy products in general were quite unknown to most Japanese until the time of the Meiji restoration. Only 15% of Japan is cultivable, and most of the country is covered by mountains, so there simply isn't the room to graze cattle – for milk, butter, cheese, beef or anything else! A curious consequence of this was observed and remarked upon by Isabella Bird.

" As animals are not used for milk, draught or food, and there are no pasture lands, both the country and the farm-yards have a singular silence and an inanimate look; a mean-looking dog and a few fowls being the only representatives of domestic animal life. I long for the lowing of cattle and the bleating of sheep."

In addition to these geographical concerns Japanese homes have never had (and many still don't have) ovens. Baking (and roasting as mentioned before in the section on meat) has never been a part of Japanese cuisine, so cakes and desserts as we know them don't exist. A traditional Japanese meal concludes with rice and pickles, or fresh fruit such as persimmons or *nashi* pear.

Confections though **do** have a place in Japanese cuisine, but the manner of their making, and the style of their eating, is totally different from what we understand in the West as dessert. As previously mentioned, they are not made with butter, eggs or milk. If cooked they are most likely steamed, not baked, and finally they are eaten in between mealtimes, as an accompaniment to green tea. Sometimes this tea is the bitter and frothy ceremonial *matcha* of the tea ceremony, and sometimes just regular *sencha*, the type of tea you drink with guests who call by in the afternoon, or offer to visitors at work. These cakes, or sweetmeats, are made from rice flour and often have a sweet filling made from beans, either the ubiquitous *azuki* bean, or white beans. Other similar cakes are made from sweet potato or chestnuts. One exception is *kasutera* (castella), a plain sponge cake, introduced by the Portuguese (and named after Castile in Spain). One of the earliest examples in Japan of the use of eggs as a raising agent in baked goods, it's been around in Japan since the sixteenth century, but is always made commercially by specialist *kasutera* makers, never at home.

Although sugar was first introduced as early as the eighth century, almost certainly from China, as were most things in those days, it was initially regarded more as a medicine than a food, and used sparingly. In any case it was a very coarse, raw brown sugar, more like molasses than the refined sugar in use today. Later, in the sixteenth century, sugar was produced from cane grown in Japan, but still it wasn't used by the general populace, and things remained this way until after the middle of the nineteenth century, and the Meiji restoration. All the traditional Japanese sweets which are today made with beans and sugar were, before this time, made without the sugar. Once the Japanese did get hold of sugar, though, it seems they didn't look back. As well as adding it to these bean-based delicacies and confections, sugar is now an ingredient in nearly every stock, broth and cooking style you can think of.

Kashi are sweets, and they can be divided into several categories: *namagashi* translates as fresh or raw, and this type doesn't keep. *Namagashi* includes jellies made with agar agar (*kanten*) and *kuzu* starch, and delicate pastes and doughs made with rice flour. *Han namagashi* are half fresh, and include things such as jellies made with sweet bean paste, called *yōkan*, and steamed buns called *anpan,* which are similar to Chinese cakes. *Higashi* are dry sweets, practically all sugar and more like candy than cakes. The crisp toasted rice cracker, called *sembei,* is also included in this category, and it can be either salty or sweet.

"A delicately graceful weeping willow hangs by the door of the sembei *shop which stands far enough back from the pavement to allow a little fountain to play before it. Only* sembei *are sold here, a particularly crisp biscuit which is made in many sizes, and may be either salt or sweet flavoured."*

Grace James, *Japanese Recollections and Impressions*

Perhaps Grace James was writing about Soka, a small town on the northern side of Tokyo which is famous for its *sembei* production. Many little old shops like the one she describes still remain, and sell the widest variety of *sembei* I've ever seen. Big round crackers coated in sesame seeds, small oblong bite sized ones with a sugary coating or a strip of *nori* sea weed encasing them, and these days some are even combined with a cheese flavoured cream (one of those hybrids of East and West which to my mind is less successful than some). Luckily Japanese rice crackers are now becoming readily available outside of Japan – even Marks and Spencer sell them, and I thoroughly recommend them as a low fat alternative to peanuts, to accompany drinking and for party nibbles.

"Cakes were served which seemed to me far too beautiful to eat, as they were decorated with a lovely, light design of weeping willow and flying swallow."

Grace James, *Japanese Recollections and Impressions*

Tsuruyahachiman is a famous and long established traditional cake shop, situated in the heart of Tokyo. Walking in to this place feels more like visiting a temple than a shop. Glass cases are filled with items of the most exquisite beauty, which reflect and emphasise the changing seasons. In autumn, little cakes are shaped like persimmons, mushrooms and maple leaves. They look similar to the marzipan confections which are popular in Europe, but instead of marzipan these cakes are made from rice flour. I first visited the shop in autumn, to research material for my film. I was breathless with delight at the verisimilitude of the cakes – the 'dried persimmons' had a fine coating of flour – just as dried persimmons develop a coating of sugar after being hung up to dry over many months. Visiting the same shop later in spring I watched the master making cakes which resembled cherry blossoms (of course) but also some crafty looking 'bamboo shoots' – complete with singed markings representing the layers of husk on the swollen root. In summer the display is different again – with *mizu yokan* predominating. This is a clear jelly, made from *kanten*, or agar agar, and in summer it has a cooling effect. Sometimes little fish shapes are set in to the clear jelly, to represent carp swimming in an icy pool – just the type of image you need to cool you down in the oppressive humidity of a Japanese summer.

The conclusion to all these observations, is that I have included only a small sample of traditional sweets here, as the making of *kashi* is specialist work, and beyond the capabilities of the average domestic kitchen. However, I have selected some recipes for desserts which, although you'd never be served them in Japan, use Japanese ingredients to make healthy and unusual alternatives to familiar puddings and sweets. Such recipes are influenced by macrobiotics, and can result in some delicious combinations.

Traditional sweets then are generally made from rice flour, mixed with water and steamed or boiled. *Shiratamako* is a refined glutinous rice flour which consists of lumpy granules when dry and is the flour most often used here.

Another kind of rice cake is made from glutinous rice itself (not flour), which after cooking is pounded to a thick sticky mass, until it no longer resembles rice at all. This is *mochi*. (See page 101 for more about how to make it yourself.) Our first recipe here is a *mochi* recipe (you don't have to make the *mochi* cakes yourself).

RICE CAKES WITH ROASTED SOY BEAN POWDER
ABEKAWA MOCHI

Mochi, made from pounded steamed rice, is supposed to contain the spirit of the rice god who is called Inari. For this reason large decorative slabs of *mochi* are placed in shrines in the family home at New Year and offered to the gods. Decorated with seaweed and pine fronds and topped with a seasonal *mikan* (or tangerine) they are supposed to ensure health and prosperity for the coming year. I can't guarantee the prosperity, but these cakes are certainly healthy, and you don't have to wait until New Year to eat them either. Small cakes of *mochi* are available dried in Japanese stores. You can reconstitute them by soaking in warm water, or simply grilling. This is a popular way of eating them, rolled in roasted soybean powder, called *kinako*, which is sometimes lightly sweetened. The more fanciful name for this is *Abekawa mochi*, Abe river *mochi*, so called because this way of eating *mochi* is said to have been discovered in the vicinity of the Abe river by the powerful Tokugawa Shogun, who believed that the golden soybean powder was real powdered gold.

4 tablespoons soybean powder (*kinako*)   4 pieces *mochi* (pounded rice cake)
2 tablespoons caster sugar (optional)

Mix together the soybean powder and sugar and spread on a plate. Place the *mochi* pieces under a grill, and grill slowly until soft and sticky, and the outside lightly crisp and brown. If you are using dried (not fresh) *mochi* it will need longer cooking to soften, so use a lower temperature grill, or soften in hot water first. After grilling dip the *mochi* pieces briefly into hot water, then into the powder and sugar mixture, coating both sides. Serve as they are, to accompany tea, or just as a snack. They are quite filling as each piece of *mochi* is equivalent to one bowl of rice.

SMOOTH RED BEAN PASTE
KOSHI AN

Although you can buy this ready made it is not so difficult to make yourself, and if you do you can adjust the level of sweetness to suit your palate (ready made versions tend to be over sweet). Reduce the amount of sugar here even further if desired.

175 g/6 oz *azuki* beans   pinch salt
250 g/ 9 oz sugar

Soak the beans overnight. The next day place them in a large saucepan well covered with fresh water. Bring to a boil and boil vigorously for 5 minutes. Drain and throw away this water. Put the beans into the saucepan again, this time with 5 times their volume of water. Bring to a boil then turn down the heat, cover, and simmer until the beans are very soft (check that they don't dry up or scorch). Remove from the heat and strain off the remaining water into a bowl – you need this water so don't throw it away. Then press the soft beans through a sieve, mixing the pulpy bean with the remaining water that you've just saved. Press well, so that you use the maximum bean pulp, and discard only rough skins, which will be left in the sieve. The watery pulp must then be put into a fine cotton bag, and excess water squeezed out. You will now be left with a very smooth bean paste. Empty this out of the bag into a saucepan with the sugar, and stir continuously over a low heat until the sugar is dissolved, and the mixture thick and smooth. Add the pinch of salt. This can now be used in a variety of confections.

CHUNKY RED BEAN PASTE
TSUBUSHI AN

175 g/6 oz *azuki* beans   pinch salt
250 g/ 9 oz sugar

Follow the instructions as for the smooth bean paste in the previous recipe, but omit the pressing through a sieve and squeezing through a bag. Simply cook the *azuki* beans until soft, then add an equal amount of sugar and stir over a low heat until the sugar is dissolved and the beans mashed up, but not smooth. This can be used to make a more robust and less refined sweet.

STEAMED RICE CAKES WITH SWEET BEAN FILLING
KASHIWA MOCHI/ SAKURA MOCHI

The word *mochi* is also used to refer to cakes made not from pounded steamed rice, but from rice flour. The result is similar to *mochi*, but easier to make. *Kashiwa mochi* gets its name from the oak leaves (*kashiwa*) in which they are wrapped. They are traditionally served to boys on The Boy's Day Festival on May 5th, as the association with the big and strong oak tree is deemed appropriate for growing boys! A similar confection, called *sakura mochi*, is wrapped in salted cherry leaves, which can be eaten, so I have substituted vine leaves here, which gives an acceptable approximation of the taste. Of course if you can get preserved cherry leaves then use them.

250 g/ 9 oz glutinous rice flour (*shiratamako*)	vine leaves to wrap
250 ml/ 9 fl oz water	4 tablespoons chunky red bean paste (*tsubushi-an*)

Mix the rice flour and water, adding the water slowly and kneading as you go. Keep kneading until you have a smooth paste, not too stiff and not too sloppy – like marzipan, or as the Japanese say, like your ear lobe. (You may need a little less or more water.) Take about two tablespoonsful of the mixture and form into flat round cakes. Wrap each one in damp muslin and place in a hot steamer. Steam over a medium heat for 15-20 minutes until the cakes are cooked through and transparent, and no longer powdery inside. They should be soft and stretchy. Leave to cool.

   Lightly sprinkle cornflour on a board and roll each cake out, flattening it until it's about 10 cm/ 4 inches diameter. Put a teaspoonful of chunky *azuki* bean paste (*tsubushi-an*) in the middle and fold over, sealing the edges so that the paste stays inside. Wrap in a vine leaf. Serve at room temperature, with green tea, or as a snack.

RICE CAKES WITH MUGWORT
YOMOGI MOCHI

When I was cooking at Daitō In Temple I would scour nearby fields and hedgerows for wild mugwort in spring, just as country families in Japan have always done. Back in the kitchen of the temple the tender young tips would be well washed, parboiled, and ground to a purée in a pestle and mortar. The purée is then mixed with rice flour and water to make these delicate little cakes, a feature of The Girl's Day Festival, celebrated on March 3rd. As mugwort contains both iron and calcium it is a most appropriate food for girls and women. You don't have to be a girl to enjoy it though. If you are collecting it yourself just make sure you pick the young tips, as the plants become tough and bitter as they mature. Dried mugwort is sold in Japanese stores and should be re-constituted with water before using. You could try substituting other green leaves, such as spinach or, if you want to use wild food, young nettle tips!

2 large handfuls of fresh young mugwort leaves

250 g/9 oz rice flour (*shiratamako*)

250 ml/9 fl oz water

3 tablespoons roasted soybean powder (*kinako*)

Wash the mugwort leaves well and soak in cold water for an hour (or longer if possible) to lessen bitterness. Parboil in boiling water for 30 seconds. Remove and plunge into cold water to keep the green colour. Drain and squeeze. Put into a *suribachi* (pestle and mortar) and grind to a paste.

Mix the rice flour and water, adding the water slowly and kneading as you go. Keep kneading until you have a smooth paste, not too stiff and not too sloppy – like marzipan, or as the Japanese say, like your ear lobe. (You may need a little less or more water.) Take a tablespoonful of the mixture and form into small balls. Place them in a hot steamer, lined with muslin, and steam over a medium heat for 15-20 minutes. The balls will have become a gooey stretchy mass. Check that it is cooked through and transparent, and no longer powdery inside. Remove from the steamer and put into the grinding bowl with the mugwort. Now this is the strenuous part – you have to knead and grind until the mugwort is well distributed amongst the *mochi,* (you can try using a food processor, although I can't guarantee the blades won't snap). Once it's fairly well mixed in, leave it to cool. Cut into small pieces. On a board sprinkle the soybean powder, and coat each piece of *mochi* in it. Eat as a snack or with tea.

Variation: Instead of coating with the soybean powder these can be grilled, toasted or even added to soups, as in the recipes for *Isobemaki* (page 104) and *o-zōni* (page 102).

DUMPLINGS WITH SWEET SAUCE
SHIRATAMA DANGO

This is another variation on rice cakes made with rice flour. In this case they are boiled, not steamed. After further grilling they are coated with a sweetened soy sauce. This is the type of snack you can find at street festivals all over Japan.

250 g/9 oz rice flour (*shiratamako*)

250 ml/9 fl oz water

SWEET SAUCE:

2 tablespoons soy sauce

2 tablespoons caster sugar

2 tablespoons *mirin*

2 teaspoons potato starch (*katakuriko*) dissolved in water, to thicken

Mix the flour and water and leave to stand for five minutes until the water is absorbed.

Then form the mixture into small balls (about a tablespoonful each) and drop them into a large saucepan of boiling water. They will sink then rise. Let them simmer on the surface for about 2 minutes until cooked through. Drain and place into cold water to cool them. Drain again, and put aside.

Now make the sauce. Put the soy sauce, sugar and *mirin* in a small saucepan, and bring to a boil. Turn down the heat then when the sugar is dissolved add the starch paste, and stir well. Simmer for a minute, stirring all the time, until thickened.

Take some bamboo skewers and put 2 or 3 rice balls onto each. Grill briefly until just browned and then dip into the sweet sauce. Serve hot or at room temperature.

Variation 1: After you have cooked the dumplings and cooled them you can simply roll them in roasted soybean powder (*kinako*) and eat them without grilling. You can even experiment with sweet coatings, such as chocolate powder, cinnamon sweetened with caster sugar etc.

Variation 2: You can make the rice balls themselves sweet by adding sugar to the rice flour paste. Dissolve 3 tablespoons caster sugar in boiling water, make up the quantity of water with cold and then add it to the flour as before.

SESAME CUSTARD
GOMA DŌFU

This sesame milk custard is the *sashimi* of Zen temple food – often served at the beginning of a meal – delicate and luxurious. Although it is referred to as sesame 'tofu' it has nothing to do with soybeans. It just looks like tofu. The ingredients are simply sesame seeds, but the luxury of this food lies in its preparation, as the traditional way of making it was quite labour intensive. Large amounts of sesame seeds were ground to a smooth paste by hand in a *suribachi*. Modern gadgets, such as a blender, make it easier, but the thickening process can't be speeded up or electrically assisted. However, the result is worth the hard work. This would make a very interesting starter, or it could be served at the end of a meal instead of a sweet pudding (you may fancy sweetening it). A tiny blob of *wasabi* paste and a drizzle of soy sauce makes a savoury style dish, or it can be served just as it is, unadorned.

You'll need a cheesecloth bag or strainer, and a square mould (such as *nagashibako*) which holds about 240 ml/ ½ pint liquid. Wet the mould and stand it in a tray of cold water before you begin.

50 g/ 2 oz white sesame seeds (toasted or untoasted)	50 g/ 2 oz *kuzu* starch (dissolved in a little cold water to make a thin paste)
275 ml/ 10 fl oz water	

Toasted seeds give a darker coloured sesame milk, but you can use either toasted or untoasted. Put the sesame seeds into a blender with the water, and whizz for about 5 minutes – until the 'meal' is very fine, and you have a smooth liquid. Now, strain this liquid through fine muslin or cheesecloth, or a fine sieve, squeezing as much of the liquid sesame 'milk' out as possible. (This can be quite messy so try not to squirt it all over the kitchen.) You need a smooth milk, without bits in it, and all being well you should have about 400 ml/13 fl oz of it. Put into a large deep heavy bottomed saucepan, and add the starch mixture. Make sure the starch is completely dissolved, with no lumps in it then put over a medium heat and keep stirring. It will start to thicken as it heats up so be assiduous in your stirring. When it boils it will become quite stiff, so you'll need to stir vigorously. A wooden spoon is better than a balloon whisk for this as the mixture is thick and stiff. The mixture will splash up the sides of the inside of the pan, and spurt and bubble. This is quite normal. Keep stirring for about 5 minutes as it thickens and becomes glossy, and big bubbles appear. Then pour into the wetted mould. Leave until set, but don't put it into the fridge, as it will harden. To serve, cut into four small squares, and place each in the centre of a small dish or plate. Place a small blob of *wasabi* paste on top, and have a drizzle of soy sauce handy. Eat with chopsticks or a spoon.

STEAMED WALNUT CAKE
KURUMI TAMAGO

One of my most treasured possessions is a book given to me by my good friend Yasko Yokoyama. It's called *Edo Ryori* (Edo Cuisine) and is a book of very old recipes from the Edo era (1600 to 1853, before the Meiji restoration). The book itself is beautifully produced, covered in traditional Japanese indigo fabric (called *kasuri*). The recipes are elegant and simple, reflecting the limited choice of ingredients in use at the time. In fact the book is divided into four sections; rice, eggs, tofu and fish, and the different ways in which so few basic ingredients are prepared is a testament to ingenuity. These two recipes, roughly translated, are from the egg section, and are probably classics of their day. Although they don't contain sugar I have included them here as they are rich, and to my mind resemble desserts (although you may want to try sweetening them).

50 g/ 2 oz shelled walnuts	½ teaspoon soy sauce
1½ tablespoons saké	2 eggs

In a dry skillet or frying pan (or sesame roaster if you have one) toast the shelled walnuts until golden and aromatic (be careful not to burn them). Transfer to a *suribachi* (grinding bowl), or food processor if you like gadgets, and grind until you have a smooth paste. Add the saké and soy sauce and mix well. In a separate container beat the eggs well then gradually add to the walnut mixture, blending well. Pour the mixture into either a *chawan mushi* cup or a square mould, ready for steaming. Place in a steamer over a high heat, and cover with a cloth. Steam vigorously until the surface of the mixture turns white, then turn down the heat and steam gently, covered, for about 8 minutes until the mixture is completely set. Test by inserting a fine bamboo skewer into the centre – when it comes out clean then the pudding is cooked. Allow to cool, then serve two small slices, or two scoops (ice cream style) on an attractive lacquer or ceramic plate. Eat with a little wooden stick or small spoon, as a snack, a starter or a dessert.

STEAMED SESAME CAKE
RIKKYU TAMAGO

25 g/ 1 oz sesame seeds	½ teaspoon soy sauce
1½ tablespoons saké	2 eggs

Follow the instructions exactly as in the previous recipe for Steamed Walnut Cake, substituting white sesame seeds for walnuts.

PERSIMMONS IN SAKÉ SAUCE
KAKI NO SAKÉ KUZUTOJI

This delightfully simple dessert is an original from Sankō In Temple, shown to me by the abbess, Koei Hoshino. Apart from the extravagant use of saké, it is the contrast of temperatures that makes it special – the fruit must be chilled and the sauce hot. Persimmons in Japan are eaten whilst they are slightly firm, so try to use firmer rather than softer fruit.

2 persimmons	1 tablespoons *kuzu*, or potato starch
240 ml/ 10 fl oz saké	(*katakuriko*) dissolved in a little cold water

Peel the persimmons and cut out the stem end and any seeds. Cut each one into 6 wedges, and place in the refrigerator for at least two hours to chill. Just before serving make the sauce. Put the saké into a small saucepan, and bring to a boil over medium heat. Simmer for 30 seconds or so to eliminate the alcohol (you don't have to do this!) then dribble the dissolved *kuzu* starch in, stirring well. The mixture will thicken, so keep stirring to prevent it going lumpy. Simmer for a couple of minutes until evenly thickened and glossy. Place 3 slices of persimmon into each person's dish, and pour the hot sauce over. Serve immediately.

Variation: You can try this with Western style fruits and alcohol, such as chilled Conference pears with hot red wine sauce, or chilled strawberries with white wine sauce. Use your imagination.

SWEET POTATO
SATSUMAIMO/ YAKIMO

Roasted sweet potatoes used to be a great treat for Japanese children, and for some reason they are also seen as a ladies' food. When I was first in Japan in the 1970s it was still common to hear the cry of the sweet potato seller. He'd roam the streets in the early evening with a little cart holding a charcoal brazier, on which he roasted whole sweet potatoes, crying '*Yakimo, oishi yakimo*' ('roasted potato, delicious roasted potato'), whereupon children would excitedly rush up with their 100 yen coins – in the same way that Western children dash out to the ice cream van. Roasting these potatoes simply, with absolutely nothing to adorn the natural flavour brings out the best in them. It's a flavour given by God. Simply wrap the potato in foil and place it directly on to the coals of a fire (a barbecue fire or a Rayburn). When you retrieve it an hour later it's transformed. The skin peels away and you can scoop out the soft sweet flesh with a spoon. Delicious. Gives a Japanese flavour to bonfire night!

SWEET POTATO AND ORANGE TWISTS
SATSUMAIMO TO ORENJI NO CHAKIN SHIBORI

This is my variation on a traditional recipe for sweet potato twists. The sweet potato purée is formed into a ball and laid on a square of damp cotton which is then wrapped around it, shaken and twisted. After carefully removing the cloth the indented pattern of the twist is left on the purée, which is purely decorative but is another of those finishing touches that the Japanese do so well, and that elevate simple food into something elegant and special. You'll need a cotton handkerchief to form the twists.

2 large sweet potatoes, roasted with the skin on (about 400 g/ 14 oz)	½ teaspoon orange zest (finely grated)
2 tablespoons caster sugar	2 tablespoons salted butter

Wrap the sweet potatoes in foil and bake either in a hot oven (220C/425F/ gas mark 7) or in hot coals for half to one hour until soft all the way through (or peel, cut into chunks and boil in water until soft). Remove the sweet potatoes when cooked and, holding them in a cloth, remove the skin, or cut in half and scoop out the soft flesh. Put into a saucepan and mash well until you have a smooth purée. Add the sugar and beat well over a low heat until the sugar is dissolved and the mixture thick. Melt the butter in a small saucepan (or small measuring pan). Add the melted butter and orange zest to the potato purée and mix well. Leave to cool in the fridge, after which the mixture should be firmer. Now you are going to attempt the creative bit. Take a level tablespoonful of the mixture and form into a small ball. Then, holding the clean piece of cloth across the palm of your left hand, place the ball of purée in the centre. Pull the cloth up around it, and shake a little, so that the purée settles in the bottom of the cloth. Gently wring the cloth. Carefully peel the cloth away, which should leave a ball of purée with a twist indentation on it. Place one or two twists on a small wooden or lacquer plate, and eat with a bamboo fork or small spoon.

Note: The flouriness and water content of the sweet potatoes may result in the mixture being too soft, in which case the twisting won't be so successful. If this is the case, don't worry. You can simply serve small scoops of the purée, ice cream style, on a plate. The taste will be just as good. You can also add a few drops of orange essence if you like.

SWEET POTATO AND CHESTNUT BALLS
KURI KINTON

225 g/ 8 oz sweet potatoes	pinch salt
75 g/ 3 oz caster sugar	6 small chestnuts, cooked, shelled and
2 egg yolks	chopped

Peel the sweet potatoes thickly and cut into thick slices or chunks. Stand in cold water for half an hour or longer, to remove any bitterness. In fresh water place in a saucepan and bring to a boil (this is an occasion when you can use your drop lid – *otoshi buta*). Simmer until soft. Strain off the water, then return the pan to a low heat, and shake the contents around over the heat to get rid of excess moisture. You need do this for only a few seconds – don't scorch them. In a separate bowl, mash the potato to a smooth purée. Then put the bowl over water, in a *bain marie* or double saucepan, add the sugar and the egg yolks, and beat well over a low heat. Add a pinch of salt. Keep stirring whilst heating, until the mixture thickens and is fluffy. Leave to cool at room temperature, then put in the fridge to chill. Take a spoonful of mixture and form into a ball with your hands. Sprinkle the chestnut pieces onto a plate and gently roll each ball of purée into the pieces, so they adhere to the surface. Serve on lacquer plates, or on an autumnal leaf, with a small bamboo fork to eat it with. This is an afternoon sweetmeat to drink with tea and celebrate autumn.

AGAR AGAR (KANTEN) JELLY

Use one bar of agar agar to 500 ml/ 18 fl oz of liquid. If using flakes, measure them by volume (they are too light to weigh accurately) at a ratio of 1 : 5 flakes to liquid, that is 600 ml/ 1 pint liquid to 8 tablespoons flakes (e.g. 4 tablespoons flakes to 300 ml/ 11 fl oz liquid). Cups would be even easier – 2½ cups water to ½ cup flakes, or 1¼ cups water to ¼ cup of flakes.

SNOWY KANTEN JELLY
AWAYUKI KAN

Kanten means cold sky, and is descriptive of the way in which this seaweed gelling agent is traditionally prepared. To create the light transparent bars of gel the processed seaweed is left outside in winter for many days, whence it freezes during the night, and the sunlight melts it during the day. This natural freeze-drying technique is the same as the one used for making freeze-dried tofu. Sadly, many commercial operations are now speeded up, mechanized and chemicalised, but there are still a few suppliers making *kanten* in the traditional way, and their products are often available at health food and organic stores. Clearspring distribute it widely.

I bar agar agar (*kanten*) or 6
tablespoons flakes
450 ml/ 16 fl oz water
350 g/ 12 oz caster sugar
I egg white

I tablespoon lemon juice
I teaspoon lemon zest
a small bunch of red currants, or 8
grapes, or 4 strawberries, to decorate

Wash the agar agar (*kanten*) bar in water, and squeeze out excess moisture. Put into a saucepan with the measured water and leave it for half an hour to soften. Put onto a low to medium heat to dissolve the *kanten* completely and, when it has, strain the liquid through muslin or a fine sieve to get rid of any impurities. (If you are using the flakes simply dissolve them in the water, there is no need to strain.) Put the liquid back into the pan along with the sugar, and bring to a boil. Simmer over a low heat until the liquid is reduced by half. Beat the egg white until fluffy. Add the lemon juice and lemon rind to the syrup and then slowly fold in the beaten egg white, mixing evenly. Pour into a wetted square mould, and leave to set – which will take an hour or two. To serve, cut into four squares and place each on an attractive plate. Decorate with the fruit placed on top – cut the strawberries or grapes in half and place cut side down, side by side. If using berries just lay a small bunch on top artistically.

RED BEAN JELLY
MIZU YŌKAN

Yōkan is a thick sweet jelly, made with bean paste and sugar and set with agar agar, which is commonly served with green tea. This lighter summer version is made with less bean paste, is therefore not as dense and I think more appealing to Western tastes. You'll need a square or rectangular straight sided mould (such as a *nagashibako*) to set it in. Stand it in water first.

I bar agar agar (or 6 tablespoons
flakes)
500 ml/ 18 fl oz water

700 g/ 1lb 9oz smooth *azuki* bean paste
(*koshi an*, page 238)

If using a bar of agar agar, wash it first under running water then squeeze out excess moisture and tear it up, putting the pieces into a saucepan with the water. If using flakes simply sprinkle them into the saucepan of water. Put on a medium heat until the flakes or pieces are dissolved. Stir lightly and keep on a simmer to reduce the liquid by about a sixth. Remove from heat and add the sweet bean paste. Put back on a high heat and whisk well whilst heating to make smooth thick purée – about 3 minutes. Pour into a wetted mould and leave to set. You can force cool by standing the mould in a bowl of cold water. Once it's cooled leave it to chill overnight in the fridge, covering lightly with plastic wrap or foil. The next day it should be quite firm, and ready to cut into smooth sided slices or squares. Serve on glass plates for a cooling effect, and eat with little wooden sticks or forks, accompanied by green tea.

Variation: the basic jelly can be flavoured and coloured with things other than *azuki* bean, by combining the water with apple, pear or orange juice, or even red wine. Just keep to the basic ratio of liquid to agar agar as given earlier. An orange flavoured jelly can be cut into small cubes and served in hollowed out orange halves. A hollowed out half melon could also be a good container for serving fruit based jellies. Use your imagination and what is available.

STEAMED EGG CUSTARD WITH GINGER SAUCE
YOSE TAMAGO

This is another recipe from *Edo Ryori* – an exceptionally simple egg custard, but served with a ginger flavoured sauce. The excitement of this dish comes from the smooth texture of the custard and 'bite' of the ginger – and the fact that it is an old historical recipe. This could be served as a starter, as it's not sweet, but if you wanted to Westernise it to make a dessert you could use water instead of *dashi* and add sugar.

4 eggs	I teaspoon saké
pinch salt	pinch salt
I teaspoon light soy sauce	½ tablespoon light soy sauce
300 ml/ 10 fl oz *dashi* (page 49)	2 teaspoons *katakuriko* (potato starch)
GINGER SAUCE:	dissolved in a little cold water
200 ml/ 7 fl oz *dashi*	I teaspoon ginger juice

Break the eggs into a bowl and mix well, but stop before it becomes frothy. Add the salt, and soy sauce. Slowly add the *dashi* at room temperature. Pour into four *chawan mushi* (steaming) cups and place in a hot steamer. Cover with a towel and steam for 2-3 minutes, until the top turns white. Then turn down the heat and steam at a lower temperature for about 10 minutes, until the egg is set. Test by inserting a bamboo skewer – if it comes out clean it's done. Whilst it's steaming you can make the sauce. In a small saucepan combine the *dashi*, saké, salt and soy sauce. Add the dissolved starch and put over a medium heat. Stir well until thickened, and keep stirring over a low heat until the mixture is clear and glossy. Take off the heat and add the ginger juice. Mix in well. When the egg custard is done, take off the heat and pour a few spoons of the ginger sauce on top of each cup. Serve hot, with small spoons to eat.

GREEN TEA GRANITA
MATCHA NO KAKIGORI

In the sweltering humidity of the Japanese summer a common refreshment is a bowl of shaved ice piled high with a topping of sweet fruit syrup, called *kakigori*. One traditional topping is a sweet green tea flavoured syrup. I have adapted this idea to make a green tea granita – deliciously refreshing and beautiful to look at. Make sure you take the granita out of the freezer regularly to break it up, otherwise it will just become a solid block of ice.

500 ml/ 18 fl oz water	2 tablespoons powdered green tea
250 g/ 9 oz caster sugar	(*matcha*)

Combine the sugar and water in a saucepan, and keep on a low heat until the sugar is dissolved, and the liquid slightly reduced. Take off the heat and leave to cool. Add the green tea powder and stir well. Pour into a shallow container which will fit in your freezer. Freeze for a couple of hours, then remove and stir the contents around with a fork, breaking up the ice to create icy granules. Place back into the freezer, and repeat the process after another couple of hours. Remove from the freezer 20 minutes or so before serving and mash up the contents a little more before spooning into glasses. Serve as it is (garnished with a mint leaf) or with a small spoonful of *azuki* bean paste (*tsubushi-an*) on top for a traditional Japanese flavour.

PRUNE AND AMAZAKE PUDDING
PURŪN TO AMAZAKE NO PURIN

Macrobiotics is an approach to life and diet which was developed by Japanese emigrés to America at the end of the nineteenth century. It was later popularised by Georges Ohsawa in the nineteen thirties, and Michio and Aveline Kushi in the sixties. Using traditional Japanese ingredients the followers of macrobiotics have developed many interesting and tasty variations on Western style foods, particularly desserts. Because they never use dairy products, or refined sugar, this pudding uses *amazake,* a traditional sweet 'pudding' made from fermented rice, as both a dairy substitute and sweetener. *Amazake* is made by fermenting rice with *kōji* (the same agent used to make miso and saké). The resulting sweet rice pulp is traditionally served in Japan at Shinto shrines to celebrate new year, when it's combined with hot water to make a drink. Brown rice and millet *amazake* are available in the West at health food stores, and this is what I have used here. As well as getting sweetness from *amazake* this pudding is made sweet with the addition of dried prunes, so there's no need for any extra sugar at all. Oat milk makes it creamy without using any dairy products, and ground almonds add a nutty flavour. It's thickened with *kuzu*, the traditional starch that is used to aid digestion, so all in all it's pretty good for you, as well as being quite delicious.

125 g/ 4 oz dried prunes, stones removed	4 heaped tablespoons *amazake* (brown rice or millet)
500 ml/ 18 fl oz oat milk	3 tablespoons ground almonds
2 tablespoons *kuzu* starch	

Soak the prunes overnight, by covering with warm water and leaving to soften. In the morning put the softened prunes and the water in a saucepan and bring to a boil. Simmer covered, until the prunes are very soft and begin to fall apart. You want squishy prunes in thick syrupy liquid – not swimming. Transfer to a blender and whizz until you have a purée.

In a large saucepan pour the oat milk and add the *kuzu*, dissolved in a little water. On a medium heat stir until it starts to thicken. Add the *amazake*, ground almonds and prune purée, and keep stirring while it continues to thicken for a further 3 minutes. Take off the heat and pour into individual dishes to set. Serve at room temperature.

PRUNE KANTEN WITH NUT CUSTARD
PURŪN KANTEN

Again, this is not a traditional pudding, but uses Japanese ingredients like agar agar (*kanten*) which is made from sea vegetable, and is used to make sweets and desserts such as Red Bean Jelly (*mizu yokan*). In this recipe I've used prunes, and served it Western-style with a custard but, in the spirit of traditional Japanese cooking and inspired by macrobiotics, I have not used dairy products, but made a nut 'milk' from almonds.

---

400 g/ 14 oz dried stoned prunes,
  soaked overnight in 400 ml/ 14 fl oz
  water
6 tablespoons agar agar (*kanten*) flakes

ALMOND CUSTARD:
125 g/ 4 oz almonds
125 ml/ 4 fl oz water
1 tablespoon cornstarch

Put the prunes into a medium size saucepan with the soaking water. Bring to a boil and simmer for 30 minutes, covered, until the prunes are very soft and falling apart. (Add more water if necessary.) Transfer to a blender and whizz until you have a smooth as possible purée. You need 500 ml/ 18 fl oz of liquid purée, so add more water if necessary. If it's not sweet enough add a tablespoon of grain syrup, such as barley malt syrup, to taste. Transfer to a saucepan and sprinkle the agar agar flakes into the purée. Put on a low heat and simmer slowly until the flakes are dissolved. Turn into a wetted mould and leave to set and cool. You can put this in the fridge to chill once it is cooled.

To make the almond custard, drop the almonds into boiling water, and let sit for a few minutes. Drain, plunge into cold water and rub off the loosened skins with your fingers. They should slip off easily. Put the almonds and water into a blender and whizz for 2 minutes until smooth. Strain this through a piece of muslin or cheesecloth, wrapping up the corners well, so that you can squeeze all the 'milk' out. Put this into a small saucepan. Dissolve the cornstarch with a little cold water and add to the milk in the pan. Bring to the boil, stirring well over a low heat, and then simmer for 2-3 minutes until the custard thickens. Leave to cool.

To serve cut the chilled prune jelly into squares or blocks, and swirl the almond custard around as attractively as possible.

CARROT AND APPLE KUZU PUDDING
SHYĀRI NO NINJIN PURIN

This pudding is only slightly sweet, from the apple juice, and can be served as a dessert, or Japanese style with tea. I thought of it when looking at different ways of using *kuzu* starch to make puddings. You can experiment with other juices, such as freshly squeezed beetroot and orange.

150 ml/ 5 fl oz freshly squeezed carrot juice (keep the resulting carrot pulp, and use for Tofu and Carrot Balls (*Maridōfu*))	100 ml/ 3½ fl oz apple juice 7 tablespoons *kuzu* starch

Combine the juices and the *kuzu* starch, making sure any lumps in the *kuzu* are broken up, and completely dissolved. Do this in a large deep saucepan, then put on a low to medium heat, and bring to a boil, stirring well. As it thickens you will have to stir more and more vigorously, and the depth of the pan will be most necessary. Do this for 5 minutes or so until the mixture is thick and glossy and has big bubbles in it. Remove from the heat and pour into a wetted mould which holds about 250 ml/ 9 fl oz of liquid. A square, metal *nagashibako* with removable lining is best. Force cool by placing the mould in a bowl of cold water, but don't put it in the fridge as it will harden. Leave to cool to room temperature then turn out of the mould. You can turn it out into a bowl of cold water if you like, and then cut it up under the water. The consistency of *kuzu* is such that the resulting jelly has an elasticity that holds it together. Cut into four and serve either as a dessert or with tea.

ORANGE AND BEETROOT 'TOFU'
ORENJI TO BIITO NO KUZU KAN

Instead of using beetroot juice this recipe uses cooked beetroot to make a purée. Again, because it's made with *kuzu* starch it's best not to put it in the fridge or it will harden.

125 g/ 4 oz beetroot, cooked 225 ml/ 8 fl oz freshly squeezed orange juice	2 tablespoons saké 7 tablespoons *kuzu* starch

Have ready a wetted mould that holds about 250 ml/ 9 fl oz of liquid, and stand it in a tray of cold water.

Slide the skin off the cooked beetroot, and chop into small chunks directly into a blender (to avoid staining your chopping board). Add the orange juice. Whizz until you have a smooth purée. Transfer to a deep saucepan. Dissolve the *kuzu* in a little cold water then add to the beetroot mixture along with the saké. Bring the mixture to a boil over a medium heat, stirring all the time. When it starts to boil, turn the heat down and continue to simmer, stirring vigorously until it is stiff, stretchy and glossy, with big bubbles. It will become difficult to stir, but keep going, as it needs to thicken for 5 to 10 minutes. Pour into the wetted mould and leave to set and cool to room temperature. Serve cut into squares, either as it is, or with a blob of *wasabi* and soy sauce.

BEVERAGES

JAPANESE TEA
O-CHA

"She prepares the tea, pours it out in tiny cups and serves it to us, kneeling in that graceful attitude – picturesque, traditional – which for six hundred years has been the attitude of the Japanese woman serving tea. Verily, no small part of the life of the women of Japan is spent thus in serving little cups of tea."

Lafcadio Hearn, *Writings From Japan*

GREEN TEA

The tea most associated with Japan is of course green tea, although the leaves come from the same variety of tea bush that we get Indian black tea from, *Camellia Sinensis*. The reason Japanese tea is green is that the picked leaves are steamed before drying. This process destroys the enzyme that turns tea black, and therefore preserves the colour. It is now being recognised that this method of preparing the leaves preserves more than just the colour however, as the health benefits of Japanese green tea drinking are now being widely documented. Recent newspaper articles in the UK have expounded the virtues of green tea for losing weight, and several scientific studies have observed anti-carcinogenic effects of green tea in mice. A 1993 study in Shanghai, China, suggested that consumption of green tea may inhibit the growth of tumors in the case of oesophageal cancer in humans, and a Japanese study in 1986 revealed lowered cholesterol levels in men drinking nine or more cups of green tea a day. It has been credited with anti-bacterial properties, reducing the effects of radioactivity, and even preventing tooth decay. So there's every reason to get brewing. 'Brewing' however is the last thing you should do with Japanese tea...

You may have wondered why Japanese tea is usually made in such tiny little pots. This is because green tea turns bitter when it gets cold or is left to stand. A small pot can be drained immediately, so tea is never left in the pot (tea cosies and tea warmers are anathema to Japanese tea). The wet leaves however, can be left in the pot and used again. Simply pour more hot water on top, so that each serving is freshly made. And this is another difference from English tea, although green tea is always freshly made, boiling water is not used. The water must be allowed to go **off** the boil, until it reaches the ideal temperature, which is said to be 80C/175F.

"A smiling girl presented me with a zen, a small lacquer table about six inches high, with a tiny teapot with a hollow handle at right angles with the spout, holding about an English cupful, and two cups without handles or saucers, with a capacity of from ten to twenty thimblefuls each. The hot water is merely allowed to rest a minute on the tea leaves, and the infusion is a clear straw-coloured liquid with a delicious aroma and flavour, graceful and refreshing at all times. If Japanese tea stands it acquires a coarse bitterness and an unwholesome astringency. Milk and sugar are not used."

Isabella Bird, *Unbeaten Tracks in Japan*

Bancha The tea which is drunk everyday, at home, in restaurants and workplaces, is called *bancha*. This is the lowest grade, coarse leaved but mild tasting. Refreshing when hot, it turns bitter when cold. To make it: just as you do in England – first warm the pot (by swilling it out with hot water). Put 1 tablespoon tea to 1 cup and leave to infuse for no longer than 2 or 3 minutes. Pour into large or small handless cups, and drink as it is, without milk, lemon or sugar.

Hōjicha is *bancha* which has been roasted, and thus has the appearance of brown leaves and twigs. It can be drunk either hot or chilled.

Kukicha is a roasted brown tea comprising only twigs and stems, which is favoured by macrobiotic drinkers. Because it contains no leaf it is low in caffeine, and, unlike other teas, it is gently simmered rather than infused. It has a pleasant earthy or smoky aroma and is refreshing both hot or cold. It is not widely available in Japanese stores but can be found in health food shops.

Sencha is medium grade green tea, obtained from younger, more tender, leaves than *bancha*. This is the tea served to guests, and on special occasions. *Sencha* is usually made in small pots whereas *bancha* is sometimes brewed in larger quantities. (In sushi shops for instance *bancha* is served in large mugs.) It is brewed in the same way as *bancha* above, with water that has been taken off the boil, to 80C/175F, but proportionately more tea is used to water – about 2 tablespoons to one cup of water. In addition it is left to steep for no longer than a minute, and the pot is then drained. More water is added to the wet leaves for the next cup, and so on. Tea cups, although small, are never filled to the brim (this is common sense when you think about it, as they don't have handles). About 80% full is about right – *hachibunmei* is the expression for the correct level of filling. The small handleless cups are presented on little wooden, carved or lacquered saucers, which tend to be objects of exquisite beauty in themselves. I counted my collection recently and discovered that I have accumulated seven different sets of saucers.

Gyokuro is the best tea you can drink outside of tea ceremony tea. The young growing leaves are specially nurtured on the bush, and only the first most tender pickings are used for this 'jewel dew' tea. It is drunk in very small amounts and carefully sipped so that the flavour is especially appreciated, and the experience savoured. It is important that the delicate flavour is not ruined by water that is too hot, so *gyokuro* is brewed with warm not hot water – a temperature of 50C/120F is said to be best.

TEA CEREMONY TEA (MATCHA) AND TEA CEREMONY (CHA NO YU), THE RITUAL

"...a thick green purée of powdered tea (looking rather like spinach) was produced in a large and ancient chawan (bowl or tea cup), not beautiful to untrained eyes, for its texture was rough and its colour muddy. The cup was first taken in hand by the chief guest who drank the prescribed three and a half sips. It was then passed – not, of course, from hand to hand, but from fukusa to fukusa (napkin to napkin) turned about, carefully wiped and admired. Each guest took a portion of the strange, clinging faintly bitter mixture, and so this part of the ceremony drew to a close."

Grace James

Tea ceremony *Cha no yu*, means hot water for tea. *Matcha* or powdered tea is made from the same young leaves that *gyokuro* is made from, but the leaves are ground to a very fine powder. Unlike all the other teas this is made not in a pot, but individually in a large bowl, for each person, with attendant ceremony. Hot water is drawn from a carved iron kettle, the bowl is warmed, and a small scoop of the delicate green powder is taken from its decorated container using a miniature bamboo ladle. The tea is whisked to a froth in the bowl, with a little bamboo brush which is cut from one single piece of bamboo stem. Swishing the whisk back and forth to create the correct amount of froth is much more difficult than it looks, especially if it is to be done elegantly (which of course it must). After the bowl is passed to you and you have drunk the bitter but surprisingly creamy and delicious contents, you must carefully examine the bowl, and murmur appropriate words of appreciation. It is incumbent upon you in fact to express admiration for the shape, colour, design, age and even price of the bowl. In many cases the price of a tea bowl will equal, or even surpass, that of a fine painting: the potter may well be a famous name, and his work much venerated.

Drinking *matcha* then is more than taking a cup of tea, it's practically a religious experience, something like a very long drawn out communion. That is exactly how it is meant to be, as the whole 'art of tea' was brought back from China by Buddhist monks who encountered it as part of their training (caffeine-rich powdered green tea was originally drunk to keep them awake during long prayer sessions on their retreats). Reinforcing the philosophical aspects of tea ceremony are the many related disciplines of painting, flower arranging, ceramics, *kaiseki* food, garden design, and poetry. All of these elements, which are so closely associated with Zen Buddhism, have developed in response to, or alongside, the tea ceremony.

SAKÉ (NIHON SHU) AND SHŌCHŪ

"Saké, when heated, mounts readily to the head, and a single cup excites the half-witted man servant to some very foolish performances."

Isabella Bird

The Japanese in common with other Asian peoples, generally have a low tolerance for alcohol, and their faces soon turn red after only a drink or two. As Isabella Bird observed, however, Japanese men tend to behave merely comically, exhibiting more benign and less aggressive behaviour than their Western counterparts, when inebriated. A little bit of banter and plenty of staggering and singing are the usual signs, at least as observed by me on various station platforms in Tokyo at midnight! Pretty much the same behaviour that so exasperated Isabella a hundred years ago. In fact wherever she went in Japan she couldn't, it seems, avoid saké, and her letters are littered with saké-related anecdotes.

"'To drink for the gods' is the chief act of worship, and thus drunkenness and religion are inseparably connected, as the more saké the Ainos drink the more devout they are, and the better pleased are the gods. It does not appear that anything but saké is of sufficient value to please the gods."

Isabella Bird, *Unbeaten Tracks in Japan*

Although here Isabella was specifically referring to the indigenous Ainu peoples of Northern Japan, a love of saké, and religious excuses to drink it, are common to all Japanese. All ceremony is accompanied by saké drinking. At New Year celebrations bottles of saké are offered to the gods at Shinto shrines, and saké is served to the visitors from gold kettles.

The drinking of saké is also an important feature of the Japanese marriage ceremony – the union is considered sealed only upon the completion of a rigorously prescribed amount of drink. In fact the marriage ceremony seems to consist of little else according to this amusing account by Isabella Bird.

"The father-in-law drank three cups, and handed the cup to the bride, who, after drinking two cups, received from her father-in-law a present in a box, drank the third cup, and then returned the cup to the father-in-law, who again drank three cups. Rice and fish were next brought in, after which the bridegroom's mother took the second cup, and filled and emptied it three times, after which she passed it to the bride, who drank two cups, received a present from her mother-in-law in a lacquer box, drank a third cup, and gave the cup to the elder lady, who again drank three cups. Soup was then served, and then the bride drank once from the third cup, and handed it to her husband's father, who drank three more cups, the bride took it again, and drank two, and lastly the mother-in-law drank three more cups. Now if you possess the clear-sightedness which I laboured to preserve, you will perceive that each of the three had imbibed nine cups of some generous liquor."

Isabella Bird

As marriages in those days were almost always arranged, and the bride and groom had little say in who they were actually marrying, perhaps this ritual was devised so that unhappy couples could tie the knot without full realisation of what they were doing, or even who they were marrying.

In any event saké drinking is always accompanied by some sort of ritual. Even plain drinking in a bar is ritualised. You must never fill your own saké cup, but should lift your empty cup lightly in order that your companion may fill it for you: in return you must keep a careful eye on his cup and fill it when empty. This presupposes of course that you have a drinking companion, and this is the point. The Japanese just love being in groups. It makes them feel secure and feel that they belong. Being alone is the worst thing they can imagine (which is why they always travel in groups), and drinking alone is unthinkable.

So what exactly is saké? Although most Westerners use the word to mean rice wine, saké in fact is the generic term for alcoholic drink, and the correct term for the rice wine which foreigners think of as saké, is *nihon-shu* – literally Japanese 'spirits'. In fact saké isn't a spirit either, as it isn't distilled. And it's not a wine – it doesn't need to be aged like wine, it just needs to ferment, like beer. The alcoholic content, at around 24%, is higher than wine but lower than spirits. All this causes much confusion to Customs and Excise people who never know how to classify it.

Saké then is brewed, from rice combined with *kōji* mold, which ferments it. The starch in the rice turns to sugar, and this sugar ferments to alcohol, at the same time. It is then refined. The whole process takes no more than two months, when it's ready to drink. In fact once a bottle is opened it should be drunk fairly quickly (which I have to say is never a problem in my house!).

Most saké is pasteurised, usually twice, but non-pasteurised saké, called *namazake* which is still 'alive' (*nama* means fresh or raw) can be found in the refrigerator section of saké shops. *Namazake* should always be drunk cold, never heated. Although saké is generally perceived as being a drink which is heated before serving, the custom of doing so was introduced only in the eighteenth century – relatively recently compared to the length of time the Japanese have been drinking it. In fact connoisseurs (called *tsu*) always prefer their saké cold, and, as just mentioned, some types of saké are specifically intended to be drunk chilled or even on the rocks. *Konodoshu* is another of them – with a higher alcohol content than most saké it is particularly appropriate for serving with ice, as the ice then dilutes it.

Nigori zake is unrefined saké which is thick and milky white – still having bits of rice mash in it. This unrefined saké would be similar to the type that is referred to in the *Kojiki* – the eighth century record, and first written account, of Japan's early history. So the Japanese have been drinking saké for a long while.

Taruzaké is saké which has been aged in a cedar tub, and thus retains the aroma and taste of the wood. At festivals and celebrations, such as at cherry blossoming viewing time, saké is often drunk cold from small square cedar cups (called a *masu*), instead of the usual ceramic cup (*choko*). At such times it's common to see huge decorated barrels of saké being cracked open with a wooden mallet amid much jollity.

To heat saké first decant some into a *tokkuri* – the small bottle which is often mistaken for a bud vase by foreigners not in the know. The bottle is then heated by standing it in boiling water on a low heat, until it reaches the required temperature. It should be hotter than blood heat, but not scalding – about 42-50C/108-122F. Heating saké releases its fragrance, and also ensures that the alcohol reaches the blood more quickly. Although it tastes lovely it has to be said that you can get a wicked hangover from drinking too much of it. The trouble is that it is so easy to drink too much, partly because it tastes so good, but also because custom dictates that it can be considered impolite to refuse when your cup is filled by your companion.

The study of saké (although possibly simpler than wine) can be quite complicated – I prefer to simply drink it! But for those of you who want to know more, there is an excellent English language book on the subject, called *Saké, a Drinker's Guide*, by Hiroshi Kondo (published by Kodansha).

Umeshu is a sweet plum-flavoured liqueur-type drink, which is popular in summer, served over ice. One brand is sold in straight-sided green bottles with several plums nestling at the bottom of the bottle. It can also be served with sparkling soda, and a ready mixed version is available in cans.

Next to saké, **shōchū** is the other indigenous drink of Japan. Unlike saké which is brewed, *shōchū* is distilled – from a variety of grains and vegetables, such as potato, barley, millet and even buckwheat, and the alcohol content is higher – up to 36%. A typical winter drink is *shōchū* diluted with hot water (ask for *oyuwari*) with an *umeboshi* plum in the bottom of the glass. In summer it can be diluted with cold water, or served on the rocks, but is commonly mixed with sweet flavoured sodas, such as lime or lemon, in which case you'd order *chuhai*. Another recent trend is to dilute it with cold brown tea – oolong tea from China usually, which gives a pleasant non-sweet drink. Unlike vodka in the UK, *shochu* is relatively cheap, and is thus popular with working men and students. It certainly doesn't have the ceremonial and religious resonance of saké, nor does it have the cachet of wine, which, as it's a foreign import, is considered fashionable, especially by young Japanese women. Because *shōchū* can be watered down (which saké generally isn't) it's a good drink to see you safely through long evenings in bars.

On the subject of bars, one charming custom in Japan, which I wish would be exported is the 'bottle keep' system. Regulars buy a full bottle (such as whisky or *shōchū*) and keep it behind the counter at their local drinking place. On each visit they just ask for their own bottle, which has their name on it, and drink as little or as much as they like. The bottle is paid for on the first visit, and on future visits money will be spent on accompanying food, additional mixers and some type of cover charge. Once the *mama-san* gets to know you she'll automatically reach for your bottle when you go in. It's little customs like this that give a huge sprawling place like Tokyo the feel of a village. In fact I often felt inspired to describe my life in Tokyo as cosy, something which I am sure most people who haven't lived there would find hard to understand. But it was true.

In the end that is how I feel about Japan, its people and of course, its food. Japan is not the austere minimalist place it is sometimes made out to be, the people are not regimented and humourless, and the food is not from another planet. It's certainly not complicated. Japanese food, like the people themselves, can be approachable and friendly. It's easy to make and easy to eat. I hope that this book will help to open up the mystery of Japanese cuisine, and in the process the heart of the Japanese people.

BIBLIOGRAPHY

Travel and historical accounts
Isabella Bird *Unbeaten Tracks in Japan* (Virago/Beacon Travellers 1984)
Sir Ernest Satow *A Diplomat in Japan 1853-64* (London 1921)
M.E. Cosenza *The Complete Journal of Townsend Harris* (Doubleday 1930)
S.Keizo (trans. C.S.Terry) *Japanese Life and Culture in the Meiji Era* (Obunsha Tokyo 1958)
Grace James *Japan Recollections and Impressions* (Allen and Unwin 1936)
Basil Hall Chamberlain *Things Japanese* (Kegan Hall, Trench and Trubner 1891 and John Murray 1902)
Lafcadio Hearn *Writings from Japan: An Anthology* (Edited by Francis King) (re-printed Penguin 1984)
Richard Gordon Smith *The Japan Diaries of Richard Gordon Smith* (Edited by Victoria Manthorpe) (Penguin 1986) © J.Austin and E.A.Tudge 1986
Donald Richie *A Taste of Japan*(Kodansha 1985)
Rafael Steinberg *The Cooking of Japan - Foods of the World series,* (Time Life Books 1970)

Food and cookery books
A special recommendation to the first five books, which have been invaluable to me in my research:
Shizuo Tsuji *Japanese Cooking a Simple Art* (Kodansha 1980)
Richard Hosking *A Dictionary of Japanese Food* (Charles Tuttle 1996)
Joy Larkcom *Oriental Vegetables: The Complete Guide for Garden and Kitchen* (John Murray, London 1991)
Koei Hoshino *The Heart of Zen Cuisine* (first published as *Good Food From a Japanese Temple*) (Kodansha 1982)
Gaku Homma *The Folk Art of Japanese Country Cooking* (North Atlantic Books, California, with Domo Productions, Colorado 1991 © Gaku Homma)
Hiroko Urakami *Japanese Family Style Recipes* (Kodansha 1992)
Lesley Downer *Japanese Vegetarian Cookery* (Jonathan Cape 1986)
The Better Home Association of Japan (Trans. Fumiko Hara) *Japanese Home Style Cooking* (Better Home Publishing 1986)
Margaret Leeming and Mutsuko Kohsaka *Japanese Cookery* (Rider 1984)
Margaret Leeming and May Huang Man-Hui *Far Eastern Vegetarian Cooking* (Columbus Books London 1985)
Linda Lee Barber and Junko Lampert *Tofu a new way to healthy eating* (Century Hutchinson 1986)
Katsuji Yamamoto and Roger W. Hicks *Step by Step Sushi* (The Apple Press/Quintet Publishing 1990)
Masaru Doi *Japanese One-Pot Cookery* (Kodansha 1966)
Kay Shimizu *Japanese Foods For Health* (Shufunomoto Co.Ltd 1974)
Sadako Kohno *Japanese Cooking* (Shufunomoto Co.Ltd Tokyo 1968)
Madhur Jaffrey *A Taste of the Far East* (BBC Books and Pavilion Books Ltd 1993)

Japanese language sources
Tomiko Shimazaki and Hiroshi Fukuda *Edo Ryori* (2001 nen sha, Japan 1983)
Koichiro Goto *Kaiseki Ryori o Tanoshimu* (San Ichi Shobo 1987)

Magazines
Kyo no Ryori (NHK, December 1978)
Shiki no aji No.14 (New Science Sha, Autumn 1998)
Kyo no shōjin ryōri No.172, Kurashi no sekkei No.74 (Chuo Kōron Sha 1986)

Macrobiotic sources
Peter and Montse Bradford *Cooking with Sea Vegetables* (Thorsons 1985)
William Shurtleff and Akiko Aoyagi *The Book of Miso* (Ten Speed Press, California 1976 & 1983)
Craig and Ann Sams *The Brown Rice Cookbook* (Thorsons 1983)
Edward and Wendy Esko *Macrobiotic Cooking for Everyone* (Japan Publications Inc. Tokyo 1980)
Wendy Esko *Introducing Macrobiotic Cooking* (Japan Publications Inc. Tokyo and New York 1987)
Tokuji Watanabe with Asako Kishi *The Book of Soybeans* (Japan Publications Inc. Tokyo and New York 1984)
John and Jan Belleme *Cooking with Japanese Foods* (East-West Health Books, Brookline MA, 1986)
John and Jan Belleme *Culinary Treasures of Japan* (Avery Publishing, New York 1992)

DIRECTORY OF SUPPLIERS

Japanese Food Shops

London

Arigato Japanese supermarket
48-50 Brewer Street
London W1
Tel 0207 287 1722 (tube: Piccadilly Circus)

Atari-ya (Finchley)
595 High Road
North Finchley
London N12
Tel: 0208 446 6669 Fax: 0208 446 6728

Atari ya (West Acton)
7 Station Parade
Noel Road
London W3 0DS
Tel: 0208 896 1552 (tube: West Acton)
*good fresh fish

Harro Service Ltd
20-22 Worple Road
Wimbledon
London SW19 4DH
Tel: 0208 944 1928 Fax: 0208 947 1961

JA Centre (Tazaki Foods)
Unit B Eley Industrial Estate
Eley Road
London N18 3BH
Tel: 0208 803 8942 Fax: 0208 884 0869

Marimo
350-356 Regent's Park Road
Finchley
London N3 2LJ
Tel: 0208 346 1042 Fax: 0208 343 0951

Miura Foods (Kingston)
44 Coombe Road
Kingston-upon-Thames
Surrey
Tel: 0208 549 8076 and 0208 651 4498
Fax: 0208 547 1216
*good selection of fresh fish

Miura Foods (Sanderstead)
5 Limpsfield Road
Sanderstead
South Croydon
Tel: 0208 651 4498
*good selection of fresh fish

Natural House
Japan Centre (Lower ground floor)
212 Piccadilly
London W1V 9LD
Tel: 0207 434 4218 Fax: 0207 287 1083

Oriental City
399 Edgware Road Colindale London NW9 0JJ
Tel/Fax: 0208 200 0848

Rice Wine Shop
82 Brewer Street London W1
(tube Piccadilly Circus)
Tel: 0207 439 3705 Fax: 0207 828 5151
(no fresh fish but a good selection of saké, frozen and
dried food and good prices)

TK Trading
Unit 6-7 The Chase Centre
Chase Road
London NW10 6QD
Tel: 0208 453 1743 Fax: 0208 453 0606
e mail: yoshikawauklyd@msn.com

Yoshino
15-16 Monkville Parade Temple Fortune
Finchley Road
London NW11 0AL
Tel: 0207 287 1733 and 0208 209 0966
Fax: 0208 458 8970

Yoshino Fish
Unit 10 Oriental City
399 Edgware Road
London NW9 0JJ
Tel: 0208 205 6500   Fax: 0208 205 9100
(tube: Colindale)

Fresh Fish (non-Japanese stores)

Chalmers and Gray
67 Notting Hill Gate London W11
Tel: 0207 221 6177 Fax: 0207 727 3907
*will deliver

Box's of Fulham
110 Wandsworth Bridge Road Fulham London SW6 2TF
Tel: 0207 736 5766 Fax: 0207 736 4509
Contact: Donal Box

Jarvis
56 Coombe Road Kingston-upon-Thames
Surrey
Tel: 0208 546 2886 Fax: 0208 546 0989

Steve Hatt Fishmonger
88 Essex Road Islington London N1
Tel: 0207 226 3963

Japanese Stores Outside London

Brighton
Midori
19 Marlborough Place
Brighton E Sussex
Tel: 01273 601460 Fax: 01273 620422
*will also do mail order

Wing Yip has a wide selection of Japanese goods
including fresh local fish and imported frozen fish and
Japanese saké.

Birmingham
Wing Yip
375 Nechells Road Nechells Birmingham B7 5NT
Tel: 0121 327 3838 Fax: 0121 3276612

Cricklewood
Wing Yip
395 Edgware Road London NW2
Tel: 0208 450 0422 Fax: 0208 452 1478

Croydon
Wing Yip
550 Purley Way Croydon Surrey CR0 3RF
Tel: 0208 688 4880 Fax: 0208 688 8786

Manchester
Wing Yip
Oldham Road Ancoats Manchester M4 5HU
Tel: 0161 832 3215 Fax: 0161 833 2798

Ledbury
Ceci Paolo The Delicatessen
21 High Street, Ledbury Herefordshire HR8 1DS
Tel: 01531 632976 Fax: 01531 631011
e mail: patriciaharrison@compuserve.com
Contact: Patricia Harrison.
*a selection of Japanese foods and kitchenware

Newcastle
Setsu Japan
196a Heaton Road
Newcastle upon Tyne
Tel: 0191 265 9970 Fax: 0191 276 2951
*good selection of fresh fish and wide range
of Japanese goods

Reading
Ayame
Unit L13 Gyosei College Acacia Road Reading Berks
Tel: 01734 3106470

Swindon
Jasmin
c/o Station House Hotel
The Avenue
Stanton Fitzwarren
Swindon Wilts
Tel: 01793 861777 Fax: 01793 861857
* fresh fish to order only

Retailers – Macrobiotic and Japanese organic foods

London
Freshlands
49 Parkway Camden Town
London NW1 7PN
Tel: 0207 428 7575
Freshlands (City)
196 Old Street
London EC1V 9FR
Tel: 0207 250 1708

Wild Oats
210 Westbourne Grove London W11 2RH
Tel: 02027 229 1063 Fax: 0207 243 0988

Bushwacker Wholefoods
132 King Street Hammersmith London W6 0QU
Tel: 0208 748 2061

Bumble Bee
30 Brecknock Road London N7
Tel: 0207 607 1936

Planet Organic
42 Westbourne Grove London W2
Tel: 0207 221 7171

Oriental City
399 Edgware Road
Colindale London NW9 0JJ
Tel/Fax : 0208 200 0848

Mail Order Organic Japanese

Clearspring Direct
Tel: 0208 746 0152 Fax: 0208 811 8893
email: mailorder@clearspring.co.uk
www.clearspring.co.uk

Clearspring have an extensive supply of Japanese foods all naturally produced and usually organic. They supply a huge range of distributors and retailers. To find your nearest retailer contact the distributor in your area from the list below:

Goodness Foods
South March Daventry Northants NN11 4PH
Tel: 01327 706611 Fax: 01327 300436

Harvest Foods
29 St Catherine's Road Bournemouth Dorset BH5 4AE
Tel: 01202 420998 Fax: 01202 417757

Nottingham (and national)
Health Stores
Queens Road Nottingham NG2 3AS
Tel: 01159 555255 Fax: 01159 555290

Scotland
Grassroots
20 Woodlands Road Glasgow G3 6RU
Tel: 0141 353 3278 Fax: 0141 353 3078

Highland Wholefoods
Unit 6 13 Harbour Road Inverness IV1 1SY
Tel: 01463 714467 Fax: 01463 715 586

South and South East
Infinity Foods Co-op
67 Norway Street Portslade East Sussex BN41
Tel: 01273 424060 fax: 01273 417739

Marigold Health Foods Ltd
Unit 10 St Pancras Commercial Centre
63 Pratt Street London NW1 0BY
Tel : 0207 267 7368 Fax: 0207 485 3247

Republic of Ireland
Munster Wholefoods
Farranfore Kerry Eire
Tel: 00 353 66 64691 Fax: 00 353 6664692

Wholefoods Wholesale
Unit 2D Kylemore Industrial Estate Kileen Road Dublin
10 Eire
Tel: 00 353 1 626 2315 Fax: 00 353 1 626 1233

National and North West
Natures Store
Unit 2 Jamage Industrial Estate Talke Stoke on Trent ST7
1XN
Tel: 01782 794300 Fax: 01782 774698

National and East
Rainbow Wholefoods
21 White Lodge Trading Estate Hall Road Norwich
Norfolk NR4 6DG
Tel: 01603 630484 Fax: 01603 664066

North
Suma Wholefoods
Unit AX1 Dean Clough Industrial Park Halifax West
Yorkshire HX3 5AN
Tel: 01422 345513 Fax: 01422 349429

South West
Seasons
8 Well Street Exeter Devon
Tel: 01392 201 282 Fax: 01392 275 764

Wholesalers organic suppliers manufacturers and producers

Soy products and organic tofu wholesaler:
Pauls Soyfoods Ltd
66 Snow Hill Melton Mowbray Leicestershire LE13 1PD
Tel: 01664 60572 Fax: 01664 410345
Mobile: 0860 667319

Fresh unpasteurised organic miso and kōji:
Source Foods
Unit 9 Cwm Business Centre Marine Street Cwm Ebbw
Vale Wales NT23 7TB
Tel/ fax : 01495 371698
e mail: sourcefoods@miso.co.uk
www.miso.co.uk
Contact: Paul Chaplin

For organic unpasteurised miso tofu tempeh and seitan (gluten):
Full of Beans
96 High Street Lewes East Sussex
Tel: 01273 472627
e mail: tempeh@globalnet.co.uk
Contact: Sarah and John Gosling

For a wide range of organic fresh sea vegetables and related seaweed condiments (including delicious seaweed salt):
Eco-Zone
65 St Quintin Avenue London W10 6NZ
Tel: 0208 962 6399
Contact: Eric Vagniez
e mail vagniez@btinternet.com

For organic quality dried sea vegetables and condiments. Will mail order from the US:
Maine Coast Sea Vegetables
Franklin Maine 04634 U.S.A.
Contact: Carl Karush
Tel: 00 1 207 565 2907 Fax: 00 1 207 565 2144
e mail: mcsv@acadia.net
www.seaveg.com

For traditional Japanese cakes and sweets:
Minamoto Kitchoan
44 Piccadilly London W1V 9AJ
Tel: 0207 437 3135 Fax: 0207 437 3191

For unusual and oriental seeds fungi and ferments to make miso and natto contact:
Future Foods
PO Box 1564 Wedmore Somerset BS28 4DP 01934 713623
www.futurefoods.com

For further information on macrobiotics contact:
Macrobiotic Association of Great Britain
377 Edgware Road London W2
Tel: 07050 138419

For organic eggs and sweetcorn (may deliver in quantity). Can be found on the Borough Market London once a month and Islington Market London N1 every Sunday.
Farmer Kit's Organic Eggs
Little Bowsers Farm
Little Walden Saffron Walden
Essex CB10 1XQ
Contact: Kit Barker
Tel/Fax 0179 527315

Organic meat (will slice thinly for Japanese dishes):
Meat Matters
2 Blandy's Farm Cottages
Letcombe Regis Wantage Oxon OX12 9LJ
Freephone: 08080 067426 Fax: 01235 772526
Will deliver free within Greater London Oxfordshire
Berkshire and South Bucks. Other deliveries are charged
according to size of order.

Organic Welsh sea salt:
The Anglesey Sea Salt Company
Brynsiencyn Lanfairpwllgwyngyll
Anglesey LL61 6TQ Wales
01248 430871 Fax: 01248430213
e mail: seasalt@email.wales.com
www.nwi.co.uk/seasalt

For dried Japanese food items and kitchen utensils and cooking instruction:
The Authentic Ethnic Cookery School
14 Redcliffe Square London SW10 9JZ
Tel: 0207 373 3651 Fax: 0207 460 0334
Contact: Tertia Goodwin and Shirley Booth

For Japanese goods and a limited selection of food items and kitchen ware:
Muji (Mujirushi Ryohin Europe)
London stores:
26 Gt Marlborough Street London W1V 1HL
Tel: 0207 494 1197 Fax: 0207 494 1193

39-41 Shelton Street Covent Garden London WC2H 1HJ
Tel: 0207 379 1331 Fax: 0207 379 1603

157 Kensington High Street London W8
Tel: 0207 376 2484 Fax: 0207 936 3665

187 Oxford Street London W1R 1AS
Tel: 0207 437 7503 Fax: 0207 437 7517

Manchester store:
137 Regent Crescent Trafford Centre Manchester M17 8AR
Tel: 0161 747 3555 Fax: 0161 747 3777

Kingston store:
Unit f3 Bentall Centre Kingston Surrey KT1 1TP
Tel: 0208 974 8741 Fax: 0208 547 2897

Bluewater store:
Unit L125 Lower Guildhall Bluewater Greenhithe Kent
DA9 9SN
Tel: 01322 624354 Fax: 01322 624355

Whiteleys store:
D1 116 Whiteleys London W2 4YN
Tel: 0207 792 8283 Fax: 0207 792 8180

Other Japanese kitchenware and tableware:
Take Ltd
45-46 Chalk Farm Road London NW1 8AJ
Tel: 0208 876 9216

24 Chiswick High Road London W4 1TE
Tel: 0208 742 0718

182 Upper Richmond Road West London SW14 8AW
Tel: 0208 876 9216

14-15 New College Parade Finchley Road
London NW3 5EP
Tel: 0207 586 0064

Utsuwa no Yakata (Tajimi UK Ltd)
Unit 22 Oriental City
399 Edgware Road Colindale London NW9 0JJ
Tel: 0208 201 3003 Fax: 0208 201 3004

GLOSSARY OF JAPANESE WORDS

abura oil

abura-age deep fried tofu 'pouch'

age deep fry

aji taste

akadashi red miso

arai to wash, but also refers to the process of refreshing fish in cold water

arame seaweed

atsuage thick deep fried tofu

awase miso blended miso

bainiku pickled plum

bentō lunch box

chawan bowl for serving rice or tea

chawan mushi 'steamed bowl' a steamed savoury custard

Chūka Chinese style

dango dumpling

dashi stock made from kombu and usually dried bonito flakes

dengaku grilled vegetables or tofu topped with a flavoured miso topping

Edō jidai Edo era 1600-1853, when Japan was closed to the outside world

Edō murasaki literally Edo 'purple', but refers to a delicious salty paste made of soy sauce and *nori* which accompanies rice

endō green bean

enka plaintive folk song

fū style, a la japonais, as in *wa fū* Japanese style

fu (2) wheat gluten

genmai brown rice

gohan cooked rice

gokan no ge a type of grace, recited by monks and nuns before eating

goma sesame

gomoku dish made up of assorted (literally five) items- such as variety rice

haigamai half refined rice, with the husk removed but the germ left intact

hanami cherry blossom viewing

hashi chopsticks

hikari mono literally 'shining thing', refers to silvery fish such as mackerel and sardines

hiki giri pulling or drawing cut

hina matsuri Girls Day or the Doll Festival, celebrated on March 3rd

hyōshigi giri clapper cut - thick rectangles

ichijū sansai rice and three - the basic meal format, comprising rice, soup and three other dishes

Inari god of rice

inarizushi tofu pouches stuffed with rice

irodashi colour giving technique – parboiling then rinsing in cold water

itamae head chef – the one who stands in front

izakaya unpretentious drinking place, which usually sells good cheap food

jidai era (as in Meiji jidai and Edo jidai)

jinja Shinto shrine

kaisō sea vegetables

kaiseki the refined style of cooking which accompanies tea ceremony

kake jiru basic noodle broth, served hot

kanpyō dried gourd skin

kappa mythical water nymph – said to like eating cucumbers

katsuobushi dried bonito fillet, shaved into fine flakes

katsura muki the cutting style whereby a root vegetable is cut into one thin continuous sheet. Not easy

kezuri shaved

kine wooden mallet used for pounding rice into *mochi*

kitsune fox

kōji grain which has been inoculated with *Aspergillus oryzae*, used as the starter for making saké, miso, soy sauce, *mirin* and *shochū* spirit

kōya dōfū freeze dried tofu

kuri chestnut

kinugoshi silken or soft tofu, made without pressing

kombu kelp seaweed – the basis of *dashi* stock

kinako roasted soy bean powder

kome uncooked rice, the grain, usually *o-kome*, with the honorific o added to reflect its lofty status

kuzu starch of the tuberous *kuzu* vine root

mama san the lady who serves

in and owns the bar – usually a lively and interesting character

maze mixed, assorted, adulterated, as in *maze gohan*

Meiji Restoration the restoration of Imperial rule and the opening up of Japan to trade with the outside world – the beginning of Westernisation, which began in 1868, under the Emperor Meiji

menrui noodles

meshi cooked rice or, casually, a meal

mijin giri a mincing cut

minshuku inexpensive bed and breakfast place, usually in the country

momiji maple leaf (as in *momiji oroshi*)

mono thing, item, as in *yaki mono* – grilled thing, *age mono* – deep fried thing

moriawase a selection or mixture

moritsuke the proper arrangement of food – actually it means 'to heap' – and should imitate natural features of the landscape

mushi to steam

mushi yaki steam grilling – these days usually wrapped in foil

nabe cooking pot, but also refers to the one-pot cooking style, where the food is cooked in an earthenware pot at the table

nagashibako rectangular metal mould with removable lining for making jellies and the like

nama fresh, raw

niku meat

nomiya drinking place, which usually sells cheap and delicious bar snacks

noren traditional half curtain hung on the doorway of a bar to indicate that it is open

okazu side dish

okoge the scorched layer of rice in the bottom of the pan – a delicacy

oroshi to grate/ grated food

oroshigane a grater

oshi giri a pushing cut – straight down

otoshibuta drop lid – wooden and fits inside the pan

ran giri 'chaos' or random cut – uneven chunks

ryōri cuisine, cooking

sainome giri cube cutting

sasagaki a shaving cut

sasami chicken breast fillet

sashimi raw fish

shibui astringent

shichimi tōgarashi seven spice pepper

shimofuri 'hoar frosting', the technique of refreshing meat and fish by pouring boiling water over then chilling in cold

shinmai new rice – the first of the season

shincha new tea – the first of the season

shio yaki salt grilled

shio zuke salt pickled

shirumono soup or broth or gravy (except clear soup). *Shiru* also becomes *jiru*

shōjin ryōri Zen temple cuisine, which is meat, fish and dairy free in other words completely vegetarian

su vinegar, as in *sushi* – vinegared rice

sudare a bamboo blind, but also used to refer to the bamboo rolling mat – more accurately called *makisu*

suimono clear soup literally 'something to drink'

sumeshi sushi rice

suribachi grinding bowl with serrated inside surface

surikogi wooden pestle used with the above

surimi fish paste – the basis of various fish products such as *kamaboko, chikuwa*

teishoku a set lunch or meal

tenzo head cook in a temple or monastery

tetsuyu dipping broth for tempura

tori chicken

ton pork (also *buta*)

tsuke jiru concentrated dipping sauce for cold noodles

tsuki giri a thrusting cut

tsukimi moon viewing, but also refers to an egg (the moon) being placed on top of food such as noodles

tsukudani a preserving technique whereby food (for example beans or sea weed) is cooked in a strong mixture of soy sauce and sugar until dry and sticky. The salt and sugar preserves them for a long time. Eaten in small quantities like a condiment

usu wooden tub used for pounding rice into *mochi* (used with a mallet called *kine*)

wa prefix meaning Japanese style

wan bowl

yakuza gangsters

yatai street stall selling food

yūgaku parboiling

zaru basket for serving noodles, or as a colander

zen low invidual table for serving food – not much used these days but popular in the 19th century

Zen branch of Buddhism characterised by its austerity and simplicity.

zuke pickling

PICTURE CAPTIONS

Facing page 64
Soups

Top
Winter Miso Soup with Onion and Daikon (*Daikon to tamanegi no* akamiso jitate)

Middle
Summer Miso Soup with Beansprouts and Tofu pouches (*Abura-age to moyashi no miso shiru*)

Bottom
Clear Soup with Tofu and Spinach (*sunomono*) (*Tōfu no sunomono*)

Facing page 65
Tofu

(clockwise from top)

Chilled Silken Tofu with condiments (*Hiya yakko*)

Tofu with Miso topping (yellow and green) (*Tōfu dengaku*)

Mixed vegetables with Tofu dressing (*Shira ae*)

Facing page 96
Four Season's Rice

(clockwise from top)

Plain boiled rice (*Gohan*)

Rice Balls (*O-nigiri and yaki o-nigiri*) (Summer)

Winter Chestnut rice (*Kuri gohan*)

Rice Bales (*Tororo Kombu no o-nigiri*) (Autumn)

Rice with green peas (*Endō no gohan*) (Spring)

Facing page 97
Noodles

Top
Fox noodles (*Kitsune udon*)

Middle and bottom
Cold Buckwheat noodles with Vegetable Tempura (*Ten Zaru Soba*)

Facing page 128

Top
Deep Fried Gluten (*Rōbai*) (wholewheat and white flour)

Middle
Creamy Plum Dressing (*Ume doreshingu*)

Bottom
Broccoli, Mushroom and Gluten salad (*Burrokori to Rōbai no sarada*)

Facing page 129
Rice, Soup and Pickles

(clockwise from top)

Miso Soup with Tofu and Wakame (*Tōfu to wakame no miso shiru*)

Daikon and Carrot instant pickle (*Daikon to ninjin zuke*)

A selection of commercially prepared pickles - *takuan*, cucumber, bamboo shoot and *umeboshi* plum.

Rice with condiment (*Furikake gohan*)

Facing page 160

Top
A selection of Rolled Sushi (*Makizushi*)

Bottom
Assorted Raw Fish (*Sashimi moriawase*)

Facing page 161

Salt Grilled Wholefish (*Sakana no shio yaki*)

'Maple Leaf' Radish condiment (*Momiji oroshi*)

Facing page 192
A Selection of Spring dishes

(clockwise from top)

Rice with Perilla leaves (*Shiso Gohan*)

Bamboo Shoots sautéed with Mange Tout and Arame

(*Takenoko to sayaendō no itamemono*)

Chicken grilled on skewers (*Yakitori*)

Spinach with Bonito Flakes (*Ohitashi*)

Facing page 193
A selection of Summer dishes

(clockwise from top)

Fine Wheat noodles (*Sōmen*)

Deep fried Aubergine with fresh Broad Beans (*Nasu no soramame ae*)

Wakame and Cucumber Salad (*kyūri to wakame no sunomono*)

Chicken breast with Vinegar, Mustard and Miso dressing (*Sasami no karashi ae*)

Facing page 224
An Autumn meal

(clockwise from top)

Rice with enokitake mushrooms (*Enokitake gohan*)

Pumpkin and Azuki Beans (*Kabocha to azuki no nimono*)

Deep Fried Tofu and Shiitake 'Pine Cones' (*Matsukasa*)

Green Beans with sesame dressing (*Ingen no goma ae*)

Facing page 225

Winter Meal (*Chirinabe*)

Cod and Tofu One-Pot (with salmon)

INDEX